FAMILY POLICY MATTERS

How Policymaking Affects Families
and What Professionals Can Do

Second Edition

FAMILY POLICY MATTERS

How Policymaking Affects Families and What Professionals Can Do

Second Edition

Karen Bogenschneider

Rothermel Bascom Professor of Human Ecology
University of Wisconsin-Madison

Family Policy Specialist
University of Wisconsin Extension

CRC Press
Taylor & Francis Group
Boca Raton   London   New York

CRC Press is an imprint of the
Taylor & Francis Group, an **informa** business

First published by Lawrence Erlbaum Associates
10 Industrial Avenue
Mahwah, New Jersey 07430

This editon published 2011 by Routledge

Routledge
Taylor & Francis Group
711 Third Avenue
New York, NY 10017

Routledge
Taylor & Francis Group
2 Park Square
Milton Park, Abingdon
Oxon OX14 4RN

Cover design by Tomai Maridou

CIP information for this book can be obtained by contacting the Library of Congress

ISBN 0-8058-6071-1 (cloth : alk. paper)
ISBN 0-8058-6072-X (pbk. : alk. paper)
E-ISBN 1-4106-1424-7 (ebook)

Printed in the United States of America

Contents

Foreword

Theodora Ooms
Center for Law and Social Policy

This book puts forward a compelling case for taking family policy seriously. Families matter—to individuals, communities, and society as a whole. In the past three decades, family life has undergone dramatic transformations. For instance, the entry of more mothers into the labor force, the rising rates of cohabitation, out-of-wedlock childbearing, and divorce have had major impacts on government and other institutions. Nevertheless, until relatively recently, families were considered a private institution beyond the reach of government. In 1971, for example, the first federal day-care legislation was vetoed by President Nixon on the grounds that it was an unwarranted intrusion into family life. Just 2 years later, however, in 1973, Senate subcommittee hearings entitled, *American Families: Trends and Pressures*, launched a new debate in the United States about whether government policies had, in fact, contributed to the recent changes in family structure and function, and about how policymakers should now respond to them.

I went to Washington in 1976 to join the staff of the newly founded Family Impact Seminar. For the next 4 years, through the White House Conference on Families in 1980, the families theme was led by President Carter, Vice President Mondale, and HEW Secretary Joseph Califano. After Reagan's election, family issues were captured by conservatives who radically redefined them. The debates that followed in the 1980s and 1990s were often highly contentious: The term *family values* was thrown around like a political football. At the Family Impact Seminar, we worked with a coalition of four national family-focused organizations, known as COFO, to move the field forward substantively and assert the broad middle ground on family issues.

Nearly two decades later, we can look back and see that some progress has been made. Family issues are now high on the policy agenda of both political parties. Some areas of consensus have been forged, and useful policies have been enacted to support and strengthen families. Researchers have learned a great deal about the changes in family formation and the diversity of family patterns. However, despite that policymaking has become considerably more family-focused, the term *family policy* is still not widely used, and few people are actively engaged in the field.

Policymakers at national and state levels are eager for information to help them enact sound family policies, but what information exists is often scattered or not in a usable form. Researchers, advocates, and government officials frequently focus only on a *part* of the family—children, mothers, fathers, or grandparents—without seeing the larger picture—how the different parts fit together or threaten to pull apart. For the most part, families continue to be "everyone's concern, but nobody's responsibility" (Ooms, 1990, p. 77).

Bogenschneider's book is the latest in a handful of seminal books that have defined the field of family policy, including Alva Myrdal (1941), Sheila Kamerman and Alfred Kahn (1978), Daniel Patrick Moynihan (1986), and Gilbert Steiner (1981). She takes a giant leap beyond her predecessors, however. The substance and scope is breathtakingly broad and filled with practical examples from real life. She goes beyond just offering definitions, descriptions, and analysis to *challenge* academics, policy researchers, and family professionals to engage actively in the formation of family-focused policy. Most important, she offers practical ideas about how to do so based on her own rich experiences as family researcher, teacher, program evaluator, and director of the Wisconsin Family Impact Seminars and the national Policy Institute for Family Impact Seminars.

When issues such as teenage pregnancy prevention, child care, child support, and marriage are of such interest to public officials, why is the field of family policy so undeveloped? Why are there only a handful of family policy courses taught in family life departments and social work schools, and even fewer in public policy schools? When increasing numbers of policy researchers in the major think tanks are working on specific family issues, why are there no units within these institutions established to encourage and pursue family policy as an organizing theme? Why are there still no groups within government agencies dedicated to examining the impact of their policies on families?

Bogenschneider discusses two major barriers that have prevented the growth of the family policy field. The first is the pervasive American ethos of individualism—first noted by De Tocqueville and, most recently, by Amitai Etzioni, Robert Bellah, and other leaders in the communitarian movement—that permeates academic research and policymaking. Individualism frames the way we collect, analyze, and present data; design policies and programs; and train professionals. In academia, it results in a high degree of disciplinary specialization. This philosophy of individualism handicaps our study of social policy problems and solutions because it forces us to look at individuals as separate from their most important context: their families, however they are defined. Families are not easy units of analysis, of course; they are complex, dynamic, messy, ever-changing systems. A family policy orientation requires one to think about individuals and families in a comprehensive way and to design holistic responses for meeting their needs.

As Bogenschneider points out, family policy requires being able to integrate information from a wide range of academic and professional disciplines. This multidisciplinary aspect of family policy would seem to present a daunting obstacle to engagement in family policy research or advocacy. Bogenschneider draws on the experience of the Family Impact Seminars, however, to illustrate how this integration can be achieved. Within each discipline and professional field, there are experts who specialize in family issues and practice—economists and policy analysts, demographers, family lawyers, family historians, family sociologists and psychologists, family health care professionals and social workers, family life educators, and many others. These people can be the gatekeepers who translate the insights of their own disciplines into knowledge that is useful to policymakers. Sometimes it is true these researchers will need coaching to do the translation, or family policy intermediaries will need to do it themselves to bridge the worlds of scholarship and policy (which is the function of groups like the Family Impact Seminars).

There are other sources of relevant knowledge to tap into when designing policies that take into account the complexity of family life. Within government departments, there are many officials who understand how best to meet families' needs from the experience of delivering programs in the real world, to real families in diverse communities. In the community, there are increasing numbers of innovative pioneers who are learning how to design and administer programs that are comprehensive, coordinated, and family-centered.

The second barrier that Bogenschneider identifies to the growth of the family policy field is, interestingly enough, family values. Family policy, more than any other area of policy, touches on deeply held personal values and experiences. In a country as diverse as the United States, this inevitably leads to controversies over such highly divisive issues as abortion and gay marriage. As a result, many other, less contentious family issues have been, and continue to be, unnecessarily polarized. In her thoughtful and original chapter 9, Bogenschneider points out that tensions between competing rights and responsibilities of individuals and families—between children and parents, mothers and fathers, dependents and caregivers—are often at the heart of family policy debates. Another main area of disagreement centers on the appropriate scope and limits of government intervention into family life. These values dilemmas, or *true paradoxes* as Bogenschneider terms them, can precipitate paralysis in policymaking when "advocates become mired in ideology, enticed by the persuasiveness of their political rhetoric, and entrenched in the self-righteous belief that their position alone represents what is true, right, and good."

The exciting challenge of family policy is to craft solutions that strike a balance between extreme positions and seek to support the well-being of the family as a system while making sure that individuals' basic needs and rights are respected and protected. This kind of creative accommodation of different perspectives and interests is, in fact, the same kind of balance achieved on a daily basis by well-functioning families. As Bogenschneider concludes, "moving toward the middle ground does not result in mediocre policies, but in more realistic policies that mirror the inherent give and take of family life."

Over the past decade, a broad middle ground has been forged about policy in such formerly contentious areas as child care, teen pregnancy prevention, earned income tax credit, child support enforcement, and welfare reform. I hope that a similar consensus can be built to address the four issues that Bogenschneider identifies as front-burner family policy debates for the new millenium: family and work conflict, long-term care, family poverty, and marriage. To move the field of family policy forward on these and other issues, she urges professionals and citizens to become actively involved, and she offers nine roles and strategies from which to choose. It is my belief that readers of this excellent book will discover, as I have, that family policy is not only important, but fascinating, rewarding, and even fun.

The fact that the publishers have decided to publish a second edition gives me a kernel of hope for the future of the field of family policy.

Foreword

Thomas J. Corbett
University of Wisconsin–Madison

As I read an early draft of *Family Policy Matters*, I was reminded of a brief, yet compelling, interchange I had recently experienced. During a lunch break at a scholarly conference, the issue arose as to the extent to which research played a role in the formulation of public policy. A former senior congressional staffer with particular expertise in welfare policy, and one personally sympathetic and receptive to the contribution of research, considered the issue only for a moment. In Congress, he noted to the assembled academics, policy is driven by two main factors: power and ideology. Research accounts for 5% of the input, with an upside potential of 10%.

Even conceding some hyperbole for effect, his cynical response cannot be easily dismissed. Few would argue that policy research drives policymaking. Those who ply the policy research trade and seriously anticipate exerting some practical impact are likely to be disappointed, perhaps even puzzled, in the end. Their efforts are similar to those who train bears to dance as a profession. Yes, it can be done, but we do gaze in wonder when we actually see it accomplished.

The author of this book has undertaken a Herculean task. Among other things, she attempts to summarize an overwhelming and growing body of literature on families and family dynamics. She provides a conceptual framework for the discipline, attempting to give this rather amorphous intellectual and policy arena shape and definition. At the same time, she addresses the practical issues faced by those who operate in what we casually refer to as the *real world*. Most important, she does all this with wit and brevity and the insight that comes from caring and experience.

Although much can be said of this work, I want to focus on three of my reactions: the professional risk involved in this type of book, some thoughts on why it is timely, and a reflection or two on its importance.

AN ACT OF PROFESSIONAL COURAGE

Her singular folly, if you will, is her adventurous journey into the nexus between analysis and practice—that nebulous intersection of knowledge producers and knowledge consumers. All too often, as she realizes, such interactions are best thought of as unconventional acts between nonconsenting adults. For an academic, her willingness to trespass on the intersection of research and (policy) practice clearly is an act of professional courage. I can speak with some experience on this matter. Throughout my career, and particularly during my tenure as Associate Director of the Institute for Research on Poverty at the University of Wisconsin, I also entertained the promise and perils of cross-walking between these diverse worlds governed by two radically distinct cultures. They have, on the surface at least, different constituencies, time frames, vocabularies, reward systems, and motivations.

For an academic, showing too much interest in the application of knowledge can be professionally self-destructive. This is true, even at the University of Wisconsin, where the concept of coterminous boundaries between academia and the state—popularly known as the "Wisconsin Idea"—was developed and promoted almost a century ago. Without question, there is risk in this effort.

Every academic located at a research university knows full well where his or her professional interests lie. All the incentives are loaded on creating new knowledge to be published in refereed journals. Thus, the rewards go to those who focus on narrow, specialized topics directed toward a tiny audience of academic peers. Equally important tasks related to translating research for the real world, and integrating findings from diverse disciplinary traditions, are typically frowned on by those who consider themselves knowledge producers. The real world, for them, is a hard and alien terrain to be avoided whenever possible.

Professor Bogenschneider and her colleagues who contributed to this work have shunned the traditional and safe route. This book takes chances. It pushes the envelope in an area fraught with hardened positions, where dispassionate analysis seldom finds fertile ground. Thus, this is a brave work—one that should have an extraordinary impact on both the purveyors of public policy and those who seek to shape or inform the policy agenda through rigorous inquiry.

WHY FAMILY POLICY IS IMPORTANT

In truth, we have always had family policy. We just did not always appreciate that fact. The similarities with poverty research and policy practice are
illuminating. As a distinct area of inquiry, poverty research and analysis
typically is dated back to the early 1960s. During that period, a definition of
poverty was developed by Molly Orshansky of the Social Security Administration, and public policy focused in on this societal challenge when President Johnson declared the War on Poverty. By the late 1960s, one litmus
test for policy proposals was, "What does it do for the poor?"

Although concern for the poor can be traced back to the emergence of
civilization, and although poverty research, as we now know it, was evident
as early as the late 19th century, the pace and sophistication of research
did not pick up until a distinct field of inquiry developed. Today, our understanding of poverty is immeasurably more advanced and sophisticated
than it was just 40 years ago.

Family policy is in much the same condition as poverty policy was some
three to four decades ago. There is a good deal of it going on, but the avenues for distilling and translating the work in ways that effectively shape
and inform policy have yet to be fully exploited. The same ingredients are
required. We need a definition of the concept, and we need a policy arena
that has defined and accepted families as a legitimate subject of public discourse.

In some important ways, practice is outpacing both policy and research
as is exemplified in the recent transformation of the nation's social safety
net for impoverished families. Welfare in the United States has been transformed since 1996. First, the underlying goal of social assistance has shifted
from partially remedying income shortfalls to affecting behavioral change
at the individual and *family* levels. Second, contemporary reform encourages the reallocation of program and policy authority to levels closer to
where families are actually helped. Moreover, the purposes of social assistance have expanded. It is now recognized that new workers, a tribute to
the success of welfare reform, must be nurtured in the labor market
through a variety of work supports; functioning two-parent families must be
promoted and strengthened; and the communities in which low-income
families reside must be strengthened. In seven upper midwest states, welfare spending on what they term *family formation and stability* purposes increased from about 6% of all TANF expenditures in 1996 to 18% in 2000.

In consequence of these changes, the contradictions, redundancies,
and narrowness among existing programs are more apparent, and so is
the need to integrate categorical programs into a coherent and compre-
hensible network that might make sense to consumers and service providers alike. Not surprisingly, experimentation in one-stop centers, complex

community networking, radical secondary devolution, and even virtual agencies has exploded.

But if there is a common thread running through the yet unfinished transformation of social welfare programs begun in the 1990s, it is permission to "think outside the box," particularly at the community level. Inexorably, and inevitably, those newly responsible for welfare programs began to reconceptualize what they were doing and for whom. They no longer obsess about isolated issues affecting individuals, but rather increasingly consider the complex of interacting challenges facing families in dynamic environments.

THE GREAT DIVIDE REVISITED

As noted earlier, I am most taken with the effort to bridge the gap between knowledge producers and consumers. Recently, I completed my tenure as a member of an expert panel organized by the National Academy of Sciences that examined data and methods for evaluating reforms in the nation's social safety net. In its final report, the panel concluded that the evaluation community had fallen short in answering basic questions about the efficacy and promise of welfare reform. Some observers were disturbed by the conclusion, pointing out that the federal government and private foundations had committed unprecedented resources to evaluating reform.

Why the diverse perspectives—so little learned despite so great an effort? Naturally, one might conclude that some observers simply do not accept the results of existing research, believing that the next study will reveal the truth. Or, as is the want of academics in general, no amount of research is enough, each study revealing the need for more.

But the story is more complex of course. Contemporary research efforts are laudable, and much has been learned. At the same time, there is a conservative dimension to evaluative efforts. They seek to isolate and estimate the independent effects of particular policies and strategies. The search was for the policy or program that would solve the welfare problem, as if there were such a magic potion. This scientific imperative, along with surprisingly high levels of control-group contamination, resulted in studies only able to identify the most modest impact at best and in a sobering sentiment that nothing works really well. Policymakers often felt that the evaluators and researchers somehow failed to capture what they were really doing. In the end, both sides often feel disenchanted—the evaluators frustrated at being ignored and those responsible for reform feeling that the researchers simply do not get it.

Family Policy Matters contains extraordinary examples of successful strategies for bridging this culture gap. As with any proposed marriage, the success of the bond cannot be based on mere mutual attraction. It takes work. I know from first-hand observation that the Family Impact Seminar strategy first developed by Theodora Ooms in Washington, DC, and more recently replicated in a number of states by Professor Bogenschneider, has been a superb venue for bringing policymakers and research together. The simple fact is that it does not matter how much analysis exists, nor how rigorous it is, if the information is not delivered to those who need it in a digestible form. The mule will starve if it cannot get to the hay no matter how much hay exists.

I hope this work receives the attention it deserves. It is one of those books written on the right topic at just the right time. The emerging focus on families will not be sustained or successful simply because it is the right thing to do. We will be successful only if we are informed and savvy. The succeeding pages contain a blueprint for how to proceed.

Preface
The Floating Opera of Family Policy

The curtain rose on Act 1, Scene 1, just as it did with any other opera. The cast members knew their roles and performed each act and scene as they had many times before. However, the plot unfolded, not on a typical stage, but on the flat, open deck of a showboat owned and operated by Captain Jacob R. Adam. The showboat, dubbed *Adam's Original and Unparalleled Floating Opera,* traversed the Virginia and Maryland tidewaters in the 1930s (Barth, 1967/1983). Rather than being moored at Long Wharf for the performance, the showboat drifted up and down the river while the opera was being performed continuously in view of the audiences seated along both banks.

The audience would catch whatever scene was being performed as the showboat floated past. Then they would have to wait until the tide ran back again to catch another scene, if they were patient and persistent enough to still be sitting on the shore.

To fill in the gaps in the plot, the audience would have to use their imagination. Or they would ask their more attentive neighbors what was going on, or inquire of viewers upstream or downstream who had detailed knowledge of a part of the opera they had missed. Or they could read press accounts of the plot and media reviews of the performance of the cast. Most times, the audience would not understand at all what was going on, or perhaps worse, they would think they knew what was happening when in actuality they did not.

The floating opera illustrates the process of creating policies to support and strengthen families. We seldom see the whole policy from beginning to end. We catch little snippets of it. We may get involved in one act or scene as a policy is being developed, but we lose track of it as it winds its way through the legislative process. We sometimes catch sight of family issues, but too often they drop out of view before we have the time or knowledge to take action. Just as it is difficult to understand an act or scene without knowing the whole plot of the opera, it is difficult to make sense of policy snippets without a holistic understanding of the field of family policy—what it is, what it is not, and what it can achieve.

This book provides a comprehensive overview of the whole floating opera—the substance of the field of family policy, and the benefits a family perspective can bring to policymaking. Drawing on hundreds of research articles and books, the volume provides a solid background on the legitimacy of a family focus in policymaking, the effectiveness of family policies, and the myriad of policy roles professionals can play.

The preface first previews the new features of the second edition and then turns to who the book is for, what makes the book timely, how the book is organized, and why professionals should care about family policy-making.

ABOUT THE SECOND EDITION

After the publication of the first edition of this book, several remarkable changes occurred in the policy landscape for families. When I was writing the first edition, it was too early to comment on some of the most significant family policies in a generation—the Defense of Marriage Act, the No Child Left Behind Act, and the Personal Opportunity and Work Opportunity Reconciliation Act. The first edition recognized the devolution of family policy decisions from the federal to state governments, but did not predict the extent of change and the short time in which it would occur. For example, by 2005 when I was writing the second edition, 40 states had enacted legislation that defined marriage as a union between a man and a woman, 40 states used government funds to provide couples and marriage education, and about half of states had some recognition of same-sex parents. Moreover, marriage or marriage-like status had been granted to same-sex couples in California, Connecticut, Massachusetts, Hawaii, and Vermont.

The impressive array of family policies passed in the last 5 to 10 years leads to questions about whether this palpable shift toward a focus on the family is permanent or merely a passing policy fad. Will family policies ebb and flow as they have in the past when periods of interest and investment have been followed by periods of benign neglect? This question is addressed in a new chapter that reflects on the roots of American social policy in the early to mid-20th century and examines whether understanding the themes and cycles of the past can shape a more enduring set of family policies in the future.

To save time for the busy professional, the second edition includes about 220 new references that strengthen the rationale for family policy, incorporate new evidence of the role that policies play in fostering well-functioning families, and update from 1990 (a) the family policies passed by the federal government, and (b) the national reports published that recommend a family perspective in policymaking. Moreover, the volume includes three new case studies of how professionals have promoted a family impact perspective, a new appendix on the procedures for conducting a family impact analysis, and an expanded discussion of state statutes and governor's executive orders that require family impact statements on policies or programs.

WHO THE BOOK IS FOR

Because family policy spans research and practice, this book is of use to those who generate research, those who advocate for it with policymakers, and those who teach it to the next generation of professionals. For researchers, the book provides the rationale for developing family-sensitive, politically relevant research questions and describes two theoretical approaches (i.e., advocacy and education) for those interested in seeing their research and ideas acted on in the policy world. For family policy instructors, the book provides the theories, definitions, research reviews, and practical examples from which good courses and high teaching evaluations are made. For practitioners, the book moves beyond theory to providing concrete roles and pragmatic strategies for overcoming controversy and influencing policies in ways that strengthen and support families across the life cycle.

This book also crosses disciplinary boundaries. Obviously, family policy is integral to family professionals, including researchers whose primary interest is the study of families (e.g., family psychologists, family sociologists, child and human developmentalists, family historians, and family demographers) and practitioners who work directly with or serve families either as educators or counselors and clinicians (e.g., clinical psychologists, Cooperative Extension Service county agents and state specialists, family life educators, social workers, and marriage and family therapists). This book will also interest scholars from a whole host of fields that interface with families, including aging, child development, economics, education, health, law, medicine, nursing, political science, psychology, public policy, sociology, and social work.

WHAT MAKES THE BOOK TIMELY

In politics, it has been said that timing does not mean anything—it means everything. The time may be right for a book on family policy because of three converging forces: Families need support, political leaders are perceived as being increasingly disconnected from American citizens, and professionals' knowledge and understanding of families and policymaking is at an all-time high.

The first element that makes this book a timely one is the urgent need for family support. Families efficiently and effectively carry out a variety of functions so important to society that they have been called the nation's best social workers (National Commission on Children, 1991a). Families economically support their members; raise the young into competent, caring adults; and care for the elderly, sick, and disabled in ways that no other institution can do or do as well. There is little dispute that families have changed dramatically in the last 25 years and now require different supports than were needed in the past.

To emphasize the extent of these changes in one important family function, childrearing, I ask audiences to indicate, by a show of hands, their response to several questions: How many of them (a) grew up more than 100 miles away from extended family, (b) were raised in a single-parent home, and (c) had a mother who worked full time outside the home when they were a preschooler. Then I ask audiences to indicate with a show of hands how many of their own children (a) are growing up more than 100 miles away from extended family, (b) live in a single-parent home, and (c) had a fully employed mother during the preschool years. These questions never fail to exemplify in a concrete way the extent of changes that have occurred in parenting and family life in only one generation.

A second reason that this book is timely is growing perceptions among experts, leaders, and citizens that American politics is more fragmented, more polarized, more shortsighted, and less intelligent than it should be (Smith, 1991) leading to a serious disconnect between U.S. leaders and citizens (Yankelovich, 1995). Some professionals believe that the political process is so flawed that it does not merit their attention or participation. In sharp contrast, others share my view that the current shortcomings in U.S. politics are a clarion call for the involvement of professionals and citizens alike. By applying their knowledge and expertise in the policy arena, professionals can contribute to a more enlightened policymaking process than now exists. Professionals have the potential to make inroads in overcoming public cynicism, powerlessness, and distrust of the policymaking process (Boyte, 2000). In so doing, they can restore the dignity and legitimacy of American politics.

Finally, science- and practice-based knowledge of what families need and how policymakers can respond is not definitive, but certainly substantial enough for professionals to make a contribution to family policy. Professionals are in the business of generating ideas, and ideas can be powerful political tools (Smith, 1991). Researchers use the methods of social science to conduct studies that sometimes confirm conventional thinking, but other times contradict common sense and challenge the status quo. Practitioners, by applying ideas in the families with which they work, produce knowledge and insight that is difficult to acquire in other ways. This book offers pragmatic processes and procedures that professionals can use to help policymakers turn these good ideas into good policies (Ganzglass & Stebbins, 2001).

HOW THE BOOK IS ORGANIZED

The analogy of the floating opera resonates with me because I sometimes feel as if I have been seated on the shores of the river watching various acts and scenes of family policy most of my career. From my first job as a county extension agent to my current job as a university professor and extension specialist, my work has been situated betwixt and between the research and policymaking enterprises. This book is deliberately and inadvertently shaped by what I have learned from 30 years of professional experience as a practitioner, teacher, and researcher, and a lifetime of personal experience as a daughter, wife, and mother. Four experiences described here unwittingly became the seeds for this book, which took a full 30 years to germinate.

In 1979 when my oldest son was born, I experienced firsthand the power of family policy in creating the conditions under which families operate. During my pregnancy, I worried about how I might reconcile a demanding job as a county extension agent with the responsibility of caring for a young child. A friend and I decided to pursue sharing my full-time job—a change that did not affect the salary for the position, but did entail additional fringe benefit costs. This job-sharing proposal required approval from the three levels of government—county, state, and federal—that funded the position. Following a lengthy approval process, permission was finally granted, but not without extraordinary effort on my part, exceptional support on behalf of my supervisors, and the courage of a rural county board of supervisors to become the first in the state to endorse a job-sharing arrangement.

Initially, I thought that my personal situation was unique and that I sojourned alone in balancing the needs of my family with the demands of my job. Yet according to recent public opinion polls, conflict between work and family is the leading concern of contemporary parents, and one that Americans believe policy could and should make easier—not just for the good of parents, but for the good of a society that ultimately depends on the character and competence of the next generation. My personal struggle to balance work and family motivated me to begin collecting evidence on how many family policies were available, what value a family perspective could bring to policymaking, and whether family issues were a legitimate focus of government. This collection of evidence, which draws on the latest research in the field, is presented in the first five chapters of the book.

Another policy experience early in my career as a county extension agent in a rural Wisconsin county taught me an unforgettable lesson: the inestimable value of relevant and timely research in policymaking. In the early 1970s, when federal money for local aging programs became available, I was asked by several senior citizens to help them develop a county commission on aging. One of the commission's first efforts was to conduct a countywide needs assessment of senior citizens in every village, city, and township. A local public health nurse and I selected a random sample of seniors to be interviewed, developed the questionnaire, and trained 40 older people, who eventually conducted 532 face-to-face interviews, 1 of every 3 senior citizens in the county.

A couple months later, the county social services committee met to decide what, if any, services the county's elderly might need. I excused myself from the meeting to see if my program assistant had finished tabulating the results of the personal interviews. When I returned, I had data indicating that the most important issue facing the elderly in this rural county was lack of transportation. These data were the impetus for the county supervisors to develop transportation services for the elderly and to write grants to help secure federal funding to defray the costs. I also prepared 13 community reports of the findings, which were used by village boards, city councils, and town boards to develop programs and services tailored to the needs of senior citizens in their respective locales.

In this, my first experience at collecting and summarizing data for policymakers, I learned that research could be a powerful political tool. The power of research, however, is magnified or mitigated by its relevance to the issues policymakers face and the questions they raise. The second section of this book reviews the latest scientific evidence on several policy issues likely to be high on policymakers' agendas in the foreseeable future: competent parenting, family poverty, health care, long-term care, marriage, and work–family conflict. Chapters 6 and 7 may be especially illustrative because they were originally published as briefing reports for Wisconsin policymakers. As such, they are organized around the questions policymakers typically ask, and written in the succinct, easy-to-understand style that policymakers prefer.

The third section of the book deals with an element of policy that may deter family professionals from working in the policy arena: the controversy that many family policies evoke. My most contentious policy experience was serving as a delegate to the 1980 White House Conference on Families. What I remember most about the conference was the bitter conflict that erupted between the political left and right. I met good-hearted, well-intentioned people on both sides of the debate who disagreed so strongly on a few issues (i.e., abortion and homosexuality) that the conflict threatened to interfere with progress on any issue. Yet amidst the controversy, delegates were able to put aside their differences and reach consensus on several policy proposals such as family impact analysis on policies and programs, and family-friendly policies in the workplace.

So now when faced with seemingly insurmountable political disagreements that cause others to despair, I remember the most important lesson that I took away from the conference—the politics of hope. The seeds of chapter 9—the theory of paradox for overcoming controversy and reaching consensus—were sown at this conference, although it took several years and many more experiences before these ideas were fully formed. Reviewers have consistently found chapter 9 to be one of their favorites because of its potential to move controversial family policies forward.

The last section of the book deals with strategies for connecting research and policymaking. Madison, Wisconsin, where my office is located, offers a visual reminder of the importance of bringing research to bear on policymaking—State Street. At one end of State Street is the University of Wisconsin, one of the largest research organizations in the country, which operates under a near century-long tradition of making the boundaries of the University the boundaries of the state. At the other end of State Street is the state legislature, which is making a number of decisions that could benefit from social science knowledge. These two institutions are only a few blocks apart in geographic distance, yet they could be miles apart in the amount of communication that occurs between the two. One way that we are trying to connect the two ends of State Street is through the Wisconsin Family Impact Seminars, a series of seminars, briefing reports, newsletters, and discussion sessions for state policymakers.

Since their inception in Wisconsin in 1993, we have held 23 seminars on topics such as juvenile crime, parenting, and welfare reform for 1,666 participants, including 99 different state legislators and 245 legislative aides from 156 legislative offices. In 1999, Theodora Ooms asked me to assume leadership of the national Family Impact Seminars founded in 1976 to build capacity for family-centered policymaking. Currently, we are providing technical assistance to 21 sites that have conducted 121 seminars in state capitols across the country: Alabama, Arizona, California, Georgia, Illinois, Indiana, Kentucky, Maryland, Michigan, Mississippi, Montana, Nebraska, New Hampshire, New Mexico, North Carolina, Ohio, Oklahoma, Oregon, Pennsylvania, Wisconsin, and the District of Columbia.

In my work on the seminars, the analogy of the floating opera reverses: Research is continually being conducted and presented on the flat, open deck of the showboat and policymakers are sitting on the shores. Policymakers try to catch the relevant snippets of research that can guide their decision making, but they are continually interrupted by the competing demands on their time and the many lobbyists seeking to influence their decisions. Professionals like me who try to connect research with policymaking are in the business of writing scripts geared to the interests and needs of policymakers; casting experts who can communicate in the clear, engaging style that policymakers prefer; and scheduling the opera at times that coincide with the legislative agenda. This book can help professionals decide what tools and technologies they can use to bring research to bear on policymaking and which approach can best help reach their goals—advocating for particular policy alternatives or educating policymakers on a range of policy options.

Chapters 13, 14, and 15 depict the educational approach, which is less well known, but nonetheless a powerful means of providing information to policymakers to guide their policy decisions.

WHY PROFESSIONALS SHOULD CARE ABOUT FAMILY POLICYMAKING

Family professionals in particular have the potential to make a unique contribution to policymaking. Family professionals are trained to look beyond the individual toward a relationship between two or more individuals and to raise the fundamental connectedness of human beings to one another, a perspective that begins in families and one that is often overlooked in U.S. policymaking. This family void in policymaking is puzzling, given that public opinion polls consistently show that families are the most important element in people's lives and given that policymakers typically strive to be responsive to the views of their constituents. What remains elusive to many policymakers is how they can best act on the public's interest in families and bring a family impact perspective to public decision making.

I have been sitting on the shore watching the floating opera for three decades, observing, experimenting, and thinking about how we could make better connections between research and policymaking. If I could, I would make family policy a public health issue akin to public regulation of utilities. If I could, I would put a family perspective in the water supply if it meant that the well-being of families would be more routinely considered in policy development, enactment, implementation, and evaluation (Keyser, 2001).

What each of us can do right now is to put families on center stage in our personal and professional lives.

There is no single force with a stronger influence on the next generation than families, particularly those able to resist the strong, gravitational pull toward self-gratification and instead selflessly invest time, energy, and financial resources in their offspring. Yet focusing exclusively on our own families with nothing expected from or owed to other families is a thinly veiled form of individualism. To make families a national priority, we must each individually and collectively take the necessary steps to make families matter in policymaking. We must move beyond our own families to create the conditions for all families to do their best in what families do best—instilling the responsibility and commitment to others on which our country was built and on which its future depends.

Many of you, even those who are experienced family professionals, will be novices in the policy world, perhaps reluctant to get involved in an endeavor in which your skills are untested, the journey could be long, and the outcome uncertain. I recall some advice from an experienced lobbyist following one of my first policy efforts. Optimism, hope, and the will to make a difference are sometimes more important than experience. Experience can be gained with time if you have the will to get involved. My hope is that readers of this book will become involved in ways, large and small, to encourage policymakers to make families matter in policymaking.

ACKNOWLEDGMENTS

This text would be incomplete without a mention of those people who inspired this book and taught me about family policy. Perhaps none is more important than the students in my undergraduate and graduate classes on whom I have tested all the ideas in this book—whose questions sharpened my thinking, whose insights enriched my writing, and whose enthusiasm reaffirmed the value of recording these ideas for other students of family policy. To make the sometimes esoteric topic of family policy come alive for students, the book includes 26 case studies of professionals who have underwritten with their lives their belief that building family-friendly policies is deserving of their dedication because it can enhance family development as surely as other professional endeavors. These case studies range from researchers who were asked by policymakers to calculate the cost-effectiveness of an early intervention program for low birthweight infants to an organization that advocates for the political, social, and cultural needs of 300,000 families. Some of the professionals highlighted in chapter 12 have brought together high-ranking state agency officials from seven Midwestern states to provide peer mentoring on implementing welfare reform, and others have formed university-based institutes to channel research and resources into policymaking.

Because my classes have been well received by students, I am making a teaching guide and CD available to instructors who adopt this book for use in their undergraduate and graduate classes. In addition, family policy instructors are also referred to the teaching section of my Web site for syllabi and teaching techniques organized by Dr. Denise Skinner, a professor and longtime family policy instructor at the University of Wisconsin–Stout (http://www.familyimpactseminars.org/syllabi.htm).

I am indebted to many colleagues, but especially to five who have unselfishly shared their insights on policymaking and research dissemination with me over the years: Tom Corbett, Mark Lederer, Marygold Melli, Theodora Ooms, and Dave Riley. In addition, the following colleagues have generously contributed their time and expertise on repeated occasions: Dick Barrows, Inge Bretherton, Shannon Christian, Jane Grinde, Rae Schilling, and Denise Skinner. I owe a special debt of gratitude to several people who have patiently tried to teach me to think like a policymaker: former Representative Peter Bock, Governor's Representative Jessica Clark, former Senator Alice Clausing, Governor's Representative Annette Cruz, Senator Alberta Darling, Governor's Office Representative Lisa Ellinger, Representative Curt Gielow, Representative Tamara Grigsby, former Representative Stan Gruszynski, former Senator David Helbach, former Senator Joanne Huelsman, Representative Jean Hundertmark, Senator Julie Lassa, Senator Mark Miller, Congresswomen Gwendolyn Moore, former Governor's Representative Melanie Ohmsted, Senator Luther Olsen, former Senator Mary Panzer, Senator Judy Robson, Senator Carol Roessler, Representative Gary Sherman, former Representative Susan Vergeront, former Representative Daniel Vrakas, former Representative Joan Wade, Governor's Representative Donna Wong, and former Representative Rebecca Young. I am also grateful to Russ Whitesel of the Wisconsin Legislative Council for alerting me to the analogy of the floating opera.

The state coordinators of the Policy Institute for Family Impact Seminars, Heidi Normandin, Elizabeth Gross, and Jessica Mills, have graciously assumed additional responsibilities during every publishing deadline for which I am grateful. The Wisconsin Family Impact Seminars would not have been possible without the work of several assistants including Nicole Anunson, Karla Balling, Bethany Brewster, William Michael Fleming, Beverly Hartberg, Carol Johnson, Kirsten D. Linney, Kari Morgan, Jonathon R. Olson, Jennifer Reiner, and Aimee Ray. I owe a special word of thanks to Meg Wall-Wild, Karen Dorman, and Mari Hansen for preparing the manuscript; to my Lawrence Erlbaum Associates editors Lori Handelman, Bill Webber, and Judi Amsel for their encouragement and advice; and to Jane Weier for her support of my administrative responsibilities.

My policy work has been generously supported by the Helen Bader Foundation, Inc. (program officers Robin Bieger Mayrl, Bob Pietrykowski, and Helen Ramon), the Lynde and Harry Bradley Foundation (program officer William Schambra), the W. K. Kellogg Foundation (program officer, Winnie Hernandez-Gallegos), the David and Lucile Packard Foundation (program officers Kathy Reich, Lisa Deal, and Mary Larner), and two private philanthropists, Elizabeth C. Davies and Phyllis M. Northway. I also wish to thank the many county Extension agents, Mary Huser, and Stephen Small with whom I partnered on Wisconsin Youth Futures. I especially appreciate the contribution of Edie Felts-Podoll, who allowed me to write about her policy experiences in chapter 13. I also want to acknowledge Robin Douthitt, Dean of the School of Human Ecology, and Laurie Boyce, University Extension Family Living Program Leader, who have generously supported my policy work in Wisconsin and across the country.

Finally, I extend my appreciation to my family, first to my own parents, who taught me by example what it means to be a caring and committed family member and how it feels to be a recipient of this care and commitment. Most of all, I extend my appreciation to my husband, Neil, and my sons, Bret and Ross, who provided the encouragement to write this book and the periodic space from family responsibilities to complete it.

Preface to Reluctant
Students of Family Policy

This book was written with the reluctant student of family policy upper-most in my mind—a description that fits most of the students in my family policy classes. The students who leave my class loving family policy as I do were the primary motivation for writing this book. Based on my experience, the prototypic reluctant student of family policy often does not know why it is important to get involved with families and policy, whether family policy can make a difference in the lives of individuals and families, what effect policy will play in their future career, and how to get started.

WHY IS IT IMPORTANT TO GET INVOLVED
WITH FAMILIES AND POLICY?

Whether diagnosed through the lens of economics, psychology, sociology, or theology, one major threat to our public life and a major crisis in our personal lives is excessive obsession with the self (Peterson, 1985). It is families that provide a moral voice with the potential to overcome the pull toward self-centeredness, greed, self-interest, and the quest for power (Responsive Communitarian Platform, 1992). It is in families that we learn the value and joy of commitment to others, even when such actions exact a personal cost. At first, we learn in baby steps by demonstrating commitment to those that we know and love, but eventually our horizons expand to being able to act unselfishly toward those we do not know in our own community and ultimately in communities across the nation and the world.

In a society based on the rights of individuals, it is easy to ignore the responsibilities that come with these rights and to snub our nose at getting involved in politics, which is too often seen as a corrupt, influence-peddling, power-driven process. However, Peterson (1985) explained that politics cannot be "abandoned" by the younger generation just because it is seen as "dirtied" at this particular point in time. Historically, politics derives from the Greek work *polis* (city), which represents everything that people do as they assume responsibility for the way society develops. Politics means working together with others toward a common purpose, and a family perspective entails examining whether that common purpose privileges individuals or whether it provides advantages for families and the collective good.

CAN FAMILY POLICY MAKE A DIFFERENCE IN THE LIVES OF INDIVIDUALS AND FAMILIES?

People just like you and me have made a difference by getting involved in family policy. Carol Lee, a 46-year homemaker and mother of three in rural Canada, was the impetus for a change in the way the Canadian government collects census data. When the national census taker came to her door and asked how many hours she worked, Carol knew that the question meant working for pay and that she would have to answer "Zero," despite the hours she spent each week on childrearing. She wrote to the minister in charge of the census and complained that it was not right to ask only about paid labor, which provided an incomplete picture of women's work. This single act of protest by a concerned citizen was the beginning of a movement to lobby the Canadian government to count the labor of homemakers in its national data collection. Four years later, the government decided to include three new questions on its census form regarding unpaid labor, specifically the time spent on home maintenance and housework, child care, and assistance to the elderly (Crittenden, 2001).

Kaki Hinton of Pfizer met for lunch with nine other corporate executives concerned about the shortage of family-oriented TV programs. Because these companies were interested in placing commercials on programs that family members could watch together, executives from Coca-Cola, Johnson & Johnson, Kellogg, IBM, and Sears ended up banding together to form the Family Friendly Programming Forum. Members of the Forum have had a real impact on the kind of shows the major networks are producing by reading television scripts, selecting those that are family-friendly, and helping underwrite the substantial startup costs of producing new programs (Bauder, 2004).

One of the most significant policy changes in my hometown in the last decade was initiated, in part, by a student attending the University of Wisconsin–Madison. Cigarette smoke causes Ira Sharenow to become physically ill, which made it difficult for him to eat out with friends. Instead of just griping about something that he knew was not right, he took the next step of working with a number of activists and lobbying organizations to establish a smoking ban in city restaurants and on the University of Wisconsin–Madison campus. The far-reaching impact of this grassroots activism is captured in the words of the president of a local medical association following a similar initiative in his community: "The passage of your legislation to restrict smoking in the workplace will probably save more lives than I will in my whole career as a physician" (cited in Adams, 1995, p. 21).

WHAT EFFECT WILL POLICY PLAY IN YOUR FUTURE CAREER?

Whether or not you decide to seek a career in which you can shape policy, it is likely that your career will be shaped by policy. For example, a teacher notices that when students enter middle school, their grades go down, their self-esteem declines, extracurricular participation drops off, and alcohol use increases (Simmons, 1987). The teacher becomes frustrated that his or her efforts in the classroom seem compromised by the structure of the school system. Should this teacher continue to do the best he or she can in a less than ideal situation, or should he or she venture into the policy arena and take steps to change the school's structure (Bogenschneider, 2003)?

Another professional works for an independent living agency coordinating services for the elderly. Many of the agency's clients care for their spouses at home rather then placing them in an institution. Medicare pays for some medications and visiting nurse services, but does not provide what caregivers say they need most: respite care. Should the professional continue to support family caregiving as much as he or she can, given the limitations of the existing law, or should he or she work to get the law changed (Bogenschneider, 2003)?

Or perhaps you are a new professional deciding what career you want to pursue. If you are interested in working with families living in poverty, do you want a job where you help people better cope with being poor by teaching stress management and financial planning skills? Or will you seek a policy-related job where you can work to change some of the conditions responsible for people falling into poverty in the first place? Do you want to work for change in one family at a time (an honorable and important profession) or do you want to make sweeping changes that can potentially raise many families out of poverty (Bogenschneider, 2003)?

HOW CAN YOU GET STARTED?

Someday, in the distant or perhaps the not-so-distant future, you may find yourself saying, "This isn't right!" or "There ought to be a law." That is how political activism often begins. You may be one injustice, one indignation, one cause, or one candidate away from political involvement (Braun & Williams, 2004).

Who knows? It may be just for such a time as this that you have enrolled in a family policy class, but the true test of the course and ultimately of your generation depends on whether you can summon up the wherewithal and willingness to venture forth into the policy arena. The well-being of families may depend on it. As aptly put by Robert F. Kennedy, "Few of us will have the greatness to bend history itself, but each of us can work to change a small portion of events, and in the total of all those acts will be written the history of this generation."

THE RATIONALE
FOR FAMILY POLICY

CHAPTER

1

Do We Need a Family
Perspective in Policymaking?

Greater than the tread of mighty armies is an idea whose time has come.
—Victor Hugo

How much do families matter in policymaking? The answer can be found in
the lives of real families. For example, in the summer of 1998, I received two
e-mail messages from friends who had recently given birth—one in this
country and one in Europe. My American friend worked at a university hospital that had more generous benefits than many U.S. employers. Yet after
returning to work following a 2-month maternity leave, she was immediately placed on mandatory overtime, despite having two preschoolers at
home and a husband who was working two jobs to make ends meet. This
experience contrasts sharply with the experience of my Austrian friend during her pregnancy and birth. She received 16 weeks of leave, during which
she was forbidden to work; if found doing so, she could have been fined.
Following maternity leave, she was eligible for an additional 18 months of
parental leave.

A poignant example of an individual versus a family perspective in
policymaking occurred in Wisconsin in 1997. As carpenters were restoring
the outside of Wisconsin's historic capitol, policymakers inside were debating whether to redesign the Healthy Start program, which provided health
care coverage to eligible working-poor families. Although many diseases are
contagious, Healthy Start provided health care to certain family members
(i.e., mothers, infants, and young children), but not to others (i.e., fathers and
older children). An expansion of this program was being debated in the state

3

legislature when the federal government passed the State Children's Health Insurance Program (SCHIP), which was designed to increase health care coverage for children. As an incentive to states, SCHIP increased the federal reimbursement rates—an offer that most states readily accepted. In Wisconsin, for example, this incentive translated into $37 million in federal funds annually, which would provide 71% of the costs of covering additional children (J. Peacock, personal communication, November 5, 1998).

The governor of Wisconsin had also introduced his own health care plan, Badger Care, which targeted poor children as well as their families. Badger Care proposed providing health care coverage for poor families that met eligibility criteria, but were not covered by Medicaid or employer health insurance. The federal government argued that Wisconsin could only use SCHIP money to cover children's health insurance costs and that Medical Assistance (MA) money must be used to cover the cost of parents' insurance. The catch, however, was that using MA funds required Badger Care to become an entitlement available to all poor families, which the governor resisted because of apprehensions about its potential cost (J. Peacock, personal communication, November 5, 1998).

Thus, the debate in Wisconsin centered around whether health insurance coverage for the poor should be child-based or family-centered. Proponents of restricting coverage to children argued that it would cost less than family coverage and thus could cover more uninsured children. Supporters of extending coverage to the entire family disagreed, citing examples that family-based coverage would bring in 75% of eligible children compared with only 45% in child-focused coverage (Bartels & Boroniec, 1998). After 2 years of consideration, the federal government finally granted Wisconsin a waiver to provide family-based health care coverage to some, but not all, working-poor families. The fact that providing family-based health coverage requires a lengthy federal waiver process is one stark example of the individualistic nature of policymaking in this country.

Most policymakers would not think of passing a law or enacting a rule without considering its economic or environmental impact, yet family considerations are seldom taken into account in the normal routine of policymaking (Ooms, 1990). State legislators report being unfamiliar with how children and families are faring in their districts and uninformed about family policies or programs that work (State Legislative Leaders Foundation, 1995). Policymakers explain that they do not have the staff or time to gather all the relevant data on the complex issues that confront them (Hahn, 1987). As a result, they rely on information from lobbyists and special interest groups (Hahn, 1987) that is often fragmented, parochial, biased, and less focused on family issues. The leaders of state legislatures across the country report being generally unaware of grassroots groups that advocate on behalf of children and families, unacquainted with child and family advocates, and seldom contacted by constituents on family issues (State Legislative Leaders Foundation, 1995). The bottom line is that policymakers typically enact policies without consulting family authorities or advocates, seeking input from families, or relying on family research (Blankenhorn, 1990; Ooms, 1990, 1995; State Legislative Leaders Foundation, 1995).

WHY DOES A FAMILY VOID IN POLICYMAKING EXIST?

This family void in policymaking is probably the unfortunate culmination of several converging forces. This chapter considers the potential roles played by some of the forces that are commonly considered the leading culprits: inattentive policymakers, unsupportive professionals, an apathetic public, slow acceptance of the idea of government support for families, and rapid changes in family life.

Does the Family Void in Policymaking Stem From Policymakers Who Are Uninterested in Family Issues or Undervalue Their Importance?

The rhetoric and written record suggest otherwise. Political interest in children and families ebbs and flows, yet according to political pundits, it may now be at its highest peak in the last 20 years (Hutchins, 1998; Ooms, 1995). In recent studies, state legislative leaders have called child and family issues a "sure-fire vote winner" (State Legislative Leaders Foundation, 1995). More important, concern for families does not pigeonhole politicians as politically conservative or liberal, as Republican or Democratic, but is so universal that it is considered simply American (Jacobs & Davies, 1991).

For example, Jimmy Carter was the first U.S. president to make strengthening families a major goal of his administration without limiting the focus to any ethnic or economic group (Steiner, 1980). President Clinton declared in his 1994 State of the Union address that the country's problems are rooted in the breakdown of our families and communities (Winkler, 1994). In the 1994 Republican Contract with America, 4 of the 10 proposals dealt specifically with families. Less than 2 years later, the Democrats made "Families First" their campaign slogan (Wisensale, 2001a). In the 1996 presidential campaign, presidential hopefuls Bob Dole and Bill Clinton battled to be the bearer of the family banner (Rosenberg & Limber, 1996). In the 2000 elections, presidential candidate Al Gore called for a family lobby as powerful as the gun lobby (Belkin, 2000). During the first 6 months of his term, President George W. Bush vowed to unveil a family-friendly agenda to give parents more time with their children and with each other (Fournier, 2001).

The 2004 presidential campaign, which pitted John Kerry against incumbent George W. Bush, was dominated by talk of war and the economy; however, television ads in several states challenged Kerry's opposition to the Defense of Marriage Act, which defined marriage as between a man and woman (Wisensale, 2005b). Thus, over the last 30 years, several high-profile politicians in both major parties have positioned family policies as important issues in their political campaigns.

Can the Family Void in Policymaking Be Blamed on Lack of Attention and Support From Professionals?

Family professionals who educate or deliver services to families have repeatedly endorsed a family perspective in policymaking, as evidenced in a number of reports issued by federal and state agencies, national commissions, nonprofit organizations, and professional associations (see Table 1.1). Of these organizations, perhaps the most influential is the bipartisan National Commission on Children, which met for 2 1/2 years, reviewed the current state of knowledge on children and families, conducted a national opinion survey, and held hearings and focus groups in 11 communities across the country. Liberal and conservative members of the Commission endorsed an agenda for children and families that contained 11 principles, 3 of which dealt with the primary role of families in rearing children and the responsibility of society to help families fulfill this obligation.

In the last two decades, significant progress has been made in family-centered prevention science (Spoth, Kavanagh, & Dishion, 2002). A number of developmental models and intervention studies have demonstrated the viability of family-centered approaches for prevention and intervention programs that target prosocial and antisocial behaviors in infants, children, youth, and adults. The conclusions of these studies are aptly summarized in the words of preeminent developmental psychologist Urie Bronfenbrenner (1986): "The family is the most powerful, the most humane, and by far the most economical system known for building competence and character" (p. 4) in children and adults alike. As examples, a solid body of evidence is emerging about the value of family approaches in promoting academic achievement, economic success, and social competence; in preventing aggressive behavior, association with deviant peers, delinquency, early sexual debut, and substance abuse; and in treating drug abuse and helping former inmates transition back into the community (Baum & Forehand, 1981; Bobbitt & Nelson, 2004; Conduct Problems Prevention Research Group, 1999, 2002a, 2002b; Crittenden, 2001; Dishion, Andrews, Kavanagh, & Soberman, 1996; Dishion, Kavanagh, Schneiger, Nelson, & Kaufman, 2002; Dishion, McCord, & Poulin, 1999; Heckman & Wax, 2004; Knight & Simpson, 1996; Kreider, 2004; Kumpfer & Alvarado, 2003;

TABLE 1.1
Selected National Reports Recommending
a Family Perspective in Policymaking

Year	Author	Title of Report
1990	National Commission on Child Welfare and Family Preservation	A Commitment to Change
1991	National Commission on Children	Beyond Rhetoric: A New American Agenda for Children and Families
1991	U.S. Department of Education, Office of Educational Research and Improvement	Policy Perspectives: Parental Involvement in Education
1992	Council of Chief State School Officers	Student Success Through Collaboration
1992	The Communitarian Network	Responsive Communitarian Platform
1993	The Communitarian Network	A Communitarian Position Paper on the Family
1993	National Council on Family Relations	Family Health: From Data to Policy (Hendershot & LeClere, 1993)
1993	National Commission on America's Urban Families	Families First
1995	State Legislative Leaders Foundation	State Legislative Leaders: Keys to Effective Legislation for Children and Families
1996	Finance Project	Building Strong Communities: Crafting a Legislative Foundation
1997	Center for Law and Education	Urgent Message: Families Crucial to School Reform
1997	Institute for Educational Leadership	Partnerships for Stronger Families: Building Intergovernmental Partnerships to Improve Results for Children and Families
1998	U.S. Department of Justice, Office of Justice Programs, Office of Juvenile Justice and Delinquency Prevention	Effective Family Strengthening Interventions
1999	Chief State School Officers	Early Childhood and Family Education: New Realities, New Opportunities
2000	National Council on Family Relations	Public Policy Through a Family Lens: Sustaining Families in the 21st Century
2001	Family Support America	From Many Voices: Consensus: What America Needs for Strong Families and Communities
2002	Institute of Medicine	Health Insurance is a Family Matter
2004	National Association of Counties	Human Services and Education Platform and Resolutions
2004	National Human Services Assembly	Family Strengthening Policy Center Introduction to Family Strengthening
2004	Office of the Assistant Secretary for Planning and Evaluation, U.S. Dept. of Health and Human Services	Indicators of Child, Family, and Community Connections
2005	National League of Cities	Strengthening America's Families: An Agenda for Municipal Leaders

Patterson & Yoerger, 1993; Resnick et al., 1997; Simich-Dudgeon, 1993; Spoth et al., 2002; Stormshak, Dishion, Light, & Yasui, 2005; Stormshak, Kaminski, & Goodman, 2002; Zigler, Taussig, & Black, 1992).

Is the Public Apathetic or Uninterested in Whether Families Are Designated as a Criterion for Policymaking?

The answer is a resounding "no." When the public is asked what is important to them, families top the list. In a recent public opinion poll, 93% of Americans rate a happy marriage as one of their most important goals (Mason, Carnochan, & Fine, 2004). Similarly, a resounding 99% of Americans reported that loving family relationships are extremely (91%) important to them—almost twice as many as rated their job as extremely important (49%) and one third more than gave this same rating to financial security (61%; Bennett, Petts, & Blumenthal, 1999).

The importance of one's family, which a 1982 survey indicated is almost identical among African Americans and Whites (Wilson, 1999), appears to be more than just pious words or hollow sentiments (Wilson, 1999). In 1989, families invested an enormous amount of time and money in their children, with out-of-pocket expenditures totaling $484 billion—substantially more than the $314 billion invested in children by government at all levels (Sawhill, 1992). In fact, the real value of the activities that families provide in such home activities as child care, carpentry, and food preparation equals that of the official economy (Carlson, 2005). This investment in family life yields a healthy return. Americans who report that their family life is going well also report being more satisfied with their life in general and with specific aspects of their life, including job performance, financial security, parenting competence, and physical health (Zill, 1993).

Yet despite this recognition of the extraordinary power of family relationships in their lives, Americans are not complacent and, when asked, express grave reservations about the state of families. For the first time in 50 years of Gallup polls, Americans ranked family decline along with ethics and morality as the most important problems facing the country today ("What's the Problem?", 1999, p. 4). In surveys, four out of five Americans believe it is harder to be a parent today than it used to be (Hewlett & West, 1998; National Commission on Children, 1991b), and more Americans chose the 1950s than any other single decade as the best historical period for raising children (Coontz, 1997). Irrespective of their income, education, ethnicity, or race, contemporary parents contend that family life is threatened by conditions such as damaging cultural messages, economic pressures, excessive work demands, social isolation, and unsafe streets and neighborhoods. Importantly, these stressors stem from conditions outside their families, the very conditions that public policy can address (Bronfenbrenner &

Weiss, 1983; Finance Project, 1996; National Commission on Children, 1991b). Most Americans would probably agree that childrearing is primarily the responsibility of families, yet they also acknowledge how government shapes the conditions that make it easier or harder for parents to do a good job. In particular, policies directed at families are more popular with the American public than child-focused policies amid worries that programs directed at children are really disguised welfare programs (Skocpol, 1995).

Thus, in policymaking, where timing means everything, promoting a family perspective in policymaking would seem to be an idea whose time has come. One would think that effect on families would be one of the first questions policymakers ask of any policy, rather than the last. If policymakers, professionals, and the public endorse the importance of families to a strong and vital society, why does family policy still take a back seat to economic or environmental policy?

Is Government Support of Families a New Idea That Has Been Slow to Gain Acceptance?

The research evidence is clear: Families do a better job of promoting competence and character in their members when they can count on the support of contexts outside their home—close friends, good schools, caring communities, and responsive government (Weissbourd, 1987). The importance of the ecological principle of the embeddedness of a family in its environment is perhaps best illustrated by drawing on examples from the natural ecology. Logging in the Northwestern woods has damaged the habitat of the spotted owl and has threatened extinction of the species by interfering with the ability of the adults to reproduce and guarantee the survival of the young. Similarly, the weakening of the ecology of families can undermine competent parenting and impair the capacity of the human species to rear its young into productive, caring adults.

In reality, providing support to families is not a new concept. For decades, parents have received support in village greens and on park benches; during barn raisings and church meetings; and at gatherings in the general store, post office, or neighborhood cheese factory. In these settings, which were once commonplace in America, parents were able to talk with each other, observe other parents interacting with and disciplining their children, and find out about community rules and standards for childrearing. Few of these customs remain, yet the needs they met and the purposes they served continue (Kagan, Powell, Weissbourd, & Zigler, 1987). The ways families were supported in the past may not be as available to contemporary families. One could argue that the ecology of family life has changed so rapidly that it has crowded out these important customs that used to provide family-to-family support and that new forms of support, primarily from government, have not been able to keep pace.

Can the Rapid Changes in Family Life Be Credited
With the Family Void in Policymaking?

Clearly, many of the well-documented changes in the ecology of family life have interfered with the time, resources, and opportunities for family members to develop these close ties to relatives, neighbors, schools, and community. For example, contemporary families are more mobile, which makes it more difficult to access informal sources of social support. Between 1995 and 2000, almost half of the U.S. population (46%) packed up and moved. Moreover, in 2000, 20% of U.S. children lived with at least one parent who had emigrated from another country (Hernandez, 2005).

In the last 100 to 150 years, considerable change has occurred in the structure of American families, changes so sudden and dramatic that family norms have not yet stabilized and societal supports have not yet materialized. For example, today about 1 of every 3 White children and 7 of 10 Black children are born outside marriage (Haskins, McLanahan, & Donahue, 2005). The teen birth rate has declined recently, but still exceeds that of most industrialized nations (Haskins et al., 2005). The divorce rate has increased from 5% of first marriages near the middle of the 19th century to about 50% of all first marriages today (Amato, 2000). The divorce rate has stabilized recently, but still is among the world's highest (Haskins et al., 2005). Given the extent of marital disruption, the number of children born to single mothers, and the sharp increase in homes headed by single fathers, about half of all children alive today will live in a single-parent home by the time they reach 15 years old, often accompanied by poverty (Smeeding, Moynihan, & Rainwater, 2004). Cohabiting couples increased 46% between 1990 and 1997, from 2.9 million to 4.1 million (Seltzer, 2000). In the 2000 U.S. Census, the nearly 600,000 homes headed by gay or lesbian couples were found in almost every county in America (Cohn, 2001). Of these households, 27% included children. Because the Census did not count the number of children, conservative estimates are that 166,000 children are being raised by gay and lesbian parents (Meezan & Rauch, 2005).

These changes in family structure have been accompanied by changes in family roles and responsibilities. For example, the decreased fertility rate and the increased longevity of family members has transformed the shape of the American population from a pyramid in 1900 (i.e., a large base of children under 5 tapering off to few family members 65 and over) to a string bean in 1990 (i.e., similar numbers in each age category). It is more likely that a 20-year-old will have a grandparent still living today than a 20-year-old had a mother still living in 1900. These extended kin can serve as a resource for children as they grow up, or they can put more strain on families exposed to protracted years of intergenerational conflict and prolonged years of caregiving (Bengston, 2001).

The increasing participation of women in the labor force in the 20th century has had ripple effects on caregiving, childrearing, family consumption, household labor, and marital relations. Between 1900 and 1980, nearly 30 years of life expectancy were added to women's lives, while work expectancy increased over 350% during the same period (Spenner, 1988). Granted, this does not mean that women in earlier times did not work, but many worked in family businesses that allowed more flexible integration of productive and reproductive work. As recently as the 1960s, many women participated in the labor force on a part-time basis, structuring their work so that family life was altered very little (Masnick & Bane, 1980). Since the 1950s, however, the sharpest increases in labor force participation have been among mothers of young children (Masnick & Bane, 1980; Moen & Yu, 1999). Between 1969 and 1987, the average employed American worked, on average, 1 extra month each year (Schor, 1991). Between 1989 and 1995, work hours continued to increase, with families raising children logging in the longest hours (Moen & Yu, 1999). By 2000, the vast majority (70%) of children lived with a mother who worked for pay (Hernandez, 2005).

These rapid changes in structure and function have had profound impacts on family life. In recent polls, Americans report feeling caught in a double squeeze—being squeezed by economic needs, yet never having the family time they desire (Daly, 2001; Skocpol, 1997). In a 2000 nationally representative poll, about one in five teens (21%) said one of their top two concerns was "not having enough time together with parents" (Global Strategy, Inc., 2000).

In sum, the adults in today's families are living in a world so substantially different from the one they grew up in that it has been likened to a new world. However, social policies have failed to keep pace with the changing circumstances of contemporary families. A new world has emerged, according to one cultural observer, but it is missing the protective ozone layer that family-focused policies could provide (Hochschild, 1992). Parents, in particular, have desperately tried to shield the young by serving as this absent ozone layer; however, doing so requires exorbitant expenditures of time and energy that can only be provided by a heroic level of parenting that all aspire to but few can achieve. A society that creates an environment so unfriendly to parents that it requires superparenting has been characterized as inhumane (Garbarino & Kostelny, 1994) and a "public health problem that warrants national attention" (Steinberg, 1996, p. 189).

Has Americans' Interest in Families Failed to Move Beyond Lip Service?

These rapid changes in living arrangements and in family roles and relations are clearly an important reason for the family void in policymaking. These changes have occurred so rapidly—most in the span of a single human lifetime—that policymakers are faced with perplexing questions of what kinds of supports are needed, for which families, and what are the most cost-effective ways to deliver them.

The take-home message of this chapter is that it is one thing to intuitively accept the importance of families to a strong, vital society, and it is quite another to consciously and systematically place families at the center of the policy process. Policymakers' interest in families is at an all-time high, yet what remains elusive is how policymakers can best act on this interest (Ooms, 1995). Social scientists are more adept at generating high-quality research than disseminating it to policymakers (Bogenschneider, Olson, Linney, & Mills, 2000), and many need training to acquire the skills for communicating research findings in an accessible, timely manner. The American public recognizes that a family impact perspective can bring an essential quality to policymaking, but no large group exists that represents family interests in politics and works to enact policies that reflect this broad, shared consensus. Thus, family issues have captured the attention of policymakers, professionals, and the public and some progress has been made. However, no one is certain what can be done, how best to proceed, or who should assume responsibility.

WHAT CAN THIS BOOK OFFER TO FAMILY PROFESSIONALS INTERESTED IN MAKING FAMILIES MATTER IN POLICYMAKING?

My intent in this book is to begin building an ozone layer for families by promoting a family perspective in policymaking in Congress, state capitols, county boards, city councils, school boards, village halls, places of worship, and the boards of directors of businesses and community organizations across the country. The policies enacted or defeated in these bodies shape the context in which families live, and thus they shape human and family development. I encourage family professionals to promote family criteria for policymaking, just like economic and environmental impacts are routinely considered in policy debate. I forward the idea of family impact analysis, which encourages policymakers at all levels to routinely inquire about the impact of laws, rules, or programs on families' well-being. This book draws on hundreds of studies from the last few decades, not with the intent of dictating a particular policy option or single professional role, but to provide a solid foundation for professionals interested in becoming more active in shaping the policy environment in which families operate.

In response to Ooms's (1990) critique that "families are everyone's concern, but nobody's responsibility" (p. 77), this book identifies fresh theoretical perspectives, specific professional roles, and concrete strategies whereby family professionals can move beyond rhetoric to pragmatic actions that strengthen and support families. The role that professionals adopt is particularly germane because we are in the socioeconomic status (SES) to which most people model and aspire (Bellah, Madsen, Sullivan, Swidler, & Tipton, 1985/1996). We have the capacity to influence the opinions of policymakers and the public. We have access to the evidence that family-focused policies are not only possible, but within our reach. The question that remains is whether we have the conviction, will, and tenacity to ensure that families secure the priority they deserve in policymaking.

I begin this book by marshaling evidence that an individualistic perspective has historically pervaded American society and that our policies, programs, and professional training lack a family focus. I provide several examples, both case studies and empirical evidence, that policymakers' image of their clients is disproportionately the individual, with families coming in only as a distant afterthought. Then I turn to defining terms, specifically differentiating *family policy* from *a family perspective in policymaking* and proposing two categories of definitions that may help policymakers tackle the thorny and potentially divisive task of defining families. Next, I address the questions of whether families matter to society and whether we know how to mount programs and policies to influence family matters. I illustrate how a family focus in policymaking could result in more effective policies and programs, using examples such as the government's role in promoting competent parenting and health care. I review how a number of family policies enacted in the mid-1990s have prompted some of the most remarkable changes in the political landscape in the nation's history and what family policies are likely to be front-burner issues in the foreseeable future.

Despite this track record of the enactment of family policies and a respectable body of evidence supporting family approaches, I examine why it has proved so exorbitantly difficult to promote a family perspective in policymaking. I review three prominent views of the demographic changes that have transformed the fabric of family life in the United States in the last quarter-century, views that are often at the heart of the controversy that stymies the progress of family-friendly policies. I propose a theoretical perspective with the potential to foster consensus by raising and recognizing the valuable considerations each of these different perspectives can bring to bear on current family policy debate. To move a family agenda forward, I look back at the history of American family policy to examine whether analysis and understanding of these past successes can inform political debate and shape a more enduring set of family policies in the 21st century. I detail in the pages of this book nine theoretical roles for family professionals in the policy arena, several case studies of each, two methods for carrying out these roles, and a family impact analysis tool (Ooms & Preister, 1988; see also Appendix A) to assess the consequences of policies and programs on family well-being. I draw on my experiences in conducting Wisconsin Family Impact Seminars and Wisconsin Youth Futures to discuss several pragmatic procedures and strategies for working with state and local policymakers. I conclude by speculating about the future of the family policy field and identifying two specific actions that we can encourage policymakers to take to transform their interest in families into concrete policy initiatives.

As Victor Hugo said more than a century ago, "Greater than the tread of mighty armies is an idea whose time has come." The time has come to join together to make families matter in policymaking.

2

Is Policymaking Focused More on Families or Individuals? Are Professionals Adequately Trained in Family Science, Theory, and Methodology?

Perhaps because of the dominance of individualism in our country, we tend to split the individual from the family, just as we have tended to split the mind from the body.

—Doherty (1993, p. 98)

The United States may be the most individualistic country in human history (Yankelovich, 1995). For example, the United States and its northern neighbor, Canada, are similar in that they are both liberal Western democracies, yet their founding principles differ substantially. In their constitution, Canadians define *rights* as "peace, order and good government," in contrast to the U.S. Constitution, which guarantees "life, liberty, and the pursuit of happiness" (Lipset & Pool, 1996, p. 38). Consistent with America's founding principles, the majority of policies in this country focus predominantly on individuals—children, youth, women, veterans, the elderly, disabled, and poor—and fail to recognize how families contribute to social problems, are affected by them, and could be valuable components of viable solutions.

In this chapter, I amass evidence of the pervasiveness of individualism in American policies and programs, citing both historical and contemporary examples. These examples are important because individualism is so ingrained in American thought and experience that it often goes unnoticed and is as difficult for Americans to describe as it would be for fish to describe the water in which they live. This chapter is central to establishing the rationale for family policy, which, in essence, is a cultural critique of the American penchant for individualism. Individualism obviously has brought many benefits to this country, but nonetheless can be detrimental if not balanced with a healthy dose of its counterpoint, familism (see Triandis et al., 1993).

From a historical perspective, the United States is one of the only countries in the world without a specific mention of the word *family* in its constitution. The silence on families (Rice, 1977) was not accidental, but a deliberate attempt by the founding fathers to avoid a patronage system based on wealth or lineage as existed in the English monarchy against which they were rebelling. In contrast, the U.S. Constitution established a system based on equality of opportunity for every individual. These individualistic principles, established early in the nation's history, have continued to permeate our policies in ways that our founding fathers might not have anticipated or intended. For example, at the federal level, 15 congressional committees and five executive branch departments have some jurisdiction over families, but none devotes its attention exclusively to families. In fact, it was not until 1981 that the word *family* was used in the title of a subcommittee of the U.S. Congress (Jacobs, Little, & Almeida, 1993). Even today the United States—with all its agencies overseeing such national interests as agriculture, defense, energy, health, labor, and transportation—has no agency with sole responsibility for families. This legislative labyrinth is replicated at the state level (Sawhill, 1992). Slightly more than half of state legislatures have a specific committee or commission that deals with family issues, but many do not (State Legislative Leaders Foundation, 1995). In fact, statutes in one state—Idaho—prohibit policies supporting children under age 5, perhaps the very family members least able to speak up for themselves.

Neither the federal government nor state governments have an explicit family policy, so policymakers pass piecemeal legislation that responds to specific individual needs but does not provide a comprehensive vision for families (Elrod, 1999). Granted, government is not totally uninvolved in or even neutral to families. A number of policies support such family functions as education, health care, and caregiving for the young, aged, and disabled. Yet a careful scrutiny of American policies illustrates that policymakers' image of their clients is disproportionately the individual, with families relegated to the periphery of policy development, enactment, implementation, and evaluation (Moen & Schorr, 1987).

In the following examples, as throughout the book, I define *policy* as the development, enactment, and implementation of a plan or course of action carried out through a law, rule, code, or other mechanism in the public or private sectors. I define policymakers broadly as those who make laws or policies at several levels in Congress and our state houses; in our counties, cities, and villages; in churches, synagogues, and places of worship; and in schools, workplaces, and communities. I begin with case studies to illustrate how a family perspective in policymaking impacts the lives of real people in contemporary families. Then in an attempt to underscore the pervasiveness of these individualistic principles, I cite examples of a lack of a family focus in (a) federal, state, and local laws; (b) workplace policies; (c) organizational practices and operating procedures; (d) professional training; and (e) data and theories.

EXAMPLES OF THE LACK OF A FAMILY FOCUS IN POLICYMAKING

Case Studies

To illustrate the family void in policymaking, we need go no further than the real-life, everyday experiences of our friends, relatives, and acquaintances. Each of these examples is a true story, but names have been changed to protect people's privacy.

> Joe and June had two teenage sons. Joe was a top-level executive in a national manufacturing company in the Midwest and his wife, June, was finishing up a doctoral degree. Joe was offered a promotion and transferred to Georgia. Because the two teenagers wanted to complete high school in their hometown, the company paid for an apartment for Joe in Georgia and flew him home every other weekend. The result? A marriage of over 25 years ended in divorce.

> Kathy, a mother of four, was laid off from a job at a manufacturing company in rural Wisconsin. When Kathy was called back to work 6 weeks later, she was placed on the night shift. She had to depart for work each day just 30 minutes after her children arrived home from school. When Kathy was hired, she was promised she would never have to work the night shift. Yet when she raised this issue with the personnel manager, he bluntly replied, "Do you want a job or not?"

> Cassie had just finished her first 2 months as a freshman in a high school of 500 students. Her parents, Mary and Steve, were looking forward to the parent–teacher conferences to see how Cassie was adjusting to her classes and what kinds of support and encouragement they could provide at home. Parent–teacher conferences were scheduled once each year on 2 consecutive days with only one evening session from 5 p.m. to 8 p.m. Mary and Steve both arranged to leave work early and arrived promptly at the school at 5 p.m. Long lines of parents were already forming outside the door of every classroom. The lines were moving so slowly that Mary and Steve decided to split up the list of Cassie's teachers. Despite this and despite having only one child in high school, they were unable to meet with each of their daughter's teachers before the conferences ended at 8 p.m.

> After the birth of her baby, Alice experienced postpartum depression. When the baby was only 1 week old, Alice's therapist suggested that she needed time away from her family. She recommended that Alice, even though she was nurs-

ing the baby, spend the weekend in a motel by herself. This therapist focused on the needs of the patient sitting in her office with no regard for how the actions of this patient would reverberate throughout her family.

Irene was a 72-year-old grandmother who was raising her grandson in a public housing project in inner-city Philadelphia. When her grandson was involved in a drug deal, Irene was notified that she would be evicted from her apartment. Pro bono legal counsel helped her keep her home on a technicality—the drug deal had occurred more than 2 miles from the housing project.

These case studies attest to the undeniable power of family policy in the everyday lives of real people—a power that can be unleashed by supportive policies or undercut by their absence. In the next sections, I look at laws that may advertently or inadvertently undermine or overlook the power of families. I illustrate these discussions with selected federal, state, and local examples.

Federal, State, and Local Laws

Federal Examples. Third-party payers such as Medicaid and private insurers cover individual treatment for mental illness, but seldom cover marital or family therapy. For example, marital therapy is typically covered only if one of the individuals receives a psychiatric diagnosis (Ooms, 1998). Marriage penalties will always exist for the poor as long as our tax system is progressive and benefits like Food Stamps, Medicaid, housing, and welfare are income-tested (Acs & Maag, 2005; Carasso & Steuerle, 2005; Garfinkel, 2004; Marshall & Sawhill, 2004). For example, if they marry, a low-income working couple whose combined income is a modest $25,000 will suffer a financial loss of $1,900 in Earned Income Tax benefits (Marshall & Sawhill, 2004).

Policies too seldom recognize the responsibilities of family members to each other. For example, for families with caregiving responsibilities, tax breaks have not kept pace with inflation. If they had, the exemption for dependents would be three times higher—at a level of $8,200 rather than the current $2,750 (Browning & Rodriguez, 2002). For families who provide long-term care to the chronically ill, disabled, and frail, Medicare reimburses eligible nurse visits to their home. Yet the services that family caregivers repeatedly say they need the most—respite care and day care to provide time away from the stresses of caregiving—are typically not covered (Ooms & Preister, 1988). Currently, nannies who are formally hired to care for children can purchase disability insurance, but children's mothers cannot. Similarly, nannies earn Social Security credits when they care for children, but mothers do not. In other respects, Social Security recognizes family caregiving responsibilities by providing benefits to widows, divorced spouses, and surviving children under age 18 (who actually are more apt to receive benefits through Social Security than through welfare programs). However, concerns about the solvency of Social Security have led to proposals to create individualized accounts that would maximize an individual's opportunity to build up personal savings for retirement, but would jeopardize existing protections for children and lower earning spouses (Reno, Graetz, Apfel, Lavery, & Hill, 2005).

Perhaps even more illustrative than the policies that do exist are those that do not. In a 1998 United Nations study of 152 countries, the United States was one of only six countries that did not have paid family leave (International Labour Organization, 1998), along with Australia, Lesotho, New Zealand, Papua New Guinea, and Swaziland (Crittenden, 2001). When filing their tax returns, business executives can deduct from their tax obligations half the cost of meals and entertainment as legitimate expenses of doing business, but employed parents cannot deduct the cost of child care (Crittenden, 2001). Typically it falls to families to fill in the gaps left by the nation's individualistic policies and practices when hospitals send patients home before they are ready, when employers demand overtime to meet company deadlines, and when government and industry provide few regulations on violent and sexual content in TV programming, movies, and video games.

State Examples. Many family policies, such as marriage, divorce, property distribution, and child welfare, are decided on a state-by-state basis (Anderson, 1995; Mason et al., 2004). According to legal scholars, family law has been shifting in the last two decades from treating marriage and families as social institutions that serve the common good to dealing with them more like private contractual arrangements (Mason et al., 2004; Regan, 1996). For example, in Wisconsin and several other states, a family has no legal status separate from its members, which makes the substance of family law one of defining and enforcing the rights and obligations of individuals in certain types of relationships (Bogenschneider, Young, Melli, & Fleming, 1993; Mason et al., 2004). In the U.S. jurisprudence system, litigation—especially constitutional litigation—undercuts arguments based on family, community, or collective responsibility (Melnick, 2005). As families have become less of a social institution in the legal tradition, spouses and family members are treated no differently than other contracting individuals (Regan, 1996).

Landmark devolution legislation in the 1990s has transferred federal authority to the states on a range of issues, including children's health insurance, family preservation, and welfare reform. One of the most notable examples is the 1996 welfare reform law, the Personal Responsibility and Work Opportunity Reconciliation Act (PRWORA). As the title of this act implies, the primary focus of welfare reform in most states is promoting personal responsibility by encouraging and facilitating recipients' wage-earning or bread-winning capacity. Less attention has been directed to the impact these reforms might have on parents' caregiving capacity and, consequently, the future prospects of the children growing up in welfare-involved families. With respect to eligibility, most states have taken steps to purge the welfare system of its historic bias against fathers and two-parent families, but 16 states still make it harder for two-parent families to receive welfare and Medicaid benefits (Garfinkel, 2004; Marshall & Sawhill, 2004).

Local Examples. Many policies that touch the lives of families are decided at local levels of government—in towns, villages, cities, and counties—and by local boards and councils. For example, cities and villages have the prerogative to pass or prohibit ordinances to establish domestic partnership licenses that extend marriage-like rights and benefits to same-sex couples. Zoning decisions, made by local and county governments, can limit a family's ability to operate a home office or home business and restrict trailer homes to certain locations, typically disadvantaged neighborhoods (Carlson, 2005).

In many states, public and private elementary and secondary schools are operated by local boards of education with the statutory authority to enact school policies and practices. Even in the face of government mandates, local boards retain considerable discretion in implementation. For example, the 1994 Educate America Act promoted parental involvement in children's schooling. States responded with a number of programs and activities that school districts could use to make parents a more vital part of their children's education. Yet the effort expended to encourage parental involvement depends to a large extent on the commitment of the local school district (Henderson, Marburger, & Ooms, 1986). The attitudes and behaviors of the staff, particularly the principal, play a pivotal role in establishing the school's climate for partnering with families and the community. For example, how strongly school officials buy in to parental involvement often determines whether parents are invited to participate in classroom activities, serve on site councils, or partner with the school in other ways. In a recent study of kindergarten teachers, the efforts schools made to involve parents were "too late, too impersonal, and too cursory to have much of an effect" (Pianta, 2004, p. 6). In fact, over 90% of attempts to involve parents during this critical transition to school entailed a group meeting or letter to parents after the school year began.

The local school board and the teachers' union are also important players because, in many states, whether a school district can have one or more parent–teacher conferences in a year is specified in teacher contracts. Teachers' unions often negotiate for clauses in their contracts that preclude the use of teachers' aides or full-time volunteers, typically parents, in the classroom (Henderson et al., 1986).

Whether after-school and summer programs are available in a community often depends on decisions made by local boards and councils of nonprofits groups, religious organizations, school boards, service clubs, and youth-serving organizations. For example, in recent studies, the reading scores of disadvantaged children have been shown to fall about 3 months behind the scores of middle-class children during the summer months. Not surprisingly, these summer learning losses, appear to add up over time. At the end of high school, the achievement gap between middle-class and disadvantaged students could be completely explained by summer learning losses and the achievement differences when the children entered first grade. Programs like the Teach Baltimore Summer Academy have been shown to avert these summer learning losses, and several out-of-school-time programs have been shown to boost student achievement (Borman, Overman, Fairchild, Boulay, & Kaplan, 2004; Harvard Family Research Project, 2003). The availability of these programs is apt to be determined locally.

Community organizations can come to the aid of families with children by providing such services as education and training, child care, and youth recreation. Local organizations can also compete for resources that are directed to families raising children. For example, in the span of only two years, the fledgling organization No Kidding grew from 2 chapters to 47. No Kidding plans social events for those who choose to remain childless. Members refer to themselves and others who they claim are enlightened enough not to have children as THINKERs (two healthy incomes, no kids, early retirement). Couples with a stay-at-home parent are disparagingly referred to as SITCOMs (single income, two children, oppressive marriage). The printable names for children include anklebiters, crib lizards, and sprogs. Policies that support children such as employer- or government-sponsored child care, the federal child tax credit, health insurance for dependents, and parental leave are thought to cheat the childless, who make up about 10% of registered voters (Belkin, 2000).

Workplace Policies

Of the 100 biggest economies in the world, over half are corporations, not countries (Wisensale, 2005a). The decisions made in corporate boardrooms affect families as surely as those made in the state house or the nation's Capitol. For example, a bankruptcy court allowed United Airlines to terminate its pension plan, affecting 121,500 workers. This ruling had obvious consequences for the workers and their spouses, but perhaps also for the extended family and possibly the taxpayers who might be called on to ante up the retirement dollars that United promised but failed to deliver.

Employers have the prerogative to grant employees time off for family-related reasons. In 2003, employers scaled back benefits responsive to family needs such as flex time, prenatal programs, and well-baby programs (Society for Human Resource Management, 2003). Employers also have the right to demand overtime hours with little or no notice. In 1994, 45% of factory workers worked overtime, the highest level reported by the Bureau of Labor Statistics in its 30-year history of tracking the data (Crittenden, 2001). In court rulings, employees have little recourse when asked to work overtime. For example, a single mother was hired to work from 8:15 a.m. to 5:30 p.m. and then was fired for refusing to work overtime. She sued for wrongful dismissal, but the Massachusetts Supreme Judicial Court ruled that an employee could be fired as long as the reason did not violate an existing public policy. Evidently, no public policy protects a parent's right to care for her child (Crittenden, 2001).

Organizational Practices and Operating Procedures

Developing family-sensitive policies and programs is necessary, but not sufficient. Steps must also be taken to ensure that agency administrators and front-line staff members develop practices and operating procedures that reflect the stated purpose of the program and carry out the intent of the legislation. Four examples are given here.

First, the Jobs for Youth/Chicago program was developed in 1979 to help young men and women, aged 17 to 24 years, move into the workforce and out of poverty. Over time, program organizers noticed that a number of parents participating in the program were involved in stable relationships with a partner and wondered if involving both partners might better meet the program's goal of increasing available income. Perhaps most surprising is that it took almost 20 years before a new program was designed using a couple rather than an individual approach to employment assistance (Gordon & Heinrich, 2005).

Second, a striking example of the impact of policy implementation emanates from the establishment of emergency shelters designed to provide temporary assistance to homeless families. In 64% of the cities surveyed by the U.S. Conference of Mayors, families often have to separate to secure accommodations (Anderson & Koblinsky, 1995). It is not uncommon for homeless shelters to refuse accommodations to boyfriends, and as many as 40% exclude adolescent sons (Jacobs et al., 1993), who must then be removed from the families and placed in foster care (Anderson & Koblinsky, 1995).

Third, as early as the 1990s, calls were heard to transform the myriad of agencies and organizations that provide early intervention services into seamless delivery systems. Yet families needing services often have to travel to different sites, fill out countless forms, and file separate reimbursement forms (Winton, 2000).

Finally, the 1981 Adolescent Family Life Demonstration Grants Program of the U.S. Department of Health and Human Services was heralded as groundbreaking because it acknowledged the valuable role that the parents of a pregnant daughter can play in lessening the detrimental effects of early pregnancy. For the first time, programs were required to involve family members in their services. Yet this innovative legislation included no guidelines about how to involve families, nor was information gathered about how successful they were in doing so.

These insensitive program practices and ill-planned operating procedures may be due, in part, to inadequacies in the training of professionals who assume policy positions or who operate agencies, organizations, or programs.

Professional Training

Families are of only marginal interest to the disciplines that traditionally influence public policy, such as economics, political science, and law. In a recent search of the top 26 political science journals from 1907 to the present, Strach (2006) found that the word *family* appeared in article titles only 61 times. That is, in almost a century, political scientists published fewer than one article per year with a family orientation prominent enough to warrant a mention in the title. Moreover, in the field of law, family policy is marginalized and frowned on as an area that top students should go into ("Interview With Gary Becker," 2002).

Policy texts rarely include an entry for child or family policy in their tables of contents (Huston, 1994), an indication that policy courses based on these texts may be more individualistic than familistic in their orientation. Two recent analyses have criticized high school and college textbooks for justifying marriage and family on the basis of what each contributes to self-actualization (Browning & Rodriguez, 2002). At the collegiate level, Glenn (1997) criticized the content of 20 recent marriage and family textbooks as being focused too much on adult individualism and too little on such issues as the benefits of marriage and the important role parents play in child development.

In all fairness, Glenn's critique proved controversial (Cherlin, 1997; Scanzoni, 1997; Skolnick, 1997), yet it raised the important question of whether professionals receive enough exposure to family influences on human development. Using school personnel as an example, only about 4% to 15% of teachers have had course work in parent involvement (Epstein, 2001). Only seven states require principals and administrators to have training in parent involvement (Education Commission of the States, 1996). Similarly, the majority of school counselors and school psychologists are trained in and practice individually focused models of service delivery that seldom incorporate parents (Forness, 2003; Strein, Hoagwood, & Cohn, 2003). Virtually none of the school staff in the four middle schools that Stormshak and her colleagues worked with had training in how to establish collaborative relationships with parents aimed at improving student behavior and school performance. When these schools experienced budget cuts, providing family support in the school was perceived as a luxury that the schools could no longer afford (Stormshak et al., 2005).

The vast majority of teachers feel ill prepared to meet the needs of culturally diverse families (Winton, 2000). Early childhood educators often do not receive training on how to include children with disabilities in the regular classroom—a situation that the families of these students say has not changed much in the last 20 years. In 1998, the U.S. Department of Education funded an exemplary model for universities to provide interdisciplinary inclusion training to personnel in community settings; however, many of the innovative training programs reverted to business as usual after the training grant ended (Winton, 2000).

Even the training of human service professionals focuses heavily on diagnosing and treating individuals, with less attention to assessing family functioning, partnering with families to reach program goals, and designing and delivering family-based interventions (Ooms, 1995). In fact, only about 10% of practitioners are using proven family strengthening programs and, of these, only 25% are implementing them with reasonable fidelity (Kumpfer & Alvarado, 2003). However, even when interventionists use proven programs and are well trained, they are often unable to be as family centered as they want to be due to bureaucratic barriers such as the size of the caseload, monitoring and reimbursement protocols, coworker perceptions, and institutional inertia (Winton & Crais, 1996).

One compelling example of the pervasiveness of individualism on the training of human service professionals emerged from a critique of therapists' training. According to Doherty (1994, 1995), who is a therapist himself, training in the Rogerian, cognitive, behavioral, or psychodynamic traditions typically focuses on the needs and interests of the client seeking treatment. For example, therapists who pose questions like, "What are you getting out of this relationship?" set up an individualistic cost–benefit analysis that seems antithetical to family commitments like faithfulness to marriage and responsibility to children. This individualistic orientation has even permeated the ranks of family therapists, many of whom are more comfortable talking about what family members deserve from a relationship than what they owe to it (Doherty, 1995). Doherty's thoughtful critique, conceptualized as it is from a family impact perspective, is illustrative because it underscores how seldom this type of analysis is undertaken.

The training of researchers deserves special consideration because they produce many of the theories and much of the data that undergird our knowledge of families—what supports families need and how effective family policies and programs are. Conducting research and analyses that take family life into account requires careful attention to protocol, measures, analytical techniques, and theoretical frameworks.

Data and Theories

The lack of a family orientation is evident in the quantity and quality of family data: (a) what data are collected, (b) who is targeted, (c) which measures are used, (d) how data are analyzed, and (e) in what ways studies are theoretically conceptualized and discussed.

What Data Are Collected. First, collecting data on some aspects of family life seems to be a low priority of state and federal governments. There is no better illustration of this bias than the effort in the 1990s to develop social indicators of societal well-being. Several federal executive agencies supported a concerted effort to identify key indicators by which to assess how well we were doing as a society, and to help guide and shape future policy development and social investments. Surprisingly, there was little debate about how to organize these social indicators and, by default, the organizing principle ended up being children, not the families in which the children resided. Even though many of the indicators discussed were based on the family concept, the major publication ended up being titled *Indicators of Children's Well-Being* (Hauser, Brown, & Prosser, 1997). Similarly, a 1997 Executive Order established the annual publication of a set of national statistics based on the health of families. Notably, the resulting publication left the word *family* out of the title: *Trends in the Well-Being of America's Children and* Youth (Westat, 2000).

The preponderance of data on children and families is based on samples that are small and sometimes nonrepresentative (Moore, 1993). Within policymaking circles, U.S. Census data are considered the gold standard, so decisions about what data to collect can have far-reaching implications. As an example, Census data are able to identify a household as a stepfamily only if the stepparent, not the biological parent, completes the form (Coleman, 1993). Also, the only category on the 1990 census form for a respondent who is not a spouse, child, parent, or sibling of the head of household is boarder (D. E. Smith, 1993), a classification that many extended family members might object to. For its data collection in 2000, the Census Bureau dropped the question on marital status on the short form, although it remains on the long form, which is distributed to only 1 of every 6 housing units.

In 2000, the Census started collecting data on unmarried partners, who were classified as households not families. The Census Bureau is not permitted to release data on living arrangements that would approximate same-sex marriage because of the Defense of Marriage Act, which defines marriage as between a man and woman. Because unmarried partners were not defined as a family type, less information is gathered and reported (Gates, 2005). For example, the Census asked if a household was headed by a same-sex couple and if the household included children, but did not ask how many children (Meezan & Rauch, 2005).

When data are collected on a larger scale, important family variables are sometimes omitted. The National Survey of Families and Households, a prominent source of family data, did not distinguish between half-siblings and stepsiblings in its first wave of data collection. In 1995, budget cutbacks prompted the National Center on Health Statistics to discontinue compiling national data from state reports on marriage and divorce, thereby limiting the capacity to describe marital trends within and across states (Ooms, 1998). Most states summarize marriage and divorce data, but the number of states that tabulate and publish detailed data that would allow tracking such trends is not known (Ooms, 1998).

In 1990, the United Nations Statistical Commission recommended that member countries prepare data estimating the value of nonmarket labor, such as the functions families perform for their members. By the late 1990s, Australia, Austria, Canada, France, Germany, Italy, Israel, and Norway had begun collecting the data, but no progress had been made in the United States (Crittenden, 2001).

Who Is Targeted in Data Collection. Most program evaluations measure outcomes for individuals rather than families. One prominent example is the 1985 report on the cost-effectiveness of eight major federal programs promoting children's well-being. Only one program, Head Start, considered the program's effect on parents (Ooms & Preister, 1988), despite the undisputed importance of parents in the lives of children. Instead of focusing only on an individual child or adult, a family orientation would entail focusing on a relationship, such as that between a child and a parent or between two adults through marriage or other partnerships.

Which Measures Are Used. Even if families become the focus of research, collecting family data is virtually impossible unless family criteria can be identified that might serve as (a) widely agreed-on outcomes of policies or programs (e.g., rates of family violence or quality of the parent–child relationship; Cohen & Ooms, 1993; Moen & Schorr, 1987), and (b) theoretically sound family processes (e.g., parental responsiveness, family involvement, or interpersonal communication skills) that may contribute to these outcomes (Haskins, 1993). Only when family variables are widely and consistently used can generalizations be drawn across studies.

How Data Are Analyzed. Analyzing variables from the perspective of the whole family system (Cohen & Ooms, 1993) is a daunting task even for the experienced researcher. For example, in a three-person family, there are six relationships (i.e., the mother–father, mother–child, father–mother, father–child, child–mother, and child–father). In a two-parent family with two children, the number of relationships escalates to 12, with substantially more if a divorce is followed by remarriage. Because the relationships of family members are not independent of each other, traditional statistical techniques such as analysis of variance (ANOVA) are not appropriate, requiring researchers to master new analytic methods such as structural equation modeling (Cook, 1994), repeated measures ANOVA, intraclass correlations, and hierarchical linear modeling (Maguire, 1999).

How Studies Are Theoretically Conceptualized and Discussed. These shortcomings in family data, measures, and analytic techniques have stymied the development of theories (Olson & Tiesel, 1993), which, contrary to conventional wisdom, are essential to policymakers (Bogenschneider & Gross, 2004; Moen & Schorr, 1987; Monroe, 1995). If policymakers are to develop workable solutions to social problems, they need theoretical frameworks that explain the causes of social problems, thereby indicating which decisions or interventions may offer the best chance for success. For example, the notion of the psychological parent, rooted in attachment theory, was frequently used by courts to make decisions about who should have complete and perhaps exclusive custody rights (Mason, Fine, & Carnochan, 2001). In aging, decisions are likely to be shaped by competing theories regarding whether cognitive development is conceptualized as a property of the individual or as having a relational component. At the other end of the life span, the universal prekindergarten movement could adopt the school paradigm that focuses on the individual or the early education paradigm that focuses on involving the parent.

The theoretical mechanisms that explain how family income is linked to negative child outcomes provide critical guidance for policy decisions (Sawhill, 1992). If low income directly jeopardizes child outcomes, then the appropriate policy response is to transfer more income to children. However, if income is simply a marker of something else, such as parents' enhanced feelings of competence and the role modeling that competent parents provide when they earn income, then earned income is more important to child well-being than are welfare transfers. Consequently, the appropriate policy response would be to help people develop the skills and work habits they need to succeed in the labor market. If lack of income produces stress or depression in parents and if this stress or depression interferes with competent parenting, then the best response may be interventions to reduce stress and enhance parenting competence, which in turn would improve child outcomes.

SUMMARY

Let me be clear that I am not arguing against the value of child data, because as Hernandez (1994) pointed out, policy conclusions may be markedly different if the unit of analysis is children rather than families. What I am arguing is that, because analyzing data from a child or family perspective yields different results, child data may be incomplete if not supplemented with family data. In fact, data from both sources may be warranted for a couple reasons. First, because 98% of children in this country grow up in families and are expected to continue doing so in the future (Steiner, 1980), ignoring the context in which the vast majority of children are raised seems shortsighted. Second, child data or data on other individuals in families are often needed to document social problems in ways that capture the attention of policymakers, the press, and the public. Yet our responses to social problems might be more effective if policymakers moved beyond the realm of the individual and incorporated family considerations into policy and program solutions.

This point leads to the obvious question about how effective policies and programs are that focus on families rather than individuals. Before turning to this question, however, I address the thorny issue of definitions—a topic that historically has hampered efforts to advance the field of family policy.

3

What Is Family Policy?
What Is a Family Perspective
in Policymaking?

There has been a dramatic transformation in the perception of the family. Consequently, we are at a crossroad between what the family was in the past, what it is now, and what it will and should be in the future.
—Henry J. Sokalski, Secretariat,
International Year of the Family (1993, p. 3)

As a family policy specialist, I often am asked to define family policy. My friends often joke that family policy begins at home with decisions about whether to leave the toilet seat up or down. Granted, that decision is a humorous example of one specific family policy, but the lack of clarity in definitions of family policy is no joking matter. Scholars have been unable to agree on how to define family policy, but they have agreed that an essential first task in moving the field forward is to reach consensus on definitions (Aldous, Dumon, & Johnson, 1980; Moen & Jull, 1995; Monroe, 1995; Wisensale, 2001b), a task that has proven so difficult that it has been likened to "swimming in molasses or nailing Jell-O to a tree" (Blankenhorn, 1990, p. 5).

On the one hand, I am surprised at how often I am asked what family policy is. I suspect that family policy teachers are asked to define their field more frequently than are teachers of economic or environmental policy. On the other hand, this void in clear and consistent definitions of family policy is not too surprising given the short and contentious history of the field. Of course, we have always had a family tilt in policymaking, but family policy did not emerge as a distinct field of intellectual interest and inquiry until the 1970s. During the 1980s, its development was stymied in the aftermath of the politically contentious White House Conference on Families. Issues like abortion and same-sex unions were so divisive that politicians shied away from even using the word *family,* and family policy was pushed off the federal policy agenda for almost a decade (Ooms, 1984).

Yet clear definitions are critically important because progress depends on identifying what the parameters are—what family policy is, what it is not, and what it can achieve (Schattschneider, 1960). Imprecise language invites impostors who borrow the politically popular, nonpartisan family label of the 1990s (Skocpol, 1997) as a Trojan horse for narrow individualistic agendas (Blankenhorn, 1988b, p. 6; Ooms, 1990). To muster broad-based political support, almost any issue whether it is cutting taxes, gun control, prayer in schools, or women's rights can be touted as being good for families (Belkin, 2000; Blankenhorn, 1990). One prominent example is the 1998 name change of the Women's Legal Defense Fund to the National Partnership for Women and Families.

Definitions of family policy have been marked by differences in their scope, source, target, and content. In regard to scope, Kamerman and Kahn (1991) defined family policy as "everything that government does to and for the family" (p. 3). Critics have contended that defining family policy broadly enough to include defense policy, economic edicts, or pollution controls results in a concept so elastic that it potentially encompasses everything and consequently loses any integrity. Conversely, Moen and Schorr (1987) defined family policy as a "widely agreed-on set of objectives for families, toward the realization of which the state (and other major social institutions) deliberately shapes programs and policies" (p. 795). Critics have contended that definitions requiring "deliberate" and "widely agreed upon" actions (Trzcinski, 1995a) are so limiting that the definition becomes virtually meaningless.

Some definitions constrain the source of family policy to actions by governmental bodies (Aldous & Dumon, 1990), thereby disregarding the large number of family policies that emanate from employers and nonprofit organizations. The target of family policy has sometimes been restricted to families with children (Aldous et al., 1980), which excludes families providing care and economic support to adults. The content of family policy has been confined by some scholars to economic issues (Seaberg, 1990), essentially overlooking several other important aspects of family functioning such as childrearing and caregiving.

FAMILY POLICY OR A FAMILY PERSPECTIVE IN POLICYMAKING?

Perhaps this confusion can be clarified by returning to the roots of the field and the early writing of Kamerman and Kahn (1978), who made a clear distinction between explicit policies, which are designed to achieve specific goals regarding families, and implicit policies, which are not specifically or primarily intended to affect families, but which have indirect consequences on them. As a parallel to this distinction, I propose both an explicit and implicit definition: family policy and a family perspective in policymaking, respectively. Both of these terms build on a broad definition of policy as a plan or course of action carried out through a law, rule, code, or other mechanism in the public or private sectors.

Ooms (1990) used the analogy of economic policy to defend the importance of an explicit definition of family policy against naysayers who contend that attempting to define a field as broad as family policy is a futile endeavor (Steiner, 1981). Although almost any policy has some impact on the economy, certain policies such as those in the budgetary and fiscal realms are similarly broad, but nonetheless are clearly understood to be economic policy.

To provide clarity to the field, an explicit definition needs to frame family policy in a way that overcomes the limitations of a scope that is too broad or narrow, a source that is unnecessarily constraining, a target too exclusionary, and a content unreflective of the many functions families perform. Thus, a definition of family policy worth its salt should focus attention on "family business" (Blankenhorn, 1990, p. 18; Zimmerman, 1988/1995). *Family policy* involves four main family functions (Consortium of Family Organizations, 1990b; Ooms, 1990): (a) family creation (e.g., to marry or divorce, to bear or adopt children, to provide foster care), (b) economic support (e.g., to provide for members' basic needs), (c) childrearing (e.g., to socialize the next generation), and (d) family caregiving (e.g., to provide assistance for the disabled, ill, frail, and elderly). Families also provide members with love and transmit cultural and religious values, but these intimate functions matter to social policy only when they interfere with the four main family functions (Ooms, 1990).

For policies that fall outside this explicit definition of family policy, and there are many, a companion implicit term, *a family perspective in policymaking,* acknowledges the important role that family considerations can play in a broad range of policy issues. A family perspective in policymaking analyzes the consequences of any policy or program, regardless of whether it is explicitly aimed at families, for its impact on family well-being (e.g., family stability, family relationships, and a family's ability to carry out its responsibilities).

To clarify these terms, Ooms (1990) offered several examples. Family policy would include issues encompassed under the four family functions such as child care, child support, divorce, family violence, juvenile crime, long-term care, and teenage pregnancy. Tax provisions that create a child-care tax credit or decrease the marriage penalty would be classified as family policy. However, a tax reform law that lowers taxes for individuals, many of whom happen to live in families, would not be considered family policy. Other issues, such as health care, housing, poverty, substance abuse, and unemployment, would not be considered family policies because they are not aimed specifically at families. Nevertheless, these issues would certainly benefit from a family perspective that examines in what ways families contribute to these problems, how families are affected, and whether families need to be involved in solutions (Ooms, 1990).

WHAT CAN A FAMILY PERSPECTIVE BRING TO POLICYMAKING?

Whatever definition is used, the term *family* makes an important conceptual distinction in policymaking circles by moving our attention beyond the individual to a relationship between two or more persons tied together by blood, legal bonds, or the performance of family functions such as caregiving and economic support. Why is using families as a yardstick for social policy better than a focus on children, women, or men? A family focus makes sense because it reflects the way the real world works. Most Americans live their lives not as individuals operating on an island unaffected by others, but in relationships. Focusing on the interests of women or men, as many organizations do, with no thought of the roles most of these women and men play as spouses, parents, and partners is incomplete, because it encourages individuals to claim their own rights at the expense of others. Focusing on children seems short-sighted when their ability to grow and develop depends on close and continuing relationships with adult members of the species. The objective of family policy is not to play off one family member against another, but rather to maximize individual contributions for the good of the whole (Kamerman, 1977).

A family impact perspective has the potential to bring an essential quality to American policymaking that no other institution or interest group does as well—commitment to others even when such actions exact a personal cost. In a society that is often focused on getting more, the family perspective reshifts the focus to giving more. In a nation built on the premise that every person is endowed with certain inalienable rights, the family perspective serves as a reminder that these rights come with responsibilities. In a culture that often uses money and material possessions as a sign of worth, worthiness in families comes from actions difficult to ascribe a dollar value to such as commitment and self-sacrifice by each for the other. In a country with a political action committee for every cause, a family perspective has the potential to counter the narrow, often self-serving agendas of proliferating special-interest groups. The family perspective provides a moral voice with the potential to overcome the threats of self-centeredness, greed, self-interest, and the quest for power (Responsive Communitarian Platform, 1992).

The family perspective is a critical distinction that is too often overlooked in policy circles. For example, any children's policy or women's policy is often incorrectly equated with family policy, even though the target of interest is an individual, not a family relationship or family unit. Family, when mentioned in policy debate, is sometimes misused to represent some, but not all, relationships in families. For example, all too often, we speak of children in a vacuum without mentioning the families in which they are being reared.

Family can be a code word for mother and child, with little or no attention to father (Blum, 1993) or grandparent (Henderson, 2004). *Family* is sometimes used as shorthand to represent the relationship of parent and child, often ignoring the relationship of the adults in families through marriage or other partnerships. The commonly used term *single-parent family* masks the role of cohabitating and noncustodial parents in the lives of their children (McLanahan, Garfinkel, & Mincy, 2001; Walsh, 1995).

Even with more precise terminology, however, we still face the question of who family policy is designed for (Ooms, 1990), which raises the thorny controversial issue of defining the family. Definitional issues, particularly those regarding same-sex marriage and grandparent visitation rights, have proven so controversial and polarizing that they have stymied progress on other family issues.

WHAT EVIDENCE OR PRECEDENCE CAN WE USE TO DEFINE THE FAMILY?

Defining family is not a matter that can be settled by research or by court cases. Researchers cannot design a study that will examine what is the best or most optimal definition of family. Research, however, can document "what is," which can help policymakers design what the best political response might be. One of the best examples is a recent study of approximately 5,000 children born to unwed parents living in 20 large U.S. cities (McLanahan et al., 2001). To the surprise of policymakers and the public alike, this study documented a high rate of cohabitation and close partner relationships among so-called single parents. When their baby was born, half of unmarried mothers were living with the father and another third were romantically involved with the father. Many of these fathers are highly involved at the time of the birth, with nearly three quarters of the mothers rating their chances of marrying the father as 50–50 or better. The mothers report that 80% of fathers provided some financial support during pregnancy, 84% had their name on the birth certificate, and 79% of children will take the father's surname. This pattern of family-like behaviors seems to reflect more than just the excitement surrounding the birth, given that 75% of the children who were living with their biological parents at birth were also living with them 18 months later, and 60% were living with them 6 years later. By revealing that the commonly used term *single parent* is often a misnomer, this study changed the terms of the policy debate—these cohabitating couples are now referred to as *fragile families*. Conceivably, fragile families may need different policy responses than the mythical single parent raising a child alone.

Moreover, there is no explicit definition of family in the law, but this does not mean that courts do not base decisions on a particular view of the family, typically a traditional one (Bogenschneider et al., 1993). The competing interests of family members come into sharp relief when grandparents petition the courts for the right to visitation with their grandchildren. In courts of family law, the rights of biological and adoptive parents to raise their children as they see fit is a "highly-guarded constitutional and common law right" (Henderson, 2004, p. 6), whereas grandparents do not have a constitutionally protected right to grandchildren as members of the extended family. Thus, based on long-standing family law tradition, parent rights are protected above all other considerations, except in cases of parental unfitness or child maltreatment. The U.S. Supreme Court has granted very limited protections to grandparent-led families and in only one known case, *King v. King* (1992), did the justices seek to balance the rights of parents, children, and grandparents. Courts have granted grandparents visitation rights in a small proportion of cases (36.5%), which suggests a gradual shift in how the family is defined in some circumstances (Henderson, 2004).

The legal definition of family is also central to court decisions on same-sex couples. Currently, about two thirds of states have adopted versions of the Defense of Marriage Act, which nullifies same-sex marriages that occur in other states (Wisensale, 2005b). In about half the states, courts have allowed members of same-sex couples to adopt their partner's children. Three recent California Supreme Court decisions ruled that former members of such relationships could be required to assume parental rights and obligations even in the absence of an adoption or a domestic partner agreement. For example, after a same-sex relationship ended, the court required the former partner to pay child support to support twins born when the women were a couple (Liptak, 2005). However, courts have not developed a single definition of the family, but instead have made decisions on a case-by-case basis. These changes in legal responses to the definition of family have been hailed by some as a long overdue recognition of changing family forms, and have been criticized by others as deliberate attempts to undermine and unravel the traditional family as we know it (Liptak, 2005).

DOES THE FIELD REQUIRE A SINGULAR DEFINITION OF THE FAMILY?

In work with state policymakers, we seldom receive requests to define what we mean by family, which leads me to believe that the definition of family need not be a barrier to achieving progress as a field. We have found that promoting a family perspective has proven more important than any specific definition of family. In fact, we believe that just as there is no single, sacrosanct definition of the economy (Coleman, 1993), no singular definition of the family may be possible. For example, thinking of the economy probably brings to mind a variety of economic structures, such as the producer-based farmer's market, the locally owned craft store, a franchised fast-food restaurant, and the multinational bank. The word *economy* encompasses a range of financial functions, such as producing goods or services to earn income, using income to purchase goods for consumption, and distributing wealth through buying and selling. Like the economy, families encompass a myriad of structures (e.g., single-parent families, stepfamilies, foster families) and engage in multiple functions (e.g., bearing or adopting children, providing economic support).

Existing definitions of family can be categorized in two ways: (a) structural definitions that specify family membership according to certain characteristics such as blood relationship, legal ties, or residence; and (b) functional definitions that specify functions that family members perform, such as sharing economic resources and caring for the young, elderly, sick, and disabled (see Bogenschneider, 2000; Bogenschneider et al., 1993; Moen & Schorr, 1987).

Both types of definitions have limitations. For example, structural definitions exclude long-term foster families, same-sex partners, and cohabiting couples who are not related by birth, marriage, or adoption, but who nevertheless carry out many family-like functions over a significant period of time. Functional definitions appear on the surface to be more inclusive because these criteria are met by long-term foster families, cohabiting couples, and same-sex partners. Yet other living arrangements that are considered to be families do not fulfill the specified family functions. For example, functional definitions would exclude a noncustodial parent who fails to pay child support or a legally sanctioned marriage where the couple no longer cares for each other, but stays together for economic reasons or for the sake of the children (Doherty & Baird, 1983).

Trying to identify only one definition of family is like trying to cheat death: It does not work, and you end up feeling foolish for trying (Doherty & Baird, 1983). Rather than seeking a single universal definition, either a structural or functional definition can be written to reinforce the intent of a specific program or policy (Eshleman, 1991; Moen & Schorr, 1987). For example, if the issue were child support, a structural definition would require financial support only from those people related to the child by blood, marriage, or adoption, whereas functional definitions would require support from any committed caregiver. If the issue were care for the elderly, structuralists would provide benefits only to those who have legal responsibility for the dependent, whereas functionalists would include any close companion who provided care. When considered in the context of specific legislation, structural definitions seem more appropriate for some goals and functional definitions for others. We believe that definitions will vary over time, across jurisdictions, and in different political contexts.

The lack of a single preferred definition of *family* may seem opportunistic or even cowardly, yet precedence exists. No legal definition of family appears in the U.S. Constitution, the federal statutes or regulations (Ooms, 1998), or many state statutes (Bogenschneider et al., 1993). In fact, the U.S. Supreme Court concluded in *Stanley v. Illinois* (1972) the court should not be constrained by a rigid or formal definition of the family unit, but should make a determination based on the facts of the case (Henderson, 2004).

Because it is not a matter that can be resolved by research, defining family is ultimately a question of values and priorities—the types of decisions that policymakers are elected to make. For some, leaving the matter to policymakers may seem unsettling and unsatisfying. Yet given the multiple goals of policies, it may be impossible to settle on a single definition that will suit all purposes, and a protracted debate over language and definition may impede progress toward more useful and pragmatic policy initiatives. Rather, it may be more prudent and productive to define families according to the intent of a specific policy or program (Moen & Schorr, 1987).

The absence of a universal definition does not mean that family definitions are unimportant. Definitions often determine who benefits from a program and who does not. For example, federal programs have often been restricted to certain types of households (e.g., single-parent households), and health insurance benefits are often available only to partners who are married, which the 1996 Defense of Marriage Act defined as only heterosexual, not same-sex, unions. Furthermore, definitions often convey societal beliefs about what is normative and socially sanctioned and, by implication, what is deviant.

Defining families and differentiating between family policy and a family perspective in policymaking are central to positioning the field as "a full-fledged adult in the policy world" (Jacobs & Davies, 1994, p. 290). Precise definitions and clear language establish parameters for the field that expand its reach so that many policies are included, but also limit its scope so that some policies are excluded.

To place this discussion of definition into context, the next chapter examines whether families matter and if they can bring a value-added perspective to policymaking. The answer to this question is central to crafting a vision for the field and articulating the value of family well-being as a criterion for policymaking.

4

Do Families Matter and What Is Their Value in Policymaking?

The family is the most powerful, the most humane, and by far the most economical system known for building competence and character.
—Bronfenbrenner (1986, p. 4)

The novel is set in England in 2021. Human males have become sterile, and the last children were born on Earth in 1995. The world did not give up hope until the last generation reached sexual maturity and tests revealed that not one of them could produce fertile sperm. Then they knew the human race was literally dying and there was no hope of a future.

Science and invention had ended except for those discoveries that could extend human life. Crops remained unsown, and landowners left their estates untended. What joy was there in planting trees and tending gardens that no one would see grow to maturity? Animals were despised because they could do without thought—something humans could not.

The elderly, no longer wanted or needed, were conducted to state-sponsored mass suicides known as the quietus. The government paid hefty pensions to the relatives of incapacitated or dependent elderly who committed suicide.

In their universal bereavement, people put away all reminders of children. Playgrounds were dismantled, toys were burned, schools were boarded up or used for adult education, and children's books were removed from libraries. The cry of a newborn baby and the voices of children could be heard only on tapes or records, which some found unbearable, but others began to feed on like drugs.

Facing a future without a future, people were filled with outrage, resignation, and apathy. Justice, compassion, and commitment were unheard echoes on the empty air. Few were interested in struggling for a just society when there was no hope of posterity for the race or for oneself.

This novel, *Children of Men,* by P. D. James (1992) underscores that much of what we do in the present makes sense because of the possibility of a future. We are diminished if we live without knowledge of the past and without hope for the future, which, for me, lies in children and the families that nurture them. The willingness of one generation to invest in the next is one of the most telling measures of the worth of a society (Bronfenbrenner & Weiss, 1983).

Sagas of family life have been a popular literary theme that has transcended the ages (Kane & Penrod, 1995), ranging from the classic novels of Leo Tolstoy to the contemporary writing of P. D. James. Television sitcoms of the last half-century have portrayed family life with all its human frailties in programs such as *All in the Family, The Brady Bunch, Coach, The Cosby Show, Dharma and Greg, Everybody Loves Raymond, Home Improvement, I Love Lucy, Malcolm in the Middle, Married With Children, The Nanny, Oh Baby, Ozzie and Harriet, Roseanne,* and *The Simpsons.*

In their writing, some scholars have romanticized the family as a "haven in a heartless world" (Lasch, 1977). Others have demonized it as an institution that stifles individualism, oppresses women, and fosters patriarchy (Stacey, 1993). Based on the reports of anthropologists, the family in one of its many forms has been part of every known human society (Eastman, 1996). In contemporary society, families are said to be the central element and source of greatest joy in the lives of the majority of Americans. Nine out of 10 married people find their greatest joy in their family, but so do more than half of single Americans and almost three fourths of those currently divorced (Mellman, Lazarus, & Rivlin, 1990). The vast majority of Americans (93%) rate a happy marriage as one of their most important life goals (Mason, et al., 2004). Moreover, in the policy realm, initiatives that focus on children and families are so politically popular (Hutchins, 1998) that families as a theme in policymaking may be at their strongest point in the last 20 years in Congress, in the states, and among the citizenry (Ooms, 1995). This enthusiasm for families implies the value of a family focus in policymaking, but what hard evidence exists that families matter to society or policymaking? This chapter addresses each of these questions.

THE VALUE OF FAMILIES TO SOCIETY

Families teach a powerful moral lesson that no other institution or interest group can teach as well. As the only institution based primarily on love and caring, families teach connectedness and commitment to others and perhaps have always done so (Kane & Penrod, 1995). The ethos of well-functioning families is commitment (Bayme, 1991; Doherty, 1995) so strong that we would give our life for another (Hewlett & West, 1998). This commitment is essential to all cultures and societies because with human offspring, more than any other, the prospects that the young will survive and develop depend on close association with older members of the species (Bronfenbrenner & Weiss, 1983; Browning, 1996; Eastman, 1996). This commitment may be even more consequential in countries like the United States, with its pervasive individualistic culture, a strong market economy, and a weak government safety net. The importance of family commitment in each domain is considered in turn.

Family Commitment in Individualistic Societies

Since the 18th and 19th centuries, nearly every family historian has written about how the culture of individualism has come in conflict with family allegiances and solidarity (Browning & Rodriguez, 2002). In his classic writing on democracy in the United States in the 1830s, Tocqueville (1945) worried that freedom was threatened by individualism. Tocqueville coined the word *individualism* to describe Americans' tendency to isolate themselves from their responsibilities to the larger society by focusing exclusively on themselves and their families, which he described as becoming enclosed in one's own heart. If unchecked, individualism could isolate people from their ancestors, contemporaries, and even descendants as they come to believe they control their own destinies with nothing expected from or owed to others.

Tocqueville observed that American individualism was tempered by religious and democratic political participation and the large number of voluntary associations he observed, but particularly by associations in the family. The family, by being the first institution to teach "habits of the heart," could counter isolationism with a larger view of public responsibility.

The individualism that Tocqueville observed in the 19th century is still pervasive in American culture today (Bellah et al., 1985/1996). In fact, independence and self-reliance have become so ingrained in American thought, mores, and cultural metaphors that it is almost invisible except to the most astute observer. Individual rights are so taken for granted by Americans that they are seldom disputed. According to Bellah and his colleagues (1985/1996), "Anything that would violate our right to think for ourselves, judge for ourselves, make our own decisions, live our life as we see fit, is not only morally wrong, it is sacrilegious" (p. 142). For example, although most religions are based on a body of believers who support and reinforce personal beliefs, religion in the United States is seen first as something individual prior to any affiliation with an institution. In a 1978 Gallup poll, 80% of

Americans agreed that "an individual should arrive at his or her religious beliefs independent of any church or synagogue" (Bellah et al., 1985/1996, p. 228). In fact, when original German hymns were imported to the New World, the word *I* was seldom found, whereas it is frequently found in hymns originating in America (J. Strandjord, personal communication, August 29, 2001).

The mythical heroes in American drama are the archetype of rugged individualists. The cowboy, exemplified by the Lone Ranger, was a shrewd sharpshooter who saved the townspeople but ended up leaving the town and riding off alone into the sunset. Perhaps an even more vivid exemplar is the hard-boiled detective who, like the cowboy, is a loner. Detectives such as Kojak, MacGyver, and Matlock are smart and relentless in detecting corruption and bringing justice to bear for the good of an often corrupt society—a society they always stand outside. What makes the cowboy and detective rugged individualists is that they have special skills they can use to save society. Yet to save society, they must remain devoid of family and community— the very associations touted as the best antidotes to unfettered individualism and powerful prophylactics for civic disengagement (Bellah et al., 1985/1996).

The consequences of individualism became even more apparent in the 1990s (Bellah et al., 1985/1996; Blankenhorn, 1990; Bumpass, 1990; Lesthaeghe, 1995). For example, the Responsive Communitarian Platform (1992) issued a call for a better balance between our rights as individuals and our responsibilities as members of families and communities. In keeping with the founding fathers, communitarians believe that democracy cannot be sustained without a citizenry willing to respect the rights of others and to assume responsibility for the collective good even when such actions exact a personal cost (Glendon, 1992).

Like Tocqueville, communitarians believe that cultivating the moral foundations for balancing obligations to self and others begin in the family. Culture provides broad parameters for acceptable behavior, but it is in families that these values are actually translated into individual actions. As exemplified in cross-cultural research, American mothers typically perceive their babies as being born dependent and parent them in ways that build independence and self-reliance, whereas Japanese mothers view babies as being born independent, so their parenting is aimed at building interdependence and reliance on the group (Barratt, 1993). For example, to build interdependence, parent–child relationships are characterized by frequent socializing, guidance, and consultation, which give the child less privacy. Conversely, to build independence, parent–child relationships are marked more by emotional detachment, which provides the child with increased privacy and autonomy (Triandis, Bontempo, Villareal, Asai, & Lucca, 1988). As one concrete example, punishment of teens in U.S. families is being grounded or forbidden to leave the house, whereas punishment of teens in Japanese families is being put out of the house (Triandis, 1994).

The Responsive Communitarian Position Paper on the Family contends that families teach moral lessons that extend beyond one's own family. In families, we learn respect for others along with self-respect, appreciation of the rights of others along with acknowledgment of our own rights, and the responsibility to serve others as well as ourselves. These moral anchors learned in families do not call for heroic self-sacrifice, but rather for the understanding that each member of the community owes something to all the rest (Elshtain et al., 1993).

Many contemporary examples exist of the individualistic tendency to privilege private interests and ignore obligations to the rest of society. A new estate planning industry has grown up that advises the elderly on how to divest themselves of resources so they can pass on their inheritance to their own family and divert the costs of their long-term care to government-sponsored Medicaid programs. At the other end of the life span, college students proudly claim to be aspiring DINKSs—a double-income family with no kids. The desire to earn high incomes and remain childless has become such a common aspiration on college campuses that it evoked an acronym of its own. In a similar vein, college students believe those charged with a crime have the right to a jury trial, but when asked to serve, they say, "find somebody else" (Braiker, 2003).

Perhaps two of the most compelling examples of individualism are (a) the highest rates of income inequality between the rich and the poor in recent U.S. history (see chap. 8), and (b) declines in the Tocquevillian life of civic engagement (Bellah et al., 1985/1996). In an analysis of American civic engagement in the 1990s, Putnam (1995) noted that voter turnout dropped by nearly 25% since 1960, attendance at public meetings fell by more than a third since 1970, union membership plummeted by about half since the mid-1950s, participation in parent–teacher organizations dropped by 40% since the 1960s, and church membership stagnated or declined since the 1970s. Many major civic organizations also experienced a sudden substantial decline in membership. Overall, associational memberships fell by about one fourth in the last quarter-century among all educational and social sectors.

Given that such associations build tolerance and social trust (Boyte & Etzioni, 1993; Wilson, 1999), declining civic engagement may account, in part, for drops in Americans' belief that most people can be trusted—down from 58% in 1960 to 37% in 1993 (Putnam, 1995). Yankelovich (1995) documented an increasing disconnect between the public and its political leaders, a trend that was not evident a decade earlier. This trend seems not to have abated given that Americans' trust in government declined for all levels of government between 1998 and 2004. Americans reporting "not very much" trust in government increased from 16% to 24% for local government, from 15% to 24% for state government, and from 30% to 33% for Congress (Gallup Organization, 2004). Overall, Putnam concluded that Americans "voted less, joined less . . . trusted less, invested less time in public affairs, and with our friends, neighbors, and even our families" (Putnam, 2002, p. 20).

Putnam's analysis has been criticized because he assessed only the quantity, not the quality, of social ties and because he omitted some relevant associations such as work-related groups that Americans may join. Yet even his critics acknowledge that the richness of social ties has declined and selfishness in the United States has increased (Wolfe, 1998). Polls show that the vast majority of Americans believe that the nation's social morality has declined. Among the core values that are eroding are neighborliness and individual obligations and responsibilities—values that Yankelovich (1995) contended are fundamentally important in a rights-oriented individualistic society like ours.

One countervailing trend to rising individualism is the increasing ethnic diversity in the United States. African American, Native American, Asian Pacific American, and Hispanic families differ in many respects, but one commonality is an emphasis on loyalty to the group and collective rather than individualistic values (Harrison, Wilson, Pine, Chan, & Buriel, 1990). Parents in ethnic minority families encourage children to cooperate, share, and recognize their interdependence with others, whereas parents in the White majority culture value competition, autonomy, and self-reliance. In a recent study, Asian and Latin American adolescents endorsed family obligations much more strongly than did adolescents from European backgrounds. These ethnic differences in values and expectations regarding obligations (i.e., assisting, respecting, and supporting their families) were a full standard deviation in magnitude and were consistent across gender, family composition, SES, and place of birth (i.e., whether the youth or parents were born abroad or in this country; Fuligni, Tseng, & Lam, 1999).

As a caveat, it is important to note that people or societies cannot be characterized as totally individualistic or familistic. Using societies as an example, Germany is more individualistic than Hong Kong. Yet in a recent study, Germans chose collectivistic perceptions 37% of the time, whereas people in Hong Kong chose individualistic perceptions 45% of the time (Triandis, 2001). Moreover, it is overly simplistic to assume that people with strong familistic tendencies are never selfish and those with strong individualistic tendencies always are. In reality, the differentiations that I am drawing here for pedagogical reasons are not as distinct or discernible as they appear on first blush. Nevertheless, it does seem safe to conclude that individualism in combination with other societal forces appears to be hard on families and interferes with the moral messages they pass on to the next generation (Browning & Rodriguez, 2002). Furthermore, the influence that individualism exerts on family life may depend, in part, on the context in which it occurs. For example, individualism may be more damaging to family life in the context of a strong market economy, the topic to which we turn next.

Family Commitment in Strong Market Economies

Curiously, gross domestic product is both an antecedent and a consequence of individualism (Triandis et al., 1988). Individualism leads to more innovation and, hence, more economic development, but a strong market economy can become so coercive that it undermines our connections and responsibilities to others (Bellah, 1990). Some cultural observers worry that the market can invade family life and reduce family functions to commodities that can be bought and sold on the private market (Browning & Rodriguez, 2002). For example, several recent examples exist of the privatization of many family functions such as adoption, child care, child support, education, foster care, long-term care, and welfare programs.

The family ethos of commitment may assume greater importance in capitalistic countries to temper the self-interest that often drives market economies (Schor, 1991). For example, between 1969 and 1987, the average employed American worked an additional 163 hours annually or one extra month each year. Some of these extra hours are obviously worked out of necessity, but not all of them are; work hours have increased irrespective of income or family structure. The extra income apparently buys more material goods, as Americans own and consume twice as much as their 1948 counterparts (Schor, 1991). Cultural observers warn that the greatest threat to strong families and a good society is an economy that becomes too coercive, creating a culture of consumerism so potent that it transforms "today's luxuries" into "tomorrow's necessities" (Bellah, 1990; Lesthaeghe, 1995; Schor, 1991, p. 122).

Consumerism has also invaded families in other ways. For example, Americans complain that spending more time at work steals time away from their families. Yet only one third report that they would refuse a job that offered more money or prestige even though it would mean less time for their family (Mellman et al., 1990). Perhaps most disturbing is emerging evidence of a cultural reversal of the meaning of work and home (Hochschild, 1997). In a qualitative study primarily of a *Fortune* 500 company, a surprising 85% of employees reported that home often feels like work, and 58% reported that work often feels like home. When asked about their performance in each setting, 86% said their performance was good or unusually good on the job, but only 59% gave these same ratings to performance in their family. This blurring of work and family, however, was not confirmed in another recent study (Becker & Moen, 1999), which pointed to the need for further research to examine whether market forces are encroaching on family life. If they are, this intrusion may be more harmful in societies where government provides few family supports.

Family Commitment in Societies With a Weak Social Safety Net

According to sociologist Richard Sennett, American is "drunk on the rhetoric of individualism" ("A Conversation With Richard Sennett," 1981, p. 79). This exaggerated belief in the individual coupled with a disbelief in government makes it difficult to create a more cooperative and supportive society. The United States has a small social safety net (i.e., government antipoverty and family support programs), which means that families are called on to be the fail safe. Compared with the education system in societies with extensive government support, the U.S. education system relies more on parents for children's school readiness. With privatized health care, hospitals send patients home before they have recuperated, assuming that families will take up the slack. With a declining union presence, employers have come to expect that families will contribute to employee productivity by tolerating long work hours; relieving the employee of routine family obligations; and taking over during special events such as the birth, adoption, or illness of a family member (Giele, 1996). When a person becomes disabled or unemployed, his or her partner provides extensive care that government might otherwise have to purchase at considerable public expense (Duncan & Magnuson, 2002). When the safety nets are smaller and less certain, families serve more prominent roles as health care providers, educators, social workers, and personnel managers for their members.

Thus, public sentiment endorsing the personal significance of families and their value as a theme in policymaking has rebounded from the lows of the 1980s. Scholarly evidence has reaffirmed the historic value of families to societies, especially in countering the self-interest of individualistic cultures, the materialistic pressures of market economies, and the meager government assistance of societies with small social safety nets. The dilemma for family professionals is that the very conditions that make family commitments so important also constitute some of the most entrenched barriers to approaching policymaking from a family perspective. According to a burgeoning number of studies, policymaking would be more effective if it involved rather than superseded families—the topic of the next section.

THE VALUE OF FAMILIES TO POLICYMAKING

Would policymaking and programs be more effective if approached through the lens of a family perspective rather than an individual perspective? Responding to this question, which may be the most fundamental component of establishing a rationale for family policy, entails addressing three separate issues: (a) How do families contribute to social problems? (b) Do we know how to mount programs to strengthen families? and (c) Can policies promote these proven family programs and processes?

How Do Families Contribute to Social Problems?

Research shows that families are an important mediating link between society and individuals, particularly children. Based on growing evidence, policies that support families by improving child management skills and building strong family relationships can, in turn, foster social competence, promote children's school success, prevent delinquency, and avert disease.

Family researchers are almost unanimous in their descriptions of competent parenting (Riley, 1994). They say competent parents develop secure attachments with their child during infancy by being available and responsive. During childhood and adolescence, competent parents are warm and responsive, but at the same time firm and demanding. Preschool children who experience secure attachments and authoritative parenting are less resistant to parental bids and more cooperative with other children. They perform better in elementary and high school and are more competent in almost everything they do (Riley, 1994).

Without a supportive family, children can attend the best schools and still might not succeed (Westman, 2003). When parents are involved in their children's education, their children perform better academically (Baker & Stevenson, 1986; Epstein, 1985; Henderson & Mapp, 2002; Steinberg & Brown, 1989; Steinberg, Lamborn, Dornbusch, & Darling, 1992; Stevenson & Baker, 1987; Westat & Policy Study Associates, 2001). Their children are less likely to drop out (Rumberger, Ghatak, Poulos, Ritter, & Dornbusch, 1990) and more likely to have good attitudes toward school and homework (Epstein, 1982). Moreover, these benefits occur irrespective of the parents' gender or education and the child's age, gender, ethnicity, or family structure (Bogenschneider, 1997; Henderson & Mapp, 2002). In fact, Nobel Laureate James Heckman attributed the Black–White achievement gap to differences in the quality of the family, home, and social circle (Heckman & Wax, 2004).

For preventing problems in children and youth, there is no better target than the family (Stormshak et al., 2002). Adolescents who were close to their families were less likely to be depressed; have sex; use alcohol, cigarettes, or marijuana; and think about or attempt suicide (Resnick et al., 1997). To give one specific example, delinquency has links to families. In longitudinal studies, researchers have learned that the strongest predictor of juvenile crime is ineffective parenting (Kumpfer, 1993). More specifically, 30% to 40% of the antisocial behavior of early offenders—who are those likely to become violent offenders later—is linked to harsh, inconsistent parenting during the preschool years (G. Patterson, 1986; Patterson & Yoerger, 1993; Yoshikawa, 1994).

Many of the major diseases of modern society are caused by lifestyle choices related to diet and exercise learned in the family (Doherty, 1992). Family stress increases the chances that preschoolers will get throat infections, teens will smoke, and adult family members will get sick (see chap. 7 for a full discussion).

Do We Know How to Mount Programs to Strengthen Families?

There is no easy answer to this deceptively simple question of whether programs can strengthen families. The answer depends not only on what programs work, but also for whom and at what age or stage they work best. Also, we need to examine dosage—how long programs must exist—and processes—why they are effective (Staton, Ooms, & Owen, 1991). Several kinds of family programs have proven effective at least for some participants in selected settings.

Home visiting has been a core component in every successful early intervention program for highly stressed or difficult-to-reach families (Weiss, 1993). Home visiting has attracted considerable attention from policymakers despite inconclusive evaluations (Gomby, Culross, & Behrman, 1999). Promising evidence has emerged, however, from the most rigorous study of nurse home visiting, a treatment–comparison experimental design that followed families longitudinally. Nurse home visiting that occurred prenatally and during the first 2 years of life actually resulted in improvements to the life course of mothers and their children 15 years later (Olds et al., 1997; Olds et al., 1998). Compared with families that received only transportation and developmental screening, the families that received nurse home visiting had lower rates of child abuse and neglect, fewer arrests of the child and mother, a delay in subsequent births to the mother, and reduced family dependence on welfare. Evaluations of other home visiting programs have shown few benefits (Gomby et al., 1999), which suggests that home visiting programs have great potential, but not every program lives up to this promise.

Programs that promoted more parent involvement in school improved children's academic achievement. In a recent meta-analysis of 20 studies of parent involvement in grades K through 5, children whose parents were more involved scored approximately two thirds of a standard deviation above the control group (Turner, Nye, & Schwartz, 2004–2005). Programs that encouraged parents at high risk or with limited English proficiency to become involved in their offspring's schooling resulted in greater school success for their children (Simich-Dudgeon, 1993; Smith, 1968). Data on the cost-effectiveness of parental school involvement are not yet available, but the preliminary evidence is strong enough to warrant policymakers' consideration. If given a choice between a 10% increase in parent involvement and a 10% increase in school budgets, Harvard Professor Robert Putnam (2000b) said he would invest in parent involvement.

When it comes to preventing delinquency, "there's no place like home" (Mendel, 2001, p. 59). Most programs to prevent juvenile delinquency focus on individuals, and few have shown lasting success (Zigler et al., 1992). However, two early childhood intervention and family support programs designed to avert school failure among children in high-risk families showed an unexpected result. They prevented delinquency. Each program provided preschool education, actively involved parents, and linked participants to community services and social support networks. At age 27, children whose parents participated in the High Scope/Perry Preschool program were less apt to be in trouble with the law than were those in the control group. They were also less likely to have received welfare or social services as adults and more likely to have graduated from high school, earned more than $2,000 a month, and owned their own home (see Fig. 4.1). For every dollar spent, the program provided a return of $7 due to fewer special education placements, reduced justice system costs, higher earnings, and reduced welfare costs (Schweinhart, 2003).

Similar results were reported in a public program, the Child-Parent Center that served 100,000 families in some of Chicago's highest poverty neighborhoods beginning in 1967. Fifteen years later, 3-year-olds who participated in the program for 1 or 2 years had lower rates of juvenile crime and violent arrests, as well as lower dropout rates, higher graduation rates, and

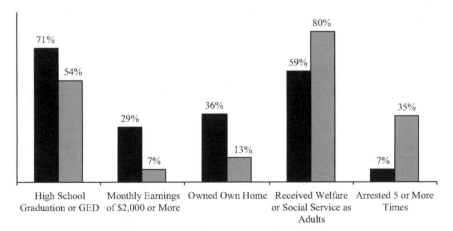

FIG. 4.1. High Scope/Perry Preschool study: Age 27 findings. *Note.* Based on results reported in Schweinhart (2003).

more years of education completed (Reynolds, Temple, Robertson, & Mann, 2001). Parent involvement yielded benefits above and beyond the child's program participation and family background. In recent cost–benefit analyses, the program provides returns of $7 for every $1 spent (Reynolds & Temple, 2005).

Results like these have led the director of research and public affairs at the Federal Reserve Bank of Minneapolis, Art Rolnick, to argue that investing money in early childhood education is perhaps the best form of economic development. For example, he estimates that the rate of return to the public for investing in the Perry Preschool Project is 12%, compared to a 7% return for investing the same amount of money in the stock market (Klein, 2004).

Strong support for family approaches has come from studies at the Oregon Social Learning Center. For example, their Parent Management Training delivers an average of 20 hours of instruction to parents, with 45 hours needed for high-risk families (Kumpfer & Alvarado, 2003). Parents learn specific child management practices including closer monitoring, conveying clear expectations for behavior, responding effectively to noncompliance, and rewarding positive behavior. Children in participating families displayed less antisocial behavior, with improvements large enough to raise the target child (and siblings) into the range of normal functioning (e.g., G. Patterson, 1986). Effects have been shown to last up to 4.5 years (Baum & Forehand, 1981).

An experimental design study of the Oregon Social Learning Center's Adolescent Transitions Program provided an even better test of the value of a family approach. Researchers contrasted a randomly assigned control group with comparison groups that were provided interventions for parents only, youth only, both parents and youth, and one group that was given only self-study materials (Dishion et al., 1996). In the long-term analysis, the teen-only group actually reported more smoking and worse school behavior than did the control group. Apparently bringing high-risk youth together, no matter how skillfully, glamorized inappropriate behavior so that participants more eagerly adopted it. Compared with the combined control and self-directed groups, the parent-only training proved most effective in improving youth behavior at school and also in reducing tobacco and marijuana use 1 year later. Contrary to expectations, no benefits occurred for the combined parent–teen intervention. Thus, interventions retain their cost-effectiveness if training parents is emphasized and aggregating young adolescents is avoided (Dishion et al., 1999).

Recently, parenting and family-strengthening programs have become more comprehensive, targeting both parents' and children's behavior often in a school or community setting (Conduct Problems Prevention Research Group, 1999, 2002a, 2002b; Dishion et al., 2002; Kumpfer & Alvarado, 2003;

Stormshak et al., 2005; Stormshak et al., 2002). In these collaborative, multidimensional, multiagency programs, parent training reduces child conduct disorder, child training improves social competence, and family practice sessions strengthen family relationships and communication (Kumpfer & Alvarado, 2003). The most effective package for enhancing parenting skills is combining parent training, which improves caregiver involvement, with home visits, which deliver participation rates of about 76% instead of the 33% that is typical in parent training (Stormshak et al., 2002).

The strongest evidence regarding the added value that a family component can bring to policies and programs emerges in the areas of child development, education, health, and juvenile crime. However, evidence is emerging in other areas as well. For example, improving family relationships helps programs reach their intended outcomes, and providing financial support to families improves family functioning. For example, in treatment programs for heroin addicts, reducing the level of family conflict was associated with less drug use (Knight & Simpson, 1996). The Minnesota Family Investment program provided additional income to working members of welfare families by boosting benefits as well as discounting 38% of earned income in calculating family eligibility. In evaluations, the program boosted family income, improved child well-being, increased marriage rates, reduced domestic violence, and stabilized marriage. To achieve these family benefits, the program cost between $1,900 and $3,900 more per family than the former Aid to Families with Dependent Children (AFDC) program (Marshall & Sawhill, 2004).

Can Policies Promote These Proven Family Programs and Processes?

Taken together, these studies provide compelling examples of the potential of family-focused approaches. Not all family approaches have been this encouraging, however, particularly evaluations of teenage pregnancy prevention programs (Kirby, 1997) and two-generation welfare programs (St. Pierre, Layzer, & Barnes, 1996). Some family-based interventions even have had unexpected adverse consequences. For example, involving couples rather than individuals in employment assistance programs resulted in better earnings gains when the program ended, but not 2 years later. This erosion in earnings gains may have resulted from the higher fertility of women living with a partner than those living alone (Gordon & Heinrich, 2005).

The best approaches for many social problems take a holistic view of the family and are comprehensive in nature, broadly addressing a family's needs for income, education, housing, or health care—all fundamental to strengthening families (Kumpfer & Alvarado, 2003). If a child goes to a failing school, remains in a neighborhood infested with crime and drugs, and lacks adult role models, a program's positive effects may quickly dissipate (Bruner, 2004). All in all, exaggerating the effectiveness of family programs to policymakers can be counterproductive, yet ignoring this demonstrated potential seems shortsighted.

What policymakers want to know is this: Can policies promote these proven family practices and programs, and how effective are they? We know that a handful of intensive, relatively expensive programs work as single-site demonstration programs. We do not yet know whether they will work if replicated on a larger scale with diverse families in different locales (Riley, 1994; Staton et al., 1991; Weiss & Halpern, 1989). We know that family-focused programs like those for preventing child abuse and juvenile crime can be expensive on a per-family basis. Yet we also know that they can be cost-effective if we factor in the cost to society of lost potential, personal suffering, law enforcement, and rehabilitation (Hawkins, Catalano, & Miller, 1992).

SUMMARY

Families do matter, and they do bring a perspective to policymaking that no other institution or interest group can do as well. In the words of Seltzer (2000):

> Families matter for individuals. What happens in our families affects how we live our lives, whether we are rich or poor, the languages we speak, the work that we do, how healthy we are, and how we feel. Families also matter for the larger social group. Family members take care of each other . . . and bear and rear the next generation. (p. 1263)

In so doing, families are an important economic unit and the only one that actually produces human capitol by socializing and educating children, providing dependable workers, and building the foundations early in life for later productivity. In fact, the investments made by families may account for three quarters of all human capital investments (Crittenden, 2001).

The rationale for family-focused policymaking has been strengthened by a growing body of research on the important functions that families perform for society and the important role that policies and programs play in fostering stable, well-functioning families. Yet the discriminating reader will note, as did Rist (1994) of the U.S. General Accounting Office, that "We are well past the time when it is possible to argue that good research will, because it is good, influence the policy process" (p. 546). For this good research on families to be acted on in policymaking, it is essential to examine whether families are perceived primarily as a private matter or as a legitimate target for government action. This topic is taken up in chapter 5.

5

Are Family Issues a Legitimate Focus of Policymaking?

Sometimes when I get home at night in Washington, I feel as though I had been in a great traffic jam. The jam is moving toward the Hill where Congress sits in judgment on all the administrative agencies of the Government. . . . There are all kinds of conveyances that the Army can put into the street—tanks, gun carriers, trucks. . . . There are the hayracks and the binders and the ploughs and all the other things that the Department of Agriculture manages to put into the streets . . . the handsome limousines in which the Department of Commerce rides . . . the barouches in which the Department of State rides in such dignity. . . . I stand on the sidewalk watching it become more congested and more difficult, and then because the responsibility is mine and I must, I take a very firm hold on the handles of the baby carriage and I wheel it into the traffic.
—Grace Abbott, Chief, U.S. Children's Bureau, 1931–1934

The legitimacy of family policy hinges on whether families are perceived primarily as a personal matter or as a proper target for policymaking. The most prominent question faced by policymakers in the 1990s was not whether families needed support, but whether support should be provided by government (Trzcinski, 1995b). Whether families are a proper issue for public policy is not a question that can be answered by science. Instead, it is a political question of values, judgments, and the priorities of the American people. This chapter addresses the legitimacy question in two ways. First, it examines recent political judgments that have been made about the development of policies to support family life. Second, it reviews the results of recent polls examining the values of the American people regarding the role of government in family life.

Much of the struggle in the 1970s and 1980s revolved around the decision as to whether families were a legitimate topic of policy debate (T. Ooms, personal communication, October 16, 1999). The 1980 White House Conference on Families contributed to legitimizing the family policy field, but all the controversy surrounding the conference led to what political observers have called a "decade of disregard" (Jacobs, 1994, p. 9). Congress became active again only in the late 1980s and early 1990s.

This chapter chronicles family policy developments since the 1990s, including private philanthropic commitments and public policy initiatives enacted by international, federal, and state governments (for a historical perspective, see chap. 10, this volume; Jacobs, 1994; Jacobs & Davies, 1994; Ooms, 1984; Wisensale, 2001a). Developments at both the federal and state levels are profiled because the 1990s have been characterized as a "Dr. Jekyll and Mr. Hyde decade," referring to the devolution of authority for policies from the federal to the state level and a simultaneous countertrend toward centralization and federal preemption of state authority (Tubbesing, 1998, p. 14). Special attention is devoted to efforts to collect family-related data because their absence has stymied progress in the field (Ooms, 1995). Obviously, the courts have played an active role in family issues, although a review of these cases is beyond the scope of this volume (see the annual review of federal and state legislative and judicial developments in the winter issue of *Family Law Quarterly*).

PHILANTHROPIC COMMITMENTS

During the 1990s, several foundations launched major initiatives that shaped the family field, influencing what issues might be legitimate topics for government actions and evaluating whether the actions taken by government actually reached their objectives for families. For example, the Edna McConnell Clark Foundation has a historical commitment to the doctrine of family preservation (e.g., cautioning the too-easy removal of children from families in which abuse or neglect is suspected or substantiated) that was later picked up by state and federal governments (T. Ooms, personal communication, October 16, 1999). The fatherhood movement was launched, in part, by the Funders Collaborative on Fathers and Families, which included the Casey, Danforth, Ford, and Mott Foundations (Carter, 1995). The Carnegie Council's Task Force on Meeting the Needs of Young Children and their Council on Adolescent Development led to several federal initiatives for children and adolescents (T. Ooms, personal communication, October 16, 1999; Zigler, 1998).

In the wake of welfare reform, 16 foundations have funded Assessing the New Federalism, an Urban Institute multiyear project to track the effects of the devolution of social welfare programs from the federal government to the states. In 1999, the inaugural issue of "Snapshots of American Families" was released, which provides a comprehensive overview of family well-being including employment, income, child support, program participation, and family life based on data from 44,461 randomly selected households and 900 low-income families with children in 13 states (see http://www.urban.org).

INTERNATIONAL INITIATIVES

International law is guided by the Hague Conventions, four of which deal with family law. The Hague Convention on the Civil Aspects of Child Abduction is in effect in 73 countries including the United States (Elrod & Spector, 2003). The primary purpose of this convention is to preserve the current custody arrangement of the child to deter parties from seeking more favorable arrangements in other countries (Elrod & Spector, 2001); moreover, children who are wrongfully abducted must be expeditiously returned through any appropriate remedy (Elrod & Spector, 2003). In 2000, the United States approved the 1993 Hague Convention on the Protection of Children and Cooperation in Respect of Intercountry Adoption, now ratified by 51 other countries (Elrod & Spector, 2001, 2003, 2004).

Two other conventions of interest to family law that are awaiting U.S. approval are the 1996 Hague Convention on Jurisdiction, Applicable Law, Recognition, Enforcement and Co-operation in Respect of Parental Responsibility and Measures for the Protection of Children and the 2000 Hague Convention on the International Protection of Adults.

FEDERAL INITIATIVES

During the last 15 years, policies were enacted to address issues such as abstinence education, adoption, child abuse and neglect, child care, children's health, children's health insurance, child kidnapping, child support, child tax credit, crimes against children, domestic violence, Earned Income Tax Credit, education, family leave, family preservation, family poverty, Food Stamps, foster care, grandparent visitation rights, Head Start, marriage, military families, out-of-wedlock pregnancies, parental abduction, partial birth abortion, paternity, same-sex marriage, servicemember's protection, telecommunications, visitation, and welfare reform (see Table 5.1). In a recent analysis of federal and state expenditures during the first half of the 1990s, Kamerman and Kahn (2001) reported a tripling of expenditures on child care, a doubling of direct cash benefits to families, and a 50% increase in family services. Using an earlier comparison point, federal expenditures for children increased from $48.6 billion in 1960 to $168.54 billion in 1997, an in-

TABLE 5.1
Selected Federal Policies Impacting Families From 1990 to 2003

Year	Law	Provisions
1990	Child Care and Development Block Grant	Provided $22.5 billion to help states improve child care; provided child care tax credits; developed a new health insurance credit for broadening Head Start eligibility; initiated full-year Head Start programming; expanded the earned income tax credit (EITC); and provided an additional EITC credit for infants (Wisensale, 2001b).
1992	Child Support Recovery Act	Made it a federal crime to willfully fail to pay child support awarded in another state; created a Commission on Child and Family Welfare with responsibilities for such issues as child custody, visitation, and domestic violence (Walker & Elrod, 1993).
1993	Family and Medical Leave Act	Provided 12 weeks of unpaid leave for a serious illness or to care for an ailing family member; ensured job security and health coverage during the leave (Wisensale, 1997).
1993	Family Preservation and Support Act	Provided almost $1 billion over 5 years (Jacobs & Davies, 1994) for community-based services, including prevention and intervention programs to avoid unnecessary out-of-home placements (Early & Hawkins, 1994; Ooms, 1998).
1993	International Parental Kidnapping Crime Act	Established international parental abduction as a felony (Elrod, 1995).
1993	Omnibus Budget Reconciliation Act	Expanded the EITC by providing an additional $21 billion over 5 years (Jacobs & Davies, 1994); addressed court reforms in foster care and adoption cases; and mandated states to establish quick paternity procedures (Elrod, 1995).
1993	National Child Protection Act	Encouraged states' criminal background checks on child care providers (Elrod, 1995).
1994	Educate America Act	Promoted parental involvement in their children's schooling (Zimmerman, 1998).
1994	Full Faith and Credit for Child Support Orders Act	Required states to enforce child support orders established in other states; required employers to comply with child support orders that noncustodial children be included in health coverage (Elrod, 1995).
1994	Federal Budget	Allocated $550 million to Head Start with full funding by 1999 (Jacobs & Davies, 1994); initiated Early Head Start (McMurrer & Sawhill, 1998).
1996	Debt Collection and Improvement Act	Denied federal loans and authorized interception of federal payments to parents owing child support (Elrod & Spector, 1997)
1996	Defense of Marriage Act	Defined marriage as a union between one man and one woman, which denied Social Security benefits to same-sex couples; stipulated that no state is required to recognize a same-sex marriage performed in another state (Elrod & Spector, 1997).

(Continued)

TABLE 5.1
(Continued)

Year	Law	Provisions
1996	Personal Responsibility and Work Opportunity Reconciliation Act (PRWORA)	Eliminated public assistance as an entitlement that ensured benefits if eligibility criteria were met. Proposed ending government dependency by promoting marriage, the formation of two-parent families, and preventing out-of-wedlock pregnancies. For families, the major federal provisions (some of which can be modified by states) are a 60-month time limit on welfare receipt using Temporary Assistance for Needy Families (TANF) funds, work requirements after 24 months of welfare receipt, the option to institute family caps that deny additional benefits to children born to parents receiving assistance, requirements that teen parents live with parents or other adults, stronger child support enforcement programs, mandates that states establish paternity for 90% of all births to unmarried women, restrictions on education and training to meet PRWORA requirements, the scaling back of food stamp benefits, a narrowing of Supplemental Security Income eligibility standards, an elimination of federally funded public assistance for newly arriving immigrants, limitations on assistance to legal residents who are not citizens, and financial incentives for states to provide abstinence education (Wisensale, 2001b; Zaslow, Tout, Smith, & Moore, 1998).
1996	Telecommunications Reform Law	Mandated that new TVs include a V-chip to allow parents to screen out programs they judge inappropriate for their children (Galston, 1996).
1997	Adoption and Safe Family Act	Provided $875 million for a 3-year authorization of the Family Preservation and Support Act; promoted adoption and moving children quickly into safe, permanent placements.
1997	Amended Individuals with Disabilities Education Act	Extended the 1975 All Handicapped Children Act to protect disabled children's rights to a free, appropriate public education alongside their non-disabled peers; required states to involve interested parties including individuals with disabilities and their families in carrying out comprehensive strategies to improve educational outcomes (Gross, 2003).
1997	Balanced Budget Act	Provided a $500 child tax credit; authorized $24 billion for state health insurance for uninsured children; restored welfare benefits for disabled legal immigrants; and initiated Hope Scholarship tax credits of up to $1,500 per year (Wisensale, 2001b).
1998	Deadbeat Parents Act	Made it a felony for anyone who crosses a state line to evade a child support obligation (Eldrod, Spector, & Atkinson, 1999).
1998	Extradition Treaties Interpretation Act	Expanded the definition of kidnapping to include parental kidnapping to help get children returned from abroad (Elrod, et al., 1999).
1998	Visitation Rights Enforcement Act	Added visitation to custody determination as specified in the 1993 Parental Kidnapping Prevention Act; added grandparents as contestants which makes grandparent visitation orders enforceable (Elrod & Spector, 2000).

(Continued)

TABLE 5.1

(Continued)

Year	Law	Provisions
2000	Strengthening Abuse and Neglect Courts Act	Provided grants to local and state courts to improve data collection and tracking of child abuse/neglect cases; expanded the Court Appointed Special Advocate Program (Elrod & Spector, 2001).
2000	Children's Health Act	Authorized new research and services on child health issues; reauthorized the Substance Abuse and Mental Health Services Administration (SAMSHA) for three years; seeks to reduce child and adult drug use, improve the health and safety of child care centers, and support comprehensive planning for school safety and youth violence (Elrod & Spector, 2001).
2000	Intercountry Adoption Act	Allowed for adoption of the Hague Convention on Protection of Children and Cooperation in Respect of Intercountry Adoption (Elrod & Spector, 2001).
2001	Economic Growth and Tax Relief Reconciliation Act	Phased in an increase in the standard deduction; widened the 15% tax rate bracket for married couples; raised by $3,000 the income level at which the EITC begins to phase down for married couples; phased in the partially refundable child tax credit at the income levels where EITC is phasing out (Marshall & Sawhill, 2004); provided families with additional options for college and retirement savings (Elrod & Spector, 2002).
2001	Revised Elementary & Secondary Education Act (No Child Left Behind Act)	Set deadlines for: expanding the scope and frequency of student testing, narrowing the test score gap between advantaged and disadvantaged students, and revamping accountability systems for making annual progress in raising students' performance in reading and math (Education Commission of the States, 2002).
2002	Promoting Safe and Stable Families Act Reauthorization	Authorized $60 million for educational and training vouchers for youth aging out of foster care, and $10 million for improving state courts' assessment of child abuse/neglect cases
2003	Jobs and Growth Tax Relief Reconciliation Act	Widened the 15% tax bracket for married couples filing joint returns; provided that the basic standard deduction for married taxpayers is twice that for single individuals; increased the amount of the child tax credit (RIA, 2005).
2003	PROTECT Act	Strengthened law enforcement's ability to prevent, investigate, prosecute, and punish violent crimes committed against children; codified the previously-established director of the AMBER Alert program, a coordinated early warning system among broadcasters and local, state, and national enforcement agencies to help find abducted children (www.amberalert.gov).
2003	Partial Birth Abortion Ban	Banned partial birth abortion, except those necessary to save the life of a mother.
2003	Servicemember's Civil Relief Act	Provided legal protections for members of the U.S. military and their dependents in the areas of termination of residential and automobile leases; evictions from leased housing; repossession for installment contracts; and 6% interest rate caps if military service affects ability to pay (usmilitary.about.com/cs/sscra/ascra2_2.htm).

(Continued)

TABLE 5.1
(Continued)

Year	Law	Provisions
2003	Amended Individuals with Disabilities Education Improvement (IDEA) Act	Preserved basic structure and civil rights guarantees of IDEA, but made significant changes in areas such as defining and specifying the requirements of "highly qualified" special education teachers, ensuring services for children who are homeless or highly mobile, aligning requirements with the No Child Left Behind Act, changing procedural safeguards and compliance monitoring to focus on student performance, and granting authority to use funds for early intervention services and to extend some services beyond age 2 (Gross, 2003).

crease of 246% during a time when the number of children increased by only 9.7%. The dollars spent on low-income children by the federal government increased more dramatically, from $5.1 billion in 1960 to $117.3 billion in 1997 (Clark, King, Spiro, & Steuerle, 2001).

In 1997, President Clinton signed an executive order requiring family impact statements on policies affecting families that, ironically, superseded a broader executive order issued by President Reagan in 1987, which required agencies to review any proposed new policies for their potential impact on families (Elrod & Spector, 1998). In 1999, President Bush issued an executive order prohibiting discrimination against parents in federal employment (Belkin, 2000). The National Governors Association has been focusing gubernatorial attention on children and families, with special attention to child welfare and low-income working families, child care, early childhood development, before- and after-school child-care programs, fatherhood, service integration, and welfare reform (see http://www.nga.org). The National Conference of State Legislatures has focused efforts on child support, child welfare, children's health insurance, education, family law, human services reform, juvenile justice, responsible fatherhood, welfare reform, and youth programs (see http://www.ncsl.org).

A new source of family data emerged in part from a national workshop calling for accessible, high-quality data on families to maximize connections to policy (see Hendershot & LeClere, 1993, for the proceedings published by the National Council on Family Relations). A 1997 executive order established the Federal Interagency Forum on Child and Family Statistics, which requires the Office of Management and Budget to publish an annual report on the condition of America's children and families based on data from 18 federal agencies (see http://www.childstats.gov; Federal Interagency Forum on Child and Family Statistics, 2000). Also, a guide to national surveys and other sources of family data was published by Westat and Child Trends (Zill & Daly, 1993).

STATE INITIATIVES

Because the word *family* is not mentioned in the Constitution, there is no U.S. family law, but rather there are 50 state family laws. Family matters such as child welfare, divorce, marriage, and property distribution are influenced by federal law, but are primarily decided state by state (Mason et al., 2004). Since 1995, several Supreme Court decisions have protected states' rights by striking down the Gun-Free School Zones Act, prohibiting rape victims from suing their attackers in federal court, barring state workers from suing employers under the Age Discrimination Act, and eliminating state workers' right to use federal disability as a basis for compensation for discrimination (Asseo, 2001). Landmark devolution legislation in the 1990s also transferred federal responsibility to states on a range of other issues, including children's health insurance, family preservation, and welfare reform (Tubbesing, 1998).

Devolution began early in the 1990s as states increasingly sought federal waivers, but it gained momentum in 1995 with the passing of the Unfunded Mandate Reform Act, which limited the ability of the federal government to mandate programs for which state and local governments must foot the bill. Devolution has provided state legislatures and governors with more responsibility and flexibility because categorical funding has been replaced with block grants (Tubbesing, 1998).

The hallmarks of devolution are, typically, greater specificity by the federal government in elaborating the ends to be achieved through block grants, more discretion for states in the means of reaching those ends, and a growing shift of services from public- to private-sector providers such as Medicare health maintenance organizations (HMOs) and for-profit vendors in areas such as child care, prisons, and welfare programs (Pratt, 1998). The trend toward devolution has been counterbalanced, however, by proposed federal child-care standards, national regulations on managed care practices (e.g., length of maternity stays), and tobacco settlements that preempt such state laws as sales to minors and vending machine sales.

In the last century, there has been a trend toward increased uniformity in family law. In some areas, the U.S. Supreme Court has set certain standards as constitutionally required. In other cases, such as child support, federal legislation has required states to adopt specific legislation as a condition for the payment of federal funds for certain social welfare programs. Finally, the Conference of Commissioners on Uniform State Laws, which promulgates uniform laws for adoption by the states, has had a significant impact on the uniformity of family law (M. Melli, personal communication, September 13, 2005). By 1998, all states had adopted the Uniform Interstate Family Support Act, which recognizes child support orders established in another state (Elrod & Spector, 2000); in addition, 41 states have established uniform standards for child custody and enforcement and 13 states have adopted uniform methods for enforcing domestic violence orders (Elrod & Spector, 2005).

States have become increasingly involved in family policy during the last 15 years. Selected examples are given here, citing first changes that occurred across states and then specific changes within states. State commissions, councils, or subcabinets were created in 30 states, primarily in the 1990s, to assign greater priority to child and family issues, facilitate better coordination among existing services, and promote child and family collaboratives (see Hutchins, 1998). In 1994, the Finance Project was formed to develop strategies for public financing and administration of community-based family collaboratives as a means to overcome rigidly categorical funding streams and entrenched bureaucratic structures. This nonprofit organization conducted policy research, provided policymaker forums and public education, and drafted sample legislation for changes in state statutes (Finance Project, 1996).

Several developments transpired in the collection of state-level family data in the 1990s. For example, due to budget cuts in 1995, the National Center on Health Statistics no longer compiles national data from state reports on marriage and divorce, which limits the ability to describe trends within and across states (Ooms, 1998). In 1990, the Annie Casey Foundation financed the publication of *Kids Count,* an annual report card comparing states on key measures of child well-being. By 1995, Casey was also financing state and substate statistics on children in every state. In 1995, *Map and Track* was launched by the National Center for Children in Poverty to track changes over time in state-initiated programs and policies for young children and their families (Knitzer & Page, 1996, 1998). In 1997, *Map and Track* also began tracking state initiatives to encourage responsible fatherhood in cooperation with the Council of Governors' Policy Advisors and the National Center on Fathers and Families (Bernard & Knitzer, 1999; Knitzer, Bernard, Brenner, & Gadsden, 1997).

In the 1998 *Map and Track* report, over two thirds of the states (34) were funding statewide programs for preschoolers, about half (24) were funding statewide programs for infants and toddlers, and half (25) were funding programs on parenting (Knitzer & Page, 1998). Despite this progress, the report concluded that state leadership was not strong enough and state investments not extensive enough. For example, only 10 states explicitly linked welfare strategies to comprehensive child and family initiatives other than child care. In 1996 and 1998, only eight states met the criteria of *Map and Track* for comprehensive initiatives, and seven states reported no state-initiated statewide programs for young children and families. State support for child care has grown substantially since the 1996 welfare reform bill. In 2001, states spent $8 billion on child care (Marshall & Sawhill, 2004), and as of 2002, 40 states had publicly funded pre-K programs for 4-year-olds and some 3-year-olds, with expenditures totaling $2.4 million (Gormley & Phillips, 2005).

In regard to fathering, state efforts have focused predominantly on financial involvement, particularly child support (Ooms, 1998). *Map and Track* reported that only four states demonstrated exemplary efforts in promoting both the financial and emotional involvement of fathers with their children. To date, state efforts focus primarily on teen fathers and low-income non-custodial fathers, with little attention to father-friendly workplace policies or fathers in two-parent families (Bernard & Knitzer, 1999).

States have also passed a number of family laws, with selected examples given here (see also chap. 8). For example, since the 1990s, every state has enacted one policy or taken on one activity to strengthen marriage, promote two-parent families, or prevent divorce (Ooms, Bouchet, & Parke, 2004). In 1999, Oregon passed legislation to allow adopted children to learn the identity of their birth mother (Elrod & Spector, 2000). By 2001, 21 states had introduced paid family leave legislation that eventually passed in 6 states in varying forms (Skocpol & Dickert, 2001). In 2002, California passed the nation's most comprehensive family leave policy. Over 13 million workers can receive up to 6 weeks of leave at 55% to 60% of wages to care for a newborn, newly adopted or foster child, or to care for a seriously ill family member including a domestic partner (Marshall & Sawhill, 2004; http://www.nationalpartnership.org). In addition, five states (California, Hawaii, New Jersey, New York, and Rhode Island) and Puerto Rico provide partial wage replacement to employees who are temporarily disabled for medical reasons, which is defined to include pregnancy and birth (see http://www.nationalpartnership.org).

THE VALUES AND PRIORITIES OF THE AMERICAN PEOPLE

Whether families are a legitimate target of public policymaking also depends on the values and priorities of American families. In a recent public opinion poll (Hewlett & West, 1998), only 6% of parents said that government was currently doing a great deal to help them. When asked how much government could be doing to help them, 47% said government could do a great deal to help them, and another 37% said government could do something to help them.

Across the board there is overwhelming support for specific family policies. For example, 85% of Oklahomans reported that a statewide initiative to "promote marriage and reduce divorce" is a good or very good idea (Horn, 2004). In polls, 73% of parents of young children and 65% of all adults support governmental financial assistance to help families pay for quality child care. What's more, 88% of parents of young children and 80% of all adults support paid parental leave (DYG, Inc., Civitas, Zero to Three, & Brio, 2000), which parents say they need; in a study of mothers who had taken almost a 12-week parental leave on the birth of their child, half wished they had taken a longer leave, but 47% said they could not afford it (Hyde, Essex, Clark, Klein, & Byrd, 1996). In a CBS poll, almost three fourths of Americans endorse extending the dependent care tax credit from parents who purchase day care to parents who care for their children at home (Carlson, 2005). If asked, most Americans would probably agree that parenting is primarily the family's responsibility, not the government's, yet these data suggest that it may fall to policymakers to help create the conditions under which parents can do their best.

Yet support for families, particularly families with children, is by no means universally held. A new organization, No Kidding, claims to represent the interests of the childless who make up 10% of the voting population. Instead of the term *childless*, which connotes loss, they deliberately call themselves *child-free*, which implies choice and satisfaction. They oppose benefits for families with children, which they believe discriminate against the childless who are not eligible for the perks, citing examples such as on-site child care, family-friendly workplace policies, and health care for dependents (primarily children). At the top of their list of targets are the federal tax code, specifically provisions like the standard deduction, and the child tax credit, which lightens the tax burden of parents.

These claims rankle parent advocates such as Sylvia Hewlett who founded the National Parenting Association as a social movement by and for parents (Hewlett & West, 1998). Equating the choice to have children to buying a boat or purchasing a pet is an example of untrammeled individualism in her view, because societies cannot exist if everyone chooses to remain childless. Hewlett, who is trained as an economist, claims that children are a poor tax shelter. Besides, we should not deny benefits to parents because we personally cannot use them, just as we would not eliminate mental health coverage because only a portion of the population needs it. The entire society benefits from well-reared children and everyone should share in their costs (Belkin, 2000).

SUMMARY

In the 1990s, so many family policy initiatives were undertaken, so many family policies were enacted, and so many Americans were supportive of government involvement that the legitimacy question appears to be answered: Families are a focus of government at all levels. This family focus in policymaking could result in either more government, as implied here, or less government. For example, in response to calls to take families into account, government could create a number of new programs to support families. Conversely, providing such support to families could negate the need for existing government services. Clearly, providing preventive services to families can help avoid the expensive interventions that result when a problem progresses to a crisis or chronic situation, such as when poorly socialized children require incarceration for their criminal acts (Consortium of Family Organizations, 1988). Whether family-focused approaches would lead to more or less government is a false debate, according to Putnam (2000b). Based on the historical record, government has sometimes been part of the problem and sometimes part of the solution.

Curiously, whether families are a target of government policy is really a moot question. Most laws, or the lack thereof, have some impact on family life. Yet debate over how and when government should intervene will undoubtedly continue.

The next three chapters shift focus and apply a family perspective to several current policy issues. Paralleling the dual definitions of family policy and a family perspective in policymaking proposed in this volume, the next two chapters specify in more detail the role that families can play in both types of policymaking. Chapter 6 focuses on family policies that help parents fulfill one family function: childrearing. Chapter 7 examines the role that families can play in health care policy. Health care is not a family policy because it is not explicitly aimed only at families, yet it could benefit from a family perspective in policymaking. These two chapters are illustrative not only because they operationalize the abstract, somewhat esoteric, concepts of family policy and a family perspective in policymaking, but also because they were originally written as briefing reports for state policymakers. Chapter 8 raises five of several hot-button issues likely to be on the legislative agenda in the foreseeable future: family and work conflict, long-term care, family poverty, marriage, and health care.

Chapter 5 is adapted from Bogenschneider, K. (2000). Has family policy come of age? A decade review of the state of U.S. family policy in the 1990s. *Journal of Marriage and the Family, 62,* 1136–1159. Copyright 2000 by the National Council on Family Relations, 3989 Central Ave. NE, Suite 550, Minneapolis, MN 55421. Adapted by permission.

II

APPLYING A FAMILY PERSPECTIVE TO CURRENT POLICY ISSUES

6

Do We Know What Good Parenting Is? Can Public Policy Promote It?

Dave Riley
Karen Bogenschneider

If a community values its children, it must cherish their parents.
—Bowlby (1951, p. 84)

If family is the foundation of society, then parenting is the process by which a society manages to maintain itself through time even while its membership is constantly changing. One generation reproduces itself in the next, not only biologically but also in its values, competencies, and character. "Culture" could not exist if this were not true. The process by which this enormous feat is accomplished is called parenting.

Despite its universally recognized, essential role in the maintenance of society across generations, parenting is often considered an inalienably private affair, too personal for government policies or intervention. Other common beliefs are that effective childrearing is

> either common sense (Everybody knows what good parents do, just ask my grandmother), instinctive (Some people are naturally good parents; either you are or you aren't and it can't be taught) or relative (Who's to say what a good parent is, anyway?). (Steinberg, 1996, p. 104)

In contrast to those beliefs, we argue that effective parenting can be defined, that it can be promoted in ways that do not oppress private values, and that government inevitably affects the quality of parenting, for better or worse, on purpose or by accident. Yet before we suggest policy ideas, we respond in this chapter to five related questions that policymakers might ask when considering whether legislation can promote competent parenting: (a) Does parenting matter? (b) Do we know what competent parenting is? (c) Can we mount effective programs to improve parenting? (d) Is parenting a proper issue for public policy or is it strictly a private matter? (e) What policy options and personal actions can promote good parenting? To answer these questions, we draw on hundreds of studies of parenting conducted in the last two decades not to offer a specific policy solution, but to provide a solid foundation for thinking about a range of policy options concerning parents.

DOES PARENTING MATTER?

Every year or two, a best-selling book gains momentary fame with proclamations that parents matter little to children's development, usually suggesting that children grow according to a fixed genetic script or sometimes that peers and other influences matter more. Some books even argue that children have a bigger impact on parents than parents have on children (a view all parents can sympathize with at times).

Researchers familiar with hundreds of studies on parenting are virtually unanimous in agreeing that genes and social influences, in addition to parents, are crucial to understanding why children grow into one kind of person or another. Yet these same scholars quickly add that childrearing by the family is still the first and foremost influence on most child development outcomes (Bronfenbrenner, 1986; Sawhill, 1992; Steinberg, 1996; Zigler & Gilman, 1990).

The best evidence for the importance of parenting comes from two kinds of studies. The first is of children who are deprived of any or most parental influence, typically children raised in orphanages (Rutter, 1995). The recent case of Romanian children who spent their childhood in orphanages with no parent-like figure, for example, reconfirms what earlier studies have shown: Most children in such situations sustain lifelong effects and many never leave institutionalized care. On the other hand, children adopted early from such institutions, into the warm embrace of adoptive parents, have normal or near-normal prospects (Rutter & the English & Romanian Adoptees Study Team, 1998). Parents matter.

The second form of data comes from experiments in which parents are trained to change their childrearing behaviors, and the effects on children's development are compared against children whose parents have not received the training. Experiments of this sort solidly prove a cause-and-effect relationship, with changes in parenting behaviors having the power to raise children's intelligence or reduce their juvenile delinquency (Kumpfer & Alvarado, 2003; Madden, Levenstein, & Levenstein, 1976; Patterson, Dishion, & Chamberlain, 1993).

As aptly phrased by Bronfenbrenner (1986), families are "the most powerful, the most humane, and by far the most economical system known for building competence and character" (p. 4) in children and adults alike. More than any other institution, families perform the magic feat of "making and keeping human beings human" (p. 3).

DO WE KNOW WHAT COMPETENT PARENTING IS?

Parenting is such a personal matter, and children are all so different from each other, that you might wonder if there can be any agreement on what competent parenting is. To a surprising extent, researchers can and do agree (Maccoby & Martin, 1983).

The greatest consensus surrounds the infancy period, when the characteristics of competent parenting are most strongly influenced by biology and least affected by culture. When their focus turns to childhood and adolescence, researchers can still provide a surprisingly coherent picture of competent parenting. The picture will have variations depending on the child's culture and gender, and the family's social class and membership. The picture is complex, and researchers are quick to admit that their knowledge is incomplete. Nevertheless, it is fair to summarize that, to a surprisingly great extent, researchers can observe normal interactions of parents with their children at home, and from these observations predict quite a bit about children's later development: their compliance with adults, cooperativeness with peers, empathy with the distress of others, school failure or success, aggressiveness across their childhood years and into adulthood, and many other outcomes.

Much of the complex picture of parenting that is painted by research findings can be summarized in terms of (a) parent–child attachment in infancy, and (b) authoritative parenting in childhood and adolescence. A secure attachment bond in infancy is the result of parenting that is sensitively responsive and reliably available to the infant (Cassidy & Shaver, 1999), and this is true across the planet. The specifics of what it means to be sensitively responsive vary across cultures, but the general pattern of findings remains fairly consistent.

Beginning in the preschool years, authoritative parenting begins to define the style of parenting that is best for most children. *Authoritative parenting* is a sometimes-confusing label for parenting that combines high demandingness with high responsiveness (Maccoby & Martin, 1983). Demandingness includes a willingness by the parent to set high expectations for the child, exert authority effectively, set rules, and act consistently. Responsiveness is expressing warmth to the child, listening to the child's point of view, engaging in verbal give and take with the child, and explaining the reasons for the parents' rules. In contrast to the authoritative style of parenting, some parents are high in demandingness but not warm and responsive (authoritarian or dominating parenting). Others are the opposite, low in demandingness but high in warmth and responsiveness (labeled permissive parenting). The fourth group is low in both demandingness and responsiveness (neglectful parenting).

Hundreds of research studies document that children who experience secure attachment relationships and authoritative parenting are much more likely than other children to do better in almost any measurable way. They are less resistant with their parents as 2-year-olds, more cooperative with peers as preschoolers, and earn better grades and get drunk less as teenagers (Maccoby & Martin, 1983). Because adolescence is the period in which children master the particulars of their own cultures, researchers have expected there might be wide variations from one culture to the next in the kind of parenting that leads to the most competent teenagers. To our surprise, therefore, researchers have found this is not the case. Studies across the world, from China to Pakistan to Germany, and within several ethnic subgroups in the United States, have found the same general pattern of findings, with the children of authoritative parents always scoring the best on whatever outcomes are studied.

Of course, the way in which a parent exerts control effectively, or expresses warmth to a child, will differ tremendously from one culture to another, and even from family to family on the same street. Cultural variations matter, in both the goals of childrearing and in the specific techniques parents use. However, the broad outline of secure attachment in infancy, and an authoritative style of parent–child interaction in childhood and adolescence, has proven to be surprisingly consistent across cultures.

CAN WE MOUNT EFFECTIVE PROGRAMS TO IMPROVE PARENTING?

A huge array of programs have been created to provide parenting education or support to parents, representing the full range of ideologies and experiences available in contemporary society. A small subset of these programs has actually been tested, and a portion of them has been found to be consistently effective in helping parents improve their abilities. We can therefore say, yes, we do know how to mount effective programs, but only a small percentage of available programs are known to be effective, and most programs lack convincing evidence of effectiveness, including some of the most widely disseminated programs.

Before describing three concrete examples of effective parenting programs, it is worth noting some of the most important ways that programs differ. We categorize programs in terms of (a) their assumed causal mechanism, (b) their stage of prevention and population targeting, and (c) their evidence of efficacy.

1. *Assumed causal mechanism.* First, programs can be arrayed along a continuum that describes their assumed mechanisms of effect, starting at one extreme with programs to provide social support to parents, and then moving to those that provide education, training, and finally therapy at the other extreme.

Obviously, this listing of program mechanisms is linked to the seriousness of need of the target parents. We know that parents in their natural settings, in the absence of any parenting programs, are more skilled and effective when they have access to supportive networks of social support (Cochran & Nieto, 1995), and in fact one of the surest predictors of an abusing family is that they are socially isolated (Salzinger, Kaplan, & Artemyeff, 1983). A series of papers by Cochran have articulated the rich variety of psychological processes by which social support can lead to better parenting, including information exchange, practical assistance, learning from role models, social control of nonnormative parenting behaviors, emotional support for the parent, and more (Cochran & Niego, 1995; Cochran & Walker, in press). This line of research suggests that parenting programs directed to the general population could simply accentuate these naturally occurring processes of social support, creating opportunities for parents to learn from each other. Some studies have found promising results for social-support, peer-learning programs, even when directed to at-risk parents. The Parents Anonymous program creates discussion and peer support groups for parents who have abused their children or feel they are at risk for abuse, and although the evaluations of these programs cannot be called convincing, they are certainly promising (Rafael & Pion-Berlin, 1999).

Many more programs are based on the assumption that parents need not just social support, but also education to change their knowledge, beliefs, and behaviors. One of the sample programs described here, which uses printed parenting newsletters, is clearly in this educational category. As the seriousness of need for intervention rises, then some programs move into a more intensive training model, most commonly behavioral training. Another of the sample programs we describe falls into this category. Finally, some parents have mental health problems, including addictions, that require therapy before any other kind of parenting intervention is likely to be helpful.

2. *Stage of prevention and targeting of the population.* This conceptualization is linked to the first. The fields of medicine and mental health have evolved a commonly used definition of levels of prevention that is useful to apply to psycho-educational programs like those for parents (Institute of

Medicine, 1994). The main distinctions are between three levels of prevention. Primary prevention is directed to everyone who has not yet exhibited the problem, for example everyone who has not yet abused their child, or every parent whose child has not already failed in school. Secondary prevention aims to prevent recurrences or exacerbations of an identified problem, and tertiary prevention treats an established problem to reduce its negative consequences. Parenting interventions are largely in the primary prevention category, with some secondary prevention programs and many fewer tertiary. An example of a secondary prevention program for parents would be a court-ordered program for abusing parents, whereas a tertiary prevention program might provide therapy to the abused child to reduce the consequences of the abuse.

Looking within the group of primary prevention programs for parents, they can be further divided in a very useful way (Gordon, 1987). First are *universal* programs, which are provided to every family in a community. The aim of universal programs is to prevent the onset of problems before they occur. School-based programs and mass media campaigns are usually universal. Second, *targeted* programs tend to be more intensive and are provided to only those families who are at risk of parenting difficulties. Targeted prevention is delivered to everyone in the risk group, before we know which ones will actually experience difficulties. The most common factor for defining a targeted, at-risk group is probably family poverty. Third, *indicated* programs are directed to individuals or families that are in crisis, already showing early signs of the problem. This is a smaller group than a targeted program, and will often require a more intensive program. When a child has begun to fail at school, or has come to the attention of the police, then the parenting program is in the indicated category.

Figure 6.1 shows how these three types of programs—universal, targeted, and indicated—typically differ in the number of families they reach and the costs per family (Andrews, 1998). Universal prevention programs, because they reach everyone, must be inexpensive on a per-unit basis. The next part of this chapter includes a successful example of this type of program: newsletters that provide instructions to parents for a cost of less than $10 per family per year. The example of an effective targeted prevention program is intensive home visiting. Such home visits cost around $3,000 per family per year, but if delivered well they can prevent child abuse in the small number of families in which such abuse would otherwise be highly likely. Child abuse, of course, ends up costing society a great deal, so these programs can be cost-effective despite their high per-unit cost. An effective program for indicated families is exemplified by a well-evaluated parent training program, described later, that creates real change for families whose children have already been identified by schools or police as too troublesome and aggressive in early adolescence. This program could also be called a sec-

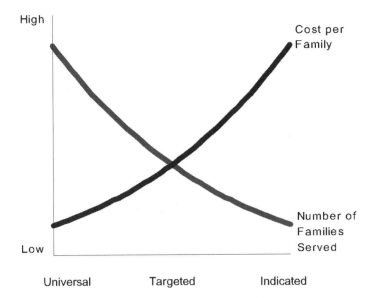

FIG. 6.1. Costs per family of different levels of prevention. *Note.* Adapted from a presentation by David Andrews, *Preventing Delinquency Through Effective Parent Training and Adult Support,* at the 10th Wisconsin Family Impact Seminar, "Building Resiliency and Reducing Risk: What Youth Need From Families and Communities to Succeed," January 1998.

ondary prevention program, because it is effective with families whose children are already law-breakers. To be effective with these families, the program must include intensive parental training that is fairly expensive, but of course not nearly so expensive as the future incarceration of these children if their families received no program.

3. *Evidence of efficacy.* How solid is our evidence that parenting interventions really work? Obviously, programs differ in this respect. Several work groups have developed schemes to categorize programs in terms of their evidence of effectiveness. Each of these efforts began with the aim of identifying and then promoting the use of evidence-based approaches to parent education. They define evidence-based approaches as those (a) with strong conceptual underpinnings (based on well-validated theories), and (b) that have been tested by research. Two U.S. federal agencies have taken a lead role in this effort. One has summarized the family-strengthening approaches to substance abuse prevention (Center for Substance Abuse Prevention [CSAP] Model Programs; http://modelprograms.samhsa.gov/). The second group, with the Office of Juvenile Justice and Delinquency Prevention (OJJDP; http://www.dsgonline.com/mpg_index.htm), reviews the effectiveness of programs in preventing juvenile crime. For an excellent review of these programs, see Kumpfer and Alvarado (2003).

Each of these groups takes care to define different levels of rigor in evaluation methods. For example, the CSAP group divides parenting programs into those that are promising, effective, and model programs. Promising programs have some evidence of positive impacts, whereas effective programs have been more strongly tested and have shown consistently positive impacts. Model programs have the added advantage of technical support for dissemination.

We provide three concrete examples of evidence-based programs. The first is a promising program (with some evidence of effectiveness) that provides education through a universal, primary prevention effort. The other two examples are model programs, already being disseminated across the country. One is a targeted intervention, whereas the other is directed to indicated families (already in crisis and exhibiting some problems).

Age-Paced Parent Education Newsletters

Because families find parenting information most useful when it is provided at needed times—not too early or too late—newsletters geared to the child's age are one vehicle for teaching competent parenting. A newsletter (or other printed material) is an information-only intervention, with no possibility of social support or individualized training. As an intervention, it assumes that written information can change knowledge and beliefs, and that this alone can lead to behavior change. Programs based on this assumption have, in practice, seldom shown impacts on parents' behaviors (Tobler & Stratton, 1997).

Several versions of age-paced instructional newsletters are distributed free to new families by the Cooperative Extension Service in at least 20 states (Cudaback et al., 1985). In Wisconsin, half of all families with newborns have received the 12 monthly age-paced *Parenting the First Year* newsletters (produced by that state's extension service) since 1990. *Age-paced* means that parents learn about 5-month-olds when their baby is exactly that age. Newsletters are inexpensive compared with home visits or parent education classes, which may make them one of the "few economically feasible methods of primary prevention in the area of child rearing" (Riley, Meinhardt, Nelson, Salisbury, & Winnett, 1991, p. 252).

A study of Wisconsin's *Parenting the First Year* newsletter found that Milwaukee-area parents reported its information and advice to be "highly useful" significantly more often than any other source, including physicians and relatives (Riley et al., 1991). In a second study of the newsletter's effectiveness, a field experiment was conducted with 1,104 Milwaukee families who had a 14-month-old child (Riley, 1997). Parents who received the newsletters, compared with those who did not, had beliefs that were significantly less like child-abusing parents. These parents also reported spanking or slapping their baby fewer times in the previous week.

Building on these results, Bogenschneider and Stone (1997) developed a series of three newsletters for parents of high school students. These researchers predicted that adolescence, like infancy, might be a sensitive period during which parenting practices are in flux and parents are more receptive to advice. In a study of 726 Wisconsin parents that compared newsletter readers to a no-newsletter control group, those parents who read all the newsletters reported monitoring their teenagers' activities more closely, being more responsive and available to their offspring, and engaging in more discussions of risky teen behaviors with their adolescents. In previous research, these practices have proven fundamental to competent parenting of adolescents; monitoring and responsiveness, in particular, are key features of authoritative parenting, the highly effective parenting style mentioned earlier. Moreover, when the newsletters featured information on local parents' reports of parenting norms and local teens' reports of risky behaviors, parents who read the newsletters were less apt to deny the alcohol use of their teen, a finding that could have important, real-world consequences. In a follow-up study, parents who were aware of their teen's alcohol use were better able to protect their adolescents from drinking and driving episodes (Bogenschneider, Wu, Raffaelli, & Wu, 1998). Every 1,000 newsletters mailed, at a cost of about $5 per family, prevented an estimated six episodes of teen drinking and driving.

An especially positive note in these studies is that the newsletters have proven as effective (and often more effective) for parents who need them most, parents in disadvantaged and highly stressed environments. In studies of the first-year newsletters, the parents who benefited most were those at greatest risk for parenting difficulties: single parents; first-time parents; and parents who were less educated, with lower income, and more socially isolated (Riley et al., 1991). Similarly, in studies of parents of adolescents, newsletters proved more advantageous to parents who faced more risks that may interfere with good parenting: a high school education or less, a family structure other than a two-parent biological or adoptive family, limited contact with relatives, and social isolation from friends (Bogenschneider & Stone, 1997).

Intensive Home Visiting

Home visiting has emerged in the last two decades as a promising strategy for promoting competent parenting. *Home visiting* is a generic term that encompasses a number of interventions (social support, education, training) by a range of program staff (from nurses to paraprofessionals and volunteers) with a variety of goals (e.g., preventing child abuse, helping families become economically self-sufficient) for diverse families (e.g., families in high-risk environments or any family with a newborn in a particular geographic locale). The common element in these programs is a series of regular visits to the home of a young child, often weekly or biweekly for the first year, with the goal of enhancing the child's well-being by changing parents' behavior through parent education, social support, and practical assistance (Gomby et al., 1999).

The first nurse home visiting programs were promoted by the Royal Army in Britain as a means of increasing the physical health of the army's eventual recruits. These programs quickly expanded their services from health practices to prevention of abuse and then to prevention of child neglect and the promotion of emotional health and intellectual development. Home visiting is based on the rationale that parents will be responsive to their child in ways that are more apt to build strong attachments and prevent abuse if they have realistic expectations of a child, know ways to respond to misbehavior, have friends and relatives they can count on, and possess the resources for coping with stressful life events.

Evaluations of intensive home visiting programs show a mixed picture; some rigorous studies show positive impacts, whereas other studies do not (Gomby et al., 1999). When benefits have been documented, the effects have not always been large, and programs have benefited some types of families more than others. Taken together, the evidence suggests that these programs have great potential, but not every home visiting program lives up to that promise.

The most promising results have been documented by the only home visiting program that has long-term follow-up data (Olds et al., 1997; Olds et al., 1998; Olds et al., 1999). Olds (1997) conducted a 15-year longitudinal study using a rigorous experimental design that compared a group receiving the treatment with no-treatment and alternate-treatment comparison groups. In Olds's program, nurses visited low-income mothers, many of whom were unmarried teens. The voluntary visits occurred in their homes prenatally and during the first 2 years of the children's lives.

Compared with low-income families assigned to an alternate program (transportation and developmental screening only), nurse home visiting, when measured 15 years later, resulted in lower child abuse rates and benefits to children's behavior and the mother's life course (see Fig. 6.2). Using data from the Elmira (New York) study of primarily White families, the 15-year-olds born to low-income, nurse-visited mothers had 46% fewer verified reports of child abuse and neglect and 56% fewer arrests. Compared with the control group, mothers visited by nurses in the study had (on average):

- 30 fewer months on AFDC.
- 37 fewer months on Food Stamps.

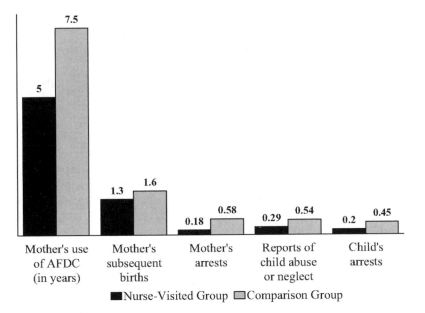

FIG. 6.2. Olds's Elmira study of nurse home visiting: Age 15 findings. *Note.* From Olds, D. L. (1997). "Improving the Economic and Social Well-Being of Families With Home Visitation Early in the Life Cycle" (pp. 33–36), in K. Bogen-schneider, T. Corbett, M. E. Bell, & K. D. Linney (Eds.), *Moving Families out of Poverty: Employment, Tax, and Investment Strategies,* Wisconsin Family Impact Seminar Briefing Report, No. 9. Madison: University of Wisconsin.

- 23 fewer months on Medicaid.
- One fifth fewer subsequent births.
- A spacing of 28 months more between first and second children.
- 69% fewer arrests (Olds, 1997).

In a follow-up study in Memphis of low-income, urban African American families, the 2-year assessments replicated some of these improvements in parental caregiving and maternal life course, although the original long-term Elmira evaluation documented more substantial gains on a broader range of outcomes (Olds et al., 1999). Because the umbrella of home visiting covers diverse programs with different populations, the varying impacts that appear to exist among studies is not surprising. According to Gomby et al. (1999), "Home visiting programs do not have the same ingredients and they will not produce the same effects" (p. 20). For home visiting, as for many other programs, policymakers need more fine-tuned evaluations that demonstrate not only whether the program works, but also what outcomes are affected, why and how effects occur, for which families, and under what conditions (Cohen & Ooms, 1993; Weiss, 1986).

State and local governments are financing home visiting through existing programs, such as Temporary Assistance for Needy Families (TANF), Medicaid, child abuse funds, and crime prevention dollars. For disadvantaged mothers in Olds's (1997) study, home-visiting programs paid for themselves by the time the child was age 4 in reduced government expenditures, primarily for AFDC and Food Stamps.

Parent Training

The efficacy of parent training can be discussed using the example of juvenile crime. In longitudinal studies, the strongest predictor of juvenile delinquency is ineffective parenting (Kumpfer, 1993). More specifically, researchers have learned that 30% to 40% of the antisocial behavior of early offenders, who are those most likely to become violent and chronic offenders later, can be tied to harsh, inconsistent parenting during the preschool years (G. Patterson, 1986; Patterson & Yoerger, 1993). Parents of these early offenders threaten, nag, and scold but seldom follow through (G. Patterson, 1986). This type of parenting teaches children to resolve conflict through coercion—specifically whining, yelling, temper tantrums, or physical attacks. This aggressive behavior leads to rejection by prosocial peers, trouble with teachers, and poor school performance (Patterson, DeBaryshe, & Ramsey, 1989). Negative consequences snowball, and these youngsters, who are poorly monitored by their parents, drift into deviant peer groups (Dishion, Patterson, & Griesler, 1994) and increase their use of illegal substances (Dishion, French, & Patterson, 1995). Over time, they fail to develop the skills for stable work or marriages that might enable them to drop out of crime as an adult (Caspi, Elder, & Bern, 1987; Patterson & Yoerger, 1993).

Based on this evidence of family and peer influences on juvenile crime, it is not surprising that programs focusing on individual youth have seldom demonstrated lasting success (Zigler et al., 1992), and may even weaken the family and thereby lead to worse outcomes for the child (Szapocznik et al., 1989). In contrast, several behavioral training programs that focus on parents and the family system as well as the child have proven effective. These include the Parents and Children Training Series (Webster-Stratton, 1982, 1990), the Helping the Noncompliant Child program (Forehand & McMahon, 1981), and the Parent Management Training program of the Oregon Social Learning Center (Patterson & Narrett, 1990). Taking the Oregon program as our example, this program has been used with aggressive preschoolers and also for families whose children have, by early adolescence, already come to the attention of school and juvenile justice officials as antisocial and delinquent.

Parents in the program receive, on average, 20 hours of training on specific child management practices that help them act more authoritatively, including closer monitoring, conveying clear expectations for behavior, responding effectively to noncompliance, rewarding positive behavior, and expressing warmth to their children. In this well-researched program, children from participating families (and also their siblings) displayed less antisocial behavior, with improvements large enough to bring participating youth into the range of normal functioning (Kazdin, 1987; G. Patterson, 1986). These results have been replicated in several studies with effects lasting up to 4.5 years (Baum & Forehand, 1981; Patterson & Narrett, 1990). Confirming the effectiveness of this program, its benefits have extended beyond the children in the family to their mothers, who experience less depression as a result of the program (Kazdin, 1987; G. Patterson, 1986).

The success of this parenting program is remarkable in several respects. First, it has proved effective with high-risk families, often with a child who is already aggressive or in trouble with the law. Second, it has proved effective not only with children 3.5 to 6 years old (63% success rate), but also with children 6.5 to 12 years old (27% success rate). The success rate with older children is impressive because it requires reversing antisocial behavior that is already well established among children experiencing school failure, rejection by prosocial peers, and encouragement by antisocial peers (Patterson, Dishion, & Chamberlain, 1993). Finally, for preventing delinquent acts among chronic male juvenile offenders, adapting this proven parenting program to the needs of foster parents has been more effective than traditional group care (see chap. 12, this volume; Chamberlain & Reid, 1998).

Summary of Program Effectiveness

Taken together, the results of these programs provide compelling examples of the potential of parent education. In fairness, however, not all family approaches have been this encouraging. Even programs similar to these three have not always been able to document similar positive impacts. These studies show the potential of parenting programs, but they do not guarantee that every program will have similar results. Although researchers caution against exaggerating the reliability and effectiveness of these programs (Moynihan, 1996; Wilcox & O'Keefe, 1991), it would also be counterproductive to ignore their demonstrated potential. Sawhill (1992) put this balanced view well: "The evidence is always mixed . . . one must weigh the risk of doing something and having it not work against the risk of doing nothing and missing an opportunity to improve lives" (p. 169).

If policymakers decided to fund only those programs they know ahead of time will work, they would cut off funding research to cure cancer or heart disease. They would discontinue peace negotiations in the Middle East and Northern Ireland because prior attempts have proven unsuccessful (Zuckerman, 2000).

IS PARENTING A PROPER ISSUE FOR PUBLIC POLICY? OR IS IT STRICTLY A PRIVATE MATTER?

The question of whether parenting is a public or private matter concerns values and judgment, not research findings. Nonetheless, let us suggest that, for most people, the best answer is that parenting is both inherently private and inevitably affected by public policy. On the one hand, our American tradition, born in reaction to the unbridled power of monarchy, has been to protect the private sphere from government intrusion. This view has moderated over time, for example, by acceptance of public intrusion into the families of child-abusing parents (originally through the use of farmers' animal cruelty laws). Still most Americans agree that raising children is the family's responsibility, not the government's.

On the other hand, families do not exist in a vacuum. Families do better when supported by close friendships, good schools, and caring communities. Some communities make it easy to raise children well, whereas others make it hard. For example, moving families out of Chicago's public housing projects and into working-class neighborhoods leads to more effective parenting in those families and far better outcomes for the children (Garbarino & Kostelny, 1995). These parents do not need parenting education nearly as much as they need a supportive community for their efforts.

Could government just stay out of the way of families, leaving parenting securely in the private sphere? This does not seem possible. Policies that affect parents deal with such issues as schools, libraries, public health, child care, workplace law, and employment programs. For example, zoning laws could make it easier to locate child-care programs inside residential neighborhoods, encouraging the formation of parenting social networks and a sense of community. Nearly every policy of government has an effect, direct or indirect, on families. Moynihan put this most aptly a half-century ago, in his foreword to Myrdal's (1941/1968) classic work *Nation and Family*:

> No government, however firm might be its wish, can avoid having policies that profoundly influence family relationships. This is not to be avoided. The only option is whether these will be purposeful, intended policies or whether they will be residual, derivative, in a sense concealed ones. (pp. vi–vii)

Just as government policies have pervasive impacts on the economy and the environment, so they also have pervasive impacts on family life. This realization has led to the development of a standard method of Family Impact Analysis of public policies (see chaps. 11 and 12), modeled after similar systems for estimating the economic and environmental impacts of policies.

Yet saying that government has an inevitable impact on parents, for better or worse, is not the same as saying that only government is responsible. Some of the changes that are needed to promote good parenting must come from parents themselves. According to one prominent social scientist, "The widespread disengagement of parents from the business of child-rearing is a public health problem that warrants urgent national attention" (Steinberg, 1996, p. 189). Parents and children long for more time together. However, many parents may find it difficult to be engaged in childrearing, according to a former president of the National Council on Family Relations, because family time has become a scarce commodity in an overbusy, overscheduled, overcommercialized society (Doherty, 2000). For example, parents feel they are losing influence to Madison Avenue advertising executives in the clothing choices of children as young as ages 7 and 8. Most educational, economic, recreational, and religious activities aimed at individuals end up pulling family members in different directions, rather than bringing them together (see chap. 12). Clearly, the promotion of more competent parenting requires attention to the realms of both personal responsibility and public policy.

WHAT POLICY OPTIONS AND PERSONAL ACTIONS CAN PROMOTE GOOD PARENTING?

Because good parenting depends on both the public and private realms, this section identifies both government policies and personal actions that can promote competent parenting. This list is not intended to be exhaustive, but hopefully it will stimulate creative thinking and constructive dialogue about how society as a whole and we as individuals can take steps to promote the type of parenting that produces the responsible citizens and productive workers on which the future of our nation rests.

Policy Options at the Government Level

Several lists of evidence-based programs have been created in recent years. These include the summaries of effective state government programs collected by the Harvard Family Research Project (1990, 1992a, 1992b, 1992c, 1994, see http://www.gse.harvard.edu/hfrp/), the Blueprints for Violence Prevention series from the University of Colorado (http://www.colorado.edu/cspv/blueprints/), and the two series already described by the CSAP, and the OJJDP. These lists largely overlap in their recommendations of specific programs that have solid evidence of effectiveness. Some of the types of programs they include are detailed below:

• Community-based family support and parent education programs can provide parents with the knowledge, skills, and social support they need to do their best in raising their children (Council of Chief State School Officers, 1989; Governor's Task Force on Family and Children's Issues, 1990; National Commission on America's Urban Families, 1993; National Commission on Children, 1991a; National Commission on Child Welfare and Family Preservation, 1990; U.S. Department of Education, Office of Educational Research and Improvement, 1991).

• Home visiting programs can help parents get off to a good start in raising their children (Governor's Task Force on Family and Children's Issues, 1990; Olds, 1997).

• Employment policies can provide paid family leave, part-time or job-sharing opportunities, and other family-friendly work policies that allow time away from work for family responsibilities (National Commission on America's Urban Families, 1993; National Commission on Children, 1991a). Because currently some employers are not required to participate, the right to family leave and other family-friendly workplace policies needs to be made more widely available to employees (Skocpol, 1997).

• Marriage education and enrichment programs have proven to reduce rates of separation and divorce, leading to a more stable environment in which children thrive (National Commission on America's Urban Families, 1993; National Commission on Children, 1991a; Renick, Blumberg, & Markman, 1992). Married parenthood can be encouraged through supportive tax policies, benefits, and marriage rules. Yet when marriages fail, systems need to be in place that ensure reliable child support payments (Skocpol, 1997). Also, mandated programs on how to coparent after divorce have been shown to reduce by half future relitigation rates over custody and child support (Arbuthnot, Kramer, & Gordon, 1997).

• Foster parents can benefit from parent training and support. A foster parent education program developed by the Oregon Social Learning Center increases the willingness of foster parents to provide care, prevents multiple foster home placements, and is more effective than group care in preventing repeat crimes among chronic juvenile offenders (Chamberlain, Moreland, & Reid, 1992; Chamberlain & Reid, 1991, 1998).

In addition to these types of specific programs, policymakers can also promote policies that lead to decent incomes, reliable child care, safe neighborhoods, quality schools, and affordable health care, which can give parents the peace of mind that allows them to focus on the important work of raising the next generation (National Commission on Child Welfare and Family Preservation, 1990; National Commission on Children, 1991a).

A family perspective can also be applied to any legislation:

• Policymakers can raise questions about how any given legislation would affect family well-being, just as the economic or environmental impacts of legislation are routinely considered in policy debate. Specifically, policymakers can ask in what ways families contribute to a problem, how they are affected by it, and whether they should be involved in the solution (Ooms, 1990).

• Policymakers can require parent or family criteria in any evaluations of programs or policies that affect families.

Possible Actions at the Personal Level

Because one cannot mandate that parents spend more time with children, or legislate cultural changes such as a greater valuing of parenting and less valuing of materialism, some activists argue that, instead of looking to government or professionals, parents must take action on their own behalf (Boyte, 1993a). One suggestion is a nonpartisan, grassroots movement generated and sustained by parents to make family life a priority and to support parents' attempts to create a better balance between time for relationships inside the family and activities outside the family (Doherty, 1999).

Following are some suggested personal actions that parents, citizens, and community leaders can take:

• Family coalitions can be organized to develop and actively pursue policies that would strengthen families and support their decision to make family time a priority (Doherty, 1999).

• Just as parents used to receive social support at market day, church meetings, and other community gatherings, communities could provide opportunities for parents to get to know each other and become familiar with community rules and standards for childrearing, such as the local norms for curfews, age of dating, rules regarding teen alcohol use, and so on (U.S. Department of Education, Office of Educational Research and Improvement, 1991). Individual families can make a point of connecting with their neighbors.

• A broad menu of parent education opportunities could be offered through businesses, civic clubs, religious institutions, and schools (Governor's Task Force on Family and Children's Issues, 1990; National Commission on America's Urban Families, 1993; National Commission on Children, 1991a; National Commission on Child Welfare and Family Preservation, 1990; U.S. Department of Education, Office of Educational Research and Improvement, 1991).

• Volunteers can establish parents' groups, organize neighborhood activities, and lend clothes, books, computers, and toys to neighbors with children (National Commission on Children, 1991a; U.S. Department of Education, Office of Educational Research and Improvement, 1991).

Balancing Public and Private Perspectives

Raising children is clearly parents' responsibility, yet it may fall to policymakers to help create the conditions under which parents can do their best. For example, government can fund family support centers that provide parent discussion groups at which parents can learn from each other about community childrearing wisdom and norms. Government can provide seed money to jump-start the formation of family coalitions, parent support groups, or public forums at the community level. These family coalitions, in turn, could develop a range of strategies to make family time a priority, which could include advocating for specific family-friendly government policies.

SUMMARY

In their importance to both policymakers and the public, child and family issues are now at their strongest point in recent decades. However, as many scholars have noted, there is often little connection between what is funded and the specific programs known to be effective or most promising (Carter, 1994). Although the knowledge created by the research community grows at a slow pace and often seems too complex or equivocal, in fact we have today some knowledge of a substantial number of well-researched, effective programs. There is no longer any excuse to jump on the bandwagon of any program that lacks solid evidence of effectiveness. We know enough, at least, to increase the odds that parenting education programs will deliver on their promise. Fulfilling this promise may depend on a dual-pronged focus of moving forward on both governmental and personal fronts.

7

Can a Family-Focused Approach Benefit Health Care?

William J. Doherty
Jared R. Anderson

Families are the hidden agent of health activity in the United States.
—Doherty (1993, p. 98)

Of all the industrialized nations, the United States has had the most difficult time conceptualizing the role of family life in the health and illness of citizens. Perhaps because of the dominance of individualism in this country, Americans have tended to split the individual from the family just as they have tended to split the mind from the body. The traditional emphasis in health research and health policy has been either on individual factors of health, illness, and health behaviors, or sometimes on the broader public health context—but in either case the family context has been peripheral.

In recent decades, however, there has been an increasing recognition among researchers and clinicians of the crucial role of family relationships and family interactions in health and illness. The two main factors in this increasing recognition appear to be the acknowledgment of the pivotal role of lifestyle factors in health and the increased awareness of the family's role as gatekeeper to the health care system. For example, studies indicate that smoking is learned first at home for many people, and that seven illness episodes are treated at home for every one that is seen by a physician (Doherty & Campbell, 1988). Families are the hidden agent of health activity in the United States.

Because many states, as well as this nation as a whole, are now struggling with a health care system mired in rising costs and increasing health care needs due to an aging population, the time for a fully integrated family perspective may finally be arriving. A growing number of health care professionals, researchers, advocates, and consumers recognize that families are a profound and powerful force on the health of individuals, and that health care in this country could be improved by supporting and strengthening family caregiving and the family's role in health promotion and disease prevention (Bomar, 2004; Elliot & Rivera, 2003; McDaniel, Campbell, Hepworth, & Lorenz, 2005). Furthermore, there is reason to believe that a family-centered approach to health care may be more cost-effective than the present approach, which focuses on individuals.

In this chapter, we first provide a brief overview of what is known about families and health issues, using the family health and illness cycle (see Fig. 7.1) as a visual depiction of the varied and pervasive ways that the family affects the individual's health and that the individual's health, in turn, affects the family (Doherty & Campbell, 1988). The model is built on the premise that all human problems are biological, psychological, and social in nature and that families are where these three domains come together. We briefly describe each category of the model and give specific examples of how health care might be enhanced by taking families into account. This model can best be read in clockwise fashion beginning with health promotion and risk reduction. The double arrows indicate the ongoing interaction between the family and the health care system. This model applies to families at all

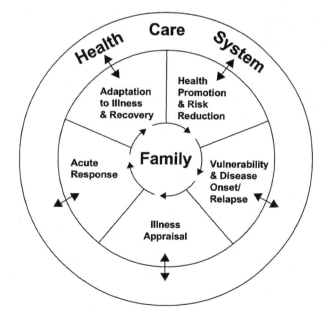

FIG. 7.1. Family health and illness cycle. *Note.* Reprinted from Doherty, W. J., & Campbell, T. L. (1988). *Families and Health.* Newbury Park, CA: Sage.

stages of the life cycle, but is especially salient to families with dependent children and frail elderly members.

This review of the family and health literature reveals many ways in which professionals can get involved at a macro policy level to make health care available to all families and at a micro policy level to ensure that the family perspective is taken into account in health promotion and illness management. We also outline the first author's work on conceptualizing how families can be mobilized in communities to be producers of health promotion for themselves and others as opposed to being only patients and consumers of professional services. Thus, health care, like parenting in chapter 6, requires both public policy responses and personal actions.

THE FAMILY HEALTH AND ILLNESS CYCLE

Health Promotion and Risk Reduction

Families are inherently involved in the promotion of health and the reduction of risky behaviors. For example, the major diseases in industrialized countries result from diet, exercise, smoking, drug and alcohol use, and failure to comply with treatment plans (Califano, 1979; U.S. Department of Health and Human Services, 2000). All of these issues are heavily family issues.

Family members influence one another's health habits. For example, children learn eating patterns in families, and most food is consumed in families. Exercise habits are acquired from families. Adolescents are more likely to smoke if either of their parents or a sibling smokes. Furthermore, family distress during early adolescence is a stronger predictor of smoking than whether parents smoke (Doherty & Allen, 1994). An individual's ability to change an unhealthy behavior depends on family support. Imagine a 60-year-old man with coronary artery disease who has never cooked for himself and needs to make dietary changes. Not surprisingly, involving his wife or other loved ones in treatment can significantly improve long-term results and can ultimately reduce health care costs (see Rankin-Esquer, Deeter, & Taylor, 2000). If families were better supported to promote health, Americans would have far better preventive health care that could prove more comprehensive and considerably more cost-effective (see Consortium of Family Organizations, 1992; Doherty & Campbell, 1988).

Vulnerability and Disease Onset or Relapse

In measures of stressful life events, family-related items such as divorce and the death or serious illness of a family member consistently rank at the top of the list as creators of the most distress (Holmes & Rahe, 1967). Studies in the field of psychoimmunology have documented more specifically how family stress makes individuals more vulnerable to illness. Widowers have been found to experience diminished immune system functioning following the death of their spouse (Calabrese, Kling, & Gold, 1987). Similarly, divorced or separated individuals have poorer immune system functioning than do matched married persons (Kiecolt-Glaser et al., 1987), and among married persons those with poorer marital satisfaction have decreased immunity (Kiecolt-Glaser et al., 1997; Kiecolt-Glaser et al., 1993; Kiecolt-Glaser et al., 1996; Mayne, O'Leary, McCrady, Contrada, & Labouvie, 1997).

Social ties benefit health, and marriage and family relationships are, for most people, the most important sources of social support (House, Landis, & Umberson, 1988; Uchino, 2004; Uchino, Cacioppo, & Kiecolt-Glaser, 1996; Waite, 1995). People, especially men, who have lost a spouse, divorced, separated, or never married, have markedly increased death rates even after researchers control for a variety of health risks (Lillard & Waite, 1995). Taken together, recent evidence on social support indicates that its absence has as detrimental an effect on health as the more widely touted cigarette smoking (House et al., 1988). Social support may exert these biological benefits through the pathway of better immune system functioning (Kiecolt-Glaser & Newton, 2001; Uchino, 2004).

Similarly, stress increases susceptibility to disease (Cohen et al., 1998; Cooper, 2005; McEwen, 1998; Segerstrom & Miller, 2004). In a classic pediatric study, bacterial throat infections in children were likely to be preceded by increased stress in the family (Meyer & Haggerty, 1962). In families with more parental conflict, 5-year-old children had higher levels of a stress hormone in their blood, even when they did not observe the conflict directly (Gottman & Katz, 1989). In addition, poor marital quality stemming from marital conflict is associated with an increase in rheumatoid arthritis disease activity (Zautra et al., 1998), early onset hypertension (Wickrama et al., 2001), periodontal disease (Marcenes & Sheiham, 1996), and a decrease in the survival rates of patients with congestive heart failure (Coyne et al., 2001). The implications of this burgeoning area of research for health care are clear: Engaging families as buffers of social support for medically at-risk individuals is one of the most beneficial interventions to promote the health of the population. Providing support to family caregivers and other burdened family members can prevent them from succumbing to illness and further consuming limited health care resources.

Illness Appraisal

Family illness appraisal refers to the family's belief about illness and family decisions about health care. The family plays a pivotal role in diagnosing the symptoms, encouraging home remedies, deciding whether professional medical help is needed, and gaining access to medical services (Campbell & Roland, 1996; Doherty & Campbell, 1988; Dowds & Bibace, 1996; Reust & Mattingly, 1996). Families have broad beliefs often based on cultural traditions about how much they can control their destinies and how trustworthy professionals are (Reiss, 1981). They also have specific health beliefs related to symptoms and treatments—beliefs that powerfully determine the individual's response to an illness episode (Brorsson & Rastam, 1993; Gottlieb, 1976).

Families' beliefs are the primary gateway to the health care system. Families usually discuss among themselves whether it is necessary to see a health professional (Dowds & Bibace, 1996; Litman, 1974; Reust & Mattingly, 1996). Over time, they generate relatively fixed beliefs about when to seek medical care—beliefs based on family history (Wright, Watson, & Bell, 1996). For example, a family that experienced the death of an infant due to a high fever in the last generation will most likely rush to the emergency room when their infant has a 103-degree fever. If this family has had six infants or toddlers in their extended family during recent years, they have experienced a one in six likelihood that a child will die from such a fever, whereas health care providers' experiences suggest a one in multiple thousand likelihood of a serious condition. Every family, then, has its own epidemiological thinking and its own internal family health consultants (Brorsson & Rastam, 1993). Therefore, it is important for health care professionals to ask about and work with the family members who are most important in shaping family health beliefs (Doherty & Baird, 1983).

Acute Response

The family's *acute response* refers to what the immediate aftermath of illness means for the family. Studies have shown that many families become temporarily overwhelmed, but reorganize themselves to cope with the crisis; they call family members together and reach out to their social support network (Danielson, Hamel-Bissell, & Winstead-Fry, 1993; Doherty & Campbell, 1988). Yet during the acute phase, the anxiety and stress level of the patient's family is often as high as that of the patient (Grunfeld et al., 2004). This level of stress often remains high as long as the patient's stress is high and sometimes longer than the patient's. For example, the biggest single predictor of the wife's level of distress 6 months after the onset of her husband's illness is how physicians dealt with the family in the hospital and whether they got the information they needed (Barbarin & Chesler, 1984).

What families want most from health professionals during the acute response to a serious illness is access and information. In some cases, the medical team informs the patient but not the family, leaving the family in the lurch and sometimes resentful of the providers (Doherty & Baird, 1983). The health care team has the responsibility to be accessible and informative—services that can be more difficult to deliver when a family lacks health insurance or has difficulty accessing needed services in a managed health care environment. In general, the key issues for the family during the acute stage of an illness are access and attention, and mobilization of internal and external resources.

Adaptation to Illness and Recovery

Families during the recovery phase often acquire a new role as caregiver for a family member—usually assigned to a wife, mother, or daughter—along with a new role of patient for the ill member. These new roles create a set of imbalances for many families—between spouses, between parents and adult children, between siblings—that makes chronic illness and disability a challenging experience for many families (Doherty & Campbell, 1988; Rolland, 1994). The family cohesiveness that was experienced during the acute onset of an illness may begin to diminish if the recovery is prolonged. The bulk of the research on families and health has been done with this phase of chronic illness and prolonged recovery. The results are quite clear: for many families, there is significant stress and burden in caring for a chronically ill or disabled member (Covinsky et al., 1994; Grunfeld et al., 2004; Vitaliano, Zhang, & Scanlan, 2003).

In studies of the impact of cancer on families, for example, the level of distress of the cancer patient decreases over time, whereas the level of stress of the spouse does not lessen over time without sufficient support (Oberst & James, 1985). Another example is that when education, support, and therapy are provided for families of individuals with schizophrenia, rates of relapse and hospital admission are decreased and medication compliance increases (Pilling et al., 2002). Adding family interventions to treatment protocol increases initial costs, but these costs can be offset by the decreased use of mental health services, lower rates of relapse, and reduced rates of hospital admission. Furthermore, during the illness and recovery phase, families have ongoing and often stressful relationships with health care professionals and the health care system. These relationships can be as chronic as the illness itself (McDaniel, Hepworth, & Doherty, 1992). Illness ends up affecting the whole family, and the quality of the lives of family members, especially the principal caregiver, is an important determinant of the ill family member's health outcomes (Campbell, 1986; Ptacek, Pierce, Dodge, & Ptacek, 1997; Schmaling & Sher, 2000).

Health professionals and society at large have significant responsibilities to assist families that are dealing with long-term illness and disability. The costs to families and society, in the form of increased family stress and greater health care utilization, are substantial. Based on increasing evidence, family-centered interventions for chronic illness are effective in managing many health problems (Campbell & Patterson, 1995).

Policy Implications

In summary, family interactions are often the invisible thread interwoven into every aspect of health and health care. Historically, families' critical role has been overlooked and undersupported. Recognition of the powerful impact of the family on the health of its members leads to many implications for the financing, organization, and delivery of health care services, including the training of health care professionals. The following illustrations are drawn from a family impact analysis by the Consortium of Family Organizations (1992):

• Proposals that expand insurance coverage should ensure that all members of the family are covered, not just the employed member. Children of the noncustodial parent also need to be covered if the custodial parent does not have coverage (p. 3).

• Incentives must be developed to encourage more physicians and other health care professionals to practice as generalists delivering primary health care and serving the whole family (p. 5).

• Health care professionals must treat families as partners in health care (p. 6).

• At the bare minimum, all health care professionals should receive training in the biopsychosocial approach to health care, which views the individual as a whole person and also as a member of a family and larger social environment. Training should teach providers how to assess the influence of family factors on health and to work in partnership with family members so as to better promote the health of their patient (p. 7).

• Plans for managed care and strategies for cost containment should include mechanisms to assess the patient's life context and the family's values, resources, and needs. With appropriate services and supports, families may often take on considerable, additional responsibilities that will help contain costs. Without these services to families, the patients will not recover as fast, and they may deteriorate and recycle back into the hospital. Alternatively, members of the family may react to the burden and stress by becoming ill themselves. Studies of the cost-effectiveness of managed care initiatives are badly needed and should include an examination of their effect on family health, functioning, levels of support, and well-being (p. 8).

TOWARD COMMUNITY ACTIVATION IN FAMILY HEALTH CARE

A fundamental limitation of most professional and policy perspectives on families and health is that they focus on patients and families only as consumers of health care services from professionals, policymakers, and social institutions. A broad critique of the professional–consumer model of social service delivery has emerged in recent years (Boyte & Kari, 1996; McKnight, 1996). The first author has extended to the health care arena the public work model of democratic renewal articulated by Boyte and Kari (1996) and their colleagues at the Center for Democracy and Citizenship at the University of Minnesota. In this model of community activation in family health care, families are seen as producers of health promotion and not just as consumers of health care services (Doherty & Carroll, 2002). Families are given opportunities to form common purpose with other families in the process of producing healthy outcomes in their communities. Families' relations with health care professionals and policymakers are characterized by partnerships that deemphasize hierarchy, with professionals serving as catalysts for the creation of community projects (Doherty, 2000; Doherty & Beaton, 2000). We have listed here the fundamental principles of this emerging model, followed by an illustration of the model in the area of diabetes care.

Principle 1: Patients and Families Are Partners With Professionals

a. The central principle: See patients and families as primary producers of health, support, learning, and healing for themselves and their communities, and only secondarily as individual consumers of professional services.

b. See professionals as partners with patients, families, and communities in promoting health and managing illness.

c. In lifestyle management of chronic illness, first tap the knowledge and expertise of patients, families, and communities, and then tap professional expertise.

Principle 2: Learning, Coping, and Healing Occur Best Within Communities

a. Identify and activate potential communities (groups of patients and families) who are concerned with a particular chronic illness or health problem.

  b. See the health professionals and the health plan as part of those communities, with assets to offer, but avoiding the risk of these professional services becoming too central.
  c. Collaboratively identify the most important health challenges and problems facing this community of concern.
  d. Call forth the resources and capacities in this community, beginning with the lived experience and human assets of the patients and families.
  e. Accentuate the sense of larger mission beyond the particular patients and families who participate in joint activities. Have a BHAG—a Big, Hairy, Audacious Goal—while starting small, local, and focused.
  f. Emphasize action groups that reach outward as well as inward.

Principle 3: A Wide Range of Stakeholders Should Be Activated

  a. Create cluster groups of families with a mission of support and outreach around the chronic illness or lifestyle issue.
  b. Create connections among the cluster groups, forming a larger community of stakeholders in community health.
  c. For special ceremonial occasions, engage families' personal networks of extended family, friends, and natural communities.
  d. Be public about all these activities to spread the vision.

Example of Community Activation of Families in Health Care

Partners in Diabetes began as a community initiative located in two medical clinics where patients, called support partners, who have lived experience with diabetes are connected with newly diagnosed and struggling patients, called members, for the purpose of support. Partners in Diabetes grew out of initial consultations between the first author and leaders within Health Partners, a Minnesota-based HMO, to develop a community engagement project focused on diabetes care. In keeping with the democratic model of engagement, professional expertise is considered "on tap" not "on top"; every participant has something to learn and something to contribute no matter their professional training. Consistent with these principles, the project was collaboratively developed by a group of providers who were deliberately diverse in terms of their discipline, and diabetes patients who represented a range of ethnic and socioeconomic backgrounds (Mendenhall & Doherty, 2003).

   This initial team of citizens that included providers, patients, and families met monthly to envision the project, develop a mission, work through issues of hierarchy and the traditional provider–consumer role, and guide the planning and implementation of the project, including development of the curriculum to train the support partners. The first author facilitated the meetings and assisted the group in maintaining the democratic, collaborative process, which took time to internalize as both providers and patients were more familiar with their roles as givers and receivers of information.

The project envisioned by this citizen group included utilizing patients with good metabolic control of their diabetes who were nominated by their physician to serve as a support partner to a member who was a newly diagnosed or struggling patient within the same clinic. Initially, 14 support partners were nominated and trained to reach out to interested members. The role of support partners included listening empathically to frustrations about diabetes, educating members about basic diabetes care and management strategies, assisting in the procurement of new technologies for measuring blood glucose, sharing healthy recipes, and in some cases cooking and exercising together (Mendenhall & Doherty, 2003). The project team met monthly to discuss the support process, consult with each other on any challenges that arose during the support process, and to develop solutions to those challenges.

The Partners in Diabetes model has been replicated both inside and outside the state of Minnesota where citizen initiatives are now being applied to newly diagnosed adolescents with diabetes, diabetes care in the American Indian community in the Twin Cities, and depression in the Hmong community. We believe the model, which we now call Citizen Health Care, could potentially be used with any medical problem where providers and patients agree that pooling their expertise and effort is important. The larger vision behind this family-centered approach to mobilizing communities is to create a transportable model for democratic engagement of individuals and families as producers of health care for themselves and others and not as just consumers of health care services. Contrast this community activation approach to the traditional one in which the professionals write grants to bring resources to the community or where professional advocates start a political pressure campaign to get a new center built. We are not saying that these two traditional approaches are without merit and are not sometimes necessary, but the new model first turns to resources within the community of families rather than immediately looking outside.

SUMMARY

This nation is still in the early stages of taking a family perspective seriously in health care policy and practice. The research base for such an approach is fully persuasive. We see the resistance to the family perspective as stemming from the traditional individualistic paradigm that dies slowly.

We now believe that those of us who advocate for a family model should work on three fronts at once: (a) macro health care policy to make good health care accessible to all families; (b) micro health care policy to ensure that families are actively involved and supported in health promotion and in dealing with illness; and (c) the activation of families to be producers of health for themselves and their communities.

8

What Current Policies and Proposals Are Changing the Political Landscape for Families?

The focus on the family as a theme in public policy is perhaps at its strongest point in the last 20 years in the Congress, the states, and among the public.

—Ooms (1995, p. 65)

For families, a number of policies enacted in the mid-1990s have prompted some of the most remarkable changes in the political landscape in the nation's history. For example, when the federal welfare reform legislation was passed in 1996, 32% of parents of children living in poverty were in the labor force. Only 4 years later, that percentage had risen to 43%—a sizable change in such a short time (Wertheimer, 2003). In 1996, Congress passed the Defense of Marriage Act, which defined marriage as a union between a man and a woman, and in less than a decade, it was enacted in 40 states (Elrod & Spector, 2005). The 2001 No Child Left Behind Act, characterized as the most significant federal education policy initiative in a generation (Education Commission of the States, 2002), charged states with improving student performance and closing the achievement gap between advantaged and disadvantaged students or risk the loss of a portion of their budgets and their student body (U.S. Department of Education, 2002). By 2004, 15 states had put in place accountability systems to assess their progress in meeting these new federal requirements (Education Commission of the States, 2002). Finally, 27 states had banned partial-birth abortion by 2003 when a ban was passed by Congress and signed into law by President George W. Bush (Partial-Birth Abortion Ban Act, 2003).

During the 1990s, several other family policies achieved prominence, albeit sometimes fleeting (see Table 5.1). Several issues are prime candidates for continuing dialogue and discussion, including child care; comprehensive, community-based family support; education; family leave; family violence; fathering; foster care; incarcerated parents; juvenile crime; and teenage pregnancy. For illustrative purposes, this chapter focuses on four family policies that are likely to be front-burner family policies in the foreseeable future: family and work conflict, long-term care, family poverty, and marriage. Moreover, this chapter discusses one other prominent issue with profound family impacts that technically is not a family policy, but would benefit from a family perspective in policymaking—health care. This chapter concludes by examining the role of family diversity in developing and sustaining family policies.

FAMILY AND WORK CONFLICT

The concern voiced most often by parents—conflict between work and family—transcends class, race, ethnicity, and family structure (Moen & Jull, 1995). Family and work conflict has been coined the "double squeeze" (Skocpol, 1997, p. 119)—a squeeze on economic resources and a simultaneous squeeze on the time and energy needed for family and community commitments (Hewlett & West, 1998). Schor (1991) explained that between 1969 and 1987, the average employed American—irrespective of income, marital status, or occupation—worked an additional 163 hours annually on the job. Because time spent on domestic labor, including housework and child care, remained almost the same, this statistic means that Americans worked, on average, one extra month each year. The time that family members spent in the labor force continued to increase between 1989 and 1995 (Center on Budget and Policy Priorities, 1998), with the longest hours being logged by families raising children (Moen & Yu, 1999).

Some Americans prefer to work longer hours (Hochschild, 1997), but many do not. They find themselves raising their children under conditions that they would not choose if they had other options (Crittenden, 2001). In a nationally representative sample of 4,554 married couples, 44% of men and 34% of women reported working substantially more hours than they preferred (Clarkberg & Moen, 1999). Only 15% reported a preference for full-time employment, although 48% worked full time, and half of these respondents worked more than 40 hours in a typical week. This preference for less than full-time employment held for all ages and education levels in this nationally representative sample (Families and Work Institute, 1995). Those people who work more hours than they prefer experience more work–life conflict, more stress, more overload, and an impaired sense of coping and mastery (Moen & Yu, 1999).

In studies of how parental work affects child outcomes, no uniform effects of parental employment have emerged. Instead, the effects appear to depend on several mediating, moderating, and developmental influences, such as the complexity of the job, the time and material resources of the parent, and demands on parental resources such as the partner's job, the number of siblings, and the birth of an additional child (Parcel & Menaghan, 1994). Increases in family income appear to benefit the child (see Perry-Jenkins, Repetti, & Crouter, 2000), but small negative effects are reported if both mother and father worked overtime (Parcel & Menaghan, 1994), if the mother worked at a low-prestige job (Raver, 2003), and if the mother worked more hours during the early years (Baydar & Brooks-Gunn, 1991; Belsky & Eggebeen, 1991; Bogenschneider & Steinberg, 1994; Harvey, 1999).

Three theoretical approaches have been proposed to guide policy responses when family and work conflict (Parasuraman & Greenhaus, 1997). First, the situation can be modified by restructuring or role negotiation through such policies as providing more flexible time schedules, improving child care, and making paid family leave a legal right. In a recent national survey, 90% of mothers and fathers wanted access to compressed work weeks, flex time, job sharing, and part-time work with benefits (Hewlett & West, 1998). Yet policies need to move beyond enabling employees to adjust their time at work or take more time away from work to changing the conditions of work that harm family life (see Perry-Jenkins et al., 2000). Some observers have called for corporate restructuring to grant the same voice to employees who invest and put at risk their human capital as to shareholders who put at risk their financial capital (Kochan, 2004). Others have advocated for a broad-based fundamental restructuring that moves beyond a "family-friendly corporation" to a "family-friendly society" (Goggins, 1997, p. 230) in which family life is more broadly supported by friends, schools, service agencies, civic organizations, and government at all levels.

A second theoretical perspective proposes that employees could learn specific techniques for better managing work-induced strain. For example, recent studies have identified specific strategies that married couples use to scale back, such as placing limits on job demands, choosing a one-job/one-career marital pattern, and trading off these strategies (Becker & Moen, 1999). Finally, a third theoretical orientation suggests modifying the meaning of the situation through personal role reorientation. Some working families are in a time bind because they want to work more hours to earn more money (Schor, 1991) or to avoid family conflicts and responsibilities (Hochschild, 1997). These findings imply the need for policies that promote personal commitments to family life and foster a cultural climate that supports these commitments.

LONG-TERM CARE

Long-term care includes a broad range of services given over a sustained period to the disabled or the frail elderly whose disabilities result in ongoing difficulties in functioning (Kane, Kane, & Ladd, 1998). Long-term care is a family issue because four of five disabled elderly living in the community rely on assistance from family and others, with three of five relying exclusively on unpaid help, usually from wives and daughters (Stone, 1999). Families make care arrangements, respond in emergencies, and assist with such daily living activities as shopping, cleaning, and meal preparation.

Long-term care needs are increasing because of the aging of the baby boomers and because of advances in medical technology that keep people alive longer. Of all the people in human history who have ever lived past the age of 65, half are alive now (Coontz, 2000). The over-65 population is expected to double by 2040, and the ratio of available caregivers to those needing care is expected to decline by almost two thirds by the year 2050 (Stone, 1999).

For caregivers, a prominent law in the last decade is the 1993 Family and Medical Leave Act, which requires employers with more than 50 workers to provide up to 12 weeks of unpaid leave to care for an ailing family member. Although federal oversight and dollars exist, long-term care is largely controlled by the states (Kane et al., 1998). In an analysis of long-term care policies in 13 states, three general strategies have emerged: (a) offsetting state spending by encouraging the purchase of private long-term care insurance, maximizing Medicare financing of long-term care, and reducing Medicaid estate planning whereby individuals manage assets to appear poor enough to qualify for Medicaid-financed care; (b) reorganizing health care delivery to make it more efficient through expanding home- and community-based options and extending managed care to include long-term care; and (c) using traditional cost-saving measures such as controlling the supply of providers and lowering reimbursement rates. Nursing homes have been the predominant long-term care providers, but younger people with disabilities have advocated for more home- and community-based options (Wiener & Sullivan, 1995). Given the rapidly rising costs, amount of need, and number of affected parties—nursing homes and other providers, health professionals, state and federal policymakers, and advocates for the disabled and the elderly—long-term care promises to remain a contentious family policy issue (Kane et al., 1998).

FAMILY POVERTY

Average household incomes did not increase between 1999 and 2004, marking the first time since Census data have been collected that incomes did not increase for five straight years (Leonhardt, 2005). At the same time, income disparity between the rich and poor has been growing. In President Clinton's and President George W. Bush's State of the Union messages, no mention was made of income disparity. In his unsuccessful bid for president in 2004, John Edwards's acclaimed stump speech on the "two Americas" raised the issue of income disparity. However, this issue, which has received little attention outside academia, has received considerable scholarly attention (e.g., Center on Budget and Policy Priorities, 1998; Hewlett & West, 1998; McMurrer & Sawhill, 1998; Wilson, 1997).

In contrast to the growth that took place in the three decades after World War II, recent economic growth has not been shared equally among all families. For example, between 1979 and 1995, family incomes rose by 26% in the top fifth of families and fell by 9% in the bottom fifth. This widening gap between the rich and poor has been consistent across African American and White households (Center on Budget and Policy Priorities, 1998; Wilson, 1997) and also across states. From 1994 to 1996, the top fifth of families with children had, on average, almost 13 times the income of the bottom fifth, with differentials among states ranging from a low of 7 to a high of almost 20. In the 1970s, no state had an income differential greater than 10, whereas in the mid-1990s, 30 states did (Larin, 1998). In a recent 2004 analysis, the income gap between the top 5% of Americans and the bottom 10% was the second widest since the Census began collecting such data in 1967 (Wollman, Yoder, Brumbaugh-Smith, & Gross, 2005). In a recent Kids Count analysis, almost half of low-income families had no liquid assets in 1999 (Annie E. Casey Foundation, 2003).

These economic trends have repercussions for families and particularly for the well-being of children (see White & Rogers, 2000). Family income is a potent predictor of children's development across income groups, with one third to one half of its impact accounted for by parenting practices, the home learning environment, and family structure (McMurrer & Sawhill, 1998). Of several policies that address family poverty, four are discussed here. First, the 1996 Personal Responsibility and Work Opportunity Reconciliation Act (PRWORA), with its provisions that address marriage, teenage parenting, fathering, child support, and family caps, was one of the nation's most significant family policies of the last decade (see its provisions in Table 5.1). Through its Temporary Assistance for Needy Families (TANF) program, PRWORA accelerated trends that transformed the culture of welfare from a focus on income support to work and self-sufficiency. By January 1999, every state had in place a new welfare system based on work (Tweedie, 1999).

Some activists believe that TANF, with its work requirements, sanctions, and marginal tax rates, is simply another name for welfare. Yet the Welfare Peer Assistance Network (WELPAN), a group of senior welfare administrators from the Midwest, believes that further shifts may be occurring toward community and family concerns, particularly the well-being of children (Corbett, 2000). Former welfare agencies are dealing with child welfare, domestic violence, education, juvenile crime, and teenage pregnancy. Work remains a major goal, but increasingly as a way of stabilizing families, improving parents' ability to function as caregivers, and encouraging fuller participation in society (Corbett, 2000).

With TANF reauthorization approaching, several major evaluation studies are measuring the success of welfare reform (see findings on the Web site of the Research Forum on Children, Families, and the New Federalism at http://www.researchforum.org). Success may be measured by reductions in caseloads, which currently have dropped by more than 60% (Dahl, 2005). In a number of studies, strong work requirements increased the number of mothers finding jobs and leaving the welfare rolls (Haskins et al., 2005).

Because of media and policymaker attention to these plummeting caseloads (Pratt, 1998), the welfare reform debate has been primarily one-generational, focusing on enhancing parents' self-sufficiency or bread-winning capacity. As an alternative, scholars have proposed two-generational approaches that simultaneously focus on parents' caregiving capacity (e.g., Smith, Blank, & Collins, 1992), arguing that if children are neglected and unable to become self-sufficient adults, the investment in their parents' employment may well be squandered (Blum, 1992). One example of such two-generational research is a recent study that showed TANF child support mandates increased the proportion of fathers paying child support, as well as the extent of contact and involvement that fathers had with their children (Mincy, Garfinkel, & Nepomnyaschy, 2005). Another example is the three-city study that followed 2,402 low-income families for 16 months as mothers transitioned off of welfare and into work. When mothers entered the workforce, their incomes increased and no negative outcomes were observed in their preschoolers or young adolescents (Chase-Lansdale et al., 2003). In fact, when mothers entered the labor force, some evidence emerged that adolescents had better mental health, enhanced cognitive achievement, and less drug and alcohol use.

Research findings have been mixed on whether TANF has increased maltreatment of children or involvement with the child welfare system. For example, in one study of 1,363 Illinois welfare recipients, the odds of child maltreatment increased among welfare recipients who received TANF but were not employed, compared to those who left TANF without work, who worked without welfare, and who combined work and welfare (Slack et al., 2003). However, in another study of 1,075 Wisconsin welfare applicants, no evidence emerged that contact with child welfare authorities was associated with welfare reform, irrespective of whether it was measured by the receipt of TANF cash assistance, the loss of this assistance, or sanctions (Courtney, Dworsky, Piliavin, & Zinn, 2005). These researchers are quick to point out that nearly all this research was conducted when the economy was strong, so more studies are needed in different economic conditions, for longer periods of time, and in states with different welfare policies.

A policy that is credited with lifting 4.3 million Americans out of poverty in 1997 is the Earned Income Tax Credit (EITC) program. The EITC targets working families with children and was expanded under Democratic and Republican administrations (Hotz & Scholz, 2000). In an attempt to reward working families and reduce reliance on welfare, a cash subsidy is provided to people with earnings up to a specific income level, but no money is granted to those without earnings. The EITC is an appealing policy to assist low-income working families because of its work incentive, relatively low administrative costs, and targeting. About two thirds of all EITC payments go to taxpayers with wages in the bottom quartile of all workers with children (Hotz & Scholz, 2000). Currently 18 states have adopted their own EITCs, which supplement the federal credit (Greenstein, 2005), and other states are considering it.

A third policy response has been to fund a broad array of investments in children, including early childhood programs, quality child care, home visiting, and Head Start. The interest of federal and state policymakers in early intervention may be due, in part, to the heightened need for child care as welfare recipients entered employment, media attention to early brain development, and scientific evidence on the importance of the early years. Of particular relevance to policy was longitudinal research linking home visits conducted prenatally and during the first 2 years of a baby's life to the mother's reduced reliance on AFDC, Food Stamps, and Medicaid 15 years later (Olds et al., 1997; Olds et al., 1998). Also, longitudinal studies of the Abecedarian Project demonstrated that high-quality, multifaceted interventions beginning early in infancy can alter the course of intellectual development. At age 21, the benefits included delayed parenthood, higher IQs, higher reading and math scores, and more years of formal education, especially for teenage mothers (Ramey et al., 1999; Ramey & Ramey, 1999).

Finally, an obvious policy question that arises from growing income inequality is whether people, particularly the disadvantaged, can move out of poverty by climbing up the rungs of the economic ladder. Economic mobility rates have remained substantial, but virtually unchanged, over the last 25 years. In the 1980s, a college education became and has remained the ticket to mobility. Families are a powerful influence on school success and increasingly so (McMurrer & Sawhill, 1998). For example, a family's SES (i.e., education, income, and occupation) is a powerful predictor of whether children attend college and, when enrolled, whether they complete a degree (McMurrer & Sawhill, 1998). Yet educational reform has focused primarily on school organization, course curriculum, instructional methods, and teacher training. Steinberg (1996) concluded that 15 years of such reforms have accomplished little because academic achievement is shaped more by the conditions of students' lives outside school. Despite evidence of a substantial family component to school success and economic mobility, family scholars have traditionally ignored educational issues (Seeley, 1985), and family advocates typically exclude education from their policy agenda (for an exception, see Lewis & Henderson, 1997).

MARRIAGE

Until recently, marriage was so politically unpopular that policymakers publicly avoided using what was disparagingly called the "M-word" (Ooms, 2002). Marriage was barely on the political radar screen a decade ago (Meezan & Rauch, 2005), but now has become one of the most widely discussed family policies with debate ensuing on two separate fronts: (a) for those who are married, the movement to strengthen marriage, support two-parent families, and prevent divorce; and (b) for those who are not, the controversy over whether same-sex partners should be allowed to marry. Each is considered here in turn.

The Movement to Strengthen Marriage

Three major demographic trends have been on the family policy radar screen. Divorce occurs in more than half of all first marriages in the United States, almost one third of all births are outside marriage, and nearly one third of children do not live with their biological father. About half of all children born today are expected to live apart from one parent during their first 15 years of life (Smeeding et al., 2004). A phenomenon underlying these trends has received increasing public attention in the last decade—the pervasive decline in marriage across all sectors of society (Ooms, 2002).

In the last 10 years, a number of federal and state actions catapulted marriage onto the political stage. According to political observers, the 1996 welfare reform law was the first federal legislation to explicitly address marriage and family formation through three little-noticed provisions that called for states to promote marriage, reduce out-of-wedlock childbearing, and encourage two-parent families (Ooms et al., 2004). After the 2000 election, President Bush declared that strengthening marriage would receive unprecedented support from his administration (Ooms, 2002). In 2001, the Administration for Children and Families in the U.S. Department of Health and Human Services committed $100 million to support research and pro-gramming on marriage education (Ooms, 2005). The Bush Administration is proposing $1.5 billion over the next 5 years to disseminate research about the benefits of marriage and to teach low-income couples how to improve their relationships and communication skills (McLanahan, Donahue, & Has-kins, 2005). Meanwhile, states and communities have initiated a number of activities to promote marriage, reduce divorce, and strengthen two-parent families. For example, 40 states have used government funds to provide couples and marriage education, often on a pilot basis; 36 states have re-vised their TANF eligibility rules to treat one- and two-parent households the same; 8 states have made significant changes to their marriage and di-vorce laws; and states are considering or enacting a number of initiatives to support premarital education, covenant marriage, and relationship educa-tion in high school (Doherty & Anderson, 2004). Moreover, governors and other senior officials in nine states have made marriage promotion a goal of their administration (Ooms, 2004).

This avalanche of interest in marriage has occurred for several reasons, four of which are mentioned here. First, married men and women are healthier, live longer, and have fewer emotional problems (Eastman, 1996; Nock, 2005; Ooms, 1998). A recent study confirmed the relation between marriage and personal happiness in 16 of 17 industrialized countries, with marriage contributing to happiness substantially more than cohabitation does (Stack & Eshleman, 1998). Second, married fathers are more apt to be involved with their children because fathers' relationship to their offspring, more than mothers', is tied to the quality of the relationship between par-ents (Doherty, Kouneski, & Erickson, 1998). Third, marriage has economic impacts in that married people work harder, earn and save more, and accu-mulate greater wealth (Forthofer, Markman, Cox, Stanley, & Kessler, 1996). Married men have higher performance ratings than unmarried men, which may be responsible for their higher earnings (Nock, 2005).

Finally, although debate continues about the effect of single parenthood or stepfamilies on child well-being, there is little question that children do well economically, socially, and psychologically if their biological parents have a strong, conflict-free marriage (Amato, 2005; Glenn, 1996; McLanahan & Sandefur, 1994). Reducing single parenthood is one promising means of moving children out of poverty, given that children raised in single-parent families are four times more likely to be poor than those raised in two-parent families (Thomas & Sawhill, 2005). Beyond poverty, growing up with both parents has other substantial social benefits for the well-being of the next generation. According to recent estimates, if the share of adolescents living with two-parent families were increased to 1980 levels, 643,264 fewer adolescents would repeat a grade, nearly half a million fewer adolescents would be suspended from school, about 240,000 fewer would have smoked in the previous month, about 200,000 fewer would commit a delinquent or violent act, and about 28,000 fewer would attempt suicide (Amato, 2005).

Marriage would seem to be a nonpartisan issue, given that 93% of Americans rate a happy marriage as one of their most important life goals (Mason et al., 2004). Moreover, most Americans, regardless of race or income, would probably agree that the best setting for raising children is when their two parents have a good or healthy marriage (McLanahan et al., 2005; Ooms & Wilson, 2004). Nevertheless, marriage policy has triggered considerable debate among conservatives and liberals alike. Curiously, conservatives who are usually skeptical about government involvement, particularly in private family matters, have been quick to jump on the marriage bandwagon, whereas liberals who usually promote government involvement are hesitant. Conservatives see strengthening marriage as a way to benefit individuals' economic and social well-being and eliminate the need for government intervention in the long run (Brotherson & Duncan, 2004). Liberals fear that marriage is a code word for an ideological agenda to deliberate women, discriminate against same-sex couples, stigmatize single parents, or force women to remain in abusive patriarchal relationships. Moreover, no marriage curriculum has been tested with low-income minority populations, which raises concerns about whether marriage education will impose White middle-class standards on culturally diverse poor people (Haskins et al., 2005; Ooms, 2002, 2005).

Supporters of the marriage initiative claim that given the support for marriage among the rich and poor alike, it should be possible to forge an approach that can build bipartisan support. Focusing on low-income people is a good starting point, according to proponents, because marriage is in the most trouble in poor families (McLanahan et al., 2005). Yet even supporters worry that the funding proposed for healthy marriage programs will divert resources and attention away from other sorely need supports for low-income families such as child care, employment-based antipoverty programs, and efforts to prevent out-of-wedlock childbearing (Ooms, 2002; Thomas & Sawhill, 2005). Despite these disagreements, there does seem to be widespread consensus that the rate of family dissolution warrants government attention because of its heavy costs for individuals, government, and society (Haskins et al., 2005; McLahanan et al., 2005; Ooms, 2002; Thomas & Sawhill, 2005). Yet debate continues over exactly what problem the marriage initiative is addressing, which is the best way to respond, and whose responsibility it is—individuals, communities, faith communities, or government (Ooms, 2002).

Acknowledging these disagreements, Ooms (2002, 2004) proposed a "Marriage-Plus" approach that is broader and more nuanced than the agenda proposed by most marriage advocates. For example, Ooms proposed that the primary goal should be promoting the well-being of children, which entails a two-pronged strategy: (a) strengthening the marriages of parents who are married, and (b) helping parents who are not to be financially responsible and to cooperate in the rearing of their children. Marriage Plus focuses on healthy marriages and taking steps to strengthen marriage "to make it better to be in rather than more difficult to get out of" (Ooms, 1998, p. 5). Marriage Plus recommends a comprehensive scope of activities that incorporates strategies known to directly strengthen marriage, as well as those that may indirectly benefit marriage such as increasing parental employment and work, reducing work stress, and preventing teen pregnancy and out-of-wedlock births. Finally, Marriage Plus is based on the principle that strengthening marriage is not the responsibility of government alone, but entails partnering as well with the business, education, faith, health, legal, and media sectors of society (Ooms, 2004).

So the marriage debate has proceeded on these two fronts. Policymakers have been faced with decisions about whether they should enact policies to strengthen marriage for those who are married and, if so, what is the best way to proceed. Moreover, policymakers have been asked to decide who should be allowed to marry and thereby receive the benefits marriage brings—tangible resources such as access to family leave, health care, and Social Security—and intangible benefits like public recognition of the commitment the couple has made to each other and the treatment this brings as a socially recognized family unit by their extended families and the community as well.

The Controversy Over Whether Same-Sex Partners Should Marry

Perhaps no recent family policy issue has been more controversial than whether same-sex partners should be allowed to marry, generating passion that parallels the days when states debated interracial marriage and no-fault divorce (Meezan & Rauch, 2005). Yet despite the amount of attention it is receiving, same-sex marriage is one of the least-studied family policy issues.

In 1981, recognition of domestic partnerships or same-sex marriage was nonexistent (Gates, 2005). By order of its high court, Vermont in 2000 enacted an extensive civil union that gave same-sex couples the same rights as married couples (Elrod & Spector, 2005). Connecticut followed suit in 2005, offering civil unions to same-sex couples, but without a court mandate. In 2004, Massachusetts became the first state in the nation to offer marriage licenses to same-sex couples, and in 2005, a constitutional amendment to ban gay marriage and create civil unions was defeated in the Massachusetts legislature in a 157-to-39 vote (Belluck, 2005). California and Hawaii also offer statuses similar to marriage that provide marriage-like benefits. A number of municipalities and states also established registries that provide some benefits to same-sex couples (Gates, 2005).

In contrast, 13 states passed constitutional amendments in 2004 banning same-sex marriage. Overall, more than 40 states enacted constitutional amendments or laws like the Defense of Marriage Act that define marriage as a union between a man and a woman (Elrod & Spector, 2005). What's more, a recent high court ruling in Massachusetts, the one state that has legalized same-sex marriage, prohibits marrying gay couples from states that ban such marriages (Belluck & Zezima, 2006).

Because family laws are enacted in family courts, the decisions can be quite divergent, with rulings made locally and sometimes dependent on the proclivities of an individual judge. With regard to parenting, in 1991, no legal recognition of same-sex parents existed in any jurisdiction. By 2005, about half of states had some recognition of same-sex parents, some established by legal mandate and others by court decree (Gates, 2005). All states allow married couples and unmarried individuals to apply for adoption. Utah is the only state that prohibits adoption by unmarried couples, whether they are heterosexual or homosexual. Only one state, Florida, prohibits homosexual individuals from adopting and only Mississippi prohibits adoption by same-sex couples. In nine states and the District of Columbia, same-sex couples can apply jointly for adoption, and in almost two dozen states, courts in the entire state or in some jurisdictions allow "second parent adoptions"—one parent (either biological or adopted) adopts the child first and a second gay or lesbian parent can file to become the second parent. In the remainder of states, only one same-sex partner can adopt and the other is not eligible for joint or second parent adoption (Meezan & Rauch, 2005).

The debate has moved beyond the statehouse and the courthouse to the classroom. In Texas, a state that bans gay marriage and prohibits same-sex civil unions, two major textbook publishers agreed to publish special health textbooks that defined marriage as a "lifelong union between a husband and a wife" ("Health Textbooks in Texas to Change Wording About Marriage," 2004).

The fault lines have been drawn over same-sex marriage. Proponents cast the issue as one of basic civil rights, whereas opponents frame the issue as a matter of morality or faith. Proponents believe that allowing same-sex couples to marry will elevate the importance of marriage and the benefits it brings to adults, children, and society. Opponents believe that allowing same-sex couples to marry will signal that heterosexual and same-sex marriage are equally good for children, when they may not be. Some scholars who reviewed the literature noted that the existing body of evidence is limited, but concluded that children raised by same-sex couples are doing about as well as children normally do. Other scholars were unwilling to draw any conclusion because they contend not a single study met generally accepted scientific standards of evidence (see Meezan & Rauch, 2005).

Like scholarly opinion, public opinion is divided. A 2005 Gallup poll showed that the vast majority of Americans (87%) believe that gays should have equal rights in terms of job opportunities and about half (49%) think that homosexual relations between consenting adults should be legal. When asked if a marriage between homosexuals should be legally recognized as valid with the same rights as traditional marriages, 37% said yes and 59% said no (Gallup Organization, 2005).

Questions of who should be allowed to marry, how to care for children and the elderly, and what society can do to economically support poor families clearly fall under the purview of family policy. The issue of health care is not considered a family policy because it affects individuals as well as families, but would still benefit from a family perspective in policymaking.

HEALTH CARE

Another front-burner issue that has hit the state and national policy stage is rising health care costs. In the first half of 2005, health care premiums grew 9.2%, which is almost three times faster than the growth in workers' earnings (2.7%). On average, in 2005, workers paid $2,713 toward premiums for family coverage or 26% of the total premium. The worker's share of the premium has remained relatively stable, but workers are now paying on average $1,094 more in premiums for family coverage than they did 5 years ago. Since 2000, premiums have increased a total of 73%, bringing the cost of family coverage to an average $10,880 in 2005. As insurance costs have increased faster than wages and inflation, it is no surprise that the percentage of businesses, particularly small businesses, offering health insurance to their workers has steadily declined (Kaiser Family Foundation, 2005). Despite this drop in employer insurance, the proportion of uninsured Americans has remained steady at about 16%, primarily because of the growth in two extensive government programs—Medicaid and military insurance (Leonhardt, 2005).

What these premium increases mean for families is that each year more families are unable to afford health insurance premiums and still pay the rent. Today the rising cost of health care threatens the economic viability of lower income families, and tomorrow it may threaten middle-income families. For many working families, rising health care costs hold down both salary increases and job growth. For senior citizens living on fixed incomes, health-related expenses ate up half of their 2004 increase in Social Security income. Perhaps no action that policymakers can take will have a bigger impact on the living standard of families than legislation to make health care more affordable, according to Dr. Arnold Milstein, who was recently recognized by the National Business Group on Health for being one of the most effective national leaders in health care innovation (Bogenschneider & Normandin, 2005).

Low-wage workers and low-income families may be hurt the most by rising health care costs (Kaiser Family Foundation, 2005). Medicaid is a publicly funded health insurance program that provides coverage to low-income children, families, seniors, and people with disabilities. Medicaid is an optional program in which states may choose to participate, but all states do. The federal government pays about 50% of the costs of medical services provided under Medicaid and as much as 80% in poor states (King, 2005). Medicaid has been the fastest growing of all state programs, accounting for about 20% of the average state's budget in 2004. As Medicaid costs have grown faster than state revenues, every state adopted at least one cost-containment strategy in 2004, the fourth consecutive year that states implemented significant strategies to control the growth in Medicaid expenditures (Smith, 2005).

As policymakers debate health care—a huge burden on government budgets that brings huge benefits to families—family policy professionals can encourage policymakers to consider how health care reform may impact the well-being of families in intended and unintended ways. For example, family professionals can alert policymakers to how health care costs are affecting families and how involving families in policy solutions could help curb costs (see examples in chap. 7). When Medicaid is being debated, family professionals can provide data that children and adults (mostly poor parents and pregnant women) represent 75% of Medicaid beneficiaries, but account for only one third of expenditures. Family professionals can use the Family Impact Checklist (see Appendix A) to raise questions about what the impact of cost-cutting strategies might be for families. For example, will eligibility criteria that make it harder for married families to qualify for health care affect decisions about whether or not to marry? Can providing additional home and community-based care as an alternative to nursing homes save money and provide long-term care options that elderly families often prefer? Will raising premium copays for low-income families deter them from accessing preventive and other medical services that may actually be more cost effective in the long run? Will the policies being debated have different effects for families as a function of their race or ethnicity—the topic to which we turn next.

FAMILY DIVERSITY ISSUES

Progress was made in the 1990s on addressing inequities of gender, race, and ethnicity, but class divisions have deepened (Bellah et al., 1985/1996; McMurrer & Sawhill, 1998; Wilson, 1997). For example, to predict the life chances of a child born in the United States in 1998, it is more important to know the parents' SES than the child's race or gender. High school completion rates of African Americans and Whites are now similar, and the earnings of African Americans have almost caught up to those of Whites with similar educational backgrounds (McMurrer & Sawhill, 1998). Nonetheless, disparities in racial wealth (i.e., the net value of assets such as stocks, savings, real estate, and business ownership) may limit parents' ability to pass along advantage to their children (Oliver & Shapiro, 1997). The disproportionate concentration of poverty among racial and ethnic minorities suggests the need for ongoing discussions of disadvantage as a function of race and ethnicity—discussions that might draw on developmental contextualism as a theoretical framework for conceptualizing family diversity (Lerner, Sparks, & McCubbin, 1999).

For research purposes, studying diversity is important to disentangle the influence of context (e.g., class, race, ethnicity, and gender) on family outcomes. For policy purposes, however, identifying similarities across diverse families is equally important. Understanding how families are different is essential to designing effective policies, but understanding how families are similar enhances the prospects that policies will muster widespread, sustainable political support (see Bogenschneider, 1999; Skocpol, 1997; Wilson, 1997, 1999). The fate of a family agenda hinges on the prospects of pulling together coalitions that transcend class and race (Skocpol & Greenberg, 1997) to promote "common solutions to shared problems" (Wilson, 1997, p. 77). A common experience across the usual divides of class, race, ethnicity, and gender is family (Carlson, 2005), and recent studies indicate enormous unity on many family policies (Hewlett & West, 1998). Issues such as child care, child support, family leave, or income disparity could well become rallying points for parent–teacher associations, unions, churches, businesses, and other community groups across the political spectrum (Skocpol, 1997).

Family policies have generated substantial political interest, although some scholars argue that the political response to family issues has not been as frequent, varied, or comprehensive as their importance warrants. The debate of family policy issues continues to generate deep-seated passion and controversy that has too often stymied the compromise and consensus needed to move family policies forward, the topic to which I turn in the next chapter.

USING THEORY AND PRACTICE TO MOVE CONTROVERSIAL POLICIES FORWARD

9

How Can We Bridge the Controversy and Move Family Policies Forward? The Theory of Paradox

As Governor, I can tell you that about 80 percent of the problems that hit my desk you can trace back to the breakdown of family structure in our society, and I think anyone who doesn't want to admit that is kidding themselves.
—Illinois Governor Jim Edgar, November 1995
(cited in Stacey, 1996, p. 13)

As a family sociologist, I can tell you that about 70 percent of the problems that hit my desk you can trace back to the breakdown of the economic and social structure in our society (the other 30 percent are probably indelible features of the human condition), and I think anyone who doesn't want to admit that is not only kidding themselves but also is shirking a personal portion of our collective responsibility in the name of the Family.
—Judith Stacey (cited in Stacey, 1996, p. 13)

Because it can generate passion so strong and controversy so divisive, the debate over family policy has been depicted as "the national family wars" (Stacey, 1993, p. 545), the "war against parents" (Hewlett & West, 1998, title page), and "generational warfare" (Skocpol, 1997, p. 123). This confrontational metaphor may be evoked because what lurks beneath the surface of family policy debate is a war of ideas with families as one of the main battlegrounds. Politicians cannot seem to agree on what conditions constitute social problems, which factors contribute to them, what values should drive policy decisions, and how society should respond. In controversial arenas, politicians tend to polarize issues by casting them in simplistic either–or terms, as black-and-white choices, or as liberal or conservative political ploys that make rousing campaign speeches and catchy 30-second sound bites. Yet these political characterizations are often inaccurate and frequently generate "more heat than light, more politics than policies, more slogans than solutions" (Bayme, 1991, p. 14).

In an attempt to overcome this polarization and break the policymaking impasse, this chapter moves beyond the stereotypic classifications of liberal and conservative that force politicians and activists into rigid, opposing camps and away from the consensus needed to enact family-friendly policies. A more fruitful approach for moving beyond the controversy may be to consider a question that defines the family policy debate and holds the potential to lend clarity, cooperation, and common ground (Blankenhorn, 1990). Because it does not fit our preconceptions of liberal and conservative, this fundamental question is often not readily apparent even to those active in the debate: What are the social consequences of the demographic changes that have occurred in family life in the United States in the last quarter-century?

This question brings into sharp relief three different theories, or worldviews, of family change. There is no dispute that families have changed, and changed dramatically, in the last 25 years (Cowan, 1993; Popenoe, 1993). Demographic data abound on the silent revolution of maternal employment; the unprecedented levels of divorce; the demographic explosion of single parenthood; the kaleidoscope of racially and ethnically diverse families; the expansion of family forms including cohabitating, gay, and lesbian couples; and the historic shift in the age structure of society due to increases in longevity and declines in fertility (see chap. 1 for details). Controversy ensues, however, in regard to how each worldview describes, explains, and interprets these changes. These worldviews are closely linked to family policy because they define which changes are discussed; the causes of these changes; their consequences for families and society; and the role of the cultural climate, economic conditions, social policy, and legal reforms.

Blankenhorn (1990) limited his discussion to two worldviews, which he called *pessimistic* and *optimistic,* but a third worldview, the *postmodern,* is also discussed here. This discussion is admittedly incomplete, however, given that there are more than three worldviews and many hybrids as well. The purpose of this discussion is not to detail every worldview, but rather to draw some of the fault lines that define the parameters of the family policy debate. In the spirit of fairness, I have renamed these worldviews because of the pejorative undertones of the term *pessimism* and the appealing nuances of the terms *optimism* and *postmodern.* These terms seem especially value-laden in America, a country sometimes considered the world's most optimistic society (Blankenhorn, 1990) and one that prides itself on its modernity. Moreover, the terms *optimism* and *pessimism* are antonyms that conjure up a simplistic notion of only two views of family change that are opposite sides of a single coin when, in reality, there are several views that differ on multiple dimensions.

In this book, I propose the terms *concerned* (instead of *pessimistic*), *sanguine* (instead of *optimistic*), and *impatient* (instead of *postmodern*). The concerned camp focuses to a large extent on the negative consequences that family changes in the last couple of decades have had, particularly for children. The sanguine camp focuses more predominantly on the positive consequences of these changes, especially for women. The impatient camp focuses on the inadequacy of these changes, calling for further change and more understanding, tolerance, and support of diverse family forms.

In this chapter, I describe each view, beginning with the concerned view and then proceeding to the sanguine and impatient perspectives. I discuss the values that underlie each view, the evidence that supports it, and the policy responses that stem from it. Granted, many sources integrate these views to varying degrees, but for the sake of clarity I try to present these perspectives in a pure, unadulterated form that clearly differentiates them from each other. In the words of philosophy professor Ben Hunt, "When we learn something new, it is almost impossible not to absolutize it in some way" (cited in Doherty, 1995, p. 165). If family policy is to move forward as a subfield of social policy, researchers and practitioners must give priority to a theoretical framework that can provide a vision for formulating family-friendly policies and practical guidance for moving the field forward (Monroe, 1995). I conclude this chapter by describing the theory of paradox, which I contend has the potential to (a) build consensus on one of the most contentious issues facing Americans—understanding what is happening to U.S. families—and (b) overcome the polarization that has often stymied progress in both implementing family policies and in promoting a family perspective in policymaking (Browning & Rodriguez, 2002).

THE CONCERNED CAMP

The concerned camp contends that families are in decline—a decline that has accelerated in the last 25 years. According to this perspective, the quality of family life would be better and the prospects for the future more secure if many of these changes had not occurred. Changes in families figure prominently in the views of the concerned. Families are considered the first and foremost influence on the development of competence and character in children and adults alike, a view consistent with scientific understanding of the role of families in human development (Bronfenbrenner, 1986).

A prominent spokesperson for this view, Popenoe (1990), identified four social trends that have impinged on families as an institution and also on one particular family form, the nuclear family: increases in maternal employment, declines in fertility, unprecedented levels of divorce, and the sexual revolution (specifically, increases in teenage nonmarital sex and unwed parenthood). Taken together, these trends have contributed to the nuclear family becoming less prevalent and to the rise in alternative family forms, such as serial families and stepfamilies, single-parent families, and unmarried couples and partnerships.

In contrast to the other worldviews, which characterize these trends merely as changes, the concerned describe them as decline. Popenoe (1990) emphasized that decline is not always negative, and he pinpointed positive aspects of the decline of the nuclear family, such as greater opportunities for women and more fulfilling marriages. Also, several of the traditional functions of the family that were taken over by the state, market, and voluntary sectors have been carried out more effectively by these institutions.

Yet Popenoe (1990) acknowledged that recent changes have weakened the capacity of families to carry out their two most important functions: socialization of children, and provision of affection and companionship (Blankenhorn, 1990; Popenoe, 1990). As families become smaller, less stable, shorter in duration, and more separated from extended family, their ability to perform these important functions is compromised. For example, children are still important, yet "their position at the top of the value pyramid is not a given anymore" (Lesthaeghe, 1995, p. 19) and they are no longer an impediment to divorce. Marital ties have weakened (Popenoe, 1990) as have the ties of parents to children (Popenoe, 1990; Uhlenberg & Eggebeen, 1986). Children have been placed in double jeopardy because both mothers and fathers began investing less in their families at about the same time. Women relinquished their role as full-time homemakers, just as fathers absented themselves from family responsibilities due to increases in divorce, desertion, and unwed parenthood (Popenoe, 1990).

Values of the Concerned Camp

The values that drive this camp are parental commitment, marital fidelity, individual responsibility, and civic participation, which they claim have been overshadowed by a cultural ethos of individualism. The cultural tilt away from commitment to children, families, and community and toward individual rights, self-reliance, and self-fulfillment has become even more pronounced in contemporary society than in recent decades (Bellah et al., 1985/1996; Blankenhorn, 1990; Bumpass, 1990). This weakening of individual responsibility is a particularly troubling trend in individualistic societies like the United States. Individualism has worked well in the U.S. in the past because its citizens have historically held a high sense of personal responsibility and obligation to others—virtues that can no longer be taken for granted (Yankelovich, 1995).

Individualism, touted as the best route to personal happiness in the 1960s, has a mixed record at best. Based on public opinion polls, the narcissism and social isolation often synonymous with individualism have culminated in a lonely, empty existence with little meaning (Blankenhorn, 1990; Yankelovich, 1989). The concerned contend that the road to happiness and a life of meaning is paved not with individualism and isolation, but with relatedness to others, investments in family, and commitments to community (Bellah et al., 1985/1996).

Because they point out the potential "dark side of modernity" (Blankenhorn, 1990, p. 15), the concerned camp is often criticized for being antiprogressive and overly cautious about accepting changes in family life (Cheal, 1991). Through the lens of the concerned, progress should not be unwittingly embraced because it does not always move you closer to the most desirable destination. For example, if you take a wrong turn, no matter how far or fast you travel, it only gets you to the wrong place quicker. The person who does an about-face is actually the most progressive (Lewis, 1996). Thus, the concerned would argue for cautious reflection on the family changes that have occurred in the last quarter-century with an eye to correcting the course when evidence suggests it is threatening the well-being of children or the vitality of family life.

Evidence in Support of the Concerned Camp

The views of the concerned camp are supported by five main sources of evidence. First, the ongoing struggle in America, captured in public opinion polls over the last 30 years, is how much freedom the individual can have (Yankelovich, 1989). In the American quest for the right balance of individualism and commitment to others, recent polls suggest the pendulum may have swung too far toward individualism. For example, in 1992, three quarters of the U.S. workforce said that selfishness was a serious or extremely serious problem in America (Putnam, 2000a). When surveyed in 1999, more than 80% of Americans called for more emphasis on community even if it meant placing more demands on individuals (Putnam, 2000a).

Second, in keeping with the views of the concerned, the American public has expressed grave reservations about the state of families and, particularly, the plight of children (Hewlett & West, 1998; National Commission on Children, 1991b). Several scholars and national commissions have voiced serious doubts about how well children are being socialized based on estimates that one fifth of children are growing up in poverty (Lerner et al., 1999) and one half of America's youth ages 10 to 17 abuse alcohol and other substances, fail in school, commit crimes, or engage in early unprotected intercourse (Bronfenbrenner, 1986; Dryfoos, 1990; Hernandez, 1994; National Commission on Children, 1991a; Uhlenberg & Eggebeen, 1986). In recent studies, even in higher income families, behavioral and emotional problems worsened in 6- to 17-year-olds (Vandivere, Gallagher, & Moore, 2004). Third, the concerned camp justifies the validity of their concerns about children by emphasizing the value to society of raising the next generation, who will become the future parents, workers, and citizens on whose shoulders the prosperity of the country depends (Bronfenbrenner, 1986; Hernandez, 1994). According to recent estimates, a child born in the United States is now worth over $100,000 to the rest of society (Preston, 2004).

Fourth, at the heart of this argument is the importance of the nuclear family. The concerned view is supported by the majority of Americans who believe that the best environment for raising children is the stable, two-parent family (Doherty, 1992), a belief consistent with scientific studies. For example, family disruptions have been shown to jeopardize child outcomes. Children who live with only one parent do less well on several measures of academic, social, and psychological well-being than do children who live with both parents (Amato & Keith, 1991; Furstenberg, Brooks-Gunn, & Chase-Lansdale, 1989; Hetherington, 1993; McLanahan & Booth, 1989). These disadvantages occur irrespective of race or education, whether the parent was married when the child was born, or whether the resident parent remarries (McLanahan & Sandefur, 1994). Similarly, a large number of studies in the 1990s document that divorced individuals are worse off than married individuals in multiple ways—lower psychological well-being, less happiness, worse health, higher stress, and more difficulties raising children (Amato, 2000). In his decade review, Amato concluded that poorly functioning people may be more apt to divorce, but that divorce also causes poor functioning over and beyond these personal characteristics.

Fifth, persuasive evidence for the concerned view comes from recent studies indicating that parental employment interferes with family time. For example, employed women spend over one third less time on child care and household tasks than unemployed women (Council of Economic Advisers, 1999). In interviewer-administered time diaries of 2,818 parents or their children, aged 0 to 12 years old, children of employed mothers spent less time eating with their families than children of unemployed mothers. This family time spent on meals was found to be associated with fewer child behavior problems (Hofferth & Sandberg, 2001). Further, in 61 recent in-depth interviews of 28 dual-earner and single-parent families (Daly, 2001), parents highly value spending time together with their children, yet given their bloated schedules they report that family time is in chronic undersupply.

The most common lament associated with the experience of family time was that there was never enough. When the 5-year-old children were asked, "Do you wish you had more family time?," they enthusiastically clamored "Yes! Yes!" When parents were asked whether they ever had too much family time, they usually chuckled and dismissed the question as ridiculous (p. 289). The primary concern of these parents was not the quality of time, but the quantity. In fact, some parents discredited quality time, calling it "liberal salve for the conscience" (p. 290).

This contradiction between parents' ideal of family time and the reality of their lives has caused pervasive parental guilt—guilt about working too much, spending too little time with the children, getting babysitters, taking time for oneself, and wanting children to go to bed. The primary impediments to finding enough family time—paid work and housework—have proved so impervious to change that many parents have given up trying to adapt their time-constrained family circumstances and instead focus on living with their guilt. Working less seems to be an option out of reach for most parents. Perhaps most disturbing to the concerned camp is the view of parents that the demands of work and child care largely are beyond their control (Daly, 2001).

The Policy Agenda of the Concerned Camp

What can be done to counteract family decline? Popenoe (1990) rejected the notion of returning to the traditional nuclear family of the 1950s, which he believes may, in contemporary society, be "fundamentally flawed" (p. 47). He recognized the value of the state in supporting families, but warned against relying too exclusively on government programs that, if not carefully designed, can inadvertently replace or weaken family functions rather than strengthen families' capacity to function.

The concerned would support policies that foster civil society—the naturally occurring sources of support in the extended family, religious institutions, neighborhood, and community—that mediate between government and families. For example, an appropriate role for government would be to create formal structures encouraging families to develop and rely on their own sources of social support that, in the future, will render the formal programs obsolete (Bronfenbrenner & Weiss, 1983). The concerned favor devolution of the power and authority of the federal government to state and local governments, which are closer to families and should be better able to develop strategies for strengthening families and civil society in ways that can be customized to local circumstances (Giele, 1996).

Because the social trends Popenoe (1990) described are evident in every Western industrialized society, he contended that they emanate not from industrialization or urbanization, but rather from broad cultural shifts. Thus, for the concerned camp, the family policy agenda is not primarily a legislative initiative, but rather a cultural campaign for family values that shape an individual's image of what families should be like and how family members should behave. The concerned call for a grassroots cultural movement that would elevate the cultural ideals of family, marriage, parents, children, and community over individualism, greed, and self-fulfillment (Blankenhorn, 1990; Popenoe, 1990).

The political agenda of the concerned camp is often dismissed because, instead of being *for* positive initiatives, it is primarily *against* family changes that many critics consider too powerful to reverse. According to Cheal (1991), "the best this camp can hope for is to prolong the life span of selected traditions for a little longer or to invent new ways of incorporating elements from the past into contemporary ways of living" (p. 47). In contrast, however, the concerned believe that broad cultural change is possible, citing the extraordinary changes brought about in relatively brief periods of time by activists in the civil rights, women's, environmental, and special education movements.

◊ THE SANGUINE CAMP

The sanguine camp views recent family changes not as symptoms of decline, but rather as indicators of the capacity of families to adapt to new social and economic conditions. Many of the changes that have occurred—increasing rights and equality of formerly oppressed individuals, and growing opportunities to seek rewarding occupations and relationships (Giele, 1996)—are seen as signs of progress that justify breaking with the constraints of traditional roles and norms (Cheal, 1991).

The sanguine emphasize the positive consequences of these family changes for individuals, especially women. As women entered the workplace in record numbers, one consequence of their resulting economic independence was the freedom to escape abusive or patriarchal relationships. When divorce or death occurred, policy changes in Social Security, unemployment insurance, divorce laws, and pensions allowed women to continue living their lives in dignity (Schroeder, 1989). Given the option of divorce, individuals who chose to remain married were more apt to experience relationships that were emotionally fulfilling. The elderly received government benefits for health and living expenses, which made them less dependent on the care of adult children. Children were seen less as the sole property of their parents, which provided them with protection against abuse and exploitation.

In contrast to the concerned and impatient camps, the sanguine do not view the consequences for children as dire (Furstenberg & Condran, 1988) or children's ability to cope as fragile. For example, the sanguine emphasize the resiliency of children in overcoming the emotional upheaval and long-term consequences of divorce (Orthner, 1990). The sanguine camp acknowledges that the recent demographic changes have not benefited individuals and families in selected segments of society (Skolnick, 1997), yet they tend to focus on those who have thrived in the midst of family change:

> The majority of first marriages do not end in divorce, the overwhelming majority of families do not experience child or spouse abuse, the majority of teenage girls do not get pregnant, the majority of adolescents do graduate from high school, and the majority of youth and adults consider themselves happy with their lives in this changing world. (Orthner, 1990, p. 109)

When considering influences on human development, the worldview of the sanguine is broader than just the family (Skolnick, 1997). The sanguine cast a wide net that includes such factors as historical changes, economic hardship, gender inequality, and emotional stress. Social problems are attributed not to the lack of resiliency in individuals or families, but rather to the lack of response from social institutions. Increasing demands have been placed on families by the nature and rapidity of the changes, which have not allowed enough time for society to respond with all the necessary countervailing supports (Giele, 1996), and has overwhelmed the family supports that public policy has put in place (Marshall & Sawhill, 2004).

Values of the Sanguine Camp

The sanguine camp believes that core American values regarding the importance of marriage, commitment, and nurturance have changed very little. Using marriage as an example, 96% of Americans express a personal desire for marriage (Orthner, 1990) and 75% believe that marriage is a lifelong commitment (Bumpass, 1990). Even among people who divorce, the majority do not give up on marriage, but remarry in search of a better union (Schroeder, 1989). The decline in marriage among African American households in inner-city communities may reflect some changes in the valuing of marriage, but is thought to be due, in large part, to the increasing joblessness of African American men, which decreases their desirability as marriage partners (Wilson, 1987).

According to the sanguine camp, family values have changed very little in the last quarter-century. What has changed dramatically are norms and standards regarding appropriate or inappropriate behavior (Orthner, 1990). Norms regarding marriage, as an example, have been revolutionized. Cohabitation before marriage has been commonly accepted, fewer people expect that marriage will last forever, and one of four children are born outside of marriage. The valuing of children has remained stable, according to the sanguine, but norms regarding who is responsible for their nurturance are in flux (Orthner, 1990). Critics of the sanguine camp, however, insist that values and norms are inextricably linked and that "you can't go on revolutionizing norms forever without changing values" (Bellah, 1990, p. 228).

Undergirding these substantial changes in norms is a valuing of greater independence and personal autonomy. Individual freedom is the core value that underlies the rationale and the policy agenda of the sanguine camp. For example, this camp shies away from policies that make it more difficult to divorce because such policies could interfere with an individual's right to self-determination and could subject women, in particular, to domination or abuse (Giele, 1996). Even in the family realm, individual variation is the norm rather than the exception. For example, Orthner (1990) explained that what is expected in family roles such as parent or spouse is less apt to be prescribed by societal norms and more apt to be customized to the particular family situation.

Evidence in Support of the Sanguine Camp

The sanguine cite three main sources of evidence for their view: public opinion polls, empirical data, and cross-cultural comparisons. First, despite concerns about the state of America's children and families in public opinion polls, the majority of parents report that their relationships with their own children are excellent (65%) or good (32%; National Commission on Children, 1991b). Employed mothers do report spending less time with their children than nonemployed mothers, but only about 5 hours less per week. When mothers work, their free time falls by about 32%, but they guard their time with their children, which falls by only 16%. Mothers who work are twice as likely to say they feel rushed, but despite the hectic pace of their lives, they are somewhat more likely to report being more satisfied with their family life than their nonemployed counterparts (Cherlin & Krishnamurthy, 2004).

Second, scholars have countered pessimistic assessments of declining child well-being, citing historic concerns about youth in every decade and calling into question the pervasiveness and consistency of the empirical data (Furstenberg & Condran, 1988; Orthner, 1990). A more optimistic picture of youth emerges when longer and more frequent data points are used, when different age groups are considered, and when African American and White youth are considered separately (Furstenberg & Condran, 1988). When data are analyzed in this way, youth are doing better in some, but not all, indicators, such as declining rates of unintentional injuries and violent crimes against and by youth. Moreover, in 2000, the teen birth rate dropped for the 10th straight year (Guttmacher Institute, 2004).

Finally, in support of their contention that families need institutional support to adapt to rapid societal changes, the sanguine cite the track record of other industrialized countries. Other countries with larger social safety nets have experienced similar increases in maternal employment, single parenthood, and divorce, yet have not witnessed a comparable decline in child well-being as evidenced by rates of child poverty, school failure, suicide, teenage pregnancy, and youth violence (Giele, 1996).

The Policy Agenda of the Sanguine Camp

For this camp, the crux of family policy is not reversing the family trends that have occurred, but rather establishing the institutional supports needed to cushion families from rapidly changing social and economic conditions (Giele, 1996). Thus, this camp advocates for broad-based policies in health, housing, and income security to create a strong government safety net that can buffer families from any negative repercussions of change. In the sanguine camp, policies tend to target individuals who, they contend, will in turn contribute to family well-being. In contrast, the concerned camp supports policies to strengthen families, which, they contend, will subsequently benefit individual well-being.

A key plank of the sanguine policy agenda is women's equality, as articulated by prominent spokesperson and former Congresswoman Pat Schroeder (1989): "If we get rid of the inequalities that hinder women, we strengthen the family at the same time. For me, building a family policy has meant finding a way to bridge the gap between public policy and the reality of women's lives" (p. 114). Critics say that equating the needs of women with the needs of families magically creates a coherent argument, but one that fails to acknowledge not only the relationships that define family life, but also the inherent conflicts that women and men face in balancing their rights as individuals with their responsibilities as family members (Blankenhorn, 1990).

THE IMPATIENT CAMP

According to the impatient camp, the tumultuous changes in family life in the last quarter-century have been insufficient in their magnitude and influence. This camp applauds the demise of the normative family and its replacement by alternative family forms, but laments that the changes have not gone far enough and that society has not come to grips with an increasingly diverse social order. For example, this camp is impatient with society's understanding of diversity in contemporary families, its valuing of this diversity, and the supports provided by social policy.

Because the concept of the family is so historically and culturally specific, this camp contends that no definition of the term *family* is possible (Stacey, 1993). They propose eliminating the concept altogether and replacing it with more generic terms such as *primary relationships* (Scanzoni; cited in Doherty, 1999), *enduring intimate relationships* (Cheal, 1991), or a *location* for resource production and redistribution (Hartman, 1981). The demise of the family should be hastened, according to Stacey (1993), because the family is not an institution, but rather an ideology with a history and a politics created by more privileged or powerful groups to advance their own interests (Cheal, 1991; Williams, Himmel, Sjoberg, & Torrez, 1995).

The family ideology implies the existence of a standard North American family: a heterosexually based, gender-normed, two-generational unit formed around a married couple (Doherty, 1999). Casting this family form as the standard infers its superiority and implies that any family that deviates from this standard is defective or dysfunctional (Williams et al., 1995). According to this view, the many children in this country growing up in other family forms may be harmed by the subtle and sometimes not-so-subtle messages that their family does not measure up.

The impatient camp points a finger at those who study, teach, or design policies for families. Much like fish trying to describe the sea in which they swim (Doherty, 1999), family experts are portrayed as participant observers who rarely call into question standard assumptions about the family (Cheal, 1991; Rapp, 1978). The impatient raise questions about how personal experience in the family and the dominant family ideology may blind researcher's understanding and bias their analysis, largely in unconscious ways (Doherty, 1999; Rapp, 1978; Smith, 1993). For example, in research designs, single-parent families, usually female-headed, are often contrasted with two-parent families who are treated as the normative standard of comparison. In practice, when a child in a nonnormative family experiences a problem in school, the problem can easily be blamed on a defective family rather than on other causes in the peer group, school, or community. The way U.S. Census data are collected may also reproduce this ideology by misrepresenting families that differ from the norm. For example, if more than one family shares a residence, only one person can be designated as the head of household. Extended family members such as an uncle or a grandmother who live in the household are designated by their relationship to the head of household in the only categories available in the census: that of spouse, child, parent, sibling, or boarder (Smith, 1993). Not until 2000 did the Census allow couples living together to identify themselves as unmarried partners (Cohn, 2001).

The Values of the Impatient Camp

The values that underlie this camp are relativism, pluralism, skepticism about progress, and a deemphasis of the individual. This camp is relativistic in the sense that they believe in no single truth, no ubiquitous moral code, no preferred family form, and no universal core to family life that can be defined as *the family* (Cheal, 1991; Giele, 1996). They would resist identifying any set of values that could be identified as core American values (Williams et al., 1995). Because truth and meaning are arbitrary, revealing themselves only in a local context (Cheal, 1991), this perspective prompts a continual questioning of assumptions and a constant searching for bias.

Fundamental to this perspective are pluralism and diversity, which they substantiate with examples of the functionality of diverse family forms. The fictive kin observed in ethnographic studies of African American families are a pragmatic mechanism for turning friends into family. Although there are no legal ties, those friends who provide care and support may be called *mommas* and *daddies.* In economically disadvantaged families, a woman who has children with several different fathers and is able to maintain relationships with these fathers expands the potential for economic support of her children (Rapp, 1978; Smith, 1993).

The impatient camp espouses a valuing of diversity, yet ironically are dogmatic in rejecting family forms based on marriage (Cheal, 1991).

> Certainly under present conditions of political, economic, social, and sexual inequality, truly egalitarian marriage is not possible for the majority. One can only conjecture whether a fully egalitarian marriage would be compatible with lifelong commitments to dyadic intimacy under utopian conditions of gender, sexual, racial, and economic justice. (Stacey, 1993, p. 547)

This camp believes that the standard North American family formed around a married couple works against gender equality by assigning women responsibility for children and casting them in a subservient role to men. This privatized model of family life keeps women in their place and portrays children as a personal responsibility rather than as a resource for the whole society (Havas, 1995).

In contrast to the sanguine camp, the impatient camp sees the demographic changes of the last quarter-century not as progress toward a state of equilibrium marked by improved well-being or increased social harmony (Doherty, 1999; Williams et al., 1995). Rather, the endpoint of change is a continual state of instability that will bring only dubious benefits, advantaging some and disadvantaging others.

The individual is less central to this camp than to the others because the individual's perceptions are shaped by experience, culture, and the dominant ideology. For example, the impatient frequently cite Jessie Bernard's (cited in Cheal, 1991) view that there are two marriages—his and hers. Because the perceptions of men and women are socially constructed, social science data based on these perceptions can be easily distorted (Cheal, 1991).

Evidence in Support of the Impatient Camp

Because of their beliefs that knowledge is relativistic and socially constructed, the impatient camp has less confidence in the objectivity of science than the other camps do. The questions that are asked, the responses
given, and the conclusions drawn are said to be jaded, sometimes unintentionally, by dominant ideologies. Because knowledge is believed to be fil-
tered through existing theoretical frameworks and cultural norms, the impatient rely more on multiple answers that emerge from case studies rather
than on single solutions reached by the consensus of quantitative data over
time. They value qualitative research and distrust sophisticated methods,
such as structural equation modeling, that control for error—an error they
contend is random and not quantifiable. They do not discount evidence
based on quantitative methods, but they also do not privilege the evidence
as more objective or scientific than other data sources (Doherty, 1999).

Support for the impatient view emanates from public opinion polls,
ethnographic studies, historical analyses, and empirical data. A 1995 Harris
poll of 1,502 women and 460 men indicated a widespread valuing of family
diversity among Americans. Only 2% of women and 1% of men defined family to mean the traditional nuclear family, and 9 out of 10 women said that
society should value all types of families (Giele, 1996). Moreover, a recent
Gallup poll concluded that about one third of Americans (37%) believe that
same-sex couples should be allowed to marry (Gallup Organization, 2005).

Writers from this camp often cite ethnographic studies like Stack's (1974)
research on family relationships in an African-American neighborhood. Some
of the relationships that Stack describes are difficult to define using the
terms of the dominant family ideology. Yet the pooling, borrowing, and exchange that occurs across households is functional in helping families deal
with crises and cope with the realities of their daily existence (Rapp, 1978;
Smith, 1993).

This camp also cites historical evidence, particularly the spotty record
in assimilating minority groups into mainstream society. As one example,
Williams and colleagues (1995) pointed out the hypocrisy of the U.S. Constitution with its high-sounding principles that all men are created equal at a
time when African Americans, who constituted one fifth of the population,
were bound in slavery.

In concert with the concerned camp, the impatient camp worries about
evidence of the grim prospects for children brought about by rapid
changes in family structure. In contrast to the concerned camp, however,
the impatient believe that children have been disadvantaged not by divorce, but by conflict-ridden marriage (Stacey, 1993). Few people question
that some families are undoubtedly so conflict-ridden and pathological that
they cannot adequately care for children. Yet critics of the impatient view

contend that the proportion of families that fall into this category may be small; with half of all children experiencing family instability, it is hard to believe that half of all parents have such conflictual relationships that they are unable to do a reasonably good job of raising their children (McLanahan & Sandefur, 1994).

The Policy Agenda of the Impatient Camp

The impatient camp argues for legal, economic, and social policy reforms, yet cautions that they should promote cultural diversity rather than cultural conformity. In the policy arena, the insidious family ideology becomes a set of blinders that obscure the family circumstances of the disadvantaged to the more privileged who are often the designers of policies and programs.

This camp claims that welfare policies are an example of attempts to recreate middle-class lifestyles and values among minorities and less privileged families who lack the resources to emulate the family patterns of the privileged (Rapp, 1978; Williams et al., 1995). To parallel the entry of middle-class mothers into the labor force, recent welfare policies have required welfare mothers to work. Yet in contrast to the employment experiences of the middle class, the jobs available to welfare mothers may not provide the salaries, training, benefits, and flexibility that allow successful integration of work and family responsibilities. Given their job prospects, some welfare mothers may be unsuccessful at moving into the workforce—a result that can lead to a trampling of the dignity of the poor (Williams et al., 1995) and also to public perceptions that the poor are undeserving, which can erode public support for welfare programs. Welfare policies may also fail, according to this perspective, because of opposition by members of the dominant group who resent bringing minorities and the disadvantaged into the mainstream (Williams et al., 1995).

To avert a system of cultural conformity that deepens class and racial divides, this perspective favors universal policies that provide benefits irrespective of work, class, marital status, family structure, or income (Williams et al., 1995). In the United States, universal programs have proved more effective than means-tested programs in maintaining widespread, ongoing political support, as evidenced by the success of programs like Social Security, Medicare, veterans' benefits, and universal public education (Skocpol, 1996; Wilson, 1997).

THE THEORY OF PARADOX

The tidal wave of change in contemporary families has generated controversial views about family policies that were unheard of in the 1950s (Cheal, 1991). If these views are as irreconcilable as they appear on the surface, this bodes poorly for the prospects of circumventing the controversy and developing policies that strengthen and support families across the life cycle. In the following pages, I propose a theoretical perspective that moves beyond the differences of these seemingly antithetical viewpoints by recognizing the validity and utility of each, thereby framing policy debate in a way that has the potential to foster compromise. In the words of Elshtain (1995), compromise is "not a mediocre way to do politics; it is . . . the only way to do politics" (p. 61).

This theory builds on Rappaport's (1981) compelling concept of true paradox—two ideas or principles that seem, at first blush, irreconcilable with each other but prove, on closer scrutiny, simultaneously valid (see Bogenschneider, 1997). Rappaport illustrated this notion with the contradiction between two widely held, but opposite, values in American politics: freedom and equality. Allowing total freedom might result in the powerful dominating the weak, thereby obliterating equality. Conversely, promoting total equality would impose more limits on some people than others, thereby constraining freedom. Thus, freedom and equality exemplify a true paradox because they are valid, yet opposing, schools of thought that are nevertheless intimately intertwined. Maximizing one of these poles necessarily limits the other. Because both poles need attention, we become one-sided when we focus on only one pole and ignore its equally compelling counterpart. In social and community life, such paradoxes are more the rule than the exception. An important role of professionals is first to discover true paradox and, if imbalance occurs, to push in the ignored direction (Rappaport, 1981).

In the worldviews of the concerned, sanguine, and impatient camps, several true paradoxes are apparent, such as a focus on children versus adults, the tension between individualism versus familism, the need for cultural versus institutional change, and whether government is the problem or the solution. To demonstrate its potential in avoiding these false debates, I apply the theory of paradox to the substance of family policy (e.g., welfare reform), a frame of reference in policymaking (e.g., a family perspective), and the locus of policy response (e.g., cultural vs. structural solutions).

Applying the Theory of Paradox to the Substance of Family Policy

The concerned and impatient camps focus on the needs of children for consistent and caring parents or parent-like figures, whereas the sanguine camp emphasizes the rights of adults to pursue personal happiness and fulfilling relationships. The tension between the competing interests of children and adults or the dependent and the caregiver are at the heart of many family policy issues, as eloquently exemplified by Corbett (1993) in his discussion of welfare reform.

Welfare reformers face the dilemma of balancing two important, yet contradictory, goals: reducing family dependency on welfare and reducing child poverty. Reaching either goal alone would be relatively simple, but attempting to simultaneously reach both goals has proven extraordinarily difficult. For example, Corbett (1993) claimed that dependency could easily be ended by eliminating welfare benefits, thereby providing the poor with no program on which to become dependent. Ending welfare programs, however, would increase the number of children living in poverty, thereby jeopardizing children's well-being. Alternatively, child poverty could be ended by increasing welfare benefits. Yet making welfare more generous would run the risk of increasing the number of welfare recipients and the prospect that they might become dependent on government assistance. Thus, the crux of welfare reform is to reduce welfare dependency by encouraging parental self-sufficiency, but to do so in a way that does not increase child poverty and harm child well-being, a policy dilemma that, in Rappaport's (1981) terms, is a true paradox.

True paradox can precipitate paralysis in policymaking. A true paradox is not always self-evident and can escape notice if advocates become mired in ideology, enticed by the persuasiveness of their political rhetoric, and entrenched in the self-righteous belief that their position alone represents what is true, right, and good. The impatient view calls into question a belief in the sanctimony of one's own position by revealing how understanding is historically and culturally situated (Gergen, 2001) and reinforced by the propensity of experts and the public alike to engage in *perceptual reductionism,* the tendency to perceive one segment of the population as representative of the whole (Corbett, 1993). For example, advocates concerned about welfare dependency fixate on adult welfare recipients, who, they contend, bear some responsibility for their family's economic situation and who, they believe, should assume some obligation for improving it. Advocates concerned about reducing child poverty, however, fixate on the children in welfare families, who are perceived as not being responsible for their plight and as having little control over it. The conceptual error of zeroing in on one image of the population and falsely assuming that it represents the whole distorts policy debate and lessens the likelihood of compromise and a comprehensive policy response.

Rappaport (1981) encouraged professionals, when faced with a true paradox, to examine whether one pole of the dialectic is being emphasized at the expense of the other. Professionals have done just that in the case of welfare reform by calling for evaluations that focus not only on the current preoccupation with reduced caseloads, but also on child outcomes such as the safety net's ability to lift children out of poverty. In the case of child care, the family's desire to have access to the child-care setting of their choice, which is often family-based care for infants and young children, conflicts with the state's right to expect quality care for the dollars invested, which is easier to monitor in center-based settings. In the case of mental health policy, the conflicting goals are stark when considering the issue of whether a mentally ill individual should be institutionalized. The individual's right to self-determination clashes with a family's responsibility to care for its members and society's obligation to protect the public. Pursuing one of these policy goals and neglecting the others may result in one-sided policies that, like a free-floating pendulum, can swing from one extreme to the other, as has occurred in movements toward and away from institutionalization, shifts in whether work is or is not required in welfare initiatives (Corbett, 1993), and the rise and fall of school busing (Rappaport, 1981).

One insight that the theory of paradox brings to policymaking is that two or more virtually opposite, yet valid, policy goals can be developed by reasonable, well-meaning people and can be pursued simultaneously. Professionals should welcome and embrace these contradictory solutions because more solutions typically mean better, not worse, policies (Rappaport, 1981). The best solutions may focus on reducing both welfare dependency and child poverty, may target both family- and center-based child care, and may provide dual options for institutionalizing some of the mentally ill and deinstitutionalizing others.

Applying the Theory to a Frame of Reference in Policymaking

As argued in this volume, a family perspective in policymaking and its orientation toward caring and commitment is valid and defensible. The theory of paradox, however, would raise the question of whether this familism is only one pole of a dialectic that has an equally compelling opposite pole. The obvious counterpoint is individualism (see Triandis et al., 1993). Focusing exclusively on familism can interfere with hard-fought individual rights, such as women's career opportunities, equal wages, and reproductive rights (Ooms, 1998). Yet unfettered individualism—as evidenced by excessive striving for occupational advancement, social status, material gains, or pleasure seeking—can interfere with the time, commitment, and self-sacrifice that solid marriages, effective parenting, and strong civil societies require (Hewlett & West, 1998). I argue that individualism is so pervasive in America that its one-sidedness justifies pushing in the ignored direction toward familism. Yet this shift does not rule out the reverse possibility that, at some future time, familism might become so rampant that a push toward more individual rights would be warranted as it is in China today (Responsive Communitarian Platform, 1992). Thus, the familism–individualism dichotomy is a true paradox that raises the ominous specter of pushing too far in either direction.

Many other aspects of a family perspective in policymaking (e.g., self-sacrifice vs. self-fulfillment, moral absolutism vs. moral relativism, family change viewed as progress or decline) can be based on divergent, yet morally defensible principles, views, or values (Rappaport, 1981). According to the theory of paradox, the optimum response may not be a pendulum swing to any extreme or a rigid either–or mentality (Gates, 2004), but an elegant integration that takes divergent perspectives into account or falls somewhere in between. Moving toward the middle ground does not result in mediocre policies, but in more realistic policies that mirror the inherent give and take of family life.

Applying the Theory to the Locus of Policy Response

A decision that often polarizes policy debate, albeit needlessly, is the source of policy responses, whether it be government, civil society, the market (Wolfe, 1989), or a cultural shift, as occurred with women's equality, civil rights, and environmentalism. One obvious fault line has been the preference among the sanguine and impatient camps for structural solutions that provide the conditions for change, and the preference of the concerned camp for cultural solutions that provide the motivation for change. For example, when considering the causes of poverty, the sanguine and impatient camps tend to attribute poverty to the conditions in which families live. In a nutshell, if society provided jobs that paid a living wage, a strong social safety net, and better living conditions, poverty and its associated ills would disappear. The concerned camp, however, cites cultural causes, contending that poverty arises because poor people have different attitudes and values than exist in mainstream society. According to this view, if the poor would just pull themselves up by their bootstraps, work hard, and believe in themselves, they could succeed.

Consistent with the theory of paradox, these two explanations are diametrically opposed to each other, and neither alone is adequate. Attitudes and values are not the sole cause of poverty, nor can social conditions fully explain everything. Moving too far in the direction of the attitudes and values perspective ends up with explanations for poverty that blame the victim. Yet relying totally on the social conditions perspective can result in government taking over responsibilities that families can better perform themselves, and overlooks the resilient individual who defies the odds and overcomes extremely debilitating circumstances. Paying attention to one pole of this dialectic and ignoring the other is clearly a one-sided approach that fails to capture the complex, multifaceted face of poverty.

In his study of poor African American men in the inner city, Wilson (1991) raised the prospect that these two explanations may be inextricably linked in a cyclic pattern that, reminiscent of the proverbial chicken and egg, has no clear cause and effect. For example, is it possible that social conditions such as racism and plummeting job prospects of poor, African American, inner-city men make it difficult if not impossible to secure employment? When these men do secure jobs, does the low pay and lack of benefits feed into negative attitudes about employment that, if expressed, increase discrimination by employers (Wilson, 1991)?

In policy circles, the extreme positions have tempered recently because both poles have gravitated toward the middle. For example, those people typically classified in the concerned camp have nevertheless recognized that this country should provide more "extensive governmental programs offering monetary support and social services for families" (Popenoe, 1990, p. 47), specifically "parental leaves for childbirth, job sharing, flexible work hours and benefits, and on-site or nearby childcare" (Blankenhorn, 1988a, p. 2). These structural supports respond to new family realities, but at the core is the concerned camp's principle of allowing parents more time with their children (Blankenhorn, 1988a). Those people typically allied with the sanguine perspective have noted that culture, although not an exclusive explanation, should not be dismissed as a contributor to problems of the poor (Cherlin, 1997; Wilson, 1991). For example, African American activist Jesse Jackson continues to advocate for structural solutions, but suggests that they be accompanied by a moral revolution as well. The power of the theory of paradox is evident in Jackson's admonition, which integrates the cultural and structural viewpoints: People are not responsible for being down, but they are responsible for lifting themselves up.

This blurring of the traditional fault lines between liberals and conservatives is epitomized in the recent proposal by Skocpol (1997) that family support for working parents would be the best focus for the Democratic Party even though it is "conservative in the best sense of the word" (p. 120). She proposed supporting the important work of families in raising the citizens and workers on whom the future of the nation depends. Her vision is conservative because she advocates for some policies to change the culture in which parents operate—taxes and benefits that encourage married parenthood and tough crime laws to make neighborhoods safe. However, her position is also progressive because she calls for policies that create the social conditions parents need, such as decent wages and benefits, job training, family leave, and child support. The irony, however, is that these liberal policies often flourish amid the family-friendly cultural climate that conservative policies typically foster.

Similarly, Marshall and Sawhill (2004) proposed a profamily agenda for the 21st century that moves beyond the polarized left–right debate by building on both the personal responsibility of parents and the collective responsibility of government, business, and civil society to support families who work hard and play by the rules. Their vision recognizes that "top-down bureaucracies cannot substitute for functioning families and neither voluntary or faith-based organizations can fully take government's place" (p. 222).

THE POTENTIAL OF THE THEORY OF PARADOX IN BRIDGING CONTROVERSY

What would a family and a family policy agenda framed by the theory of paradox look like? This theory has the potential to frame new conceptualizations of the family, shape the political agenda, and mobilize political action, each of which I discuss in the following sections.

The Potential for Conceptualizing the Family

The theory of paradox would not endorse the extreme position of romanticizing the family as a "haven in a heartless world" (Lasch, 1977) or the equally extreme position of demonizing families as an instrument of oppression, patriarchy, and abuse (Stacey, 1993). Families would not be viewed through the lens of simple nostalgia or gloom and doom, but rather as a source of some of life's most exhilarating joys, devastating sorrows, and much in between (Ooms, 1990).

According to this theory, not everyone would belong to the same kind of family. The resulting family policy agenda would not support the extreme conformity of the concerned camp or the excessive relativity of the impatient camp, but would absorb and integrate the best thinking of both views. In accord with the concerned, there would not be an undiscriminating acceptance of all family forms as functionally equivalent, and in accord with the impatient camp, there would not be an exclusionary rejection of family forms other than those based on marriage. Family forms would be assessed based on their capacity to foster the responsibility and commitment that appears to be the engine for producing competence and character in children and adults alike. Ideas would not be dismissed solely because they emerged from middle-class lives, nor would we "accept at face value the historic claims of the middle class to speak for everyone" (Featherstone, 1979, p. 43).

Family life, by its nature, would revolve around commitment. Marriage or partnerships would not be built on an unbending, steel-like commitment that traps people in stifling relationships nor on a commitment of such fragile metal that it fractures under mild stress. Commitments to children who depend on the care of adults, however, would resemble titanium steel that does not yield to stress, persists despite duress, and continues even when the relationship of the parents is broken. Marital commitments would not be broken casually and, when children are involved, would be acceptable to the community only after conscientious involvement in marriage or partner education, parent training, family therapy, or support groups (Doherty, 1992). Others have proposed that no-fault divorce should be available to some couples, but not to those with children (Galston, 1997).

The Potential to Shape the Political Agenda

Family policy activists should conduct a painstaking perusal of family issues in an attempt to discover true paradox. When it is found, it can be addressed in one of the following two ways: (a) pushing in the ignored direction, or (b) simultaneously pursuing two opposing, yet valid policy goals.

Pushing in the Ignored Direction. One compelling example of discovering true paradox and pushing in the ignored direction is the motivation for this volume. The detailed review in chapter 2 of whether policies are oriented more toward individuals or families concluded that individualism is so pervasive in this country that a push in the ignored direction—toward familism—is sorely needed. The ideal, however, is an elegant integration of these two perspectives that cannot be reached by a zealous commitment to either extreme.

Similarly, family policies that derive from the theory of paradox would not be based on the self-sacrifice advocated by extremists in the concerned camp or the self-fulfillment advanced by zealots in the sanguine camp. For example, in the debate over long-term care, policies would be established that assist families in providing care for the disabled or the elderly without requiring total self-sacrifice of other personal, family, or occupational pursuits. Yet policies would not allow a singular focus on self-fulfillment by absolving individuals of any responsibility to care for and assist family members who experience long-term difficulties in functioning.

Moving toward the middle ground is not mealy-mouthed politics that leads to mediocre policy, but is often the only way that policy gets done in the real world. The fertile middle ground is more apt to emerge out of policy debate framed by the theory of paradox, because the theory recognizes the validity and utility of opposing views. Adherents to the theory are expected to respect, not reject out of hand, views different from their own, because diametrically opposite views can be developed by reasonable, rational, well-meaning people.

Simultaneously Pursuing Two or More Virtually Opposite, Yet Valid Policy Goals. As discussed earlier in this chapter, Corbett (1993) claimed that the crux of welfare reform is the attempt to reach two valid, seemingly contradictory policy goals: reducing child poverty and reducing family dependency on welfare programs. Similarly, helping parents better balance conflicting commitments to work and family may require simultaneously pursuing structural and cultural policy responses. For example, structural supports such as parental leave or flex time could provide parents more opportunities to spend time with their children. In contrast, promoting a cultural shift that places a high priority on childrearing might provide parents with the motivation to spend time with their children. Ironically, these seemingly antithetical policy goals, which are often touted by opposing political camps, would each be more likely to be effective if implemented in concert with the other. For example, workplace benefits are more apt to materialize in a cultural climate that values parenting. Conversely, when the cultural climate values parenting, parents will be more likely to take advantage of benefits available at work.

Consistent with the theory of paradox, most social issues have more than one decent solution (Rappaport, 1981), and the most desirable response may have both structural and cultural elements. The bottom line is that we should embrace multiple solutions because the more policy solutions, the better the chances of achieving the comprehensive responses that complex problems often entail. Instead of arguing over contradictory solutions, we should pause to examine whether the controversy is masking a true paradox. If so, two seemingly antithetical solutions may both be valid, which could foster common ground rather than contentious gridlock.

The Potential to Mobilize Political Action

The biggest challenge this theory presents to family policy activists is not understanding its logic or rationale, but being able to operationalize its premises, which may be at odds with prior training and experience. Recognizing the validity of views different from their own is no small feat for professionals whose training, experience, and ideology suggest that there is a single view that should be advocated to all and a single approach that is true, correct, and right. For example, the concerned camp needs to dampen its discomfort with government policies, the sanguine camp has to temper its distaste of cultural solutions, and the impatient camp needs to forgo its passion for relativity enough to join with the concerned and the sanguine and, in so doing, muster the broad-based consensus required for political action. An equally difficult task is recognizing true paradox, which requires the perceptiveness to look beyond the obvious and the courage to go against the grain of popular thought. The advice offered by Rappaport

(1981) is that "those who are interested in social change must never allow themselves the privilege of being in the majority, else they run the risk of losing their grasp of the paradox. . . . When most people agree with you, worry" (p. 3).

Although its pursuit is not easy, the beauty of paradox is that once glimpsed, it "burns to be said" (Rappaport, 1981, p. 7). Discovering true paradox can create a sense of urgency that can breed public outrage and mobilize political action. It can help avert the pendulum swings from one extreme to the other that generate public cynicism about the capacity of policy to do the right thing to strengthen families. Perhaps most important, each camp can contribute to building the fertile middle ground from which compromise and consensus can spring forth. For example, we can look to the concerned camp to document social problems and to the sanguine and impatient camps for policy responses. Unless we are willing to admit that problems exist, policy responses will not follow (Gallagher, 1990). Yet even dire problems will not spawn political action unless policy solutions are forthcoming (Kingdon, 1995).

Even when there are feasible solutions to apparent problems, political action will not follow without citizens willing to step out of their comfort zone and into the political arena. According to communitarian Amitai Etzioni, you cannot wait for people to be perfect; you must be willing to work with whatever people are interested in the problem, even when they share only part of your agenda (Braiker, 2003). What's more, you must do so in the spirit of finding constructive solutions to the problem, rather than trying to one-up people and win an argument (Marsh, 2004). Family issues have a unique power to spawn strange bedfellows. A case in point is the coalescing of feminist organizations, minority groups, and child and family advocates to encourage fathers to shoulder the economic responsibilities of fathering (Ooms, 1990).

Is the Theory of Paradox Pollyannaish or Politically Feasible?

The theory of paradox is not a pie-in-the-sky proposal by ivory tower academicians, but a tool for overcoming polarization by seeking and straddling the center. Consistent with the observations of policy pundits, "the strongest gravitational force in Washington" is "the relentless pull toward the center" (Smith, 1991, p. 207). Disagreements have been greatly exaggerated, according to political observers. The fault citizens find with politics is not that it is too complex, but rather that it oversimplifies, polarizes, and fails to examine the vast gray areas between the extreme positions (Hahn, 1994).

A broad middle ground exists among the public that could push family policies forward (Ooms, 1995; Skocpol, 1997). The American public tends not to gravitate toward one extreme or the other and longs for less political posturing and more consensus building to create a bipartisan family agenda (Bayme, 1991; Yankelovich, 1989). In fact, Skocpol (1995) claimed that "the only progressive vision that has any chance of social effectiveness and political viability in the foreseeable future" (p. 312) is an effort aimed at family security that would support work and responsible parenting in single- and two-parent families. Blankenhorn (1988a) concurred that a national family agenda is "neither liberal nor conservative . . . the core issues facing the American family . . . will fit the strategic need of either party. Thus, it is twice blessed: good policy and good politics" (p. 2). To push forward a family agenda, the theory of paradox would warn against becoming too simplistic, self-righteous, or one-sided. "Finding the right balance . . . is what democratic discourse is all about" (McMurrer & Sawhill, 1998, p. 93).

The theory of paradox offers a creative vision for the design of family policies that circumvents the tired debates and paralyzing stalemates of the past. Yet Skocpol (1995) cautioned that program ideas are not transformed into legislation based on predictions of public support. For ideas to wind their way through the legislative process, pragmatic political strategies are needed. Because political strategizing for families is not a new idea, we can build on the track record of policies enacted throughout the 20th century that have successfully provided ongoing support to families. This is the topic of the next chapter.

10

What Can We Learn From the Roots of American Social Policy About Building Enduring Family Policies in the 21st Century?

Karen Bogenschneider
Tom Corbett

The essence of doing science is discovery. And that means more than un-covering new facts. The important thing may not be new facts. It may more likely be new ways of thinking about old facts.

—Priestley (1980)

Although it is not always recognized, public policy discourse in the United States has always had a family tilt: an underlying, often unexpressed premise that families are the basic building block in society, to be relied on, protected, and nurtured. The American colonies imported the Elizabethan Poor Laws as the framework for a system in which the extended family was the fundamental societal unit responsible for impoverished individuals. The local town became the responsible jurisdiction only if the family failed in its primary role. Even then, town leaders would try to find and often provide financial support to other families in the community willing to care for the indigent.

It is one thing to intuitively accept the importance of families to a strong and vital society. It is quite another, however, to consciously and systematically place families at the center of the policy process. To do so, we must shift the nature of discourse from appreciating families to prioritizing them as worthy of study, investment, and political action. Families need to be viewed as an area of study that deserves federal support and encouragement, a specific population to be assessed as an indicator of societal health, and an explicit object of and criterion for evaluating the impact of policies and programs.

The field of family policy is young in terms of both intellectual inquiry and policy formation centered on the family concept. According to Kamerman and Kahn (1978), the field of family policy was formally conceived in the 1970s, during the Senate's landmark hearings on American families. Acceptance of family policy as a field made little headway in the 1980s, in part because of divisive ideological debates that surfaced during the controversial 1980 White House Conference on Families. Despite these birth pains, family policy evolved into a legitimate field of empirical and theoretical inquiry during the 1990s (Bogenschneider, 2000, 2002; Ooms, 1995).

The 1990s began with the question of legitimacy: Are families a legitimate focus of policy attention and public investments, or are families a private matter? When the decade drew to a close, this question appeared to have been answered by the policy initiatives, political judgments, and priorities of the American people. Across the political spectrum, with important exceptions, a consensus emerged that government had a legitimate role in nurturing and protecting well-functioning families and that the private sector also had responsibilities.

During the last 15 years, federal policymakers enacted an impressive range of innovative policies regarding adoption, child abuse, child care, child support, domestic violence, education, family leave, family preservation, family poverty, same-sex marriage, and welfare reform (Bogenschneider, 2000, 2002). According to Knitzer and Page (1998), over two thirds (34) of the states funded programs for preschoolers, and about half funded programs for infants and toddlers (24) and parents (25). In addition, policies increasingly were examined in terms of their potential effects on family formation and stability—the marriage penalties built into certain tax policies (e.g., the Earned Income Tax Credit) being one example. In the first half of the 1990s, federal and state expenditures on child care tripled, direct cash benefits to families doubled, and family services saw a 50% increase (Kamerman & Kahn, 2001). These family policy initiatives and laws appeared to reflected the values and priorities of the American people as expressed in public opinion polls. When asked how much government could be doing to help them, 47% of parents said that government could do a great deal to help them, and another 37% said that government could do something to help them (Hewlett & West, 1998).

The 1990s also saw an impressive number of private philanthropic commitments, some influencing the choice of issues for government actions and others exploring whether government actions achieved their family-focused goals. For example, the Edna McConnell Clark Foundation's commitment to family preservation (e.g., cautioning against the too-easy removal of children from families in which abuse or neglect is suspected or substantiated) subsequently was reflected in many state and federal policies (T. Ooms, personal communication, October 16, 1999).

Although no single formal decision was made, it was apparent that families had emerged as a legitimate focus of government policy in the 1990s. The shift was remarkable. A generation before, President Richard Nixon had vetoed a federal child-care bill as an unwarranted governmental intrusion into a family concern. Child care now has become the largest single expenditure under the federal cash assistance program, TANF. Thirty years ago, the role of government in collecting child support was minimal; child support was deemed a private matter between the parties involved. Now both Democrats and Republicans readily agree to expansions of the public role in ensuring that child support is collected when children do not reside with both parents.

This question remains: Is the palpable shift toward a focus on the family permanent or merely a passing policy fad? Political observers claim that interest in family policy issues is now at its highest peak in 20 years (Hutchins, 1998; Ooms, 1990). Yet despite this popularity, the term *family policy* is still not widely used by policymakers, journalists, or the public. Moreover, few academics are actively engaged in the field in the sense that they explicitly structure their research agendas around family policy. In fact, a review of the history of family policy from the early 20th century to the present warns against undue optimism. Historically, interest in family policy has ebbed and flowed; periods of interest and investment in family matters have been followed by periods of benign neglect. Families have often drawn considerable political attention, but arguably they have failed to secure a sustained niche in American public policy.

In this chapter, we examine three major efforts over the past century to establish family policy in the public arena and ask whether the themes and cycles of the past will dictate the future. Can analysis and understanding of the roots of American social policy inform political debate and shape a more enduring set of family policies in the 21st century? Like Cairns, we believe that we are as much "determined by history as we are makers of it" (Cairns, 1983, p. 90). The past may not be prologue. We are not necessarily doomed to repeated, short-term waves of interest in family policy, particularly if we can carefully draw insights from the history of family policies that might help us shape the direction and dissemination of our research, the design of our policies, and the operation of our institutions.

The three examples that follow illustrate how family policies have waxed and waned over the century. Embedded in these scenarios are some of the origins of contemporary family policy: the activism of middle-class women between 1890 and 1920, the child- and family-saving movement from 1900 to 1930, and the Social Security Amendments of 1939. From these examples, we extract six themes that may be instructive in designing more enduring family policies in the future.

THE ORIGINS OF FAMILY POLICY
IN WOMEN'S ADVOCACY, 1890–1920

The rapid industrialization, massive immigration, and urbanization of America in the 1880s and 1890s were accompanied by social conditions such as unemployment, low wages, homelessness, and poverty. A relatively unregulated workplace led to high rates of injuries and death (Sklar, 1993). Unhealthy living conditions, particularly in urban settings, contributed to high mortality rates among infants and children (Lindenmeyer, 1997). In 1890, 9% of children lived with one parent, and most of these single parents were widowed mothers (Gordon, 1994). Single mothers who lost a breadwinning husband were typically thrust into dire economic need (Skocpol, 1997). In the first decade of the 1900s, when a living wage was $8 per week, single mothers could earn about $2 to $4 per week. To earn enough to afford food and housing, children without fathers were over six times more likely to be pressed into the workforce (33%) than children with fathers (6%). The impulse of early reformers was to separate highly vulnerable children from their impoverished families and place them in what they considered more suitable family situations or institutions. In fact, the primary reason for institutionalizing children, in one Massachusetts study, was the inability of mothers to support them. By the end of the 19th century, single mothers and their children were perceived to be a social problem of such magnitude that they needed public attention (Gordon, 1994).

To an extent unparalleled anywhere else in the world, government's response to the problems of working-class mothers and children was shaped by American women reformers, particularly middle-class women. The agenda of these women activists extended beyond motherhood to the workplace. Nowhere else in the world did protective labor legislation focus so directly on women, and nowhere else were women so involved in its enactment. The success of these women's groups in restructuring America's social and political priorities at the local, state, and federal levels can be attributed to their success in mobilizing grassroots, class-bridging coalitions that lobbied for benefits for working-class mothers and children, many of whom were unable to lobby on their own behalf (Sklar, 1993).

This track record may have been due, in part, to the unprecedented growth in female literacy in the United States compared to anywhere else in the world between 1790 and 1850 (Crittenden, 2001). By 1890, about 56,000 women were pursuing a college education and, in lieu of graduate school, many leaders of the social reform movement chose to live and work in settlement homes in working-class immigrant neighborhoods. These settings provided a venue for collecting data and experimenting with the design and implementation of welfare programs and policies (Koven & Michel, 1993; Sklar, 1993). This knowledge and skill was subsequently put to use in the nation's women's clubs (Sklar, 1993). In the last quarter of the 19th century, literally hundreds of local women's organizations formed national associations (Koven & Michel, 1993), including the Congress of Mothers, the Daughters of the American Revolution, the National American Woman Suffrage Association, the National Council of Catholic Women, the National Consumers' League, the National Council of Jewish Women, the National Women's Trade Union League, and the Young Women's Christian Association (Sklar, 1993).

The most important women's organization, the Woman's Christian Temperance Union (WCTU), was formed in 1875 as an umbrella organization with 39 departments, 25 of which did not deal with temperance. In Chicago, the WCTU maintained two nurseries, an industrial school, a mission, a medical dispensary, and a lodging house for men. In 1890, the General Federation of Women's Clubs pulled together a vast number of local networks that addressed a range of topics. For example, in 1893, the federation resolved that each club should appoint a standing committee to inquire into the labor conditions of women and children, and another committee to investigate state labor laws. By 1919, the General Federation of Women's Clubs represented an impressive grassroots network of 800,000 women (Sklar, 1993).

During the peak of American industrialization between 1900 and 1920, these middle-class women's organizations worked in collaboration with male professionals to pass an array of social policies to protect current and future mothers and their children that men had been unable to enact on their own: campaigns for compulsory education, protective labor legislation for women, and child labor (Sklar, 1993). Most of these campaigns were family policy in the truest sense because they focused, not only on the child or the woman, but also on the state's interest in preserving families (Gordon, 1994) and on the parents', usually the mother's, responsibility for the child. These associations were responsible for local initiatives such as establishing kindergarten, playgrounds, libraries, and maternal and child health programs, but also influenced legislation at the state and regional levels (Skocpol & Dickert, 2001). The most important of the issues they addressed were compulsory school attendance (passed by every state by 1918), mothers' pensions to support impoverished widows (enacted by 44 states), limits to the hours that women wage earners could work (46 states), and minimum wages for women workers (15 states). Curiously, during the same time period in which these laws were passed to protect women and mothers, proposed benefits and regulations for male workers often were defeated (Skocpol, 1995). Later, these policies for women workers were extended to wage-earning men and non-wage-earning women and children (Sklar, 1993).

These progressive-minded women activists challenged the rigid determinism of social Darwinism by working to change the social conditions in which families operated (Gordon, 1994). Experts contributed to these early reform campaigns with studies and reports that exposed social problems (Smith, 1991). For example, the Bureau of Labor Statistics published 19 volumes on their investigation of the predicaments faced by many women and child wage earners (Lindenmeyer, 1997). In addition, the writing of Samuel McCune Lindsay and G. Stanley Hall in the early 1900s helped establish childhood and adolescence as unique periods of development that deserved special attention.

Quite remarkably, this political activism at the turn of the century occurred at a time when a woman's sphere of influence was almost universally accepted as the home and a full two decades before women had the right to vote. The lexicon of these early reformers helped legitimize women's involvement in policymaking by domesticating politics. For example, in the words of Frances Willard, "[G]overnment was only housekeeping on the broadest scale" (cited in Stage, 1997, p. 28), and according to Ellen Swallow Richards, women could move into the larger world and "clean it up, as if it were no more than a dirty house" (cited in Stage, 1997, p. 30). Historians have noted, however, that this movement was not entirely altruistic in that it created new jobs and positions of power for women and tended to advance White, middle-class notions of women and childrearing. It operated primarily in the North and mostly separately from the activism of Black women (Sklar, 1993).

The commitment of these women's organizations to grassroots organization and social reform waned in the 1920s. Professions like home economics and social work lost their spirit of systemic social change and focused more on skill building, individual pathologies, and therapeutic treatment modalities. This narrowing of professional mission reflected larger societal trends: a shift toward greater individualism following World War I; the Hoover era's emphasis on individuals, standards, and profitability; a backlash against women's reform efforts outside the home; the end of the Progressive Era; and the rise of Frederick Taylor's scientific management theories (Stage, 1997).

THE ORIGINS OF FAMILY POLICY
AS "CHILD AND FAMILY SAVING," 1900–1930

Children slowly became more prominent as a distinct population of social policy interest over the last half of the 19th century. Theodore Roosevelt, U.S. president from 1901 to 1909, pored over turn-of-the-century census data, which he thought signaled family decline. Between 1890 and 1910, the number of Americans who divorced tripled. Between 1880 and 1920, the U.S. birth rate fell by over 30%. Because immigration rates were high, this led to concerns, particularly in some geographic regions, over the decline in the proportion of native stock. In 1918, the infant mortality rate was double that of western Europe, 80% of pregnant mothers did not receive prenatal care, and 23,000 mothers died in childbirth (Carlson, 2002a). Given these trends, Trattner (1999) noted that a focus on children and family once again became paramount to many social reformers of the time:

> The fate of the world is determined by the influences which prevail with the child from birth to 7 years of age. . . . All the problems go back to the child—corrupt politics, dishonesty and greed in commerce, war, anarchism, drunkenness, incompetence. (p. 109)

The establishment of the Children's Bureau is often regarded as the first political victory in a series of family- and child-saving policies. In the words of Florence Kelley, feminist social reformer and a founder of Hull House in 1903, "If the government can have a department to take such an interest in the cotton crop, why can't it have a bureau to look after the nation's child crop?" (Carlson, 2002a, p. 15). The U.S. Children's Bureau was established 9 years later with support from a number of women's associations. Julia Lathrop, its first director, was also the first woman to head a federal agency, albeit one with a small budget of $25,640 and a staff of only 15. To advance the bureau's agenda, Lathrop mobilized thousands of volunteers in settlement houses and women's clubs (Carlson, 2002a).

Building on the Progressive Era's faith in research and education, the Children's Bureau organized a grassroots movement to save babies through better mothering and family life (Ladd-Taylor, 1993). The Children's Bureau published books, organized 50,000 girls in 44 cities into Little Mother Leagues, elevated Mother's Day to a national holiday, and spearheaded a National Baby Week. In 1917, with war looming on the horizon, Lathrop helped develop an innovative compensation plan designed to maintain decent living standards for families. Half of the wages of soldiers and sailors were paid directly to their wives and children, and a family allowance was provided on a sliding scale of up to $50 per month for families with 4 or more children. Death and disability benefits were also provided for widows and children (Carlson, 2002b). Perhaps the greatest accomplishment of the Children's Bureau, however, was the passage of the 1921 Sheppard-Towner Act.

The American Medical Association fiercely opposed the bill as "German paternalism" and "sob stuff." However, women's organizations . . . actively sought its passage, forming "one of the strongest lobbies that has ever been seen in Washington." When a powerful Congressman blocked the measure in a House Committee, Florence Kelley appeared before its members and compared Congress to King Herod and the slaughter of the innocents, asking, "Why does Congress wish women and children to die?" (cited in Carlson, 2002a, p. 17).

The Democratic, Socialist, Prohibition, and Farmer-Labor parties endorsed the act, as did Republican presidential candidate Warren Harding. The Sheppard-Towner Act won an easy victory, in part, because Congress was nervous about facing newly enfranchised women voters for the first time (Ladd-Taylor, 1993).

Eventually 45 of 48 states participated in the program (Carlson, 2002a). During its 7 years of operation, the bureau distributed 22 million pieces of literature, held 183,000 health conferences, established 3,000 prenatal centers, and visited 3 million homes. By 1929, the Bureau estimated that its childrearing information had benefited half of U.S. babies. Moreover, the Children's Bureau was the federal leader in statistics, providing most Depression-era poverty data and serving as a primary consultant for the establishment of the Bureau of Labor Standards. Job applicants to the Children's Bureau had to be able to design a study of a major social problem and create a table from raw statistical data (Gordon, 1992).

Yet even though the Sheppard-Towner program remained broadly popular with American women and retained most of its political support from women's groups, it was vigorously opposed by the male physicians and bureaucrats who had come to dominate children's health policy (Ladd-Taylor, 1993). Congress never made the program permanent, and it was unable to secure access to stable funding, as Social Security had done via the trust fund. The program was eliminated through legislative maneuvers in 1929.

THE ORIGINS OF FAMILY POLICY IN THE SOCIAL SECURITY AMENDMENTS OF 1939

Franklin D. Roosevelt assumed the presidency in the midst of an economic depression that followed closely on the heels of the stock market crash of 1929. In March 1933, one third of the U.S. labor force was out of work. Between 1928 and 1932, when Hoover was president, rates of birth and marriage each declined about 20%. These work and family trends led to starkly different interpretations by the two prominent ideologies of the time: the Hoover technocrats and the American Maternalists of the 1920s.

In 1930, Hoover appointed a number of distinguished social scientists, referred to as Hoover technocrats, to the President's Research Committee on Social Trends. According to their report, released in 1933, falling birth rates were evidence of the failing of the family, particularly the housewife, who arguably could contribute more by entering the labor force. The report claimed that most family functions—care of the elderly, child care, cooking, education, health care, laundering, religious acts, and sewing—could be better and more efficiently carried out by experts in corporate, state, or charitable bodies that were organized according to industry guidelines. As summarized by Carlson (2002b):

The frail nature of the family meant that "schools, nurseries or other agencies" would need to enroll a "larger proportion of the very young children in the future" so as "to conserve childhood in the midst of rapidly shifting conditions of family life." Only "society" has the new expertise needed to grapple with "developing the personality of its children." . . . Concern should no longer focus on family strength. . . . Instead, attention should be on "the individualization of the members of the family." (p. 4)

These views, which were endorsed by business leaders, were perceived as an attack on family life by the Maternalists, a motherhood movement with roots dating back to the settlement house movement. Maternalists believed that the ideal family—the breadwinning father, mother at home, and their children—was being threatened by industrialization. The cornerstone of the Maternalists' policy agenda was a family wage: a living wage for the father so that the mother could stay home to raise the children (Carlson, 2002b). This Maternalist defense of the value of women's traditional labor against the forces of industrialization undergirded the New Deal domestic policies of the Roosevelt administration and continues to shape the American welfare state to this day.

The New Deal has been criticized by feminists as creating female dependency through patriarchal policies, a debate that extends beyond the purposes of this chapter. The New Deal did come to reflect the Maternalist perspective on social policy—a perspective consistent with views of the family that were widely accepted at the time. When asked in a 1936 Gallup poll if wives should work when their husbands had jobs, a resounding 82% said no, leading George Gallup to contend that this issue was one that voters were "about as solidly united as on any subject imaginable—including sin and hay fever" (cited in Carlson, 2002b, p. 6). Even unmarried women reformers of the day, Gordon (1992) noted, "did not . . . contradict the prevailing premises that children and women needed breadwinner husbands, that children needed full-time mothers, that women should choose between family and career" (p. 34).

We consider here how these Maternalist views of the family shaped only one New Deal policy, the Social Security Act of 1935, which is considered the foundation of U.S. public social programs to this day and the origin of one of the country's most effective antipoverty policies. In the original act, Old Age pensions were funded by contributions to individual accounts. With overwhelming political support, the Social Security Act was amended in 1939 to add survivor and dependent benefits.

Old Age pensions were thus transformed from a program for an individual worker to a social insurance program for the entire family unit. Widowed mothers received 75% of the pension their husbands would have received, as long as they did not remarry or earn more than $15 per month. Surviving children received half of the benefit their fathers would have received. An aged woman who had been married for at least 5 years and was not divorced was eligible for 50% of the pension her husband would have received, whether or not she herself had a work history. Thus, the 1939 Social Security Amendments established the American welfare system on the family wage, marriage, and a nonemployed mother at home. Those who deviated from these family norms through divorce, deliberate childlessness, illegitimacy, or maternal employment incurred financial penalties (see Carlson, 2002b).

The New Deal is one example of how an individualistic society appears to justify social programs by explicitly acknowledging recipients' service to the nation; for example, rewarding mothers for bearing and rearing children. The legislation was based on the premise that mothers deserved to be honorably supported if a breadwinning husband was not available (Skocpol, 1995). In the words of Molly Dewson, who served on the Social Security Board:

> [When] you begin to help the family to attain some security you are at the same time beginning to erect a National structure for the same purpose. Through the well being of the family, we create the well being of The Nation. Through our constructive contributions to the one, we help the other to flourish. (cited in Carlson, 2002b, p. 10)

Experts played a new, more active role in the design of the New Deal. Roosevelt attracted hordes of intellectuals to Washington by establishing various advisory and planning agencies, including his legendary Brain Trust. He also reorganized the Executive Office in the late 1930s in ways that ensured that his successors would have access to intellectual resources. By 1938, when most of the New Deal programs were in place, more than 7,800 social scientists were working in the federal government.

IMPLICATIONS FOR BUILDING ENDURING FAMILY POLICIES

Over time, demographics (concerns about family decline), economics (the Great Depression), intellectual fads (social Darwinism), and advocacy (particularly by women's organizations) played key roles in how social policy and family issues were framed and deliberated. National policy in the United States has always been cyclical in character. For example, it has cycled between individual and structural explanations for social problems, whether policy should be protective of rather than mainstream women and children, and whether government policies should be proactive or remedies of last resort. Political pushes to strengthen families and use them as instruments of social change have often been followed by periods of neglect when the family was viewed as the exclusive province of the principals themselves. Consequently, it proved challenging to sustain the promise of an activist family policy perspective over the course of the 20th century.

Some challenges to a sustained family policy perspective may well persist. Yet we think that family professionals must deconstruct the repeated rise and fall of family policies over the past century to identify circumstances that hold the promise of bringing family policy into the mainstream of social policy debate so that it has a status commensurate with that of economic policy or poverty policy. Indeed, the similarities between the development of poverty policy and family policy as legitimate fields of study are illuminating.

As a distinct area of inquiry, poverty research and analysis is typically dated back to the early 1960s, when a definition of poverty was developed at the Social Security Administration and public policy was directed to this societal challenge by President Johnson's declaration of the War on Poverty. By the late 1960s, one litmus test for policy proposals was "What does it do for the poor?" Although concern for the poor can be traced back to the emergence of civilization itself, and although poverty research, as we now know it, was being practiced as early as the late 19th century, the pace and sophistication of research did not pick up until a distinct field of inquiry developed. Today, our understanding of poverty is immeasurably more advanced and nuanced than it was 40 years ago.

Family policy is in much the same condition that poverty policy was in the 1960s. There is a good deal of it going on, but ways of distilling and translating the work to shape and inform policy have yet to be fully exploited. We still need a generally accepted definition of the concept. We need a policy arena that continues to accept families as a legitimate subject of public discourse. This will require more than wishful thinking and good intentions. We need to reflect on the history of family policy and learn from the past how to fashion a better future. In this final section, we offer six precepts on which family professionals can build so that family policy may be more firmly established as a field and an enduring set of family policies can be constructed for this century.

Family Policies Move Forward When Legitimated by Relevant Research and Theory

One impetus for the development and enactment of family policy in the past was clear data that family structure was changing in deleterious ways, some evidence that family integrity was being compromised, and a theoretical rationale for understanding the consequences of these changes for society. For example, family policies were enacted early in the 20th century when Progressive reformers were able to document trends that high numbers of women were dying in childbirth, infant mortality rates far exceeded those of other industrialized nations, and incidences of child labor were escalating. Child labor reformers were able to justify their advocacy, in part, by drawing on theories that conceptualized childhood and adolescence as distinct periods of development that warranted special protections. New Deal legislation emerged when one third of Americans were unemployed, with obvious repercussions for family stability and well-being. Advocates framed their support of this legislation on Maternalist thinking that provided a conceptual link between the well-being of the family and the well-being of the nation.

What this means for today's family professional is that good data can help policymakers determine whether social action is needed, either by identifying problems or by refuting contentions that problems exist (see Bogenschneider & Gross, 2004). Moynihan's (1941) claim, stated more than 60 years ago, that data may be more important for family policy than for other aspects of social policy still holds true: "Family matters, in other words, are not a subject for which there is a well-established alarm system that alerts the larger society to dangers as they arise. Something truly alarming has to happen" (pp. xii–xiii).

Moynihan's words capture an important, often misunderstood, element of policymaking: Data are more apt to evoke public interest and a political response when they point out potential risks or a pending crisis. Rightly or wrongly, policymakers tend to deal with outliers, such as child-abusing parents, crime-committing youth, or students that need special education. Data are more apt to be policy relevant when they spotlight risks to the individual and, perhaps more important, the prevalence of these risks in the population (Scott, Mason, & Chapman, 1999). For example, the increased risk of mental retardation is similar for individuals born premature or postmature (88% and 81%, respectively). Yet premature births have a greater impact on society than postmature births because they are five times more common. If problems are known to pose substantial risk to a significant segment of the population, research findings can elicit public outrage and catapult issues onto the political agenda.

For family policy purposes, however, our thinking needs to move beyond examination of the risks to and outcomes for the individual, a focus that is so pervasive in our culture and in our theory and research methods that it almost goes unnoticed. For example, theory has the potential to impede the progress of family policy, as exemplified by the individualistic, industry-driven recommendations of Hoover's panel of social science technocrats and the efficiency-based tenets of Taylor's scientific management theory. Perhaps there is no better recent illustration of this individualistic bias in science than the effort in the 1990s to develop social indicators of societal well-being. Several federal executive agencies, with substantial input from the academic community, supported a concerted effort to identify key indicators by which to assess how well we were doing as a society and to help guide and shape future policy development and social investments.

Looking back, it is curious that there was so little debate about the underlying basis for organizing the social indicator initiative. By default, the organizing principle ended up being children, not the families in which the children resided. Arguably, the major intellectual work to come out of this effort was titled *Indicators of Children's Well-Being,* even though many of the indicators discussed were based on the family concept (Hauser et al., 1997). Moreover, a 1997 Executive Order established the Federal Interagency Forum on Child and Family Statistics to publish a set of national statistics from 18 federal agencies on the health of families. The resulting annual publication conspicuously left the word *family* out of the title: *Trends in the Well-Being of America's Children and Youth* (Westat, 2000).

This omission may be attributable, in part, to the individualistic focus of data collection. Employment statistics make no distinction between an unemployed father of nine, a teenager looking for a part-time job, and a senior citizen supplementing pension and Social Security incomes (Moynihan, 1986). When researchers document the increasing number of Americans working long hours, are they careful to point out whether these long hours occur in families raising children and whether one or both parents are working overtime? Only when data analysts, program designers, and evaluators deliberately examine the family's role in social problems will results emerge like those in recent interventions to prevent youth crime and substance use—that interventions are cost effective only when they emphasize training of parents and avoid bringing together high-risk youth, no matter how skillfully (Dishion et al., 1999). Collecting family data, developing family theory, and designing family programs is no simple task. As Ooms notes in her foreword to this volume, "Families are not easy units of analysis; they are complex, dynamic, messy, ever-changing systems. A family orientation requires us to think about individuals and families in a comprehensive way and to design holistic responses for meeting their needs."

The Family Perspective Is Influential When Relevant Research and Theory Are Communicated to Policymakers

Theodore Roosevelt, who has been called the first American president to philosophically describe the importance of family life to the nation, was influenced to a large extent by census data that, he believed, spelled out a crisis in family life (Carlson, 2001). The 1912 Children's Bureau was a pioneer in collecting quantitative data about the need for and effectiveness of its programs and in translating the numbers for public consumption. Florence

Kelley articulated the meaning of the data by using analogies that contrasted policymakers' interest in the nation's cotton crop versus its child crop, and compared Congress to King Herod and the slaughter of the innocents. Moreover, a number of family policies were triggered, in part, by the Bureau of Labor Statistics' turn-of-the-century studies portraying the predicaments faced by women and child wage earners.

Extrapolating from the past, social scientists can no longer trust that research and theory will somehow find their way into the policymaking process (Rist, 1994). We need to devote as much energy and as many resources to developing practices and procedures for disseminating rigorous analysis into the policymaking process as we have devoted to generating high-quality research and publishing it in the leading journals. A three-pronged approach is needed: (a) directing more attention to the science of translation and to ways in which information can be packaged to meet policymakers' unique information needs; (b) encouraging a family impact perspective in policymaking, whereby policymakers consider the effects of policies on families as well as the potential benefit of taking the role of families into account; and (c) taking systematic steps inside the academy to encourage and reward efforts to connect research to policymaking outside the academy.

We are familiar with two promising models: the Family Impact Seminars and the Welfare Peer Assistance Network (WELPAN). The Family Impact Seminars are a series of seminars, briefing reports, newsletters, and discussion sessions that provide state policymakers with nonpartisan, solution-oriented information on current issues that affect families, like child support, health care, juvenile crime, and welfare reform (see chap. 14). Policymakers report that the seminars have increased their knowledge of research on family issues in ways that are useful in decision making and have shaped the development and enactment of public policies. We have further been able to substantiate that, because of the legislators' participation in the seminars, they are more apt to see the practical value of research and to consider how pending legislation affects families.

WELPAN regularly brings together state-level welfare officials for discussion about common problems and solutions, and for exchange of views with researchers and policymakers (see Corbett et al., 1998). From this dialogue have emerged some common solutions to shared problems as well as new insights that might not have been apparent without the dialogue. For example, in several reports, WELPAN members have identified and supported a shift in the direction of welfare policies toward family promotion and stability purposes (WELPAN, 2002c). WELPAN has also invested considerable time thinking through how to deliver coherent and comprehensive services for disadvantaged families by blending discrete, categorical programs in innovative ways (WELPAN 2002a, 2002b).

Family Policies Move Forward When Policymakers and the Public Support Structural Rather Than Individual Explanations for Social Problems

Throughout the nation's history, we have wavered between structural and individual explanations for social problems. The examples in this chapter suggest that family policies were more likely to have been enacted when more comprehensive structural explanations for social problems were in vogue. For example, it was hard to blame the high rates of infant mortality on individuals when they affected the rich and poor alike. The death of male breadwinners was difficult to attribute to individual choice and behavior. When one third of the nation's workers were unemployed, it was hard to imagine that so many were unwilling or unable to work.

Whether political candidates use individual or structural explanations does not always depend on their political party or the constituency they represent (Ross & Staines, 1972). For example, the Sheppard-Towner Act was passed when Republican Warren Harding was elected president, and the New Deal was enacted when Democrat Franklin Roosevelt assumed the presidency. Structural explanations for social problems seemed more apt to emerge during political campaigns and at the time of a change in administration. Challengers for political office tend to have a vested interest in structural or systemic explanations of social problems that point out the inadequacies of the current officeholders. In contrast, it is typically more politically expedient for incumbents to defend the system by arguing that their administration has contributed to a good quality of life with few problems. Any problems that are difficult to deny are attributed not to the administration, but rather to the actions of certain individuals or groups. The aftermath of Hurricane Katrina provides a contemporary example: the Republican administration criticized the poor for not heeding warnings to move out of harm's way, and the Democrats criticized the administration's Federal Emergency Management Agency for failing to respond as quickly and appropriately as the gravity of the situation warranted.

Beyond political considerations, research can often bring about change by determining whether social problems are driven more by structural or individual factors. For example, at the turn of the century, data collected in the settlement houses demonstrated the feasibility of government intervention on behalf of families. Public opinion polls in the 1930s demonstrated widespread support for the family focus of the New Deal legislation. Historically, debates about particular public policies have been linked, not only to public perceptions about what government should do, but also to beliefs about how effective government intervention can be (Skocpol, 1995). Thus, research is relevant to family policy when it identifies the success of prior programs or policies that address family factors, the receptivity of the public or affected organizations to family-oriented political responses (Rist, 1994), and the probable consequences of familistic versus individualistic policy interventions (see Dishion et al., 1999).

Family Policy Moves Forward When There Is a Broad Interdisciplinary Focus on Families

Between 1900 and 1920, female middle-class activists adopted a comprehensive agenda that included compulsory education, child labor, and protective labor legislation for women. The Sheppard-Towner Law of 1921 encompassed activities ranging from parent education and home visits to prenatal centers and health conferences. By including the terms *survivor* and *dependent,* the 1939 Social Security Amendments explicitly transformed the American welfare state from a system that focused narrowly on the individual to one that incorporated the individual's most important context, the family.

By its very nature, a family focus leads policymakers toward an integrative perspective. How do diverse policies and systems interact with complex family dynamics to affect families? One recent example is the refocusing of welfare policy on behavior and community rather than on merely handing out checks. This has prompted many policy analysts to think more broadly rather than merely zeroing in on specific problems and service strategies; we now think about how families function overall rather than focusing on specific issues such as lack of child care or Food Stamps. What does it take to change fundamental behaviors such as work, fertility, parenting, or family formation? Focusing on the family with its complex set of individual needs and relationships pushes thinking outside the box where the interactions among issues and systems become more apparent. A family focus demands a sophisticated, cross-disciplinary approach to policy challenges.

Think for a moment about how we typically organize our policy and analytic spheres. The policy world is structured into what we might call program and system arenas. Narrowly targeted programs have separate funding streams and program requirements. Legislative committees are organized and segregated around relatively narrow jurisdictions, and most executive departments are equally specialized. Similarly, the academic world is divided into disciplines and subdisciplines; synthesis and interdisciplinary work remain the exception. The field of evaluation is expert driven and dominated by experimental methods, which are most powerful for examining narrowly defined programs and policies. In a time of shrinking portfolios, the philanthropic community is targeting its resources to increasingly narrow and specific priorities.

If family policy is to become more than kissing babies (Jacobs & Davies, 1994), we must restructure how we organize our policy and intellectual worlds—break down program arenas, reorganize legislatures and executive agency expertise, transform academic reward systems, make some fundamental changes in how we evaluate policies, and encourage funding priorities to move toward a more holistic emphasis on the family system. A real focus on family policy also demands rethinking how we train professionals and how our institutions do business. Ooms, in her foreword to this volume, aptly asked:

> Why are there only a handful of family policy courses taught in family life departments and social work schools, and even fewer in public policy schools? When increasing numbers of policy researchers in the major think tanks are working on specific family issues, why are there no units within these institutions established to encourage and pursue family policy as an organizing theme? Why are there still no groups within government agencies dedicated to examining the impact of their policies on families?

Family Policy Moves Forward When There Are Formal Structures in Place

The Children's Bureau and Roosevelt's Brain Trust are prime examples of formal policy structures. Over 50 years ago, the Council of Economic Advisers and the Joint Economic Committee were established to help the nation set and reach its economic goals. No such entity exists with sole responsibility for families. This is unfortunate given that leaders today, according to Smith (1991), are far more dependent on their immediate counselors and bureaucratic experts. Such a council could give the family visibility, access to the key levers of power, a forum around which to bring together diverse and separate public entities working on relevant family issues, a locus for integrating policy- and family-relevant research, and a central agenda-setting body for developing a plan of action and assigning responsibility. Would a Council on Families have any real power and influence, or would it be a small cog in a big bureaucracy? A Council on Families could wield power, according to Moynihan (1986), who argued that the 1946 Employment Act, which established the Council of Economic Advisers, might have been more important than any jobs bill:

> The mere declaration of policy was an event; it marked acceptance of a social responsibility. . . . The point was not what answers were provided, but what questions were posed. . . . It would be enough for a national family policy to declare that the American government would be formulated and administered with this object in mind; and finally that the President, or some person designated by him, would report to the Congress on the condition of the American family in all its many facets. (pp. 10–11)

Family Policy Moves Forward When There Is Broad-Based Citizen Activism

In the early years of the Progressive Era, "social policy—formerly the province of women's voluntary work—became public policy" (Barker, cited in Stage, 1997, p. 18). Women's advocacy for labor legislation between 1890 and 1920 helped establish the constitutionality of government interventions on behalf of working families (Sklar, 1993). Julia Lathrop's success in the political arena can be attributed to the endorsements that she solicited from liberal and conservative organizations like the General Federation of Women's Clubs and the National Congress of Mothers, which later became the Parent Teacher Association (PTA; Skocpol, 1995, 1997). According to Skocpol (1995), successful U.S. social programs tend to emerge from partnerships between government and voluntary organizations, typically those organized at the local, state, and national levels. Considerable leverage can be exerted by organizations that can coordinate concerted political pressure across legislative districts.

In the United States, most organizations that include families in their advocacy promote an agenda with a particular political cast. Is it Pollyannaish to think that liberal and conservative advocacy groups would ever join forces for the ultimate good of the whole family unit? Could advocates from any political persuasion rally around a first step, encouraging policymakers to routinely ask, "How would this policy or program affect families?" Family issues, because of their fundamental importance to a wide range of constituencies, have a unique capacity to generate unexpected alliances in ways that mirror the inherent give and take of family life (Bogenschneider, 2002).

CONCLUSION

Families have always played an important role in public policy deliberations in the United States, but one that has not always been explicit and fully acknowledged. Family-centered policymaking has enjoyed periods of robust support followed by years of benign neglect. The reasons for our ambivalence toward families in public policy probably can be inferred. Children are politically safe; they do not bear responsibility for their circumstances, at least during their early years. In contrast, the adult members of families are held responsible and sometimes judged harshly. This line of reasoning tends to draw our attention to selected individual targets, leading to fractured and disconnected policies that fail to appreciate the all-important interactions among family members. This individualistic focus has also undercut political support for family policies because of voters' apprehension that programs for children are merely disguised welfare programs (Skocpol, 1995).

If we want the current period of interest in the family and its primary role in ensuring social well-being to endure, we should look to earlier periods in which activist social policies drew on the family as both a focus of attention and a source of inspiration. The vacillation between family policy feast and famine of the past may not be prologue if we draw on these lessons from earlier periods of the nation's history as guidelines for the future. Professionals can build more enduring family policies in the 21st century by conducting research and developing theories that are more policy- and family-relevant, and communicating these to policymakers in ways that will entice them to be more research- and theory-sensitive. Professionals can conduct studies, design theories, and develop programs that deliberately include structural and family factors and encourage political participation, especially when such factors are in vogue. Family professionals can encourage a broad, interdisciplinary focus on families through top-down approaches like developing formal structures to elevate the status of families in policymaking and by bottom-up approaches that encourage broad-based citizen support and activism.

It takes only a moment's reflection to realize that policymakers do not have a choice about whether to affect family life; they already do through their action and also their inaction. This chapter identifies several steps that professionals can take to elicit policy decisions that are more informed, deliberate, and self-conscious about their impact on families. We believe that the potential exists to build a set of family policies in the 21st century that are more explicit, expected, and enduring.

Chapter 10 is adapted from Bogenschneider, K., & Corbett, T. (2004). Building enduring policies in the 21st century: The past as prologue. In M. Coleman & L. H. Ganong (Eds.), *Handbook of family diversity: Considering the past, contemplating the future* (pp. 451–468). Copyright 2004 by Sage Publications, Thousand Oaks, CA. Adapted by permission.

11

What Can We Learn From the Past About Methods for Moving Family Policy Forward in the Future?

Families mattered in the past, they continue to matter in the present, and they will matter still, in the uncertain years of our future.
—Cowan, Field, Hansen, Skolnick, and Swanson (1992, p. 481)

Two recent historical analyses offer two methods for moving the field of family policy forward. Paralleling the explicit and implicit definitions of family policy posited in chapter 3, Skocpol (1995) proposed a specific, broad-based family policy that would promote family security, whereas Ooms (1995) recommended a series of efforts aimed at promoting a family perspective in policymaking across a broad range of issues. In keeping with the spirit of the theory of paradox, these two alternative methods of promoting a family agenda should not be viewed as contradictory, but should be embraced as complementary approaches that can be pursued concurrently to reach the shared goal of strengthening families. I begin this chapter with Skocpol's proposal for a specific family policy and then turn to Ooms's recommendations for a family perspective in policymaking.

PROMOTING A SPECIFIC FAMILY POLICY

Skocpol (1995) claimed that "the only progressive vision that has any chance of social effectiveness and political viability in the foreseeable future" (p. 312) is an effort aimed at family security that would support work and responsible parenting in single- and two-parent families. Skocpol believes that this family security proposal is politically feasible not only be-cause it embodies both conservative and liberal elements, as I described in chapter 9, but also because it is consistent with the characteristics of other broad-based U.S. social programs. In her historical analysis, Skocpol dispelled the stereotype of the United States as a policy laggard by point-ing to several examples of U.S. social policies that successfully provided security and support to a broad range of citizens. First, I briefly describe these policies and identify their common characteristics. I then use these commonalities as touchstones to assess the feasibility of enacting other family policies.

Successful U.S. Social Programs

The United States provided the world's first system of universal public edu-cation, which was considered the most inclusive in the industrialized world (Skocpol, 1995). Following the Civil War, the United States became a "de facto world leader" (Skocpol, 1996) in providing veterans with generous dis-ability and old age pensions, which by 1910 were reaching more than a third of all elderly men in the North and many widows and orphans. In the early 20th century, a number of benefits were provided to mothers and children. For example, 48 states limited work hours for women, 44 states authorized benefits for impoverished widowed mothers, and the 1921 Sheppard-Towner Act provided maternal health education through the Children's Bu-reau. During its 7 years of operation, 22 million pieces of literature were dis-tributed, 183,000 health conferences were held, 3,000 prenatal centers were established, and 3 million homes were visited. By 1929, the bureau esti-mated that its childrearing information had benefited half of U.S. babies.

The 1935 Social Security Act and its Medicare expansion in 1965 provided the framework for the country's most effective antipoverty program. The 1944 GI Bill and its successor provided millions of veterans with free medi-cal care; generous disability pensions; and grants or loans for homes, busi-nesses, and farms. Half of the 16 million veterans who served in World War II also qualified for loans to support education and training.

Common Characteristics of Successful Social Programs

Skocpol (1995, 1996, 1997) identified four common characteristics of these successful American social programs. First, the programs were viewed as a reward for service to the nation or as a way to prepare citizens for public service. For example, public schools were widely perceived as a means to prepare youth for service and for citizenship in a democracy. The Civil War pensions and the GI Bill benefits were popular because they were viewed as unequivocally honorable, being earned by recipients for their service during a time of war. With little stigma attached, Civil War pensions eventually reached 90% of surviving veterans. The mothers' and children's programs were seen as a reward for the service that mothers provided to the country in bearing and rearing children at a time when it was not unusual for women to die in childbirth. Social Security and Medicare were thought to be earned through contributions that recipients made during a lifetime of work. Thus, this individualistic society appears to justify social programs as a reward for service or an investment in expected service.

Second, all these successful programs provided benefits to a cross-class constituency through the same policy rubric. Universal public education, Social Security, Medicare, veterans' benefits, and the mothers' and children's programs all delivered slightly more services to the economically disadvantaged, but also provided a range of services to beneficiaries irrespective of income. The Sheppard-Towner Act, designed by Julia Lathrop, chief of the Children's Bureau, was aimed at both the poor and middle class for fear that a program targeted only to the poor would eventually suffer from scarce resources.

Third, these successful programs emanated from a relationship between the government and voluntary organizations. These voluntary organizations often evolved from broad social movements and were typically organized at the local, state, and national levels, much like our triage levels of government. For veterans' benefits, the Grand Army of the Republic supported Civil War benefits, and the conservative American Legion pressured Congress to enact the GI Bill. The General Federation of Women's Clubs and the National Congress of Mothers, which later became the PTA, promoted the passage of women's and children's programs and helped administer these programs through their local network of clubs. Their state and national conventions brought women together to set a common agenda that served as the basis for pressuring politicians to enact programs. This activism by women is quite remarkable given that it occurred even before women had the right to vote. Social Security flourished, in part, through the Townsend Movement, with more recent support stemming from the American Association for Retired Persons (AARP), which, unlike the other voluntary organizations, does not have an organized local and state presence.

Fourth, these successful programs were able to tap into resources in a secure way. Schools convinced local and state governments to support them. Social Security taxed workers and developed its own trust fund. Veterans' benefits were the beneficiary of wars, which not only are typically big revenue raisers, but also are seldom followed by declining rates of taxation. In contrast, the mothers' and children's programs were unable to secure stable funding and have continued to be poorly funded.

Using These Commonalities as Touchstones for Enacting Other Family Policies

The four common characteristics identified by Skocpol (1995, 1996, 1997) can be used as touchstones to assess the feasibility of enacting other broad-based family policies.

1. For a family policy agenda to be successful, it would first need to articulate the valuable service that families provide to society, such as raising children, caring for the elderly and disabled, and instilling competence and character in family members. In our aging society, the value of children and their caregivers may increase because the number of workers for each retiree is expected to decrease from 3.7 in 1970 to an estimated 2 in 2030 (Moen, 1996).

2. Family policies would have the greatest chances for success if built on the principle that Skocpol (1995) called "targeting within universalism" (p. 253)—the practice of making room for the less privileged in universal programs that benefit all. The most widespread and long-term programs have provided benefits to the advantaged and disadvantaged through the same policy mechanism.

3. Family policies are more apt to flourish if promoted through a voluntary association, preferably one with a local, state, and national presence. Obvious candidates are the PTA, with a membership of about 6 million in 23,000 local units, and the General Federation of Women's Clubs, with a U.S. membership of about 146,272. Or perhaps a new grassroots movement will spring up with the passion and conviction of Mothers Against Drunk Driving, the Sierra Club, or Common Cause (Browning & Rodriguez, 2002).

4. Finally, Skocpol (1995) predicted that, to ensure the secure resources that underlie successful social policies, Americans would be willing to pay more taxes for programs addressing widely felt needs that benefit not only the disadvantaged, but also their own families and friends.

PROMOTING A FAMILY PERSPECTIVE IN POLICYMAKING

In contrast to a broad-based social program, Ooms (1995) proposed a focused effort to promote a family perspective in policymaking on a broad range of issues and at several levels and stages of the policy process. Policymakers' interest in families is at an all-time high, yet what remains elusive is how policymakers can best act on this interest. What is needed is better packaged information and more tools to help policymakers design, analyze, and implement policies that strengthen families. The single strategy that has sparked the most interest among policymakers and scholars alike is family impact statements.

What Is the History of Family Impact Statements?

In her historical overview, Ooms (1995) dated this interest back to the landmark 1973 hearings on the state of American families chaired by Senator Walter Mondale of the U.S. Senate Subcommittee on Children and Youth. Testimony by distinguished scholars such as Urie Bronfenbrenner, Margaret Mead, and Edward Zigler called for family impact statements that, like environmental impact statements, would routinely assess the impact of government policies and programs on family well-being. Members of the subcommittee believed that the idea held promise, but concluded that it should be researched more thoroughly before developing legislation requiring its adoption.

In response, the Family Impact Seminar (FIS) was formed in 1976 to explore "the substantive, political, and administrative feasibility" of requiring family impact statements (Ooms, 1995, p. 2). The first FIS director, A. Sidney Johnson, and its prominent 24-member board spent the next few years talking to many people experienced with the government machinery for conducting environmental impact statements. They developed a framework and methodology for conducting family impact statements and piloted it in three in-depth national studies and 12 community-level field projects.

This study and pilot testing were summarized in a pamphlet that was subsequently mailed to all the delegates of the 1980 White House Conference on Families. The pamphlet concluded that "our experiences convince us that the process of family impact analysis is increasingly effective in revealing how public policies affect families and in recommending ways they can be improved" (Ooms, 1995, p. 2). Because the environmental impact statement mechanism was seen as highly regulatory and intrusive, FIS did not recommend requiring family impact statements on all government actions, believing that it should first be piloted on a voluntary basis in the private sector. Instead, FIS proposed establishing independent, nonpartisan commissions for families at the local, state, and national levels and that one of their functions should be preparing family impact statements on a limited number of existing policies. In addition, they urged advocacy, consumer, and service organizations to conduct family impact analyses of programs and services, including self-assessments.

Delegates to the White House Conference on Families enthusiastically endorsed this family impact proposal as one of their top six recommendations, with 80% of the delegates giving it their highest recommendation. Despite this enthusiasm from the family constituency, however, the proposal proved to be premature. During the 1980s, the idea of family impact statements was occasionally proposed in Washington in various forms, but was never enacted. At the federal level, President Reagan issued an executive order in 1987 that required agencies to review any proposed new policies for their potential impact on families, but the order was never seriously implemented (Ooms, 1995). In 1997, President Clinton signed an executive order requiring family impact statements only on policies affecting families, which ironically superseded the broader executive order that President Reagan issued earlier (Elrod & Spector, 1998).

What Is the Current State of Family Impact Statements?

Calls for family impact statements continue to come forth in every decade in this country and abroad. For example, Australia introduced the family impact statement as early as the 1980s, and is committed to reintroducing family impact statements a quarter-century later. According to the Minister for Family and Community Services, the impetus for this interest in family impact is recent strong economic performance and a budget surplus, which means the government can return a social dividend to families in terms of better quality health care, education, and family assistance. As these new proposals are developed, the family impact statements will require ministers to acknowledge and take into account their impact on families (Patterson, 2005).

In 2000, Family Support America produced a position paper on what America needs for strong families and communities. Consensus was achieved in a 3-day meeting attended by 101 experienced parent leaders, family support practitioners, and government officials representing the country's geographic, political, cultural, and racial diversity. Because of their shared belief that families are the nation's greatest asset, they called for legislation that required all federal laws and policies to be formally reviewed and assessed to determine the intended and unintended effects on families. These assessments would be made available for public commentary prior to the passage of a federal law or policy (Family Support America, 2000). Family policy professor Steven Wisensale also recently recommended that Congress adopt family impact statements, but with a new target—corporate America. Wisensale (2005a) recommended legislation that would require that corporate family impact statements be filed by any company that shuts down, files for bankruptcy, downsizes, or declares its pension plan underfunded.

Some states require family impact statements. For example, in 1998, Nebraska passed a law that requires the state to declare a family policy to "guide the actions of state government in dealing with the problems and crises involving children and families" (Neb Stat. Section 43-532). In addition,

Nebraska statutes identify the guiding principles for family policy (Neb Stat. Section 43-533) and require an annual statement of efforts to carry out this policy and these principles by any department, agency, institution, committee, and commission of state government (Neb Stat. Section 43-534). According to a 2005 analysis by Erin Pettegrew of the Ohio Legislative Service Commission (E. Pettegrew, personal communication, April 2005), Louisiana requires state agencies to submit a family impact statement prior to adopting or implementing rules (La. Rev. Stat., Section 49.972). Utah state law requires the Department of Human Services Board of Child and Family Services to produce a family impact statement that "determines the impact of a rule or policy on families. Those assessments shall determine the impact of the rule or policy on the authority of parents to oversee the care, supervision, upbringing, and education of children in the parents' custody" (Utah Code, 62A-4a-119).

In January 2000, Governor Owens of Colorado issued Executive Order D 001 00, which requires state agencies to "consider families as a factor in their decision making." The order explicitly states that "[t]his policy does not require or encourage any subdivision of state government to promulgate rules or regulations or to generate bureaucracy in any form." State agencies are required to include the following criteria in their decision making:

1. Does this action by government strengthen or erode the stability of the family and the marriage commitment, in particular?
2. Does this action strengthen or erode the authority and rights of parents in the education, nurture, and supervision of their children?
3. Does this action increase or decrease family earnings? Do the proposed benefits of this action justify the impact on the family budget?
4. Can this activity be carried out at a lower level of government, by civic and faith-based organizations or the family itself?
5. What message, intended or otherwise, does this program send to the public concerning the status of the family?
6. What message, implicit or explicit, does this action send concerning the behavior and personal responsibility of youth and the norms of our society?

Ooms (1995) reported that Illinois required that the state social services plan include family impact statements. The states of New York and Washington created guiding principles for family policy. The governors' offices in New York enacted some family impact requirements, although in a cursory fashion. Ooms reported that she has not had the resources to follow up on these leads, but her impression is that most of these proposals were not enacted or, if enacted, not seriously implemented.

This failure to establish a mechanism for systematically preparing family impact statements can be attributed to a number of political, philosophical, and procedural factors (Ooms, 1984, 1990). Politically, the election of Ronald Reagan stalled Jimmy Carter's promise to start a profamily policy agenda. Moreover, the 1980 White House Conference on Families proved to be so politically contentious that it moved family policy off the federal agenda for almost a decade. Philosophically, progress on any family issue was stymied because of the long-standing tradition of individualism in America, fear over government intrusion into the privacy of family life, and hesitation about establishing a large, cumbersome bureaucracy. Procedurally, the idea of family impact statements was constrained by inadequate training among policy staff conducting the analysis, a shortage of family data to aid in the assessment of impact, and the complexity of developing statements that accurately reflect the diversity of families in the United States.

What Tools and Strategies Are Available to Promote a Family Perspective in Policymaking?

According to Ooms (1995), the second director of the Family Impact Seminar (FIS), the idea of family impact statements is too limited a concept. What is needed is a broader family impact framework that includes a range of tools and educational strategies to help policymakers analyze the consequences of any program or policy for its impact on family well-being. This broader vision of promoting a family perspective in policymaking was initiated and has been kept alive by the FIS. The family impact framework and its accompanying principles and checklist have become a way of thinking for FIS, and this broader view permeates everything the organization does.

FIS began as a program of the George Washington University and later moved to the Institute for Education Leadership of the National Center for Family Studies at Catholic University of America and then to the Research and Education Foundation of the American Association of Marriage and Family Therapy. In 1991, FIS became an independent, nonprofit 501C organization. In 1999, its mission was transferred to the University of Wisconsin–Madison under my leadership (see chap. 12) and is now known as the Policy Institute for Family Impact Seminars.

Throughout its 30-year history, FIS has published family impact analyses of proposed legislation, laws, and policy implementation and has collaborated with community organizations to conduct family impact assessments of local programs and policies. FIS conducted 40 seminars for federal policymakers and round-table meetings for federal officials to help them implement family-centered legislation up until 1999, at which time the focus shifted to state policymaking. Through early 2006, the 21 sites affiliated with the Policy Institute have conducted more than 125 family impact seminars in their state capitals (see description of the Policy Institute for Family Impact Seminars in chap. 12). The organization has also developed and assembled a number of diagnostic tools for assessing the family sensitivity of schools, communities, adolescent treatment programs, family services, and early care and education programs and policies (see Snyder & Ooms, 1999, and http://familyimpactseminars.org/impact.htm).

One tool that has been widely used is the Family Impact Checklist, which includes six basic principles and 34 questions that serve as criteria for assessing any policy or program for its impact on family well-being. A Family Criteria Task Force, comprised of politically diverse members from the Consortium of Family Organizations (COFO), met for more than a year to draw up these principles and questions (Ooms & Preister, 1988). The checklist, which has proven useful to people from across the political spectrum, was updated in 2000 by the Policy Institute for Family Impact Seminars and reprinted by the National Council on Family Relations (2000). The latest version of the checklist is available in Appendix A and at http://www .familyimpactseminars.org/ipfcheck.pdf.

The Family Impact Checklist is based on the six following principles that can be used as criteria for assessing policies as they are being developed, enacted, and implemented: (a) policies and programs should aim to support and supplement family functioning and provide substitute services only as a last resort; (b) policies and programs should encourage and reinforce marital, parental, and family commitment and stability especially when children are involved; (c) policies and programs must recognize the interdependence of family relationships, the strength and persistence of family ties and obligations, and the wealth of resources that families can mobilize to help their members; (d) policies and programs must encourage individuals and their close family members to collaborate as partners with program professionals in delivery of services to an individual; (e) policies and programs must acknowledge and value the diversity of family life and not discriminate against or penalize families solely for reasons of structure, roles, cultural values, or life stage; and (f) families in greatest economic and social need, as well as those determined to be most vulnerable to breakdown, should be included in government policies and programs.

To illustrate their usefulness, selected findings from recent family impact analyses indicate the insights they can bring to policy debate. For example, the principle of family commitment and stability includes this question: How does the policy or program strengthen or weaken parental and marital commitment? A family impact analysis that applied this question to the mental health benefits of health insurance policies in one eastern state revealed that individual therapy was covered, but marital or family therapy was not. Another family impact question assesses whether the policy or program provides incentives or disincentives to marry, separate, or divorce. In a recent analysis, it was found that consumer health savings accounts might be more attractive to individuals than families, especially if some family members are significantly less healthy than others. With these health plans, single people have a $1,000 minimum deductible, but no one receiving family coverage can have a separate deductible lower than the minimum family deductible of $2,000. This means that the deductible for the unhealthier partner would be twice as large if he or she were married than single (Fronstin, 2005).

Family impact analyses were also designed to delve both broadly and deeply into whether or not families should be involved in solutions. For example, in a cost–benefit analysis of 42 crime prevention and rehabilitation programs, those for juvenile offenders provided a better return for taxpayers' dollars; in fact, three of the four most cost-effective programs were family based (Aos, 2003).

How Can Professionals Conduct a Family Impact Analysis?

Family impact analysis critically examines the past, present, or probable future effects of a policy, program, or service on family stability, family relationships, and family members' ability to carry out their responsibilities (Ooms & Preister, 1988). Nye and McDonald (1979) conceptualized family impact analysis as a research enterprise. Ooms (1995) agreed that the process may entail an in-depth empirical study or even a computer simulation. Yet family impact analyses may also serve as a conceptual framework for research or practice or, in the absence of research evidence, as a process for informally estimating the likely consequences of a particular program or policy on family well-being.

Family impact questions have proven useful across political party lines for: (a) reviewing rules, legislation, or laws to point out how legislation does or does not address families' needs; (b) helping prepare questions or testimony for hearings, board meetings, or public forums; and (c) evaluating programs, services, and operating procedures of agencies or organizations to identify ways in which they are strong in their support of families, and what gaps exist in the services they provide (Ooms & Preister, 1988). Family impact analysis checklists provide specific criteria that can help in assessing how policies, programs, and organizations can better promote family stability and commitment. Whereas family impact analysis can be used for any of the three purposes just listed, the procedures for conducting these assessments vary according to their intended audiences and formats (see procedures for conducting a family impact analysis in Appendix B).

Family Impact Analysis of a Policy or Proposed Legislation. To conduct a family impact analysis of a policy or proposed legislation, professionals use the Checklist for Assessing the Impact of Policies on Families. Not all questions on these checklists will be relevant for all topics. Thus, the task for those interested in assessing family impact is to evaluate which questions and principles are most applicable to the issue at hand. A family impact analysis typically does not reach a recommendation either in favor of or opposed to the legislation, nor dictate particular policy responses; instead, it typically raises several considerations of the ways the program supports and fails to support families. The weighing of these often-conflicting considerations is left to the discretion of the policymakers elected to make these decisions.

For example, as we prepared a recent Family Impact Seminar on Medicaid in Wisconsin, we asked whether the eligibility criteria for some of the Medicaid programs provided an incentive to marry or not to marry. The experts that we approached were quick to acknowledge that questions regarding family impact were important, but seldom asked and not easily answered. Eligibility for SeniorCare (Wisconsin's prescription drug program) is based on the federal poverty guidelines, which are based on family size. For an elderly couple, it would probably be easier to meet the income guidelines if they live together rather than marry. For BadgerCare (Wisconsin's SCHIP program that covers low-income children and parents), if a mother and father live with their child, they are eligible for health care benefits whether or not they are married. If a parent and a partner (not the other parent) live with the child, the partner does not receive coverage unless they marry. However, if they marry, it is possible that the joint income of the couple could disqualify them from BadgerCare by raising the family's income above the cutoff (Normandin & Bogenschneider, 2005).

Using Family Impact Analysis for Developing Testimony and Preparing Questions for Hearings. Family impact analysis can also be useful in preparing questions or testimony for hearings, board meetings, or public forums. Asking about family impact when policies are being developed, implemented, or evaluated can bring a unique perspective to policy debates or program goals by underscoring the importance of families as institutions that foster commitment to others. For example, in a hearing on the issue of foster care policy, family impact analysis would suggest the importance of raising questions about whether or not the policy offers incentives—either explicit or implicit—for others to take over family functioning when doing so may not be necessary. Additionally, the family impact checklist would prompt questions about how to involve informal social support networks, such as community, neighborhood or faith-based organizations in families' lives. Reviewing the family impact questions can help family professionals uncover how policy goals work with or against family well-being and identify questions that may be germane to encouraging a family impact perspective on the issue.

How to Conduct Family Impact Analysis of an Organization or Program. The purpose of family impact analysis for organizations or programs is to identify ways in which the services and operating procedures of agencies or organizations are and are not supportive of families. For this purpose, professionals can use the general Family Impact Checklist or any of the specific checklists for assessing the family friendliness of a school, community, adolescent treatment center, or state's child and family services plan. Family impact analysis of a program or organization is most successful when it is conducted by those involved. These stakeholders not only have a vested interest in seeing the program maximize its potential, but they also possess intimate knowledge of the program that outside evaluators may not have access to. An organizational analysis can best be conducted with a broad group of stakeholders strategically selected to represent the diversity of the organization. For example, when we conduct a family impact analysis of a middle school using the Family/School Partnership Checklist, county extension educators bring together 25 to 30 parents, teachers, youth, school administrators, parent–teacher organization representatives, and community leaders to complete the checklist (see the summary of how to conduct a family impact analysis in Appendix B). In one Wisconsin middle school, the family–school partnership assessment revealed that parents were not as involved in volunteering in the school as they might be; in response, the school board decided to hire a parent volunteer coordinator. A year later, 1,503 volunteer hours were recorded at the school—almost five times more than the previous year.

What Strategies Are Needed Beyond Family Impact Analysis?

As these examples show, the family impact analysis approach primarily builds a "policy watchdog vs. policy development capacity" (Pittman, Irby, & Ferber, 2000, p. 5). This may be actually what is needed to strengthen the policy muscle of family professionals, and to provide the spark for developing a broader, more coordinated vision of a family perspective in policymaking. To fully achieve the family impact vision, however, a cadre of family professionals is needed who are committed to serving families in a number of capacities, including (a) reframing policy issues into research questions; (b) conducting policy-sensitive, family-relevant research; (c) collecting and monitoring family trends and their implications for policy; (d) assessing the impact of actual and proposed policies on families; (e) gathering evidence on the effectiveness of family-focused policies and programs;

(f) promoting the development and enactment of policies that are attuned to family well-being; (g) developing innovative methods of connecting family research and policymaking; (h) designing equally innovative methods of evaluating the effectiveness of dissemination efforts that are not expected to have large, immediate, or singular impacts; (i) fostering the effective implementation of family-focused policies; and (j) collaborating with like-minded individuals and organizations to reach these goals.

As Steiner pointed out as long ago as 1980, family policy has no bureau or cabinet in the executive branch. Thus, in the highest echelons of government, there is no internal leadership on family policy, nor continuing attention to ensuring that the family perspective is forwarded and defended in political decisions (Steiner, 1980). The leadership for these functions could be provided by a cabinet-level Council of Family Advisers similar to the Council of Economic Advisers, a recommendation from the COFO that seems as relevant today as in 1988 when it was first proposed. The momentum for mobilizing and maintaining access to the levers of power at the highest levels of government may need to come from family professionals along with the families they represent.

SUMMARY

Too often in our zeal to be progressive, we plunge forward without taking the time to review what efforts have gone before and to build on what the pioneers in the field have learned. These complementary historical analyses of the work of Skocpol and Ooms offer pragmatic guidance for mustering the political support to move a family policy agenda forward. In keeping with the theory of paradox, these two methods and alternative sets of criteria should not be held at arm's length as competing approaches, but should be embraced as complementary tools for assessing family impact. Both share a common goal of strengthening and supporting families, although one set of criteria assesses the prospects that family policies will be enacted and the other assesses the family sensitivity of any legislative proposal, policy, program, or implementation procedure.

Both these methods provide a vision for family policymaking. However, this vision can materialize only if family professionals consider policy roles, approaches, and strategies to help us reach the prize—policies that strengthen and support families across the life span.

PART IV

STRATEGIES FOR GETTING INVOLVED IN FAMILY POLICYMAKING

12

What Roles Can Family Professionals Play to Build Family Policy?

Knowing is not enough, we must apply. Willing is not enough, we must do.
—Johann Wolfgang von Goethe

For professionals willing to get involved, what does it mean to do family policy? What roles can professionals play in building family policy? There are many. Some roles entail direct contact with policymakers, and others are far removed from the policymaking process. Some involve generating the research and ideas that can influence policymaking, and others involve disseminating this research and ideas to policymakers. Some professionals engage citizens in family policymaking, and others educate the next generation of family policy professionals.

In this chapter, I expand on previous scholarly work to develop a theoretical framework for conceptualizing roles that professionals can play in building family policy (Bogenschneider, 1995; Boyer, 1990; Nye & McDonald, 1979). Each of these roles is illustrated with two or more case studies that attempt to capture the excitement of getting involved in the policy arena as well as some of the challenges it entails. The content of this chapter is especially pertinent for the enthusiastic scholar, practitioner, or student of family studies who, curiously, is sometimes a reluctant student of and participant in efforts to build family policy. Would-be policy participants are too often unfamiliar with the myriad of policy roles that exist, unacquainted with career options in the policy field, and unaware of the vast potential that family policy holds for strengthening and supporting families across the life span.

This chapter describes nine roles that professionals can play in the policy arena:

1. Research for family policy formulation.
2. Family policy implementation.
3. Family policy evaluation.
4. Family research integration.
5. Family research dissemination.
6. Family impact analysis.
7. Teaching family policy.
8. Citizen engagement in family policymaking.
9. University involvement in family policy scholarship.

The focus of this chapter is not on doing good (Boyer, 1990), voluntary community service performed in off-hours (Boyte, 2000), or engaging in public debate on one's own behalf (Kingston & Levine, 2004). Instead, this chapter conceptualizes policy roles as part and parcel of the work of professionals, particularly those who feel that the family profession calls them to contribute to the public good.

These roles are not as easily separable as this chapter implies, and I am certain that there are other excellent examples. My intention in this chapter is to illustrate that building family policy is not just one function, but many interrelated functions that occur in both academic and applied settings.

RESEARCH FOR FAMILY POLICY FORMULATION

Researchers can help build family policy by conducting studies that help policymakers determine whether social action is needed, either by identifying social problems, refuting contentions that a problem exists (Nye & McDonald, 1979), or serving as an early warning signal that sounds an alarm when potentially troubling trends arise (Moore, Brown, & Scarupa, 2003). In the realm of family policy, research can examine whether families are fully achieving their functions of family creation, economic support, childrearing, and caregiving (Ooms & Preister, 1988).

If families are not fulfilling one of their functions, such as economic support of their members, research can guide family policy by providing causal knowledge on factors that contribute to family poverty. For example, the contributing factors could include access to education and training, individual values and attitudes, parenting practices, social isolation, as well as the economy, job market, and welfare system. Research can identify which of these factors are amenable to policy interventions (Weiss, 1986), the success of prior programs or policies that address one or more of these factors, the receptivity of the public or affected organizations to various policy responses (Rist, 1994), progress in meeting accountability-based standards in a specified time period (Moore et al., 2003), and the probable consequences of different policy alternatives.

Continuing with my example of family poverty, some of the viable alternatives are child-care subsidies, health insurance, home visiting, school vouchers, tax credits for low-income families, and tax subsidies for employers. Of particular utility to policymakers as they weigh various alternatives are cost–benefit analyses that help quantify the economic trade-offs of competing approaches (Rist, 1994). For social problems that fall outside the realm of family policy, research can often shed light on the value of a family perspective in policymaking by specifying whether families contribute to social problems, how they are affected by them, and whether policies would be more effective if they involved families or family considerations in the solution.

Perhaps one of the best ways to summarize the value of research in policymaking is by heeding the adage "What gets measured, gets done" (Moore et al., 2003, p. 5). Several streams of basic and applied research have been useful to policymakers, and I have included three examples here. First, I cite some recent examples of how basic research has been used in policy debate. Second, I describe the experience of a group of researchers in Florida who, in working on a specific policymaker's question, learned that epidemiological research methods can provide data in a form more pertinent to policymakers. Third, I describe an applied program of research that has been developed specifically to advance the perspective of children and families into policymaking.

Case Study: Using Basic Research
in Family Policy Debate

Some policy observers contend that research has influenced family policy more extensively than is commonly believed. Politicians such as Senator John D. Rockefeller IV credit the base of knowledge developed and synthesized by the National Commission on Children with providing the momentum for policies such as the 1993 expansion of the Earned Income Tax Credit (EITC) program, the 1996 strengthening of child support enforcement, and the 1997 partially refundable child tax credit (Rockefeller, 1998). Also, the 1994 Early Head Start (EHS) Program for children ages 1 to 3 was launched, in part, by the accumulation of decades of research on the importance of the early years (Zigler, 1998). Research was cited in the debate of family issues such as employment programs (Haskins, 1991), family leave (Trzcinski, 1995b), youth violence prevention (Zuckerman, 1999), TV and Internet violence regulation (Wilcox &

Kunkel, 1996), marriage (McLanahan et al., 2005; Ooms, 2002), and welfare reform (Haskins, 1991).

Court decisions about whether gay and lesbian couples should have the right to adopt children have been informed by recent studies of the well-being of children raised by same-sex couples (Patterson, 2000). Research on custody decisions influenced court decisions to make joint custody the preferred custodial arrangement (Mason et al., 2001).

Ongoing basic research is essential because progress in social science research can take years to achieve, whereas progress in policy development can occur within weeks (Gallagher, 1990). When an issue comes to the attention of policymakers, there is seldom time to commission and complete a study. Instead, policymakers draw on research that has already been completed, which for years may have been viewed as less essential, but can quickly and unexpectedly become highly relevant as illustrated by the recent interest in anthrax after it was mailed to several public officials (Sherrod, 1998).

Case Study: Using Epidemiological Methods to Understand the Benefits of Early Intervention for High-Risk Infants

Some interesting insights into how research data could be analyzed in ways that are more useful to policymakers emerged from the experience of a group of researchers at the University of Miami in Florida who were approached by government officials with a specific policy question (Scott et al., 1999). These policymakers wanted to know the potential benefits of an early intervention program for low-birthweight infants who were at high risk for mental retardation. Based on 1994 figures, the annual cost for programs for mentally retarded youth in Florida was approximately $8,580 per child compared with $3,411 for a nonspecial needs child. The 42,000 children in Florida eligible for these programs were costing the state an additional $200 million annually. The policymakers were faced with the question of whether to fund an intervention that could prevent a large number of placements in programs for the mentally retarded.

As the researchers worked with the policymakers to answer this question, three limitations of typical methods of data analysis became readily apparent. First, in contrast to traditional regression and analysis of variance (ANOVA), epidemiological methods are far superior for differentiating risk to the individual from risk to the population. For example, a risk may have a large effect on an individual who experiences it. However, because it is a rare occurrence, it may have a relatively small effect on the state. Using traditional research methods, the researchers found that premature birth increased the risk of mild retardation by 88%, and a postmature child (born after the due date) had a similar increase in risk, at approximately 81%. Although the risk to the individual was about the same for premature and postmature births, epidemiological methods revealed that premature births had a greater impact on the state because they constituted a larger proportion of births than did postmature births (21% compared with only 4%).

Second, the researchers became aware of the need to use alternative methods for assessing the impact of rare events (Scott et al., 1999). Policymakers often deal with what researchers would call the tails of the distribution or outliers in the population—violent youth, children with serious developmental disabilities, and severely dysfunctional families. What is true for these exceptional situations may diverge dramatically from what is true for the population as a whole. To illustrate this point, the researchers ran the correlation between birthweight and SAT scores in a sample of 27,952 Florida children. Their analysis revealed a correlation of .08, which means that birthweight accounted for less than 1% of the variance in SAT scores in the total sample. Yet when the researchers zeroed in on the low-birthweight babies, epidemiological methods revealed a 40% increase in the odds that these children would fall in the very low range of math ability. Thus, epidemiological methods of analysis revealed that an intervention might have little effect if applied to the total population, but could have a marked impact if targeted to the segment of the population that could benefit most.

Third, researchers are typically hesitant to categorize or dichotomize continuous data because it almost always results in a loss of information and statistical power. Yet policy decisions are typically dichotomous in nature, with policymakers often facing an up or down vote on delivering services, providing programs, or establishing eligibility criteria. Thus, the decision of whether to dichotomize data should depend on the specific question being asked so that the question drives the analysis rather than the analysis driving the question (Scott et al., 1999).

Thus, researchers can increase the utility of their research by employing epidemiological methods that provide data more pertinent to policymakers, such as the prevalence of a problem, its risk to the population, and the potential cost savings of policy responses. For a discussion of epidemiological methodology and instructions for calculating a risk ratio, odds ratio, and population-attributable fraction, see the excellent discussions by Scott and colleagues (1999) and McCartney and Rosenthal (2000).

Case Study: Collecting and Analyzing Data on Policies and Programs Across States and Communities (Map and Track)

Policymakers are particularly interested in comparing how their constituency stacks up to a similar city, county, state, or region. Curiously, this information is not always readily available, despite its usefulness to policy-makers as a guide to developing new programs or revamping existing ones. The *Map and Track* series was launched by the National Center for Children in Poverty to track changes over time in state-initiated programs and policies for young children and their families (Cauthen, Knitzer, & Ripple, 2000; Knitzer & Page, 1996, 1998). This research provided information on all 50 states regarding how young children are faring across the country. In 1997, *Map and Track* also began tracking state initiatives to encourage responsible fatherhood in cooperation with the Council of Governors' Policy Advisors and the National Center on Fathers and Families (Bernard & Knitzer, 1999; Knitzer et al., 1997). *Map and Track* was suspended in the early 2000s, but is currently being revamped.

An overview of some of the research findings illustrates its implications for policymaking. In the 2000 *Map and Track* report, about 60% of the states invest in programs for infants and toddlers and 80% in programs for preschoolers, yet five states do not fund any child development or family support programs. States are funding four main types of programs for families with children from birth to age 6: family resource centers, home visiting programs, school-linked parent education and involvement programs, and block grants that support a range of early childhood programs addressing local needs. Since the 1998 *Map and Track* report, state spending on child development and family support programs increased by almost 90% to over $3.7 billion, with large increases from nonstate revenues such as federal TANF funds, tobacco settlement funds, or funds raised through lotteries, gambling fees, or cigarette taxes.

Yet funding has been uneven across states, with 6 states spending more than $200 per child under 6 years of age and 14 states spending $20 or less. One future challenge faced by states, according to discussions with 300 key informants, is that family economic security is largely missing from efforts to enhance the well-being of young children. For example, in some states, families with incomes as low as $7,000 pay state income taxes, whereas in other states families do not begin paying state income taxes until their income is as high as $33,000 (Cauthen et al., 2000).

The exact opposite has occurred in regard to fathering: State efforts have focused predominantly on financial involvement, particularly child support (Ooms, 1998). *Map and Track* reported that only four states demonstrated exemplary efforts in promoting both the financial and emotional involvement of fathers with their children. To date, state efforts focus primarily on teen fathers and low-income noncustodial fathers. Little attention is being paid to fathers in two-parent families or to strategies such as father-friendly workplace policies (Bernard & Knitzer, 1999).

In the wake of welfare reform, 16 foundations funded Assessing the New Federalism, a multiyear Urban Institute project to track the effects of the devolution of social welfare programs from the federal government to the states. Data are being collected and analyzed on state health, income support, and social service programs for low-income residents in 13 states (see their Web site at http://www.urban.org).

FAMILY POLICY IMPLEMENTATION

Another role for family professionals has surfaced with the increasing recognition that passing family-friendly legislation is necessary, but not sufficient, to ensure that policies are sensitive to and supportive of families (Ooms & Preister, 1988; Winton & Crais, 1996). Steps must also be taken to ensure that policies are implemented in ways consistent with the legislation's intent. That is, how policies are implemented may be as important as what kinds of policies are enacted (Cohen & Ooms, 1993). Implementation is the difficult and complex task of transforming policy goals into programs, operating procedures, and regulations (Rist, 1994), a process that could benefit from professional involvement in several ways. Professionals can contribute to implementation planning by making available the results of existing research on the success or lack thereof of previous implementation efforts. Professionals could also improve implementation by educating program administrators and front-line staff on the content, skills, and actual strategies needed to successfully work with families.

Also, when policies are being operationalized, different types of data could be collected and analyzed to examine whether resources are being effectively and efficiently used to reach the intended outcome (Rist, 1994). For example, research can assess various aspects of the implementation process, such as whether the intended audience is being reached, which services are being delivered, the consistency of implementation across sites, and how the program is affecting families (see Carasso & Steuerle, 2005). As the implementation swings into full gear, researchers can provide ongoing monitoring of the situation—whether the condition improves, deteriorates, or remains the same—so program managers can make midcourse corrections. Implementation research of this genre reveals not only how "programs shape people but how people shape programs" (Institute for Research on Poverty, 1992, p. 11). This ground-level view can best be achieved, according to Rist (1994), through qualitative research methods such as case studies, focus groups, program monitoring, and process evaluations.

I include here three examples of the important roles that professionals have played in the implementation of family policies. The first example entails collecting qualitative data to influence one state's implementation of the 1993 law passed by Congress to provide family support and preservation services. The second example details the effectiveness of bringing together high-ranking state agency officials to share their experiences in implementing the 1996 federal welfare reform legislation. The third example describes the strategies used by professionals in the National Governors Association (NGA) to focus attention on the needs of children and families.

Case Study: Gathering Data to Aid Policy Implementation (Implementation of the Federal Family Preservation and Family Support Provisions in Kentucky)

In 1993, Congress approved almost $1 billion for community-based family preservation and family support services, including intervention programs for preventing unnecessary out-of-home placements and prevention programs for promoting the well-being of children and families. Funding was provided for states to conduct needs assessments to guide the development of 5-year plans intended to reform the current delivery system for family services. To assess the strengths and weaknesses of existing services, states were encouraged to seek input from stakeholders such as service providers, professional organizations, advocacy groups, community leaders, parents, and other family members.

In Kentucky, the Department of Social Services contracted with the University of Kentucky to conduct this needs assessment. According to Dyk (1995), the university designed the study, developed the individual and focus group instruments, trained the focus group leaders and scribes, analyzed the data, summarized the responses of the 15 district committees, and identified patterns and trends in the data. During a 3-month period, 97 focus groups were held across the state of Kentucky, including 39 groups of parents or family members, 21 groups of service care providers, 19 groups of children in out-of-home care, and 18 groups of community leaders. Overall, 838 people participated, including 307 family members, 209 service care providers, 198 children, and 124 community leaders. Each focus group made recommendations to the district planning committees, and the recommendations of these 15 committees became part of the state family preservation and support plan (Dyk, 1995).

Across all focus groups, one dominant theme was that the family is in crisis, and that as an essential unit in society, it must be preserved and supported. All groups strongly recommended a one-stop service delivery center, which would make it easier to access resources, streamline paperwork, minimize duplication of services, and facilitate a more coordinated and comprehensive response to family needs. From the focus groups emerged some of the barriers to family self-sufficiency, including the lack of affordable quality child care, inadequate transportation and housing, limited education and job training, and unavailability of health care benefits in many jobs. Service providers identified the need for temporary income support to help families of limited resources handle crises. Children living in out-of-home facilities identified the need for more permanency in placements, easier access to social workers or confidants who understand their unique challenges, and opportunities for continuing relationships with their siblings and biological parents when possible. Because of this thorough needs assessment, Kentucky was selected by the federal evaluator as the state in which to study consumer involvement. According to the professor who designed the needs assessment, "It was exciting to be a part of the grassroots effort to impact policy and programming for families" (P. H. Dyk, personal communication, December 5, 2000).

Case Study: Bringing Together High-Ranking State Agency Officials (Welfare Peer Assistance Network)

The Welfare Peer Assistance Network (WELPAN) was formed in anticipation of the passage of the 1996 welfare legislation that radically transformed welfare policy and positioned states as key players in welfare formulation and implementation. With support from the Joyce Foundation, high-ranking welfare officials from seven Midwestern states began meeting on a quarterly basis to dialogue about their experiences in designing, implementing, and evaluating welfare reform. The concept is simple, according to cofacilitators Tom Corbett (2000) and Jennifer Noyes. Corbett is former director and Noyes a researcher at the Institute for Research on Poverty at the University of Wisconsin–Madison. Most knowledge transfer technologies are hierarchical in nature, designed to disseminate information from subject matter experts to practitioners in the field. Instead, WELPAN employs a horizontal strategy of bringing together similarly situated peers who face like challenges to dialogue about their experiences and share what has worked in their respective locales. Resource people occasionally meet with the group, but in keeping with the spirit of WELPAN, the emphasis is on allowing ample time to discuss the implications for state implementation of welfare reform.

From this dialogue have emerged some common solutions to shared problems, as evidenced by the WELPAN report on principles for evaluating welfare reform (Corbett et al., 1998). Also, WELPAN has resulted in the discovery of some new insights and perspectives that might be more readily apparent to those doing welfare reform than those studying or teaching about it. For example, based on their report (Corbett, 2000), WELPAN members contend that welfare has undergone a cultural shift from a focus on income support to work and self-sufficiency. Further shifts may also be occurring toward community and family functioning, particularly the well-being of children. WELPAN members have invested considerable time thinking through how to move away from conventional siloed services and toward delivering coherent and comprehensive services to disadvantaged families by blending discrete, categorical programs in innovative ways (Midwest WELPAN, 2002a, 2002b, 2002c). More recently WELPAN has directed attention to accountability and how to move beyond process measures to client-based outcomes.

In anticipation of the reauthorization of the federal welfare reform law, the WELPAN network met in Washington, DC, to share their unique perspective on welfare reform with some key actors in reauthorization, including officials from the National Conference of State Legislatures, National Governors Association (NGA), U.S. Census Bureau, U.S. Department of Health and Human Services, and welfare advocacy groups. WELPAN members envision a number of future activities designed to extend its influence beyond the Midwest. The WELPAN concept has obvious implications beyond this issue and these participants.

Case Study: Fostering Peer Mentoring Among Policymakers (National Governors Association)

The NGA was formed in 1908 after the governors met with Theodore Roosevelt to discuss conservation issues. Initially, the association brought together governors so that they could discuss mutual concerns and act collectively. More recently, the NGA Center for Best Practices provides a bipartisan forum for exchanging views on the programs and policies that states are investing in and for sharing information on state innovations and best practices. Because child and family programs often have multiple funding streams with a complex mix of oversight from local, state, and federal governments, governors are in a unique position to provide leadership for a more coordinated, comprehensive state response. Over the years, the NGA has coordinated a number of initiatives to focus gubernatorial attention on the needs of children and families. For illustrative purposes, I have included only selected examples here.

The NGA brings together governors with similar interests to facilitate peer-to-peer technical assistance. In one network focused on young children, former governor Bob Miller of Nevada asked the nation's governors to share information about their programs that support the healthy development of children and toddlers. Thirty states responded with 66 programs. An independent panel of judges selected eight governors who were recognized at the 1997 annual meeting as leaders in providing services to young children and their families. To facilitate cross-state fertilization, a follow-up conference was also planned that profiled these award-winning programs and provided opportunities for states to learn from each other about what works and why. NGA also coordinated a meeting to extract best practices in implementing comprehensive support systems for young children and families based on the experience of nine states. Five states (Illinois, Maryland, Ohio, Washington, and Wisconsin) are also involved in building public and political will for state education policy.

The NGA also identifies emerging issues, responds to requests from governors' offices, and publishes briefs on state efforts on a number of child and family issues, such as child welfare and low-income working families, preventing teen pregnancy, promoting responsible fatherhood, strengthening families, providing health care coverage for uninsured children, and creating integrated services for children and families. For further information and a list of their documents, see their Web site at http://www.nga.org. The National Conference of State Legislatures provides similar services to state legislators, as described on their Web site, http://www.ncsl.org.

FAMILY POLICY EVALUATION

Professionals can play an integral role in building family policy by conducting evaluation studies that use (a) appropriate outcomes, (b) good designs, (c) realistic interim indicators, and (d) valid and reliable measures. Policy evaluation is often synonymous with program evaluation because programs are often the means through which policies are operationalized. By definition, family evaluation research means assessing whether programs or policies meet their stated outcomes for families (Nye & McDonald, 1979), yet most program evaluations measure outcomes for individuals rather than families. For example, in a 1985 report on the cost-effectiveness of eight major federal programs promoting children's well-being, only Head Start examined the impact of these programs on parents, although parents are widely considered the first and foremost influence on child development. In addition to parents, the unit of analysis in family policy evaluations could be the relationship to siblings, other family members, relatives, or partners (Institute for Research on Poverty, 1992).

Outcomes that might be considered family outcomes include out-of-home placements, domestic abuse, the quality of parent–child relationships, and the home environment. Yet documenting only that a program or policy reaches its intended outcome is too simplistic. Policymakers and policy implementers typically need to know which families are reached, under what conditions, and why and how the program is effective (Cohen & Ooms, 1993; Weiss, 1986).

Experimental designs that randomly assign families to treatment and comparison groups are considered the gold standard in evaluation research because they prove, to a reasonable degree of scientific certainty, that the program actually causes the outcome (Moore et al., 2003). Because experimental design studies are expensive, time-consuming, and sometimes impractical, researchers like Clara Pratt, an endowed family policy professor at Oregon State, have called for alternative research designs such as the emerging use of social indicators to evaluate the effectiveness of policies and programs (see the case study on results-based accountability).

Using good designs to assess outcomes for families is necessary, but still does not provide all the information that policymakers and policy implementers typically need. Because many family outcomes are long term in nature and become evident only after several years of program operation, we also need to strengthen our capacity to conduct formative evaluations that identify interim indicators of successful programs. Formative evaluation provides policy implementers with useful information that can suggest midcourse program corrections. The preliminary results provided by formative evaluation can also be useful to policymakers because they are more in keeping with governments' annual or biennial budget cycles. For example, if the goal is reduced family violence, the interim indicators might be home visits to at-risk families, access to social support, participation in parent education classes, and utilization of existing services. Moreover, we must not lose sight of the importance of identifying which single interim indicator is most critical to reaching the intended outcome and whether comprehensive approaches are needed.

Program evaluators must also examine the importance of family-sensitive program practices and which aspects of family support or involvement may be responsible for a program's success (e.g., involving family members in planning, implementation, and ongoing feedback and evaluation; providing families with full information and a range of options; and adapting programs to cultural values and strengths). Good policy evaluation can help disentangle whether the effectiveness (or ineffectiveness) of the policy is due to its design, the way in which it was implemented, the extent to which families were involved, or some combination thereof (Rist, 1994).

Finally, family evaluation research is virtually impossible unless we can identify and agree on family criteria that might serve as valid outcomes, interim indicators, and program practices as well as reliable and generally accepted ways of measuring them (Cohen & Ooms, 1993). For basic research, fine-tuned measures are needed that assess specific aspects of family functioning, whereas for program or policy evaluation, less complex measures may be warranted to make it easier for programmers to collect data from large numbers of families. To this end, researchers need to consider how to utilize alternative data sources such as case records and the observations of front-line staff (Pratt, 2000). Agreeing on and widely using a core set of family measures (Cohen & Ooms, 1993) would expedite the progress of family research because findings could be more readily compared and integrated across studies. Moreover, familiar and well-recognized family indicators could raise the profile of family issues by generating regular media coverage, just like indicators such as the gross national product and the consumer price index do for economic issues (Moore, 1999).

To illustrate the diversity of efforts within family policy evaluation, I cite here three examples. The first example is an evaluation of a specific program that uses an experimental treatment and control design. In the second example, I describe the efforts of one state in instituting a results-based accountability system to evaluate the effectiveness of its programs and policies. The third example is a collaborative effort to develop a common evaluation design and a standard set of child and family indicators for evaluating the effectiveness of welfare reform across several states.

Case Study: Comparing a Family Intervention
to a Nonfamily Intervention
(Oregon Social Learning Center's Treatment Foster Care)

This evaluation study, which has direct relevance to policymakers, employed an experimental design to compare the effectiveness of a family-focused versus a group-based treatment for male juvenile offenders. These boys, ages 12 to 17, had histories of serious chronic delinquency, and all had been placed out of their homes at least once before. They averaged 14 previous criminal referrals, including more than four previous felonies, and served an average of 76 days in detention. Researchers at the Oregon Social Learning Center compared two treatments: placing boys in secure or community-based group care facilities or placing them in the homes of trained foster parents (Chamberlain et al., 1992).

The two treatments differed in several important respects. Teens assigned to group care usually lived with 6 to 15 youth in residential settings that employed shift staff. In contrast, boys in treatment foster care lived with a foster parent who was carefully selected, supported, and trained for 20 hours in parent management skills such as supervision, encouragement, discipline, and problem solving. Youth in group care spent more time with peers, whereas youth in foster care spent more time with adults. Teens in group care had more influence on setting house rules, establishing expectations, and participating in disciplinary decisions than did teens in foster care. Teens in group care attended in-house schools, and teens in foster care attended public schools. Group therapy occurred weekly in group care, whereas it was not offered at all in treatment foster care. In group care settings, family therapy was encouraged, but families could commute to the program sites only about once a month or less. In foster care, the boy's biological family participated in weekly family therapy, and frequent home visits were encouraged, beginning with 1- or 2-hour visits and increasing to overnights.

In the program evaluations, treatment foster care was more effective in reducing delinquent acts and serious crimes among chronic juvenile offenders than was traditional group care. One year later, the youth in treatment foster care spent, on average, fewer than half as many days in detention and about a third less time locked up in state training schools than did youth in group care. Youth in treatment foster care ran away less frequently and completed their programs more often than did youth in group care. The program also worked for hard-to-reach older offenders and for youth with severe mental illness (Chamberlain & Reid, 1991). During the year after their program, teens in foster care spent nearly twice as much time living with parents or relatives—a major goal of both types of treatments—than did boys in group care.

Program evaluations like this one can provide guidance for designing policy responses by identifying not only programs and policies that work, but also those that have no evidence of effectiveness. This solution-oriented research is the kind of research most often requested by the Wisconsin policymakers with whom I work and the most often praised when it is well presented. Of particular interest to policymakers are estimates of cost-effectiveness, especially those conducted by independent firms. According to the independent Washington State Public Policy group, for every $1 spent on treatment foster care, taxpayers have saved more than $17 in criminal justice and victim costs by the time the youth is 25 (Aos, Phipps, Barnoski, & Lieb, 1999).

Based on these results, the researchers concluded that it is feasible and safe to place serious youth offenders in trained and supported foster families in the community. Not only were the youth taught to be responsible members of the family, but the treatment foster parents also used parent management skills to encourage youth to attend school regularly, do their homework, and improve their relationships with teachers and prosocial peers. Well-trained foster parents can re-create the powerful socialization forces of functional family life, which has the potential to set even hard-to-reach youth on a more positive life path, while saving substantial amounts of money in the treatment system and in victim costs. After 16 years of experience conducting the program, the researchers have been pleased by the response from strong, tightly knit families that were willing to accept training and supervision so they could provide a positive family experience for delinquent or disturbed youth (Chamberlain, 1999).

Case Study: Using Results-Based Accountability to Measure State Progress Toward Child and Family Goals (The State of Oregon's Benchmarks Initiative)

More than 15 years ago, the state of Oregon launched its Benchmarks Initiative. Benchmarks is the foundation for a results-based accountability system that identifies both long-term, statewide goals and measurable indicators (benchmarks) of Oregon's status relative to these goals.

The Benchmarks Initiative was initially proposed by a former governor with the intent of making the state more economically viable, but the initiative ultimately led to a broad set of economic, educational, social, and quality-of-life goals that detailed an ambitious vision for Oregon's future. Three broad goals and 90 related benchmarks were defined. All were state or local population-level indicators such as unemployment rate, miles of clean river, or rates of teenage pregnancy. Oregon policymakers believed that progress was more likely if the state tracked efforts to reach a limited number of goals.

State agencies further specified these goals and indicators to guide their work. For example, in 1995, the Oregon Commission on Children and Families defined four child and family goals: strong nurturing families, healthy thriving children, positive youth development, and caring communities (Pratt, 2000).

To measure progress toward these child and family goals, 20 benchmarks were selected to track the well-being of children and families. These benchmarks included rates of alcohol, tobacco, and other drug use; child maltreatment; school dropout rates; family access to health care; family poverty; immunization at age 2; juvenile crime; prenatal care and infant mortality; readiness to learn at age 5; reading and math success; and teenage pregnancy.

To connect these statewide goals and benchmarks with local services and programs, a number of program outcomes were defined that would apply to a broad range of program activities and participants. Based on a review of research by Oregon State University, each program outcome was empirically linked to the desired goal or benchmark. For example, to achieve the statewide goal of healthy, thriving children and the statewide benchmark of reduced child maltreatment, each program must achieve outcomes relevant to their participants and activities. These outcomes could be increased family access to basic resources, increased parent use of nonpunitive guidance strategies, increased speed and success of permanent placement for children whose families are not safe, or reduced drug and alcohol abuse among higher risk parents.

In this results-based accountability model, programs are not held accountable for results over which they have no control or that are unrealistic given the scope or time period for which programs are funded. For example, a local child maltreatment prevention program may be effective in reducing child maltreatment, but because it serves only a small number of high-risk families, it will have little immediate impact on the state benchmark of child maltreatment.

Using the evaluation of Oregon Healthy Start, Pratt and Katzev (1997) explained how the program outcomes have been linked to goals and benchmarks. Healthy Start offers support to families with newborn children and targets intensive services to those facing more stress and higher risk for negative outcomes. Eighteen of Oregon's 36 counties have the Healthy Start Program. In eligibility assessments, about two thirds of the families were at lower risk for poor outcomes and subsequently received short-term basic services. One third were eligible for intensive services (although resources were available to fully serve only about 50% of these families). Because Healthy Start cannot serve all Oregon families, statewide benchmarks are not effective indicators of the program's success. Thus, program outcomes were selected that aligned with Oregon's important goals and benchmarks. As illustrated below, these outcomes subsequently are tracked among the higher risk families and children that receive intensive services.

• For the state benchmark of immunization rates at age 2, over 90% of Healthy Start's babies from high-risk families are up to date with immunizations in comparison with only 71% of Oregon's 2-year-olds.

• For the state benchmark of school readiness, the Healthy Start program tracks rates of normal development among served children and rates of appropriate early intervention among Healthy Start-served children in higher risk families. Overall, about 90% of children in higher risk families are developing normally, and 100% of children whose development is outside the normal range participate in early intervention services.

• For the state benchmark of reduced child maltreatment, Healthy Start tracks both confirmed rates of maltreatment and family-level risk factors (including domestic violence rates, drug use, and guidance techniques). Program data indicate that risk factors improve particularly among families served over longer periods of time. Maltreatment rates are higher than those in the general population, but are similar to rates found among other programs serving higher risk families.

Oregon is only one of several states using results-based accountability. No single definition of results-based accountability exists, and the terms and definitions vary from state to state. The Harvard Family Research Project has taken the important step of publishing a resource guide that profiles the key components of results-based accountability in

18 states and describes the similarities and differences in their systems (Schilder, Brady, & Horsch, 1997). For policymakers or policy implementers interested in instituting results-based accountability, a resource guide and background materials are available on the Harvard Family Research Project Web site at http://gseweb.harvard.edu/~hfrp/index.html.

Case Study: Developing Child and Family Indicators (Child Trends's Guide to Evaluating the Effects of State Welfare Policies on Children)

Throughout its 25-year history, the nonprofit, nonpartisan research center Child Trends has been committed to bringing the perspective of children and families to large-scale survey research. Recently, the center worked with a group of states interested in monitoring the effects of welfare programs on children and families. In collaboration with the U.S. Department of Health and Human Services, other federal agencies, private researchers, several foundations, and state representatives, Child Trends worked for over a year to develop a common design and standard set of child and family measures. These measures assess outcomes indicating the development and well-being of children and their parents as well as the pathway variables through which children may intentionally or unintentionally be affected by welfare reform. Agreeing on a common set of measures makes it easier to compare results across states and provides data that could well be an important influence on the next generation of welfare reform policies.

Many of the measures deal with individual child or adult outcomes, yet several deal with family relationships. For example, the guidebook includes measures for marital status; paternity establishment; living arrangements of the child; frequency of parental contact with the child; child abuse or neglect; domestic violence or abusive relationships; family routines; aggravation and stress in parenting; parental monitoring; parent–child conflict; emotional support and cognitive stimulation provided to the child; stability of child care; and changes in residence, school, and marital status. The states will use four methods to collect these data: administrative records, telephone surveys, in-home surveys, and self-administered questionnaires. For ordering information on the guidebook, *A Guide to Evaluating the Effects of State Welfare Policies on Children,* check the Child Trends Web site at http://www.childtrends.org.

FAMILY RESEARCH INTEGRATION

As important as the scholarship of discovering new knowledge through basic and applied research is the scholarship of integrating research findings for the purposes of (a) generating new insights that become apparent only when one looks across studies or disciplines, and (b) distilling information of particular relevance to specific audiences (Boyer, 1990) such as policymakers. Busy policymakers typically do not have the staff or time to find and read research studies on the myriad of complex issues on which they must vote. Policymakers are also unable to screen research for quality or differentiate between long-standing, well-accepted findings and new findings that appear promising but need replication. Thus, another important role that family professionals can play in the policy arena is to provide concise, comprehensive reviews of research that capsulize the most important findings and draw implications for policy.

Reviews that integrate findings across studies and disciplines are particularly useful to policymakers given the increasing specialization in academia, the narrow jurisdictions of most Congressional and state legislative committees, and the proliferation of special interest groups that seek to advance a single point of view (Small & Bogenschneider, 1998; Weiss, 1986). Policymakers are particularly interested in well-replicated findings that identify malleable factors likely to be influenced by policy (Bogenschneider et al., 2000). Family professionals can also provide organizational frameworks for conceptualizing public issues and particularly for conceptualizing issues from a family perspective—a perspective that is notably absent from the narrow individualistic agendas of many special interest groups, think tanks, and political action committees.

Many examples of research integration exist. The two examples cited here illustrate the diversity of formats (i.e., journals and briefs) and the diversity of sources (i.e., a journal initiated by a foundation and a group of professional associations).

Case Study: Providing High-Quality Research to Policymakers, Practitioners, and the Media (The Future of Children Journal)

Over its 15-year history, *The Future of Children* has developed a reputation as being a purveyor of easily accessible, high-quality research. Originated by the David and Lucille Packard Foundation in 1991, it is now being published by The Woodrow Wilson School at Princeton University and The Brookings Institution. The journal, currently published twice a year, seeks to promote effective policies and programs for children by providing policymakers, service providers, and the media with timely, objective information based on the best available research. Each issue typically includes several articles penned by leading experts on topics related to children's well-being such as marriage, school readiness, and immigrant families. The hallmark of the journal is that it offers comprehensive, cross-disciplinary articles on the issue in an accessible format.

In addition to the journal, the Packard Foundation also produces a policy brief, which includes a synopsis of each journal, an analysis of the issue, and policy recommendations. The journal and policy brief can be downloaded free from the organization's Web site at http://www .futureofchildren.org, and bound copies can be purchased. An e-mail newsletter is also available that provides periodic notices about new publications and a new subscription service.

Case Study: Writing Research Briefs for Policymakers

In 1995, three professional associations—the Society for Research on Adolescence, the Society for Research on Child Development, and the International Conference on Infant Studies—worked together to write five research briefs to inform policymakers and the public about the current state of knowledge on several high-profile child and family issues. It is not surprising that these organizations took the lead in writing these briefs because their membership conducts some of the best research available on child and adolescent development. What is surprising, however, is that professional associations do not translate research for policymakers more frequently. A policy working group and the executive directors of these three organizations prepared briefs on child care, job loss, nutrition, teenage parenthood, and violence. In keeping with their billing as briefs, these summaries were about one page in length (see examples in Brooks-Gunn, 1995).

FAMILY RESEARCH DISSEMINATION

In the apt words of Rist (1994), "We are well past the time when it is possible to argue that good research will, because it is good, influence the policy process" (p. 546). Similarly, there is no assurance that reports that integrate research, no matter how useful, will be put to use by policymakers if they are not read and absorbed. To turn good research and good ideas into good policy (Ganzglass & Stebbins, 2001) requires more than a slick report delivered to the desk of a policymaker. What is needed is strategically designed, precisely implemented delivery mechanisms geared to the unique information needs of policymakers.

Granted, good research integration and good research dissemination overlap to some extent. Many of the organizations that integrate research for policymakers are also on the forefront of developing innovative methods of disseminating their products to those in a position to apply them to policymaking. Yet all too often, so much effort goes into producing a high-quality research integration that too little energy and resources remain for disseminating the product to policymakers. Thus, it seems important that any theoretical framework worth its salt would devote equal attention to generating rigorous research, producing high-quality research integration, and developing innovative technologies for disseminating it to those in a position to use it. For the purposes of this book, *research integration* means providing concise, comprehensive reviews of research that capsulize the most important findings and draw relevant implications for policymakers, whereas *research dissemination* means promulgating this work broadly with the intent of seeing it used in the policy and public arenas.

Scholars disagree about the influence that research has on those who design, enact, or implement family policy, with some claiming the impacts have been many and others claiming they have been minuscule (see Bogenschneider, 2000). Most would agree, however, that the impact of research on family policymaking is less than its importance warrants, although they offer seemingly divergent explanations for this state of affairs.

Some policymakers lament the difficulty of making decisions with incomplete, biased, or insufficient information. For example, William Ruckelshaus, a former administrator for the Environmental Protection Agency, once said he had only 10% of the information he needed to make decisions (Rist, 1994). Other researchers contend that policy analysis is a growth industry (Dunn, 1994) that has produced a glut of information—the sheer volume and complexity of which has overwhelmed most policymakers, who lack the staff and time to keep informed on all the issues that confront them.

Oddly, both explanations may simultaneously be true. Conceivably, the hundreds of sophisticated research studies being produced and the volumes of excellent policy reports being written may never reach the desks of policymakers, particularly those in the 50 states, the 3,141 counties, and the countless local municipalities across the country. To the contrary, it could be that the studies do reach policymakers' desks, but that the volume is so great that it limits the ability of even the most conscientious policymakers to read them, let alone absorb their implications for policy (Corbett, 2000). According to Quinn (2001), "In the Internet age, policymakers suffer at once from too much and not enough information. What they need is the right information" (p. 54), provided in the right format at the right time.

Ironically, academics often overlook and sometimes even shun the media (McCall, 1988), a powerful vehicle that can provide access to audiences of a few thousand up to several million. For example, 99% of all U.S. homes have a radio, 98% have a TV set, and 97% of all cars used for commuting have a radio. According to estimates by the American Newspaper Publishers Association, nearly 63 million Americans read a daily newspaper and 52 million read a local weekly paper (Children's Defense Fund, 1990). Obviously, disseminating research through the media offers widespread access to Americans in all walks of life, yet the media differs from other venues in the functions it serves, the audiences it reaches, and the message it delivers.

According to McCall (1983), what the media does best is create aware-ness, telling people what to think about rather than what to think. Aware-ness is important in policymaking circles because, in the apt words of Glo-ria Steinem, "There are no good laws without good awareness" (1973; cited in McCall, 1993, p. 16).

For policymaking purposes, creating awareness is particularly important for two audiences: policymakers who set the legislative agenda (Kingdon, 1995) and the public who, when aware of a social problem, can evoke the at-tention of policymakers. As an example of the influence of the media on policymakers, legislators and agency officials are sometimes more likely to read reports in the media than those produced by their own agencies. One prominent example of the media's influence on the public is the CBS docu-mentary on hunger in America, which publicized this previously obscure is-sue and, in so doing, galvanized public support for the expansion of food as-sistance programs in the 1970s (Hayes, 1982).

The appeal of the media is the large audiences that it reaches, yet its downside is that the same message is indiscriminately delivered to all. The uniformity of the message is the media's greatest limitation, yet in a curious sort of way can also be its greatest asset in policymaking. Media has the po-tential to mobilize public support for an issue, because it simultaneously captures the attention of both policymakers and the public (Zigler, 1993).

Three diverse examples of research dissemination are presented here: mailing family impact newsletters to state policymakers; promoting social science research and policy through convening, consulting, mobilizing, partnering, and communicating with policymakers; and disseminating re-search through the media. These examples differ in format, ranging from organizing seminars to disseminating newsletters and from testifying at hearings to joining coalitions. They also differ in their focus: Two are strate-gically targeted at specific audiences and one indiscriminately disseminates the same message to a mass audience.

Case Study: Delivering Family Policy Newsletters to State Policymakers (The Family Matters Newsletter Written by the Wisconsin Family Impact Seminars)

Professionals have long known that one way to connect research and policymaking is to provide information in formats that policymakers pre-fer. In the summer of 2000, to get a better understanding of how policy-makers prefer to receive information, the Wisconsin Family Impact Semi-nars (WISFIS) interviewed eight legislators and one governor's office staffer who all served on a WISFIS advisory committee (82% response rate). These advisors were familiar with the seminars, briefing reports, and discussions that WISFIS was already providing and were asked to rank eight different avenues that WISFIS could use to keep them informed: a short newsletter, links to useful Web sites, follow-up meetings, Web-accessible audio of seminar speaker presentations, satellite seminars, networking opportunities with legislators from other states, overnight retreats, and poster sessions. The most popular choice by a wide margin was a short family policy newsletter. We responded by producing a newsletter for state policymakers that we call *Family Matters*.

Since the first issue of the *Family Matters* newsletter in 2001, we have produced 13 one-page newsletters on topics such as why families are high on policymakers' agendas, how a family-centered approach could curb rising health care costs, what government's role is in the child-care marketplace, why family involvement in education is important, and how mothers' incarceration affects children's development. We have self-consciously tried to differentiate this newsletter in several ways from the many others that policymakers receive, six of which are discussed here. First, we target the newsletter specifically to state policymakers, both by selecting topics that are primarily a state (not a federal or local) issue, and by including policy solutions that are being discussed in state legislatures. Second, we are scrupulously nonpartisan in the selection of content for the newsletter and in the way that we present it. For example, we feature issues of interest to both political parties, and we write about them using an educational rather than an advocacy approach. Instead of advocating for a specific policy option, we present a range of policy alternatives, particularly those being debated or enacted in other states.

Third, we examine policy issues from a family perspective, which to our knowledge few organizations do, and none that are educational rather than advocacy-based. As we plan a newsletter, we ask ourselves in what ways families contribute to the problem, how families are affected by it, and whether family approaches would result in better solutions. Fourth, we carefully screen the research featured in the newsletter to ensure that it is high quality, solution focused, and not readily available to policymakers. Fifth, we strive to write in accessible language and we organize the writing according to the policy questions that state legislators are currently considering. Sixth, to strengthen the connections between the university and the legislature, we feature in each issue a University of Wisconsin professor whose research is relevant to issues legislators are currently discussing. In sum, when we are writing a newsletter, we strive to keep these differences, which we think of as our market niche, uppermost in our minds.

We have not conducted a formal evaluation of the newsletters, yet we did interview 11 legislative and gubernatorial advisors (100% response rate) in the summer of 2005. Most of the advisors reviewed a sample newsletter during the meeting and underscored how useful the information was. However, several were frank in mentioning that because of the volume of mail they receive and the screening of mail by their staffers, the newsletters were not reaching their desk. Several advisors recommended that we send two copies: one to their office and a second to their home (where they would be more likely to see it). Our advisors also had excellent suggestions about ways to improve the format of the newsletter to capture their attention and to make it look less like junk mail (e.g., calling it a policy brief, prominently displaying the topic on the mailing label, explaining in the first paragraph why policymakers should care about the topic or the person featured in the newsletter, supplementing the hard copies with an e-mail version, addressing a personal copy to the staffer in their office who specializes in the issue, and avoiding a font that is too small and a format with too little white space).

We have responded to these suggestions and will evaluate the effectiveness of these newsletters again. In the meantime, copies of all the *Family Matters* newsletters are available on our Web site, http://www .familyimpactseminars.org/newsletters.htm, and can be copied and distributed if WISFIS is notified.

Case Study: Convening, Consulting, Mobilizing, Partnering, and Communicating With Policymakers (Consortium of Social Science Associations)

Many professional associations carry on policy activities, which are exemplified here by the Consortium of Social Science Associations (COSSA), an organization supported by more than 100 professional associations, scientific societies, universities, and research institutions. COSSA is an advocacy organization, but most of its activities could be conducted from an educational perspective as well (for distinctions between advocacy and education, see chap. 13). According to Executive Director Howard Silver, COSSA carries out many of the functions of a lobbying organization, except that it does not contribute campaign money.

Since its incorporation in 1982, COSSA has developed a number of avenues for promoting federal funding of the social and behavioral sciences; representing the social and behavioral sciences before Congress, the executive branch, the social and behavioral science community, and the wider science and public policy community; and disseminating research to policymakers. For example, COSSA sponsors three Congressional seminars each year on current issues such as enhancing educational performance, detecting deception, the genetics revolution, health and retirement, and risk and crisis communication. The members of COSSA also participated in a science fair, poster exhibition, and reception on Capitol Hill organized by the Coalition for National Science

Funding. This evening event, complete with refreshments, attracted 200 staff and 12 members of Congress. The fair featured a booth on poverty research by the Panel Study of Income Dynamics at the University of Michigan, a geological exhibit in which participants could create their own earthquake, and displays that required onlookers to don three-dimensional glasses.

COSSA is perhaps most well known for its biweekly newsletter, *Washington Update,* which tracks social science policy for 1,600 readers in universities across the nation, on Capitol Hill, and in federal agencies. Each year, the newsletter features a comprehensive analysis of the president's budget requests for more than 40 federal agencies that support research in the social and behavioral sciences. COSSA carefully monitors legislation of interest to its members, which entails testifying before appropriations committees in Congress; commenting on drafts of legislation or rules; meeting with congressional, executive, and agency staff; consulting with the media; and partnering with like-minded coalitions. In its 1999 report, COSSA listed 23 coalitions and committees that it worked with to advance the concerns of its constituents and to voice the potential contributions of social and behavioral science. COSSA also mobilizes the wider science and policy community on relevant issues, such as the 10-month struggle in 1999 over the Shelby Amendment, which required federal grant-making agencies to ensure that all their grantees make their data available to the public under the Freedom of Information Act. COSSA monitored the 2000 Census dispute over scientific sampling and worked to save the Javits Fellowship program, which supports graduate students in the social sciences. In the past few years, COSSA has also defended data access and quality, human subjects protection, and peer review.

Case Study: Disseminating Research Through the Media (National Council on Family Relations)

Several organizations, such as Child Trends, have been effective in working with the media. Although the National Council on Family Relations has only recently increased its media efforts, its work is featured here because it focuses specifically on family issues. Through the diligent efforts of former editor Robert Milardo, one or two news releases are distributed to major news outlets as each issue of the *Journal of Marriage and Family* (JMF) and *Family Relations* are published. For example, an article in the February 2000 issue by Harriet Presser on "Nonstandard Work Schedules and Marital Instability" made the front page of *USA Today.* Harriet Presser also appeared on the *NBC Nightly News* in an interview with anchor Tom Brokaw. An article in the February 1999 issue of

JMF by Reed Larson and David Almeida on the transfer of emotions such as anger, depression, and happiness between family members received widespread coverage. The story was carried by ABC News, American News Service, the *Atlanta Journal Constitution,* Columbia News Service, *Pittsburgh Post Gazette, The Oregonian, Ottawa Citizen, Redbook,* Scripps Howard News Service, *USA Weekend, Washington Times,* Voice of America, and other TV and radio stations. The press release was also carried in the foreign media in such outlets as *Maxim* in the United Kingdom and the *Tehran Daily News.* This media coverage is the immediate response to a particular press release. According to R. M. Milardo (personal communication, December 2000), press releases often have a delayed effect as they are picked up by magazine writers or authors working on books for the mass market. Since JMF began issuing quarterly press releases, the journal has received an average of two media queries per week.

FAMILY IMPACT ANALYSIS

Another role for family professionals is to conduct family impact analyses that critically examine the past, present, or probable future effects of a policy, program, or service on family stability, family relationships, and family members' ability to carry out their responsibilities (Ooms & Preister, 1988). Evaluation research typically focuses on whether the stated goals or objectives of a program are being met, whereas family impact analysis extends this line of inquiry by examining how the program goals may be counterproductive by producing negative consequences for families sometimes in inadvertent or unintended ways (Nye & McDonald, 1979).

In 1976, a Family Criteria Task Force comprised of members of the Consortium of Family Organizations (COFO) began developing a set of six family impact principles and an accompanying checklist of questions. In 2000, the checklist was updated by the Policy Institute for Family Impact Seminars. (Copies are available in Appendix A and on our Web site, http://www.familyimpactseminars.org/ipfcheck.pdf.) The principles underlying family impact analysis include encouraging parental and marital commitments and stability, providing support so family members can fulfill their responsibilities, recognizing the strength and persistence of family ties, ensuring family empowerment and partnership, respecting family diversity, and supporting vulnerable families (Ooms & Preister, 1988). To illustrate, the principle of family membership and stability includes this question: Does the policy or program recognize that major changes in family relationships such as divorce or adoption are processes that extend over time and require continuing support and attention? In recent years, the government has allocated resources to encourage families to adopt children who are hard to place (e.g., handicapped, abused, or older children). Family impact analysis revealed that virtually no resources are devoted to providing the education and support that families need to make these challenging adoptions succeed (Ooms & Preister, 1988).

A family impact analysis of policies surrounding intercountry adoption revealed that adoption policies have different effects on different families. Ittig (2004) conducted a family impact analysis of adoption policies and a content analysis of the views expressed by congresspersons and other key policy developers at congressional hearings related to intercountry adoption. Over the course of seven hearings, the situation of birth parents was seldom presented: no advocacy groups advanced their interests, no participant self-identified as a birth parent, and no person specifically spoke on their behalf. When birth parents were discussed, they were characterized as being unable to care for their child, overburdened by a large number of children, or unqualified to function as a parent because of addiction, lack of education, or character flaws. Those speaking at the hearings never mentioned the emotions of the birth parent such as love or care for the child, whereas by contrast *loving* was the most common term used to describe adoptive parents. Several participants spoke of the child's right to a family, but the family referred to was usually the adoptive not the birth family. Ittig speculated that the voice of birth parents was less apt to be heard at the hearings because they have less power in the policy process given their typical status as disenfranchised populations in struggling nations.

Because family impact analysis, like environmental impact analysis, is a technical exercise, it may be most useful if conducted by professionals with considerable knowledge and expertise on families or by those who have been trained in the process (see chap. 11). Based on his experience as the former director of the Australian Institute of Family Studies, Mc-Gurk (1995) emphasized the importance of implementation. Australia established family impact statements in some parts of the country as early as the 1980s, but their value depended on the quality of the statements, how and if they were used in decision making, and whether a system of accountability was established.

Several tools have been developed for assessing how policies, programs, or institutions affect family well-being; some of these tools can be broadly applied and others are more suitable for specific purposes (see http://familyimpactseminars.org/impact.htm). For example, as described in one of the following case studies, family impact analysis of a broad range of policies and programs can be conducted using the family impact analysis principles and checklist. This section also includes two other case studies that describe diagnostic tools for conducting family impact assessments of schools and communities. A final case study describes how to teach family impact analysis to the public. (A primer on conducting a family impact analysis can be found in Appendix B.)

Case Study: Conducting Family Impact Analysis of Policies
(The Family Impact Checklist)

In the early 1990s, COFO published six issues of *Family Policy Reports* that aimed to assist policymakers in evaluating legislation and social programs from a family perspective. Using the family impact principles and checklist, each report assessed the impact of a specific legislative proposal on family well-being to determine whether it would help or hurt, strengthen or weaken family life. For example, the October 1990 *Family Policy Report* analyzed an initiative to support home-based long-term care, the Comprehensive Health Care Act, H.R. 4253, introduced by Representative Mary Rose Oakar, a Democrat from Ohio (COFO, 1990a). The analysis was limited to the section of the bill that specifically addressed home- and community-based care.

These four- to six-page reports typically described the legislation, analyzed it using the family impact principles and checklist, and offered recommendations based on the assessment. For example, the *Family Policy Report* on long-term care recommended that the debate be reframed to include family members who provide the bulk of long-term care. According to research studies and the testimony of family caregivers, the single most important factor in how well the elderly, disabled, or chronically ill adjust and whether they need to be institutionalized is the way in which family members respond. Thus, the report proposes that the central policy question for controlling costs and improving the quality of long-term care is this: "How can we support, supplement, and strengthen family caregiving?" (COFO, 1990a, p. 1).

The report concluded that the legislation was an important and constructive step in providing public funds to support long-term care. The bill was supportive of families by providing family counseling, therapy, and information and education services. However, the bill did not provide two other services that families say they need: respite care and adult day care. The bill was also silent on whether professionals such as case managers are expected or required to work collaboratively with families as partners in providing home- and community-based care.

COFO's first *Family Policy Report* introduced the concept of a family perspective in policymaking, and subsequent reports addressed drug abuse legislation, two child welfare bills, the child care and development block grant program, and health care reform. COFO has disbanded, but at the time these reports were written, the organization included the American Association for Marriage and Family Therapy, the American Association of Family and Consumer Sciences (formerly the American Home Economics Association), Family Support America (formerly the Family Resource Coalition), the Alliance for Children and Families (formerly Family Service America), and the National Council on Family Relations. These family impact reports are now housed at the Policy Institute for Family Impact Seminars at the University of Wisconsin–Madison (http://www.familyimpactseminars.org). The family impact analysis process has tremendous potential for use in assessing policy and legislation at the state and local levels as well.

Case Study: Using Family Impact Analysis to Improve Family Involvement in Their Child's Schooling (The Family–School Partnership Checklist)

It started with the best-selling Family Impact Seminar book, *Beyond the Bake Sale: An Educator's Guide to Working With Parents* (Henderson et al., 1986). This book evolved from a two-state field study that demonstrated the importance of parental school involvement to children's school success. Since that time, a number of studies have demonstrated that when parents are involved, students get better grades, score higher on achievement tests, attend school more regularly, drop out less often, and have higher personal aspirations (Baker & Stevenson, 1986; Epstein, 1985; Henderson & Mapp, 2002; Rumberger et al., 1990; Steinberg et al., 1992). As one step toward building stronger family–school partnerships, the book includes a checklist for gauging the school's current relationship with families and the community. The Policy Institute for Family Impact Seminars integrated this checklist with one designed by Joyce Epstein of the National Network for Partnership Schools (Epstein, Sanders, Simon, Salinas, Jansorn, & Voorhis, 2002).

The checklist is basically a self-assessment of how family-friendly the school is, based on current research on the factors that magnify or mitigate parental school involvement (Epstein et al., 2002; Henderson & Mapp, 2002; Henderson et al., 1986). In Wisconsin, this checklist was incorporated into the Families, Schools, and Communities United for Students (US) Project, developed specifically to build stronger family, school, and community partnerships.

In the US Project, county university extension family living educators bring together a partnership team that includes 20 to 30 community stakeholders such as the principal, administrators, teachers, parents, youth, school board members, school staff, representatives of the PTA/PTO and booster clubs, liaisons to strategic planning committees or site councils, extracurricular leaders, coaches, representatives of youth-serving organizations such as 4-H and Scouts, and community leaders. The partnership team uses the checklist to conduct a self-assessment that identifies where the school's support for families is strong and what gaps exist. Using these results, the team identifies strategies for building stronger family–school partnerships and develops action plans for the team's top three to five priorities.

The Family–School Partnership Checklist includes six separate components that Epstein identified as the six essential practices for effective partnership programs—parenting, communicating, volunteering, learning at home, decision making, and collaborating with the community (Epstein et al., 1997)—and also physical characteristics of the school (Henderson et al., 1986). The 65-item checklist asks the respondents to rate items such as how well the school (a) creates flexible volunteer opportunities; (b) trains volunteers so they can use their time productively; (c) provides a parent or family room for volunteers and family members to work, meet, and access resources about parenting, child care, tutoring, and related topics; (d) assists families in helping students set academic goals, select courses, and programs; and (e) has clear two-way channels for communication from home to school and from school to home.

In six middle schools in Wisconsin, the US Program has resulted in a number of actions to strengthen parents' involvement in their child's schooling and to build stronger partnerships among families, schools, and communities. For example, one school hired a parent volunteer coordinator and in 1 year's time, there was a fivefold increase in the number of hours volunteered at the school. To develop stronger, more stable parent–teacher relationships, policies were put in place in another school to ensure that students have the same homeroom teachers for both seventh and eighth grade. To improve parent–teacher communication, one school developed a parent handbook to clarify expectations, and another initiated a newsletter that is mailed or e-mailed to parents. A parent resource room was established in one school library and a directory of county services available to parents was developed and distributed to new families.

For schools interested in improving their track record in parent involvement, this Family–School Partnership Checklist includes practical steps that families, schools, and communities can take. This assessment helps focus the partnership team on strategies that research suggests are important and helps avoid wasting time on strategies that already exist in the community. The checklist results can also be used in evaluation by providing baseline data on the school's assets and liabilities, which can be useful in measuring improvements and assessing progress. The checklist can also be found on the Web site of the Policy Institute for Family Impact Seminars at http://www.familyimpactseminars.org/ipfcheck.pdf.

Case Study: Using Family Impact Analysis to Foster Family-Friendly Communities (Family Friendly Community Checklist of the Premier's Council in Support of Alberta Families)

In recognition of the 1994 International Year of the Family, the Premier's Council in Support of Alberta Families developed a checklist to assess how responsive communities are to family well-being. The checklist identifies specific aspects of communities that can contribute to or detract from family well-being. For example, items on the checklist include improving safety on a playground, training program staff to be more sensitive to family needs, making buildings more accessible to parents with strollers, and involving seniors in a neighborhood child-care center. Completing the checklist for a specific community pinpoints areas where community support for families is strong as well as areas that might need improvements. Involving community citizens in this assessment process can raise the profile of families and stimulate dialogue about specific steps communities could take to be more supportive of family well-being (Huemmert, 1995).

In Canada, the checklist has been widely used by realtors to help families choose family-friendly communities in which to live. In addition, the Alberta chapter of the College of Family Physicians has endorsed the checklist (Huemmert, 1995). In the wake of devolution in the United States, family-friendly community assessments may be particularly important, because authority for child and family issues is increasingly being shifted from the federal government to the state and local levels. (For a copy of the checklist, see http://www.familyimpactseminars.org/ffccheck.pdf.)

Case Study: Teaching Family Impact Analysis to the Public (The University of Minnesota 2005 Children's Summit)

Attendees at the University of Minnesota's Children's Summit 2005, *Smart Policies, Strong Families,* used the Family Impact Checklist to practice family impact analysis. As part of University of Minnesota President Robert Bruininks's Presidential Initiative on Children, Youth and Families, the Summit addressed the impact of policy on family functioning. One of the goals for the Summit was to equip participants with knowledge about how to assess public and private policies and programs for their potential impact on families. Madge Alberts, Program Coordinator for the Children, Youth and Family Consortium, provided this overview and analysis of their experience.

The Summit began with a series of speakers providing the context for thinking about policy from a family perspective including the demographics of Minnesota families; a video highlighting the experience of one family who had a child with special needs and the challenges they faced navigating the many social service systems required for the care of the child; and in light of the video, a follow-up discussion of the context in which families operate.

With the content of the speakers' presentations as background, Michael Benjamin, Executive Director of the National Council on Family Relations, introduced the Family Impact Checklist, which had been provided to all conference attendees. Benjamin provided a brief tutorial for how to use the checklist by applying it to the legislative proposal for government-sponsored casinos in Minnesota.

After the tutorial, participants were divided into 10 groups of 10 to 15 attendees to practice using the checklist by assessing the impact on families of a specific policy or program. The groups were allotted an hour for this task. Groups were facilitated by individuals who had been trained in the use of the checklist prior to the Summit. Facilitators also received a summary of the policy or program they were to analyze, a list of resources to learn more about the issue, and an agenda for their session. A University of Minnesota faculty member who was familiar with the policy or program area was assigned to be a consultant for each facilitator. In addition, each group had a "reality checker," a person from the community who was asked to raise questions regarding potential consequences for families and communities that could occur when policies play out for real. Facilitators had a fairly significant role in that they were required to participate in the training, familiarize themselves with the policy or program, and lead the group discussion.

State and federal policies or programs, current or proposed during the 2005 legislative or congressional sessions, were the basis for the family impact analysis exercise. They included housing for the long-term homeless, alternative response (Child Protection Services), the Family and Medical Leave Act expansion, all-day kindergarten, the Adoption and Safe Families Act of 1997, early childhood family education, moving the responsibility for extracurricular activities out of schools into communities, and consumer-directed community supports.

Following the family impact analysis exercise, groups reconvened in a large group session to debrief about the experience. Almost without exception, the comments during the feedback session indicated that attendees found the experience to be very valuable. Attendees felt they had learned at least a little about how to use one particular tool to assess policies and programs from a family perspective. Some expressed that they heard new sides of an issue they had not considered before; in fact, one participant said that because of the exercise, she had completely changed her position on an issue that she had previously felt strongly about. Others suggested that policymakers needed to be trained in the use of the checklist.

In a follow-up evaluation, 75% of the returned surveys indicated that attendees ranked the family impact analysis exercise as above average or outstanding. Many commented that they would have liked more time; they felt they just barely got started when it was time to end. Some did not like being assigned to a group, and others said they learned a lot about an issue they previously did not know much about.

The conference wrapped up with a town hall meeting format, with participants expressing their thoughts and comments about the day. Appreciation for the checklist came up again, with the suggestion that it needed to be brought to communities.

The planners of the Summit learned a number of useful things from the exercise:

- To be most effective, facilitators must understand the use of the checklist, be thoroughly versed in the issue they are analyzing, and be strong group facilitators. More training for facilitators would be provided if the exercise were to be repeated.
- Facilitators must be prepared to deal with sidetracks and individual agendas that might arise related to the policy or program being discussed.
- Facilitators gained new skills themselves in the process of preparation for the Summit. One facilitator expressed that she was so impressed with the checklist and its usefulness that she now incorporates the checklist regularly into her work.
- Groups can become very heated, particularly if the issues are value-laden.
- It takes more than 1 hour to do a thorough job of practicing family impact analysis.
- The checklist is a "sleeper" policy and program analysis tool that needs to be publicized more.
- It would be a benefit to families and communities if policymakers and policy implementers knew how to use the checklist to assess policies and programs.

For more information about the Children's Summit, go to the Summit Web site at http://www.childrenssummit.umn.edu.

TEACHING OF FAMILY POLICY

Several of the professional roles for building family policy entail teaching. For example, professionals involved in family policy dissemination may teach policymakers, professionals involved in family policy implementation may train administrators and front-line staff, and professionals involved in fostering citizen engagement may provide policy education for the public. For the purposes of this chapter, family policy teaching refers to the instruction of undergraduate and graduate students in colleges and universities. Family policy courses have flourished, in part, because of requirements that students must have a background in family policy to be certified as family life educators by the National Council on Family Relations.

In many respects, the teaching objectives in a family policy course are no different than in any other course: promoting critical thinking, acquainting students with rigorous scientific work in the field, and helping students learn to express clear logical arguments orally and in writing. Yet family policy, because of its political nature, may pose some unique challenges to those who teach it. For example, every time a professor teaches a course on family policy, different elections are being held and different legislation is being debated. Over time, what may be most helpful to students is for teachers to present theoretical and conceptual frameworks so students can think about policymaking in ways that transcend particular issues, advances in scientific knowledge, and shifts in the political climate.

The teacher of family policy must also decide whether to approach the class from an advocacy or educational stance. Some teachers provide information primarily from one political perspective that they believe most strongly supports family well-being. Other teachers believe that defining and addressing family problems often involves ranking the needs and interests of one group in society as more important than those of another, and that science alone cannot supply these value judgments. Thus, these teachers discuss a range of political perspectives and policy alternatives to allow students to form their own positions on current issues (for a full discussion of the advocacy and educational approaches, see chap. 13).

Because many students have little previous policy experience, teachers of family policy often attempt to demystify the policymaking process by requiring students to observe settings where policies are enacted or to get involved in an issue of their choice (Anderson & Skinner, 1995). For example, one teacher required students to plan a conference to develop policy recommendations for the Governor's Child Care Task Force (Quoss, 1992). Students are often encouraged to write letters to the editor on family policy issues, to read the daily newspaper, or watch C-SPAN's unedited, round-the-clock political coverage. Some teachers require students to attend a government policymaking session, judicial proceedings, advocacy meeting, political forum, or board meeting of a nonprofit organization. Brief class reports of these meetings emphasize the range of policy decisions that affect families, the number of settings in which these decisions are made, and the myriad of roles that policy may play in students' future professions (for examples, see Bogenschneider, 2006; Skinner & Anderson, 1993).

I present here two case studies. One highlights a compendium of the syllabi of family policy courses taught by teachers across the country. The second describes a particular course that directly involved students and interested community members in the policy process.

Case Study: Teaching College Classes on Family Policy (A Syllabi Handbook Published by the National Council on Family Relations)

In 2004, three experienced teachers of family policy—Denise Skinner, Elaine Anderson, and Bethany Letiecq—edited a second edition of *Teaching Family Policy: A Handbook of Course Syllabi, Teaching Strategies, and Resources* (Anderson, Skinner, & Letiecq, 2004). This compendium includes 34 undergraduate and graduate syllabi aimed at enhancing the teaching of family policy courses by encouraging the exchange of ideas on their focus, objectives, requirements, and readings. These syllabi differed in their content, scope, and aims. For example, the content of most of the courses was structured around family policy, although three included family law and one dealt exclusively with family law. The majority of courses included a broad-based examination of how policies affect family development, although others focused more narrowly on community services and gender equality. In terms of scope, most concentrated on family policy in the United States, although two had a comparative or international focus. All the courses aimed to help students understand family policy or law, broadly construed, although two focused on teaching students how to conduct family policy research and one focused on teaching students to become advocates for communities and families.

In addition to syllabi, the handbook includes teaching strategies; an annotated bibliography; student training, internship, and employment opportunities; and Web sites related to family policy. For information about purchasing copies of the handbook, check the National Council on Family Relations Web site at http://www.ncfr.org.

Case Study: Teaching College Courses That Provide Hands-on Policy Experience (University of Wyoming's Child Care Think Tank Course)

In the spring of 1990, Bernita Quoss (1992) of the University of Wyoming was preparing to teach her resident on-campus course, the Child Care Think Tank. She hoped to make family policy come alive by planning the course around current legislative proposals, specifically the current efforts to enact a national family leave law and Wyoming's implementation of the child-care guarantee in the 1989 Family Support Act. When child-care leaders in the state heard about the course, they contacted Quoss about the possibility of providing a similar off-campus course to facilitate the work of the Governor's Child Care Task Force. This request posed two dilemmas. First, the time was short. With the resident on-campus course scheduled in January and the Governor's Report due in June, was it feasible to pull off two simultaneous courses? The second dilemma was philosophical. Should a university design a course around an ongoing political issue in the state?

Quoss responded to these dilemmas with an innovative solution. Students in the resident course collaborated with the instructor to design the off-campus course as a statewide conference for professionals interested in developing recommendations for the Governor's Child Care Task Force. Professionals in the off-campus course would develop recommendations for the Governor's task force and be encouraged to organize locally for continuing advocacy.

Initially, the eight students in the resident course—four undergraduates and four graduates—met with the instructor to establish goals and objectives for the statewide conference, identify potential participants, and determine what technical information the participants and the Governor's task force would need. Developing this technical information constituted the student assignments for the class—assignments that were engaging because they were to be used for an important political purpose in the real world. For example, students volunteered to complete a literature review on the effect of the quality of child care on children's development, compare the state's plan for the child-care guarantee to the recommendations of the Children's Defense Fund, summarize a survey conducted for a state agency on existing child-care services, and conduct a content analysis of parent responses solicited by the task force. The director of the university's child-care laboratory received the challenging assignment of documenting the level of need for child care in the state. One of the resident students designed a format for providing succinct summaries of this information in the conference brochure. At the conference, the resident graduate students facilitated discussion sessions for identifying child-care needs and concerns, and the undergraduate students served as recorders. One of the resident students also provided training for school-age child-care providers preceding the conference.

As outcomes of the resident course, the students planned and held a statewide conference for 125 participants. The Report of the Governor's Task Force on Child Care was completed and delivered to the governor a few weeks after the conference. Professionals in the off-campus course were able to complete the formidable task of gathering the information needed for making recommendations to the governor in a short time span with limited resources. Three communities formed local child care and family task forces to conduct local needs assessments. One unexpected outcome was that the university renegotiated the job description of the instructor to allow more time to promote policies for children and families.

Despite these positive impacts, Quoss (1992) cautioned professionals that "such an opportunity should not be rejected easily, but neither should it be sought casually" (p. 43). Time and resources are needed beyond those typically extended to teachers of resident family policy courses. For example, this collaborative policy project required at least a year of groundwork to establish the necessary connections in the child-care community, the university, and the Governor's office. Lead time was also needed to collect and develop the technical materials required to support the students' work. The university also provided additional resources, including a work-study student, time and resources of the university's conference planning office, and funds from a department-administered grant.

CITIZEN ENGAGEMENT IN FAMILY POLICYMAKING

According to Doherty (2000), professional efforts to create public policies for families is incomplete without parallel attempts to engage families in public problem solving. The call for citizen engagement is as old as Tocqueville's writing on the value of American political participation in the 1830s and as contemporary as the 1992 Responsive Communitarian Platform, which calls for a better balance between our rights as individuals and our responsibilities as members of families and communities. Over the past several years, "democracy has largely become a spectator sport," according to Boyte (1993a, p. 172), who directs a citizenship training program at the Hubert Humphrey Institute at the University of Minnesota. Americans have come to see government as something that is "for" the people rather than "of" and "by" the people, as the founding fathers intended (p. 174). Boyte argued that we need to reinvent citizenship by redefining politics from something that government is solely responsible for to include public problem solving, whereby citizens work together to solve common problems. Collaborative public problem solving differs from traditional advocacy, which attempts to secure resources for a low-resource group from a high-resource group (Doherty, 2000).

Expanding the definition of politics to include public problem solving carves out a dramatically different set of roles for professionals. For example, if politics is viewed as primarily influencing elected officials, professionals would work directly with policymakers or help citizens understand the legislative process, gain access to policymakers, and learn lobbying skills. If politics is also viewed as public problem solving, professionals need to teach citizens how to develop problem-solving relationships with others (e.g., listen and speak well, engage in public give and take, negotiate, bargain, understand other's self-interest), and how to establish systems for demonstrating accountability (Boyte, 1993a, 1993b).

Yet working to foster civic engagement is more than just a shift in the types of materials produced for the consumer. It also entails a fundamental shift in mindset to viewing families as producers of knowledge and wisdom, and to respecting their commitment and capacity to create changes of lasting civic value (Doherty, 2000). This public work has the potential to shape the environment in which families operate, but it has other important side effects as well. Getting involved in public problem solving is often triggered by self-interest, but the process of working together with a diverse mix of people often teaches tolerance of opposing views, mutual respect, and social trust (Boyte, 1993b; Putnam, 1995). People become citizens as they engage in public problem solving (Boyte, 1993b).

In the apt words of Boyte (1993b), "while professionals—like politicians—have important roles in solving the problems of our society, they cannot begin to solve them alone" (p. 85). We can extrapolate from Boyte's model that the momentum for supporting healthy, well-functioning families not only trickles down from federal or state initiatives, but also bubbles up from grassroots groups that bring together diverse families to work on common concerns. I describe here three examples of citizen involvement in family policy—one new and one well-established effort from this country and a 70-year-old effort from abroad.

Case Study: Engaging Citizens on Family Issues (Family Life 1st)

Using Boyte's (1993a, 1993b) model of citizen involvement, a group of parents and community leaders in Wayzata, Minnesota, are fighting for influence over their children's lives against forces more powerful than most individual parents (Doherty, 2000). Increasingly, these parents have found themselves competing for time with their own children in an overcommercialized, overbusy, overscheduled society. Active marketing of clothing to preteens, for example, has preempted parental influence on the clothing choices of children as young as ages 7 and 8. Most educational, economic, recreational, and religious activities are aimed at individuals, thereby pulling families apart and encroaching on family time. One prime example is the exaggerated emphasis on athletics at the expense of family time. Parents complain of coaches who threaten to bench athletes who miss practices even on holidays such as Mother's Day or Thanksgiving.

Time in structured sports is a relatively new phenomenon, consuming twice as much of children's time in 1997 as 16 years earlier (Doherty, 2004). Parents and children alike are worried about the toll their bloated schedules take on family life. For example, in 1997, the amount of time that children spent each week in a conversation with anyone in their family was, on average, a mere 45 minutes. Not surprisingly, one in five teens reported that one of their two chief concerns is not having enough time together with their parents. Many parents (about 4 of 10) report that their children's heavy schedule of homework and activities makes their job as parents harder (Doherty, 2004).

To make family life a priority, parents themselves have generated and sustained a public grassroots movement, aptly named Family Life 1st (Doherty, 2000; Doherty & Boyte, 1999). Thus far, Family Life 1st has created a vision of a desired future for family life in the community based on the rationale that "the family can only be a seedbed for current and future citizens if it achieves a balance between internal bonds and external activities" (Doherty & Boyte, 1999, p. 28). Family Life 1st has conducted interviews of stakeholders such as parents, coaches, organizational leaders, community activists, and clergy. The intent is not to create villains or scapegoats, but to create a better understanding of the problem, foster allies, and develop a set of policies that respect families' decisions to make family time a priority.

Family Life 1st is acquiring political clout by publicly recognizing local supporters of family life and generating media attention for their efforts. For example, a Family Life 1st Seal of Approval has been created to acknowledge those individuals and organizations that support parents' attempts to create a better balance between time for relationships inside the family and time spent on activities outside the family. The first Seal of Approval was awarded to a youth football program that cut its practice times in half. The program leveraged the Seal to help gain credibility with a benefactor who is helping an inner-city neighborhood start a youth football program. Family Life 1st has used the national TV networks and major print media outlets to influence local and national conversation on this "unspoken problem" (Doherty, 2000, p. 323). Early in 2000, the organization began working with other communities who want to start their own Family Life 1st initiative (for further information, see http://www .familylife1st.org).

Case Study: Engaging Citizens in Public Deliberation (National Issues Forums)

Since 1982, National Issues Forums (NIFs) have brought people together to deliberate about important issues and help them make informed choices about the direction the country or their community should take. Rather than promoting a particular policy alternative, the forums provide an opportunity for participants to weigh the trade-offs of several policy options. The forums and study circles are convened by more than 4,000 civic and educational organizations across the country, including civic groups, churches, community colleges, the Cooperative Extension Service, high schools, and libraries. This network of NIF groups focuses on issues such as abortion, education, immigration, juvenile crime, political reform, and poverty. In 1995, one of the featured topics was the troubled American family.

There is no typical forum in length, number of participants, or format. The format ranges from small study circles to large gatherings modeled after traditional town meetings. However, the forums do differ from everyday conversations, adversarial debates, or public opinion polls in a few respects. First, the policy options are presented in a neutral, nonpartisan way that encourages participants to take a fresh look at their own opinions by considering the perspectives of others and by examining their basic principles and beliefs as individuals and community members. Second, participants typically receive issue books that provide background on the topic and offer several alternative courses of action. Finally, moderators encourage participants to discuss different approaches to an issue; weigh the benefits, drawbacks, and trade-offs of each approach; and seek common ground that might serve as a basis for action.

As a result of the forums, a public voice often emerges about the direction the participants want government to take. To help set the government's compass, the results of the forums held around the country are shared with policymakers and public officials. For example, the American Association of Family and Consumer Science conducted a number of health care forums in classrooms and communities across the country and, in spring 2004, the outcomes were presented to members of Congress, federal agencies, and the national media (Matthews, 2004). The forums often help participants reach sound informed judgments on issues, better appreciate positions different from their own, and decide what personal actions they can take (NIF Institute, 1996). Also, as a result of attending these deliberative forums, individuals or groups may take steps to address problems outside the realm of government.

Case Study: Developing a National Movement for Families (The League of Large and Young Families—The Bond)

From the country of Belgium comes an impressive example of a family movement working for and with families to provide services and advocate on behalf of their political, material, social, and cultural needs. The League of Large and Young Families, known as the Bond, is a pluralistic, nongovernmental organization that began in 1921 when families were not high on the political agenda in Belgium. The Bond is a large, firmly established, highly visible association that unites 310,000 families, or more than 1 million men, women, and children, in Flanders and Brussels. Families pay membership fees of about 1,008 Belgian francs (or about $25 per year), but receive 1.5 times this fee in membership discounts provided by more than 15,000 merchants for food, shoes, toys, clothing, and furniture.

Despite the emphasis on large families in its name, the Bond prides itself on being open to families of all sizes, any structure, and in every stage of the family life cycle. The association is so named because of its origins after World War I, when Belgium lost an estimated 25% of its population. Being pluralistic means that the movement must be apolitical, aphilosophical, and entirely independent (L. De Smet, personal communication, December 19, 2000). The Bond maintains its independence, in part, because its primary source of income is the membership fees paid by its members; government and business make only minor contributions to its budget.

The vision of the Bond is not to wait for the government to respond to family needs, but to organize families to work on their own behalf. The 120 paid staff are supported by 14,000 volunteers who are elected to their positions every 6 years. The Bond maintains a presence throughout Belgium because of its organization into 5 provinces, 33 regions, and 1,100 local branches.

The Bond has three main aims: to promote solidarity between families, to promote the interests of all families, and to work toward a family- and child-oriented climate in society. To reach these aims, the Bond (a) organizes political action on behalf of families, (b) promotes social life at the local level, and (c) provides direct services to families.

Politically, the Bond develops a long-term policy agenda for a family- and child-friendly society in consultation with its member families and volunteers. In the short run, the Bond painstakingly monitors current developments to identify policies and practices that may threaten family life. Typically, the Bond works on less controversial issues that are likely to receive widespread support from its membership. For example, a frequent high-priority issue is the drive to preserve and even improve the child allowance, a government subsidy paid to parents to support child-rearing. Because the federal government is always looking for cost-saving measures, preventing cuts in the child allowance requires constant vigilance and frequent effort. The organization's political successes include implementing tax reform, making family impact reports compulsory, resisting the lifting of a ban against advertising immediately before and after children's TV programming, laying the groundwork for children to be heard in divorce proceedings, ensuring the rights of grandparents to see their grandchildren, and supporting initiatives for balancing work and family.

To achieve these political successes, the Bond schedules meetings with ministers to present its agenda; organizes lunch meetings with the press, politicians, and organizations to discuss legislative proposals; represents families on advisory boards and management committees dealing with family problems at the local and national levels; organizes rallies; interviews the political parties on their priorities and prints their responses in its weekly mailing to the membership; encourages regional representatives to contact politicians; establishes commissions to study important aspects of family policy; follows economic and social trends with an eye toward implications for formulating new policies; and prepares press releases and leaflets for distribution.

In addition to these political activities, the Bond promotes social life at the local level. The Bond organizes family day trips; provides educational programs for parents and grandparents; provides quality children's films; organizes children's clubs and workshops on gymnastics, volleyball, and badminton; and organizes recreational sports for young and old. For example, in 2000, the Bond enrolled 22,483 young children in swimming.

In terms of direct services to families, the best known service is babysitting. In 2000, volunteers cared for 200,000 children. In 2000, elder care services were provided to 19,565 senior citizens. The Bond provides summer camps for children ages 6 to 15, operates two holiday centers in Belgium, and offers camps and vacations in Austria. For more than 30 years, a newsletter has been provided to parents with issues targeting pregnancy and early childhood. In 2000, 1.25 million copies were delivered, with the costs supported primarily by advertisers. A new magazine was launched to provide information and guidance to parents of 12- to 16-year-olds, and a free magazine is also distributed to 71,212 seniors. The Bond makes counseling available to its members, offers consumer advice, and organizes 256 cultural programs for children, youth, and families.

The Bond differs from advocacy groups in the United States in several respects. The Bond focuses on families, whereas U.S. organizations tend to be focused on individuals, as exemplified by the American Association for Retired Persons (AARP) and the National Organization for Women (NOW). The Bond appears to advocate for families of several political persuasions, whereas U.S. organizations tend to promote a particular political agenda, such as the liberal *Children's Defense Fund* and the conservative *Focus on the Family*. In contrast to the U.S. communitarian and environmental movements, which are organized primarily on a national level, the Bond is organized at the national, state, and local levels. The Bond is primarily funded by membership fees, but receives some support from government and business, in contrast to U.S. organizations such as the American Federation of Women's Clubs and the American Legion, which are supported solely by dues-paying members.

Perhaps the most telling statement about the value of the Bond comes from those who know it best. According to General Director of Socio-Cultural Sectors, Luke DeSmet (1995), "If there wasn't a Bond in Belgium, someone would have to invent one."

UNIVERSITY INVOLVEMENT IN FAMILY POLICY SCHOLARSHIP

Of all the nation's institutions that should include policy efforts in their missions, this section singles out universities because they are uniquely positioned in several respects to contribute to the formulation, implementation, and evaluation of family policy. First, since the passage of the Morrill Act in 1862, public land grant universities have a legislative mandate to pursue scholarship not only for the benefit of science, but also for the benefit of the people (Small & Bogenschneider, 1998). According to Magrath (1998), all our universities, not just those that are technically land grant institutions, are in the people-serving business, and taking steps to build family-friendly policy is just one way that universities can serve the people. Second, universities produce the lion's share of research in this country, which positions them as the primary repository of new knowledge that has the potential to inform policymaking (Kellogg Commission, 1999). Finally, universities can play a distinctive role in policy issues, many of which are contentious, because of their reputation for being unbiased and untainted by political motivations (Small & Bogenschneider, 1998).

In an era of devolution of federal authority to states and localities, governors and policymakers have increasingly turned to universities for assistance, but have not received the help or leadership they expected (Bonnen, 1998). Scholars claim to be interested in how their research could influence policy, yet these connections are seldom made.

Individual faculty can choose and often do choose to serve in many of the policy roles identified previously in this chapter. Yet creating a university infrastructure and providing resources to support outreach could serve to intensify faculty involvement and commitment to addressing the problems of contemporary life, including those that can be remedied in part by policy (Todd, Ebata, & Hughes, 1998). Just as universities provide laboratories, classrooms, and personnel to support their research and teaching functions, universities can elevate the status of outreach by providing physical space, financial backing, grant-writing assistance, editing and design services, and grant management support.

A university infrastructure can also prompt other actions that provide incentives for engaging in outreach scholarship. For example, a university that rewards outreach activity in faculty merit and promotion decisions helps create a campus climate that portrays outreach as an expected faculty responsibility, not as an optional activity fulfilled only after meeting the requirements of research and campus teaching. Also, by showcasing faculty whose outreach work is exemplary, a university can provide concrete examples of the many ways in which scholarship can be relevant and also how relevance can be scholarly (for examples from universities across the country, see Lerner & Simon, 1998b).

Clearly, examples of university involvement in family policy could be drawn from several universities across the country, but the three university infrastructures highlighted here were chosen because of their diversity and their focus on child and family policy (see other examples in Lerner & Simon, 1998b). The first example describes a within-university structure that provides the nucleus from which a number of department-crossing, discipline-breaking initiatives have evolved. The second example describes how several universities in a single state joined forces so they could better respond to requests from the community. Finally, the third example is an institute that has brought together scholars from universities in several states to provide peer assistance in developing innovative strategies for connecting research and family policymaking. These three structures vary in form and scope, but in many respects they share a common vision. The ultimate goal of these university initiatives is not solely to develop a new project, but rather to foster a new way of life for universities that culminates in changes in institutional culture and practices (Brabeck et al., 1998).

Case Study: Building Intra-University and University–Community Collaboration (Office of Child Development)

The University of Pittsburgh Office of Child Development (OCD), one of the first interdisciplinary units specializing in university–community collaborations for children and families in a large research university, was born in 1986 in response to two independent planning processes. In the mid-1980s as part of their bicentennial celebration, the University of Pittsburgh convened a meeting of 120 faculty, administrators, policymakers, industrialists, philanthropists, and community leaders to explore how the university and community could work together to improve the Pittsburgh region. At the same time, an interdisciplinary group was formed on campus to consider ways of bringing together faculty who had interests in children and families, but who had little contact with each other and even less contact with community human service providers. Both groups reached a similar recommendation: An office was needed to serve as a point of contact for facilitating interdisciplinary training and research, and for promoting university–community collaborations pertaining to children and families. The result—the OCD—was originally conceived to differ from the more typical research center in that it would not conduct research or provide services, but would primarily facilitate collaborative projects. However, collaborations that were funded wanted the OCD to manage the projects, so the OCD ultimately became both a facilitator and manager of projects (McCall, Groark, Strauss, & Johnson, 1998).

In its first 15 years of operation, the OCD, codirected by McCall and Groark, has been awarded more than $130 million in grants. An additional $40 million has been awarded to other agencies with the OCD's help in planning, implementation or administration, and technical assistance. Seed money provided by the OCD resulted in another $20 million of funding to other faculty and agencies in the region.

Although the OCD does not engage in advocacy, one of its main purposes is to provide objective background information, needs assessments, white papers, and evaluation services of particular relevance to policymakers. For example, the OCD assessed the state's needs for early childhood services; conducted the statewide needs assessment for family support, family preservation, and home visiting services; copublished the *Kids Count* fact book, which provides county-by-county data on the health, education, welfare, and economic status of Pennsylvania's children and families; and operated Starting Points, a nonpartisan project that strove to maintain consistent support for children and families despite transitions in political power.

Among its accomplishments, the OCD codirected 1 of 10 Child Abuse and Neglect Training Grants in the country; operates one of the Early Head Start (EHS) programs involved in the national consortia and conducts the Pittsburgh EHS evaluation and research project; codirected one of the five original Interdisciplinary Child Welfare Training Grants; operated 1 of 16 Drug and Alcohol Prevention Task Forces for Runaway and Homeless Youth; and operated 1 of the 24 original national sites of the Comprehensive Child Development Program. Currently, OCD's projects fall into four programmatic divisions: service demonstrations, planning and evaluation, policy initiatives, and interdisciplinary education, training, and research (see http://www.pitt.edu/~uclid/ocd.htm).

The OCD staff also conducts a core set of activities designed to (a) focus attention on child and family issues, (b) bring university and community partnerships together, and (c) provide an atmosphere for fostering collaborative projects. The OCD publishes a newsletter, writes special reports for policymakers, distributes requests for grant proposals, sponsors workshops, disseminates data on children and families, provides technical assistance, and publishes directories of personnel and services.

Case Study: Building Cross-University Collaboration
(The Florida Inter-University Center for Child,
Family, and Community Studies)

The Florida Inter-University Center for Child, Family, and Community Studies (IUC) may be the first center in the country that brings together several institutions of higher education in a state for the purpose of improving child and family well-being. Discussions began in the spring of 1993, with official approval by the board of regents in 1996. The center is a multidisciplinary team of 35 faculty from five institutions who have banded together to benefit children and families by conducting applied research, designing and delivering educational programs, using research to guide and inform local and state policies, and evaluating the outcomes of policies for children and families. The director is located at the University of Florida, and an associate director is housed at each of the other four universities—Florida A & M University, Florida State University, the University of Miami, and the University of South Florida (see Beaulieu, Mullis, & Mullis, 1998). Each of these institutions provides local affiliates with seed money, and IUC collaborations have also secured grant funding for work on such issues as family violence, workforce preparation, and human capital development from a variety of state, federal, and private sources.

This cross-university, multidisciplinary collaboration permits the IUC to assemble a group of faculty who can quickly respond to emerging local and state needs. For example, following a conference on child and family services in Florida, the cochairs of the Florida House of Representatives Select Committee on Child Abuse and Neglect requested an overview of what is known and not known about the long-term impacts of child abuse. As an outgrowth of these presentations, the leadership of the House Select Committee asked what a study of the long-term effects of child abuse would cost. In an hour-long meeting, a budget for such a study was developed and language was written to incorporate these costs as an amendment to the state budget. One week later, the Florida House and Senate passed the budget, and 2 months later Florida's governor signed the budget into law with funding for the study intact.

During its 1996 legislative session, the House Select Committee also asked the IUC to present testimony on the involvement of noncustodial parents in the lives of their children. As a result, the IUC was asked to help draft legislation to create the Commission on Responsible Fatherhood, which would compile state information on father absence, identify barriers to father involvement, describe successful involvement strategies, and suggest ways that existing state and community resources could support responsible fatherhood. The bill was passed by both the Florida House and Senate in May 1996. The IUC was also the principal contact for a 1996 law that established select county extension offices as the sites for supervised visitation between noncustodial parents and their children. Furthermore, this bill authorized cooperative extension offices to design and deliver parenting education to the parents involved in supervised visitation.

Ongoing efforts of the IUC include preparing and disseminating newsletters, policy briefs, and research updates; developing and managing a statewide database; developing educational resources; creating a clearinghouse of child and family resources; and sponsoring an annual statewide conference on high-profile child and family issues.

Case Study: Building Cross-State Collaborations (Policy Institute for Family Impact Seminars)

Because ideas are powerful political tools and because research produces policy-relevant ideas, the Policy Institute for Family Impact Seminars (PINFIS) aims to connect research and state policymaking and promote a family perspective in research, policy, and practice. In 1999, the Institute assumed the mission of the Family Impact Seminar, which was founded in 1976 to build capacity for family-focused policymaking. The Institute develops and disseminates resources to researchers, policymakers, and practitioners. To assist researchers and policy scholars, the Institute is building a national network to facilitate cross-state dialogue and resource exchange on strategies for bringing research to bear on policymaking. To assist policymakers, the Institute disseminates policy reports that provide a family impact perspective on a wide variety of topics. To assist those who implement policies and programs, the Institute has available a number of family impact assessment tools for examining how responsive policies, programs, and institutions are to family well-being. Further information on the Institute is available from its Web site at http://www.familyimpactseminars.org.

One of the Institute's first initiatives has been to provide technical assistance to professionals interested in establishing seminars in their own states. Family Impact Seminars are a series of seminars, briefing reports, and follow-up activities for state policymakers such as state legislators, legislative aides, legislative service agency personnel, governor's office staff, state agency representatives, university faculty, and family professionals. Based on a peer mentoring model, the network brings together professionals from the 21 states that are currently planning or conducting seminars: Alabama, Arizona, California, the District of Columbia, Georgia, Illinois, Indiana, Kentucky, Maryland, Michigan, Mississippi, Nebraska, New Hampshire, New Mexico, North Carolina, Ohio, Oklahoma, Oregon, Pennsylvania, Wisconsin, and Wyoming. These professionals, based in universities or the support bureaus of state legislatures, share strategies for connecting research and policymaking with an eye toward disentangling those strategies that have cross-state validity from those that are more state-specific.

Although still preliminary, the results of the initial evaluations of the first seven sites are promising. The District of Columbia has conducted 34 seminars; following one seminar, a participant organized a seminar on food security that is still active (see Mayer & Hutchins, 1998). Since its inception in 1994, California has held more than 20 seminars, each attended by between 125 and 200 participants. The seminars and policy discussions have had important impacts on state policy innovation. For example, the seminar series on teenage pregnancy prevention resulted in increased funding and a new state program within the Department of Health Services, and the seminar on fathering led to state legislation on strategies for supporting absent fathers' participation in their children's lives.

In Wisconsin, 23 seminars have been held since 1993, attracting 1,666 participants, including 99 different state legislators and representatives of 156 legislative offices. In follow-up phone interviews, legislators report using seminar information to evaluate pending legislation (81%), share with colleagues (66%), identify contacts for further information (52%), incorporate into speeches or presentations (48%), and develop new legislation (22%). Following two seminars on prescription drugs, several features of other states' prescription drug programs discussed at the Seminar were incorporated into Wisconsin's newly enacted law. Because of their participation in the seminars, 86% of state legislators who attended a child-care seminar said that they were "quite a bit" more likely to consider how legislation they are developing might affect families, and 71% said they were "quite a bit" more likely to see the practical value of research. (See chap. 14 for a full discussion of impacts.)

Michigan has held 12 seminars on topics such as children's health insurance, children of incarcerated parents, Medicaid, prostituted teens, and welfare reform. Using retrospective pretest methodology, participants at the child-care seminar reported knowing significantly more about early intervention programs, child care, and after-school care after the seminar than before (each paired sample t test significant at $p < .05$). A program featured at a seminar was subsequently mentioned in the governor's state of the state address. In Indiana, eight seminars have been sponsored by a consortium of universities and family-serving organizations. On a scale of 1 (*poor*) to 5 (*excellent*), the first Indiana seminar received an overall rating of 4.2 and an objectivity rating of 4.4. One seminar attracted 20 legislators, and one legislator was so impressed with the seminar that she volunteered to serve on the advisory committee. Following the seminar, the director was invited to address 20 legislators at a Women's Leadership Training. Oregon's first seminar, cosponsored by the House Revenue Committee, was attended by 70 participants. Following the seminar, the legislature passed and the governor signed a refundable child-care tax credit, one of the policy options raised at the seminar.

SUMMARY

This chapter was written with the reluctant participant in family policy uppermost in mind. Some of my colleagues and many of the students in my required family policy class fit this description. Students often major in family studies and faculty often work in a family studies department because they seek a meaningful profession that can benefit individuals and families. Yet the prototypic reluctant participant in family policy, whether student or colleague, often does not know what family policy is, how it can benefit families, which roles family professionals can play, and what career options exist.

In this chapter, I propose a theoretical framework that identifies nine roles that professionals can play in the policy arena: research for family policy formulation, family policy implementation, family policy evaluation, family research integration, family research dissemination, family impact analysis, teaching family policy, citizen engagement in family policymaking, and university involvement in family policy scholarship. This theoretical framework is designed to illustrate the possibilities for getting involved in building family policy and the potential this involvement holds forth for families. My intention with these case studies was to spark interest in doing family policy by giving concrete examples of several exciting ways in which policy initiatives shape the conditions in which families operate and, in so doing, shape family life as surely as our other professional endeavors.

These case studies were also intended to illustrate that building family-friendly policies is a complex task that demands professionals with diverse training, skills, and expertise. Building family policies requires professionals working in a number of settings to discover new knowledge, assist in policy implementation, evaluate policies and programs, integrate findings across studies, disseminate research to policymakers, analyze policies and programs for their impact on family well-being, inspire students of family policy, and engage citizens and academics in the policymaking process (Boyer, 1990). Professionals involved in the policy arena can work in the nation's capital or in statehouses, courthouses, city halls, or boardrooms across the country. They can be found in research laboratories, classrooms, and community centers. Policy work requires the skills of researchers, translators, evaluators, teachers, group facilitators, analysts, writers, organizers, promoters, and coalition builders.

Yet professionals who serve primarily in one role or setting often do not understand or value the work performed by those serving in other capacities or circumstances. For example, professionals in applied roles are often quick to criticize researchers for not asking policy-relevant and family-sensitive questions, just as researchers are quick to criticize practitioners for simplifying or sensationalizing the findings of their studies and for failing to evaluate their programs. Instead of pointing fingers, we should welcome the multiple approaches and diverse skills of those in research and applied positions because they are essential for a complex, interactive, multiply determined undertaking like building family-friendly policy. Without good research, there is little worth applying (Wittrock, 1993). Without good application, research gathers dust on the shelf with little chance that it will be used in ways that strengthen families and better the human condition. Thus, building family-friendly policies requires a wide repertoire of professional roles exercised across multiple fronts as policy is being developed, enacted, implemented, and evaluated.

Students often leave my class less reluctant to get involved, but keenly aware that doing family policy is, at this stage in the development of the field, often an act of faith. As is evident to the astute reader, few policy efforts have been evaluated using the rigorous methods of social science, and little hard evidence exists that the time and effort invested in these roles pay off. The professionals who serve in these roles believe in what they do and are confident that their efforts are benefitting families or will benefit them in the future. In the words of Smith (1954):

> To believe in something not yet proved and to underwrite it with our lives: it is the only way we can leave the future open. Man, surrounded by facts, permitting himself no surmise, no intuitive flash, no great hypothesis, no risk is in a locked cell. Ignorance cannot seal the mind and imagination more surely. (p. 256)

The case studies in this chapter describe professionals who have underwritten with their lives their belief that building family-friendly policies is deserving of their dedication because of its potential to shape family life. This dedication conveys an important message about the meaning of work that bears mentioning here. At the heart of the work of the true professional is the root word *profession,* which has historically been viewed as a calling, but more recently has been replaced by the concept of a job or career. According to Bellah and his colleagues (1985/1996), a job or career provides a means to our own advancement or that of our employer, whereas a calling is work that has meaning in and of itself outside the profit or advancement that it brings. More than just the mastery of technical skills, a calling contributes to the public good and, in so doing, contributes to a sense of self and a moral purpose in life. In a job or career, one's sense of self tends to be separate from the work one does, with commitment being contingent on the benefits one gets in return. In contrast, one's sense of self can be defined by a calling in which one derives meaning and purpose from work that responds to the needs of others or connects workers to those who reap the benefits of their labor.

This chapter would not be complete, however, without a couple caveats to the reader. In some respects, this chapter may be an underestimation of the work that professionals do to build family policy, whereas in other respects it may be an overestimation. This chapter builds on previous work in proposing a theoretical framework for articulating the roles that professionals can play in building family policy (Nye & McDonald, 1979). Clearly, this brief exposé is not a definitive statement of the broad array of roles that professionals play, and it obviously omits many fine examples of excellent work being done in family policy. Thus, this chapter may unintentionally serve to underestimate the scope, complexity, and impact of family policy efforts currently underway.

At the same time, however, the number of roles identified and the many case studies described may inadvertently exaggerate the amount of effort being put forth. What is not readily apparent is that many of these efforts occur in isolated pockets around the country, and others are one-shot efforts that have been discontinued due to lack of funding or the loss of a charismatic leader. In summary, the effort being expended to build family-friendly policy is dwarfed by the amount of need and the importance of the work.

The purpose of this chapter has been a fledgling attempt to describe what family professionals can do to build family policy. The next chapter addresses how these roles can be operationalized using two fundamentally different theoretical approaches: advocacy and education. Whether the role is teaching, disseminating research, building citizen coalitions, or working with the media, the nature of the work and the outcomes may be qualitatively different depending on which approach professionals employ.

13

Which Approach Is Best for Getting Involved in Family Policy: Advocacy or Education?

If the methods of social science were utilized, we could develop more sci-entific lawmaking. Legislatures could operate like laboratories with laws enacted as a "series of exhaustive experiments."
—Lester Ward (1893, cited in Smith, 1991, p. 32)

The place of [experts] was "advisors to the leaders" . . . and politicians were free to use or reject that advice as they saw fit. "They were leaders" . . . [and] "I was an intellectual."
—John Commons (1934, cited in Smith, 1991, p. 36)

Good ideas are powerful political tools (Smith, 1991). For more than 100 years, experts have tried to figure out ways to bring good ideas to bear on policymaking. In 1893, Lester Ward, a self-taught man who worked his way up to the chief paleontologist in the U.S. Geological Survey, envisioned leg-islatures operating like laboratories, with scientists directly and deliber-ately influencing lawmaking. John Commons, a central figure in Wisconsin policymaking in the early 1900s, concurred that science could benefit policymaking. Unlike Ward, however, Commons believed that the approach of experts should be much less visible and more educational. In his 30 years teaching economics and working primarily on state legislation in Wiscon-sin, he perceived the intellectual as a behind-the-scenes advisor to political leaders who were free to accept or reject his expert advice (Smith, 1991).

Historically, Americans have been intrigued by how expertise might be used to improve the way we govern ourselves, but little consensus has been reached on which approaches are best for connecting expertise and policymaking (Smith, 1991). Should experts become advocates or educators? This age-old question remains compelling and demands constant revisiting and reflection. Whether experts are conducting program evaluations, organizing seminars, preparing press releases, teaching classes, testifying at hearings, or writing for policymakers, these policy efforts can be approached from either an advocacy or educational perspective.

Chapter 12 identified a number of roles that family professionals can play in the policy arena. In this chapter, I argue that these roles can be operationalized quite differently depending on whether a professional acts as an advocate or educator. For example, program evaluation can be a pursuit of knowledge for understanding—the impartial search for truth regardless of what the data show. Conversely, program evaluation can be a pursuit of knowledge for advocacy—the intent to enact a particular policy or program by using data to demonstrate its success rather than question its impact (Shonkoff, 2004). Instructors can approach college teaching as advocates by providing course material primarily from one preferred political perspective. Or instructors can approach the course as an educator and incorporate materials from across the political spectrum, thereby forcing students to think critically and reach their own conclusions. Thus, the focus of this chapter is not *what* to do in the policy arena, but rather *how* to do it.

Any meaningful reflection on the best approach for connecting expertise and policymaking must begin with clear definitions of family policy advocacy and family policy alternatives education. To distinguish these approaches from each other, I have used real-life examples to illustrate how the professional can become involved in policymaking as an advocate or educator. The chapter concludes by helping the family professional sort through which approach might be most appropriate, taking into account who the effort will benefit, which issue is being targeted, what kind of job the professional holds, and how consistent the approach is with the professional's personal skills, knowledge, and communication style.

WHAT IS FAMILY POLICY ADVOCACY?

Because the term *advocacy* is often loosely used in contradictory ways, it can muddy discussion if not clearly defined. For my purposes, *family policy advocacy* means to campaign for an underrepresented group or a particular policy alternative that may potentially enhance family well-being. The advocate examines options in light of his or her own value system, using a personal interpretation of the scientific evidence with the aim of promoting a single policy option that he or she deems most desirable for families (Barrows, 1994; Bogenschneider, 1995; Nye & McDonald, 1979). Put simply, the intent of the advocate is to persuade. In the apt words of a think tank that uses an advocacy approach, "the aim is self-consciously to shape and influence the debate in line with a preconceived set of ideas or principles rather than simply to pursue research questions in whatever direction they may lead" (Smith, 1991, p. 206).

Advocacy is guided by a number of ideas and assumptions about the role of values in the political process, the way the democratic system works, and the potential of timely citizen action to shape political decisions. For example, when the scientific evidence is incomplete, advocates do not shy away from drawing conclusions about what the social problem is or making value judgments about which policy alternative is most desirable. Advocates then commit their time and effort to lobbying for this single policy alternative, because they believe that the political process responds to pressure from those interested in or affected by the issue. Because family policy advocates believe there is a direct benefit to the families they represent, they are typically driven by a sense of urgency that motivates them to respond strategically and promptly to the ebb and flow of the political process.

For professionals who have a particular policy option they want to enact into law, advocacy is the approach most likely to achieve this goal. The following policy initiative is clearly advocacy, because like-minded individuals and groups shepherded through the political process a specific policy option that they deemed best for families.

Advocacy in Action: The Special Morning Milk Amendment

Congress debated whether poor schoolchildren who received a free or subsidized carton of milk at the midmorning milk break and again at lunch were double-dipping into the public purse. In 1983, Congress responded by eliminating federal support for the morning milk break—a federal program administered by schools to provide milk for schoolchildren. Through this program, children who could afford it purchased a carton of milk, and poor children received free or reduced-price milk. The consequence of Congress's cut was that the average daily milk consumption of Wisconsin schoolchildren through this program dropped by 80%, from 390,000 half-pints in 1981 to only 71,254 in 1985. Parents did not know about it. Farmers did not rally. Children are typically least able to speak up for themselves. As a result, the federal morning milk program was phased out despite a surplus of milk in the state at the time. Somehow it did not seem right to eliminate free milk for poor children, especially in Wisconsin, which prides itself on being the nation's dairy state. Advocacy efforts often start when enough people believe that there should be a law or something ought to be done to make things right.

Because I was an unemployed graduate student during this time, paying my own way through school, I was free to proceed on this issue without the constraints that employment often brings. I signed up to work on the project as an internship, which meant that I paid for course credit but was not compensated. I was supervised by the director of the Children's Audit Project, Pat Mapp, who had previously worked with a Democratic and Republican state legislator on the Special Milk Amendment, legislation to reintroduce the school milk program in Wisconsin with state funding.

My first assignment was to gather background information on the nutritional status of children, which seemed a straightforward question, but proved elusive. After convincing my instructor in a social policy course that this analysis would be an appropriate final paper, I produced a 58-page background paper on the bill that overviewed the nutritional status of children, the nutrients available in milk, the impact of hunger on learning, the fit of the special milk program with other child-feeding programs, and several policy options for improving children's nutritional status. Not surprisingly, the paper concluded that the Special Milk Amendment was the most desirable policy option if targeted toward those at the greatest nutritional risk: low-income children. The Special Milk Amendment, I argued, was cost-effective, simple to administer, and consistent with prevailing public sentiment that parents should assume primary responsibility for feeding their children. My social policy professor thought this position was supported well enough to assign the paper a good grade, but questioned whether the school breakfast program might actually be a better policy option for improving children's nutritional status.

Undaunted by my professor's lukewarm response, Pat Mapp and I met with the Democratic and Republican legislators who were interested in sponsoring the Special Milk Amendment. Despite the conclusion of my research paper that the special milk proposal should be targeted toward low-income children, one of the state legislators was adamantly opposed to programs for only poor children. With no further debate, the initial proposal was drafted for all schoolchildren in Wisconsin with a $3 million price tag. One of the legislative aides condensed my 58-page paper into a 2-page fact sheet that intentionally omitted the information on the elevated nutritional risk among poor children.

My next responsibility was to pull together a statewide coalition of endorsements. Eventually 22 organizations signed on to support the bill, including several agricultural organizations, the Hunger Task Force of Wisconsin, the Wisconsin Nutrition Project, the Children's Trust Fund, the Wisconsin Education Association, the Wisconsin Association of School Boards, the Wisconsin School District Administrators, and the Wisconsin Extension Homemaker Council.

Because we did not get started until April, it was too late to introduce new legislation, so we lobbied to attach our proposal as an amendment to the state budget. After the issue was referred to the Democratic Assembly

Education Committee, we targeted a phone campaign on the four members of this committee, lobbying them to include the Special Milk Amendment in their package of recommendations to the Democratic Assembly Caucus. Convincing this committee to incorporate the proposal into its budget recommendations would greatly enhance the chances for passage. After losing this vote, we expanded our efforts to the entire Democratic Assembly. A major setback occurred the morning of the Assembly Caucus vote, when our Democratic sponsor changed his mind about introducing the legislation. He actually traded away his sponsorship of the Special Milk Amendment to garner political support for another pet project. With some 11th-hour maneuvering by Pat Mapp, the Speaker of the Assembly introduced the legislation with an inspiring "Let's do it for cows, let's do it for kids" speech. The Caucus passed a scaled-down $820,000 version that targeted free or subsidized milk to poor children, which ironically was the initial recommendation of my policy analysis.

Remarkably, the Democratic Assembly passed the amendment 3 months after we had opened the file on the issue and a mere 6 weeks after we had solicited organizational endorsements. It typically takes 5 years to get a new bill passed in Wisconsin, but we were able to expedite the usual time frame for a couple reasons. First, the process was shortened because Pat Mapp and the two legislative sponsors had engaged in some groundwork on the issue during the previous legislative session. We were also able to move more quickly because the organizations that joined the coalition brought to the table their legislative infrastructure—lobbyists, phone banks, and political connections.

When the budget was passed by both houses of the Democratic-controlled legislature, we felt confident that the Special Milk Amendment would soon be signed into law by the Republican governor. To our surprise, we heard rumors from reliable sources close to the governor that he planned to veto the amendment. I immediately called all 22 organizations, many of which had phone banks, and asked them to contact the governor in support of the Special Milk Amendment. Interestingly, some of the organizations that had been the most helpful with the Democratic Assembly forewarned me that they had little influence with a Republican governor. The Governor eventually signed the budget bill, including the $820,000 Special Milk Amendment, which was heralded as one of the only new spending initiatives in the 1988–1989 biennial budget.

The Defining Characteristics of an Advocacy Effort

This policy effort clearly falls into the advocacy camp. We were driven by an urgent belief that eliminating milk for poor kids was not right and by our fear that the interests of children and families would not be adequately represented. Despite inconclusive scientific evidence, we endorsed a single policy option that we concluded was most desirable and took steps to persuade policymakers to see our point of view. We knew that child and family advocates in the state were less powerful, low budget, sparsely staffed, and loosely organized, so we deliberately teamed up with the powerful, organized, skilled advocates who had the infrastructure and connections that successful advocacy requires. Then we meticulously tracked the bill through the entire legislative process and solicited support from those who could respond on short notice at critical junctures.

WHAT IS FAMILY POLICY ALTERNATIVES EDUCATION?

In contrast to advocacy, the family policy alternatives education approach does not lobby for a single policy, but attempts to inform policy discourse by clarifying the potential consequences of several policy alternatives. Whereas the aim of the family policy advocate is to persuade, the aim of the family policy alternatives educator is to educate by presenting research findings objectively without relaying personal preferences. The value judgments and ultimate decisions are entrusted to the people and to a number of policymakers elected to make these decisions rather than to a single person such as Plato's philosopher king or, in this case, the expert (Barrows, 1984, 1994). This approach dates back to Thomas Jefferson's view of the role of education in a democracy and underlies the successful operation of long-standing Congressional support bureaus such as the Congressional Budget Office, the Congressional Research Service, the General Accounting Office (Bimber, 1996), and similar units in many state governments.

This approach rests on a pluralistic view of society, a trust in the democratic process, a belief in enlightened self-interest, and a recognition of the limitations of social science knowledge (Barrows, 1994). Alternatives education is based on the premise of a pluralistic society, in which a variety of interests exist that are represented by policymakers with a range of political and value perspectives. Alternatives education requires the belief that, when conflicts arise among these diverse interests, the democratic process will produce better policies more often than will administrative fiat or decrees by a single individual. The educator must trust the democratic process enough to give up control (which, of course, the educator never has anyway) and forego attempts to influence the outcome in ways that are consistent with the educator's personal knowledge and values. The educator believes in the principle of enlightened self-interest—that policymakers and citizens, when given good information, will make the right decisions most of the time.

The educational approach may be more responsive to the needs of policymakers. According to a psychologist elected to Congress, what policymakers need is not more information, but more objective and valid information (Strickland, 1996) from reliable, unbiased sources. Proponents of the educational approach value the contributions of social science knowledge, yet also acknowledge its limitations in identifying social problems or differentiating among policy alternatives. For example, family policy alternatives educators criticize use of the term *social problem* because there are few social problems that affect everyone equally. Rather, social problems are better characterized as social conflicts between those who benefit from a social condition and those who do not (Barrows, 1994; Rule, 1978), or those who face greater or lesser risk from a social condition. For example, in the case of legislating caps on family size for welfare recipients, what welfare recipients perceive as a problem may be diametrically opposed to the perceptions of citizens who belong to taxpayer alliances. Even among welfare recipients, the views of long-term recipients may diverge dramatically from those who receive benefits for a short time. Thus, defining a social problem often involves ranking the needs and interests of one group in society as more important than another, which is not susceptible to proof through empirical inquiry (Rule, 1978). The role of the educator is often to describe how the perceptions of social problems may depend on the vantage point of different interest groups.

Even when interest groups agree on the problem, however, reasonable people can disagree on an appropriate course of action (Barrows, 1994; Rule, 1978). Barrows (1994) contended that even when everyone agrees on the known facts, reasonable people might disagree on the interpretation of the facts; even in situations where the facts lead to only one interpretation, different value orientations may lead to different policy recommendations. For example, in my research in one Wisconsin community, 54% of 12th graders reported drinking alcohol at least once a month. This finding alarms some citizens, who view this level of alcohol use as a serious social problem, whereas others contend it is a predictable manifestation of normal adolescent limit testing. Obviously, science alone cannot identify whether a particular set of circumstances such as the level of adolescent alcohol use constitutes a social problem.

Even if everyone agreed that underage drinking by a majority of high school seniors is a social problem, citizens often disagree about how best to respond. Some citizens claim that teen drinking is a matter that should be handled in the privacy of the family, whereas others argue for comprehensive community responses that stiffen underage drinking laws and restrict alcohol availability. In the words of Barrows (1994),

> Scientific knowledge, the wisdom of the university, cannot be used to determine the 'correct' policy choice for society because science cannot supply the value judgments that rank the interests of one group as more important than the interests of another (p. 3)

Thus, instead of assuming that the expert has indisputable facts, correct interpretations, and ideal values, the alternatives education approach contends that conflicts among competing interests are best worked out through political negotiation and compromise (Barrows, 1994). The educator feeds into political decision making by objectively supplying expert knowledge on the issue and building understanding of different points of view.

The most frequent criticisms of the educational approach revolve around objectivity and political neutrality. Is objective, bias-free policy education ever possible? Of course not, according to Barrows (1994). If complete objectivity can never be achieved, critics question the legitimacy of even striving to be objective, which policy educators warn is like throwing out the baby with the bath water. Policy educators do not reject the ideal of objectivity, as is fashionable in some intellectual circles, just as we would not reject the ideal of justice because it cannot be perfectly attained (Glenn, 1993).

If education is as objective and unbiased as possible, does that mean it is a politically neutral act? No policy effort is ever politically neutral (Barrows, 1994). Inevitably, there is bias in the issues we choose to work on because we are attracted to issues that we think are important. Moreover, providing information on an issue, no matter how objectively, favors some groups over others. For example, even perfectly objective information on a tax referendum favors passage, because people who are informed are more apt to vote "yes" than people who are uninformed. Policy education is inevitably more advantageous to individuals and groups who are less informed than to those who are more knowledgeable. In some situations, providing objective education on an issue builds understanding of different points of view, which can foster compromise and consensus. Thus, policy educators strive for objectivity, fully recognizing that complete objectivity is never possible and that, even if it were, education is not a politically neutral act.

Alternatives Education in Action: The Adams County School Breakfast Program

The issue of the Adams County School Breakfast Program arose, as most public issues do, when people said something should be done (Flinchbaugh, 1988). In one of the poorest counties in Wisconsin, teachers and staff noticed that children were coming to school hungry. They approached the county extension family living educator and together the group decided to conduct a survey to gather hard data on the extensiveness of the problem. The data substantiated their observations: 45% of all children under the age of 13 went to school without breakfast.

An interested group of teachers, staff, parents, and the extension family living educator in Adams County, Edie Felts-Podoll, decided to alert the school board to this problem. Although the group favored a school breakfast program, they decided that the most effective way to approach and solicit the school board's involvement on the issue was through the alternatives education model. In keeping with the tenets of the educational approach, they developed seven different policy alternatives for addressing the problem of hungry schoolchildren: (a) provide parent education classes in nutrition, (b) provide a school breakfast program subsidized by the U.S. Department of Agriculture (USDA), (c) locally subsidize low-income families so they can afford to serve breakfast to their children, (d) delay bus schedules and school day starting times so families have more time to serve breakfast, (e) have families provide a "sack breakfast" for children to eat on arrival at school or during midmorning break, (f) send children who wish to eat breakfast to a local restaurant, or (g) do nothing. Doing nothing is an unattractive option to most activists, but is always an alternative that the educator should place on the table. For each of these alternatives, the group developed a list of potential consequences (see Table 13.1). For example, the consequences for establishing the USDA-subsidized school breakfast program were as follows: (a) all children will have the opportunity to eat breakfast at school; (b) taxes may rise; and (c) the school system may have to adjust bus schedules, cooking, and maintenance staff to accommodate such a program.

In response to the groups' presentation, the school board agreed that children coming to school without breakfast was a problem that warranted a response. After considering the alternatives raised, the school board voted to provide nutrition classes for parents, which were subsequently taught by the teachers and the county extension educator. The issue did not come to an end, however, following the completion of the policy education effort. Six years later, the school superintendent called and asked the county extension educator if she still had the data about children coming to school hungry. She was asked to present the data to the school board that evening, at which time they passed a school breakfast program. Ironically, the school breakfast program had been the policy option that the original group of teachers, staff, and parents had hoped the school board would adopt 6 years earlier.

The Defining Characteristics of an Educational Effort

This effort was clearly an educational approach. Instead of relying on political pressure, the group provided a range of options to the school board as objectively as possible and trusted the decision to the democratic process. Scientific knowledge was able to inform the debate by specifying the number of schoolchildren who skipped breakfast and the importance of good nutrition. Scientific knowledge, however, was not complete enough to indi-

TABLE 13.1

The Adams County School Breakfast Program

Problem: Forty-five percent of all Adams County children under the age of 13 go to school without breakfast.

Alternatives:

A. Provide parent education classes in nutrition.

Consequences: 1. Parents in greatest need may not be reached.
2. Parents may increase their nutrition knowledge and provide better meals for their family.
3. Education concept may appeal to the parent group who will promote it with other parents and develop into a support network.
4. Parents may become more conscious of need and consequently feed their children breakfast.

B. Provide a USDA-subsidized school breakfast program.

Consequences: 1. All children will have the opportunity to eat breakfast at school.
2. Taxes may rise.
3. School system may have to adjust bus schedules, cooking, and maintenance staff to accommodate such a program.

C. Locally subsidize low-income families so they can afford to serve breakfast to their children.

Consequences: 1. Some needy families may not accept the stipend because of "pride."
2. Some families may now be able to purchase food for breakfast.
3. Local tax base may rise.
4. Subsidies may not encourage parents to feed their children if the reason is not economic.

D. Delay bus schedules and school day starting times so families have more time to serve breakfast.

Consequences: 1. Children will have more time in the morning to eat breakfast if they desire.
2. Parents will have more opportunity to interact and encourage breakfast.
3. School day will end later in the afternoon and conflict with extracurricular activities.

E. Have families provide a "sack breakfast" to eat on arrival at school or during mid-morning break.

Consequences: 1. Sack breakfast may not be provided if food is not available to child.
2. Sack breakfast may not be provided if parent and/or child lacks skills to prepare meal.
3. Sack breakfast will provide breakfast to children who prefer not to eat immediately upon rising.
4. Before-school or mid-morning breaks would have to be incorporated in the school schedule.

F. Send children who wish to eat breakfast to local restaurant.

Consequences: 1. Only children with money can afford to eat out.
2. Local restaurants may compete for business.

G. Do nothing about the problem:

Consequences: 1. Some children (45%) will continue to come to school hungry.
2. Some children may have learning deficits due to lack of breakfast (Iowa breakfast studies).
3. Problem will not be brought to the attention of those who make public policy.
4. Conflict will be avoided.

Note. Reprinted from Edie Felts-Podoll, unpublished fact sheet.

cate a single best policy response, nor could it provide the value judgments that policy decisions often entail. Using the alternatives education approach avoided confrontation and contributed to a positive interchange with the policymakers, which resulted in a request for further information several years later.

HOW DISTINCT ARE THE ADVOCACY AND ALTERNATIVES EDUCATION APPROACHES?

Advocacy and alternatives education are clearly different approaches, but they are not totally distinct from each other. Because the policy alternatives educator can never be totally objective and because the most effective advocates often educate policymakers on the downside of their position, advocacy and education overlap to some extent. For example, the premise of this book and the aim of the Family Impact Seminar is to promote a family perspective in policy debate. Is promoting a family perspective in policymaking an educational approach, or is it more akin to advocacy? It is both. It is advocacy in the sense that it strives to promote an underrepresented perspective—that of families. Yet it could be implemented with either an advocacy or educational approach. Promoting a family perspective on an issue could be advocacy if only family solutions to social problems are presented, and individual or community solutions are excluded. Promoting a family perspective in policymaking is educational if the family solutions are raised, not as the only or best alternatives, but as one of many competing responses. The educator would promote a family perspective by raising questions, not giving answers about whether families should be involved in the solution.

Although there may be some overlap between advocacy and alternatives education, the professional must still recognize the distinctions and understand the implications when making decisions about which approach to use in policy efforts. The county extension educator in a small rural county, for example, advocated for the establishment of a child-care center in that county. This advocacy effort made it literally impossible for her to later serve as an educator on this issue. No matter how objective her presentation was of alternatives for addressing the local child-care shortage, the community knew that she supported child-care centers. Once you cross the line from education to advocacy, policymakers remember your advocacy stance and view all further information from you as potentially tainted and biased. Therefore, using both approaches is difficult because it requires you to inform policymakers as to whether you are wearing the hat of an advocate or educator. The danger, of course, is that you would be accused of disguising an advocacy effort under the mantle of education, which would destroy your credibility. Credibility as an educator requires a reputation of being objective and unbiased, which allows you to be effective with policy-makers of all political persuasions.

WHAT ARE THE POTENTIAL CONSEQUENCES OF THE ADVOCACY APPROACH?

I have detailed here some of the potential consequences of the advocacy approach. These consequences are not classified as pros and cons or positives and negatives, because advantages to one person or group may be disadvantages to another.

- Because the advocacy approach is widely used and well understood, individuals or organizations need little explanation about its purpose and often are familiar with its potential for achieving political ends.
- Advocacy has been called a *feel-good* activity because of the exhilaration a person feels when efforts are rewarded by the passage of a law or rule that will often benefit many families. According to E. Felts-Podoll (personal communication, August 2000), working as an advocate can become almost seductive. The constituents for whom you are working come to love you for forwarding their perspective into the political arena. In contrast, the educational role can engender hostility from all sides because you bring to the table alternatives that some groups wish were not part of the discussion.
- Because advocacy has a clear, unambiguous goal, it is easy to track the effectiveness of the effort and evaluate its outcome. For example, a bill's progress can be monitored to determine whether it gets forwarded out of committee, passed by both houses, and signed into law.
- Advocacy may be inappropriate for researchers because of their training in the scientific method. Advocacy often entails making a case on one side of an issue, whereas the scientific method ideally embodies an even-handed consideration of facts on all sides of an issue and, in particular, a willingness to disprove one's own hypothesis or personal position.
- When social scientists take advocacy positions, the objectivity of research may be called into question. The mystique of the scientist is often the ability to remain dispassionate and objective in the midst of a political fray. If scientists become involved in advocacy, it may reinforce stereotypes that researchers "cook" their numbers to validate their personal views or the political predilections of those who support their research.
- Taking sides on an issue, as advocates do, can undermine future credibility with the opposing parties. Each stance may alienate more individuals or groups, which over time could limit a person's ability to form the political

alliances on which successful policy work depends (Barrows, 1994). A blatant example occurred when a national professional association endorsed a
political candidate. When that candidate was defeated, the person who was
elected to the office was unwilling to work with the organization.

• If professional associations adopt an advocacy agenda, this could
change the nature of the organization and preclude members from networking and debating diverse points of view. For example, the board of one national professional association took some specific stands on controversial issues that resulted in infighting among the conservatives and liberals in the
organization, which of course interfered with constructive dialogue on issues. If an organization's board has the authority to decide what political
stands the organization takes, members with strong political views may end
up jockeying for board positions. Organizations that take stances on issues
may also curtail membership among policy educators, who may be skeptical
of joining an organization that takes political positions for fear such connections could undermine their reputation for being objective and unbiased.

• To assess whether advocacy will pay off requires a realistic appraisal of
whether an individual or organization has the political muscle, will, and infrastructure to deliver votes in the consistent way that politicians value (Barrows, 1994).

WHAT ARE THE POTENTIAL CONSEQUENCES
OF THE EDUCATION APPROACH?

Individuals or organizations considering the advocacy and education approaches to getting involved in the policy arena must weigh the consequences of advocacy with the consequences of the alternatives education
approach, which are detailed here. As in the previous section, the consequences are not classified as pro and con or as benefits and drawbacks.

• Because the alternatives education approach is less common than advocacy, its uniqueness may bring a fresh perspective to policymaking. According to Smith (1991), many think tanks and other actors in the policy community have promoted a specific agenda, which has polarized debate rather
than fostering discussion and consensus building. Given current conditions,
the most valuable contribution to political dialogue may not be generating
novel new policy options, but rather providing a forum for engaging in dialogue on existing policy options outside the typically contentious political
environment (Smith, 1991).

• Because advocacy efforts can alienate the opposing parties, the objective nonpartisan educational approach may be more desirable for policy ef-

forts that aim to (a) work with policymakers from a range of values and political perspectives, (b) build bridges across a diverse spectrum of viewpoints, and (c) maintain effectiveness over time regardless of which policymaker is in office and which political party is in control (Bimber, 1996).

• Educators face a more difficult challenge in evaluating the success of their efforts than do advocates. Advocates promote a specific policy or legislative initiative and track its progress through the legislative process, whereas educators provide research-based information that is not expected to have large singular impacts on a multiply determined process like policymaking. In essence, the education approach strives to document "knowledge creep," whereby research slowly and continuously seeps into policymaking in ways that are difficult to trace (Weiss, 1990).

• Because it is less common than advocacy, policy education is more difficult to explain to policy novices who are less likely to be familiar with concrete examples of its potential for influencing policy debate (see examples in chap. 14).

• Policy education may be less effective than advocacy for relatively powerless groups whose views may be obscure or unknown to the educator. Representative democracy works only if all alternatives are on the table, so each can receive a fair hearing (Barrows, 1994; Laue & Cormick, 1978).

• The policy education approach may be more difficult to execute than advocacy because the educator must be conversant on a broad range of policy alternatives. Moreover, educators must be able to perform the arduous task of fairly and objectively describing policy options that may contradict their personal beliefs. Those educators who hold strong ideological views can find it difficult to turn over control of the issue to the democratic process. Also, educators must resist the temptation of using knowledge to influence the decision in ways they personally deem most desirable.

WHICH APPROACH SHOULD YOU USE TO GET INVOLVED IN POLICYMAKING?

Family professionals involved in policy issues often assume different roles, such as consultant to a coalition of citizens interested in a specific issue, or spokesperson for a specific interest group. The family professional can operate in these capacities from the stance of either an advocate or educator. For example, the advocate would work only with coalitions with like-minded views and would offer to policymakers only scientific evidence consistent with the coalition's perspectives. In contrast, the alternatives educator would consciously strive to work with groups with different political perspectives and would offer policymakers evidence on all sides of an issue. When representing the positions of an interest group, the advocate would present only data that portray this group in a favorable light, whereas the alternatives educator would also provide evidence that might depict this group less favorably.

Which approach is best? In some of their pioneering work on policy roles for professionals, Nye and McDonald (1979) argued that advocacy is never an appropriate role for the researcher or, by implication, for any professional who claims to be objective. In contrast to this view, however, I contend that there is not a magic bullet—a single optimal approach for a professional's involvement in policymaking. The most desirable approach may vary by the intended beneficiaries, the issue, the professional's job context, and his or her personal communication style. For some professionals, advocacy may be the best approach for reaching policy goals, whereas for others, alternatives education may be more suitable.

Appropriate Advocacy Efforts by Professionals

Despite the admonitions of Nye and McDonald (1979), advocacy may be an appropriate professional role when it contributes to the ability of relatively powerless groups to be represented in the decision-making process. The democratic process is enhanced when professionals take steps to ensure a proportional voice to the underrepresented (Barrows, 1994; Laue & Cormick, 1978). For some issues, scientific evidence falls overwhelmingly on one side of an issue (Barrows, 1994), or the policy debate uncovers those occasional win–win situations when all interest groups would be better off with a particular policy choice (Price, 1989). On such occasions, advocacy for one becomes advocacy for all.

Advocacy may be more appropriate in some professional job contexts than others. For example, some professionals are hired with the sole intent of advocating for particular policies or lobbying for a specific interest group. Finally, some professionals are most comfortable communicating in the persuasive marketing style that successful advocacy often entails.

Appropriate Educational Efforts by Professionals

With other interest groups, issues, and job settings, family policy alternatives education may be the more desirable option. For professionals interested in or responsible for working with more than one interest group or for developing long-term relationships with policymakers from a range of political perspectives, the educational approach is more apt to build trust and confidence than the advocacy approach. A democratic system such as ours typically resists and resents political decisions made by single-minded advocates, strong-arm politicians, or technocrats (Rossi & Wright, 1985).

For most issues, research is seldom comprehensive and definitive enough to serve as the sole determinant of a policy decision (Weiss & Bucuvalas, 1980). According to Seeley (1985), social science research is valuable in analyzing "what is," but limited in shaping social policy, which is often a value-based decision about "what ought to be." Thus, given this limitation of social science knowledge, a prudent approach for the professional may be educating on several policy options rather than advocating for one.

In some job settings, political activities are limited by state and federal laws, private or public funding, or organizational policies regarding legislative practices. For example, to maintain tax-exempt status, privately funded organizations and charities are required to severely restrict involvement in partisan politics and influence peddling (Knitzer, 1976).

Finally, working as an educator requires some soul searching regarding the match between this more dispassionate approach and the knowledge the professional has on the issue, the fit of their communication style with the educational approach, and the potential consequences of using the even-handed educational approach improperly. Would-be educators need to ask themselves these three questions:

1. Do I have the skills, ability, and knowledge to approach this issue from an educational perspective? The educational approach requires the skills to facilitate an even-handed discussion on controversial topics and a base of expert knowledge not only on one policy option, but also on several sometimes-obscure alternatives.

2. Do I want to work on this issue in a more neutral, scientific manner? Some professionals are unable to work as educators because their communication style is more confrontational and their personal views are held so strongly and passionately that it is difficult to set them aside. Conceivably, their views on one particular issue could be so strong that they would interfere with their capacity to be a good educator. For such issues, it may be best to find someone else to provide the alternatives.

3. What could happen if I use the educational approach improperly? If educators inadvertently violate the spirit of the approach and make their personal views obvious, this transgression could have negative repercussions for their job and perhaps their employer as well. For example, the position of one county extension educator was eliminated, in part, because of the fallout over a policy education program in which the educator's personal views on a controversial land use issue became known.

SUMMARY

Connecting knowledge and power is not a new concern, but one that has intrigued experts throughout the 20th century. The question of whether family policy advocacy or alternatives education is better for connecting knowledge and power has no single right answer. The best approach requires taking into account the intended beneficiary of the policy efforts, the issue under consideration, the professional's job context, and the professional's personal skills, knowledge, and communication style.

The previous chapter identified roles that professionals can assume in the policy arena, and this chapter presented two approaches for operationalizing these policy roles. The next chapter describes a specific policy role for professionals interested in influencing state policymaking (i.e., organizing Wisconsin Family Impact Seminars), which uses a specific policy approach (i.e., alternatives education). Chapter 15 describes another role for professionals interested in influencing local policymaking (i.e., engaging citizens in policymaking through Wisconsin Youth Futures), which also uses the alternatives education approach. Drawing on these examples, each of the next two chapters identifies several pragmatic lessons for connecting research and policymaking at the local and state levels.

CHAPTER

14

How Can We Connect Research With State Policymaking? Lessons From the Wisconsin Family Impact Seminars

Karen Bogenschneider
Jonathan R. Olson
Jessica Mills
Kirsten D. Linney

Far and away the best prize that life offers is the chance to work hard at work worth doing.

—Theodore Roosevelt

With a few notable exceptions, the history of the utilization of social science knowledge in the past 50 years yields few examples of research being used to inform policymaking (DeLeon, 1996; Strickland, 1996). Why has social scientists' ability to generate high-quality and increasingly sophisticated research outpaced their ability to disseminate research into the policymaking process? This conundrum, which has defied explanation for a half-century, merits attention now when the climate is receptive. Policymakers, many of whom were educated in universities (Zigler, 1998), are requesting high-quality research to guide their decisions (Farley, 1996; Melton, 1995; Miller, 1996; Strickland, 1996). Researchers are intrigued by the possibility of seeing their findings acted on outside the walls of academia (Smith, 1991; Zigler, 1998), and outreach specialists are committed to developing innovative strategies for connecting research to the pressing problems that confront and confound America's youth and families (see Lerner & Simon, 1998a).

This chapter describes one technology for research dissemination: the state Family Impact Seminars (FIS), an ongoing series of seminars, briefing reports, and follow-up discussions designed to increase the utilization of research in policymaking. Modeled after the FIS series for federal policymakers (Ooms, 1995), the state seminars provide objective, solution-oriented research on current issues and promote family well-being as a criterion for policymaking, just as economic and environmental impacts are routinely considered in policy debate.

We begin this chapter by reviewing the history of the utilization of social science research in policymaking. Then we present four theoretical perspectives that attempt to explain the underutilization of social science research in policymaking. Next, we describe the FIS model and the preliminary impacts of conducting the seminars in Wisconsin. Finally, we identify 10 lessons about strengthening connections between research and policymaking that have been fundamental to the success of the seminars and that may have relevance for those professionals interested in replicating the seminars or linking research and policymaking in other venues as well. We conclude by drawing implications for theory and practice.

HISTORY OF THE UTILIZATION OF SOCIAL SCIENCE RESEARCH IN POLICYMAKING

The use of social science research in policymaking has had a rather short history. Prior to World War II, government officials did not completely disregard data from social science research, but they seldom based decisions on such information (Bulmer, 1987; Pettigrew, 1985). Technological developments during the wartime years—penicillin, radar, the bomb—raised confidence in scientific methods and expectations that research could be used after the war for improving health, well-being, and the standard of living. From the early 1960s to the early 1980s, hundreds of millions of government dollars were channeled into the expansion of social science research endeavors, and it appeared as if a stable partnership between social scientists and policymakers was being formed (Booth, 1988; Weiss, 1986).

This initial enthusiasm failed to acknowledge, however, several constraints of utilizing research in policymaking that became evident in efforts like the War on Poverty (Smith, 1991). By the early 1970s, it became apparent that research results were not having the direct effects on policy that had been hoped for (Pettigrew, 1985; Weiss, 1986); by the early 1980s, the subsequent disenchantment led to significant cuts in government funding for social science research. Since that time, the use of social science research has appeared to be more haphazard than systematic (Gagnon, 1990; Lindblom, 1980; Patton, 1997), and social science data have often been ignored by government decision makers.

THEORIES REGARDING THE UTILIZATION OF SOCIAL SCIENCE RESEARCH

Four theories have been proposed to explain the apparent underutilization of social science research in policymaking—three that focus on the futility and one on the promise of establishing a research–policy connection. One theory focuses on the nature of policymaking, contending that it is a fast-breaking, self-serving, influence-driven process incompatible with the methods of social science, which are more time-intensive, intellectual, and rational. Conversely, a second theory focuses on the limitations of social science knowledge. Because of their reservations that research is often incomplete and circumstantial, many social scientists are unwilling to communicate their research findings to policymakers to guide decision making. A third theory contends that the underutilization of social science knowledge is an artifact of a democratic, free-market system, which lacks institutional structures for integrating knowledge and power (Wilensky, 1997). Finally, a fourth theory attributes underutilization to a communication gap between researchers and policymakers, who are portrayed as two communities with different goals, information needs, values, reward systems, and languages. Each theory is described here in more detail.

The Political Nature of the Policymaking Process

The idea that social science research can directly impact the policymaking process, coined the *hypodermic model* (Pettigrew, 1985), assumes that decisions are made in a rational manner. In recent years, however, scholars have acknowledged that decisions are made in a political context and that research serves at best as one factor among many that policymakers consider. Typically, lawmakers weigh competing factors, such as values, career aspirations, media attention, and constituent views (Booth, 1988; Gagnon, 1990; Kingdon, 1995; Nelson, Roberts, Maederer, Wertheimer, & Johnson, 1987; Weiss, 1986). For example, policymakers are unlikely to support policy alternatives, even those with substantial empirical support, if they are unpopular with constituents. Ignoring constituent views could jeopardize reelection bids (Arnold, 1990; Mayhew, 1974). Also, policymakers must make informed decisions on an array of issues in a fast-breaking, fluid environment. This situation slants decisions to information sources that respond more rapidly and decisively to the urgency of the political process than social scientists typically do (Strickland, 1996).

Limitations of Social Science Knowledge

During the 1950s and 1960s, when the relation between social science research and policymaking appeared most promising, social scientists were heavily influenced by a positivistic paradigm. Researchers believed that social science knowledge could be discovered and understood in a systematic, objective manner (Prus, 1992). Social scientists adopted research methods similar to those used in the physical sciences, with the intention of unlocking universal truths about social phenomena. Researchers believed that such knowledge could be generalized across contexts and time. Such objective information could be used as a basis for policy decisions (Doherty, Boss, LaRossa, Schumm, & Steinmetz, 1993; Prus, 1992).

Shortly after this initial enthusiasm, however, it became apparent that social scientists were unable to deliver on these inflated promises. The fundamental assumptions of the positivistic paradigm came under scrutiny. Social problems, in particular, proved notoriously difficult to define and solve (Sarason, 1978). Scholars also contended that human behavior, with its great variation and complexity, resists reduction to simple universal laws (Howard, 1985; Prus, 1992). According to a past president of the Association for Public Policy Analysis and Management, forecasts or projections were based on unreliable data and were almost always wrong (Aaron, 2000). Because two "experts" could reach diametrically opposed conclusions (Aaron, 2000), social scientists began questioning the utility of traditional scientific methods. Researchers influenced by postpositivistic thought realized that their own values and biases might interfere with their ability to conduct objective investigations. With evidence so imperfect and incomplete, some scholars doubted whether social science knowledge could be a useful guide to action in the policy arena (Tittle, 1985).

Few Centralized Institutions for Integrating Knowledge and Power

All rich democracies produce a cadre of academics, yet some have better track records than others for linking research findings to policy decisions (Wilensky, 1997). This research utilization results not from the supply or rigor of social science knowledge, but from closer ties between research and policy deliberations. For example, better research–policy connections exist in centralized, corporatist systems such as Austria, Germany, Japan, Norway, and Sweden, and, to a lesser extent, Belgium and the Netherlands (Wilensky, 1997). In the United States, research utilization is also limited by ambiguity about the proper role of government in addressing social problems (Aaron, 1978) and, in particular, apprehension about governmental intrusion into the privacy of family life (Ooms, 1984). To more effectively integrate research into policymaking in this country, there needs to be a more centralized government, less fragmented policymaking, more dialogue among national labor and employer federations, and a more clearly defined role for government in family policy (Wilensky, 1997).

Communication Gap Between the Two Communities of Researchers and Policymakers

In his review of the two-communities theory, Caplan (1979) suggested that underutilization of social science research results from limited understanding and communication between social scientists and policymakers, who have different goals, information needs, values, reward systems, and languages. For example, social scientists generally conduct research for the sake of discovery, whereas policymakers utilize research for the purpose of developing pragmatic means of solving problems (Booth, 1988; Caplan, 1979; Linquist, 1990; McCall, 1996).

Adherents to the two-communities theory also enumerate obstacles to communication between researchers and policymakers. Social scientists employ increasingly complex methodologies and complicated statistical procedures, which are difficult to explain to lay audiences (Booth, 1988). Many researchers do not know how to present their findings in ways that might influence policy decisions (DeLeon, 1996; Scott et al., 1999). Instead, they generate lengthy research reports that contain discipline-specific language aimed at other scientists that is not readily understood by those outside academia (Nelson, Roberts, Maederer, Wertheimer, & Johnson, 1987; Patton, 1997; Weiss, 1990; Weiss & Bucuvalas, 1980). This communication pattern perpetuates itself, in part, because translating research findings into accessible formats provides small payoffs and few short-term benefits in academic circles (Boyer, 1990; DeLeon, O'Keefe, VandenBos, & Kraut, 1996; Lynton & Elman, 1987; McCall, 1996).

Is the Use of Research in Policymaking Futile or Promising?

In summary, the first three sets of theories attribute underutilization of social science research to structural factors that are difficult to change. Indeed, it is unlikely that policymaking will develop into a rational reflective process, that scientific knowledge will progress to fully understanding the complexity and variability of social problems, that researchers will develop methodologies that completely overcome the biases inherent in their studies, or that more centralized institutional and governmental structures will emerge. Thus, these theories suggest the futility of using social science research to directly impact the policymaking process.

However, we adhere to the more moderate view of many policymakers (Miller, 1996) and scholars (Mark & Shotland, 1985)—that research can have at least some incremental impact most of the time. Thus, we build on the two-communities theoretical framework, which suggests that behavioral factors are at least partially responsible for the underutilization of social science research. According to this perspective, one major factor that contributes to poor research–policy connections is the apparent communication gap between researchers and policymakers.

Family Impact Seminars are one example of a technology, based on the two-communities theory, that has sought to bridge the communication gap between social science researchers and policymakers. We argue that this theory can be operationalized quite differently depending on whether an advocacy or educational orientation is used (see chap. 13 for a complete discussion of these two orientations). Dissemination efforts based on an advocacy orientation provide only research that is consistent with the views of a particular researcher, policymaker, political party, or ideology. In contrast, the orientation known as alternatives education, which undergirds the seminars, entails presenting a range of policy alternatives as objectively as possible without relaying personal preferences. The value judgments and ultimate decisions are entrusted to a number of policymakers elected to make these decisions rather than to a single person (Barrows, 1984, 1994; Bogenschneider, 1995).

THE FAMILY IMPACT SEMINAR METHOD

The seminars are an ongoing series of seminars, briefing reports, newsletters, and follow-up discussions that provide objective, solution-oriented information aimed at bringing a family focus to policymaking. The seminars, which address topics such as welfare reform, competent parenting, teenage pregnancy, and juvenile crime, emphasize the benefits of taking into account the role of the family in addressing social issues (Ooms & Preister, 1988). They typically attract 45 to 90 state policymakers, including legislators, legislative aides, governor's office staff, legislative service agency personnel, state agency representatives, university faculty, and administrators of family-serving organizations.

Logistically, the seminars begin early in the day, before committee meetings begin, and offer a complimentary continental breakfast. Following the advice of state legislators, the seminars are held in or close to the state capitol, which provides easy access for state legislators. The format for the 2-hour seminars consists of three 20-minute presentations by a panel of premier researchers, policy analysts, and program directors, with about one fourth of the time allocated to discussion. For each seminar, a CD is prepared, and a background briefing report summarizes state-of-the-art research on the issue in a succinct, easy-to-understand format. Several opportunities are also provided for engaging attendees in dialogue on the issues and identifying common ground.

If the seminars were as simple as organizing meetings for policymakers, social scientists would have experienced more success in linking research to policymaking in the past half-century. The preliminary impacts of the seminars, summarized in the next section, depend on careful attention to several pragmatic practices and procedures, such as (a) developing diverse delivery mechanisms; (b) providing a nonpolitical forum for discussion; (c) identifying timely topics; (d) selecting engaging speakers to present high-quality research; (e) drawing policy implications that span the political spectrum; and (f) targeting the unique information needs, work culture, and writing preferences of policymakers.

PRELIMINARY IMPACTS OF THE WISCONSIN FAMILY IMPACT SEMINARS

In Wisconsin, 1,666 participants, including 99 different state legislators and 156 legislative offices, have attended at least 1 of the 23 seminars conducted since 1993. Each seminar attracts an average of about 70 participants. On a scale of 1 (*poor*) to 5 (*excellent*), the overall participant rating of each seminar has been above 4, with high ratings on relevance to needs, usefulness to role, and objectivity (see Fig. 14.1). As shown, these high ratings have been consistent across topics, speakers, and participants. Legislators' en-

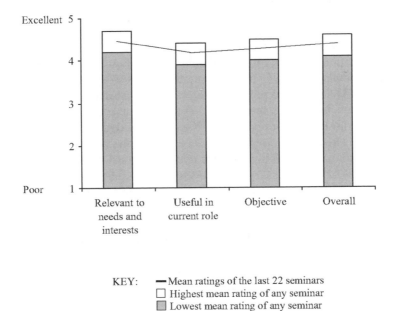

KEY: ▬ Mean ratings of the last 22 seminars
         ☐ Highest mean rating of any seminar
         ▨ Lowest mean rating of any seminar

FIG. 14.1. Average participant ratings of 22 Wisconsin Family Impact Seminars (1993–2006). *Note.* 1 = not relevant, useful, or objective; 3 = somewhat relevant, useful, or objective; 5 = very relevant, useful, or objective.

thusiasm about the seminars is exemplified by comments such as, "These seminars have been one of the better uses of my time since I've been in the state legislature these past seven years," and "These early morning meetings usually put me to sleep, but not this one. I was very surprised and found it to be very worthwhile for setting goals and direction for legislation." Moreover, this enthusiasm has been translated into action. When the seminars were held on session days, the assembly delayed its starting time twice to allow state representatives to attend.

To examine how much information participants learn from the seminars, we use retrospective pretest methodology that emerged from our collaboration with Clara Pratt and Sally Bowman of Oregon State University/Extension. The retrospective pretest method helps address a common reliability issue faced by evaluators when the information from the seminar helps participants realize that they knew less about the topic than they originally thought. So at the conclusion of the seminar, participants are asked to report their level of understanding on specific items after the seminar as well as their level of understanding on these same items before the seminar. Using paired sample t tests to compare the differences between these two reports, participants in a seminar on early childhood care and education reported knowing more about each of the four items after the seminar than before, with each test significant at $p < .001$. As shown in Figure 14.2, three items measured participant understanding of the research presented at the seminar, and one item measured understanding of how this issue affects families.

To assess the usefulness of the seminar compared to other information sources, telephone interviews of all state legislators who attended the long-term care seminar ($N = 18$) were conducted 6 to 8 weeks after the seminar. Based on pilot interviews of 21 state legislators in 1995, the seminar organizers predicted that legislator ratings of the usefulness of the information sources would range from constituents, who were deemed most useful, followed by the seminars and newsletters or print materials, to lobbyists being the least useful. Trend analyses were conducted to determine whether the mean ratings of usefulness followed this hypothesized trend. These analyses excluded seven legislators who were attending their first seminar because most had been in the legislature for only 1 month. As hypothesized, state legislators rated the seminar as the second most useful of four information sources ($M = 3.98$), with constituents the most useful ($M = 4.55$) and print materials ($M = 3.56$) and lobbyists ($M = 3.75$) the least useful. Although the order of print materials and lobbyists was reversed from the hypothesis, the means were close enough for the trend analysis to be significant, $F(1, 39) = 10.12$, $p = .003$ (see Fig. 14.3). The trend was also significant when newsletters ($M = 3.44$) were substituted for print materials, $F(1, 38) = 6.46$, $p = .015$.

In the same telephone interviews, 81% of legislators reported using the information to evaluate pending legislation, 66% to share with colleagues,

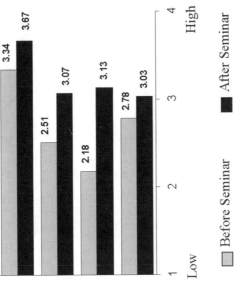

How the quality of child care affects children's development (p < .001)

Why the private marketplace does not work as well for child care as for other industries (p < .001)

How child care programs differ across states (p < .001)

How parents can be involved in child care programs (p < .001)

FIG. 14.2. How much participants learned from a Wisconsin Family Impact Seminar on early childhood care and education using retrospective-pretest methodology. *Note.* Based on the 17th Wisconsin Family Impact Seminar, which was on early childhood care and education and was attended by 75 participants (response rate = 80%).

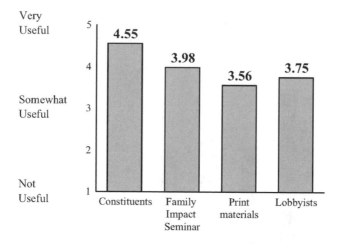

FIG. 14.3. Average legislator ratings of usefulness of information sources. *Note.* Based on a linear trend analysis from 11 legislators attending the 12th Wisconsin Family Impact Seminar on long-term care, $F(1, 39) = 10.12$, $p < .003$.

52% to identify contacts for further information, 48% to incorporate into speeches or presentations, 44% to influence state policymakers, and 20% to develop new legislation.

In surveys and other contacts, seminar organizers discover specific ways that legislators use information from the seminars. For example, after attending a seminar on youth substance use, one legislator formulated an opinion on a pending cigarette tax. Following two seminars on prescription drugs, legislators reported that they used seminar information to draft new legislation, help them critique and modify proposals, sort out poor proposals, and discuss the issue with advocacy groups. Eventually, several features of other states' prescription drug programs discussed at the seminar were incorporated into SeniorCare, a new law enacted by the Wisconsin legislature.

Policymakers other than legislators report applying information from the seminars in several ways. For example, a state agency official reported that a seminar presentation by a leading scholar and follow-up discussions led to a proposal for pooling early intervention funds, similar to a model being used in another state. A Wisconsin Supreme Court representative reported that research presented at one seminar was used to develop a pilot program to prevent teen pregnancy and keep female adolescents from entering the juvenile justice system. Information from the seminars was incorporated into both the state juvenile justice plan and the state teenage pregnancy plan. On two occasions, briefing reports were used as the basis of K–12 resource guides on Wisconsin families mailed to all teachers and administrators in every school district in the state. As offshoots of the state seminars, 25 seminars have been held for local policymakers, one for 75 board members of Wisconsin foundations, and another for trial court lawyers and judges in cosponsorship with the chief justice of the Wisconsin Supreme Court. Additional impacts are incorporated into the next section (see also Bogenschneider, 1995).

Moreover, we have also found that the seminars have changed policymakers' attitudes toward families and research, based on phone interviews following the child-care seminar (67% response rate). Because of their participation in the seminars, 86% of state legislators who attended the seminars said they were "quite a bit" more likely to consider how legislation they were developing might affect families, and 71% said they were "quite a bit" more likely to see the practical value of research.

THEORIES AND PRACTICES FOR CONNECTING RESEARCH AND POLICYMAKING

Based on this preliminary evidence of the effectiveness of the Wisconsin seminars, we have identified 10 lessons for strengthening the connection between research and policymaking. These strategies derive from political science theory and several methods of process evaluation, including post-meeting questionnaires completed by 75% of the participants at 23 seminars; 10 sets of follow-up telephone calls 6 to 8 weeks after seminars to participants in 13 seminars (response rates ranging from 25%–71%); and 85 personal interviews with state legislators, governor's office representatives between 1997 and 2005.

Develop Varied Delivery Mechanisms Geared to the Diverse Learning Styles of Policymakers

Consistent with the adult education literature (Tough, 1971), the seminars have proved that policymakers are not a homogeneous group, but have different learning styles and prefer information in varied formats. In Wisconsin, attendance by state legislators has ranged from 9 to 28 members per seminar, with an average of 14—a level that policy observers consider impressive (Shonkoff, 2000). The 18th seminar was attended by 110 participants, including 28 legislators and 35 legislative aides. An additional 5 legislators attended the luncheon, bringing the total to 33. During the day's activities, 59 legislative offices were represented. Another 15 ordered copies of the briefing report or audiotape, which means this seminar reached 74 legislators and their staff—more than half of Wisconsin's 133 legislative offices.

In evaluations, 100% of the participants preferred the seminar and briefing report format over a briefing report alone. Of the legislators not in attendance, typically 10 order a complimentary copy of the briefing report. Briefing reports are also made available to other policymakers and the public at a nominal cost. On the advice of a Wisconsin legislator who commutes long distances to the capitol, CDs of the seminar are made available, which are typically requested by five or six legislators.

Recognizing the strong oral tradition in legislative bodies (Bimber, 1996), the seminars' organizers have developed alternative delivery methods for building on legislators' preference for the spoken over the written word (Massad, Sales, & Acosta, 1983). Following the seminars, about 30 to 40 participants attend one of two 75-minute discussion sessions moderated by professionals with expertise on the topic. Because committee meetings limit legislator attendance at these discussions, the organizers hold a 75-minute roundtable luncheon for legislators to interact with the seminar speakers. Ten legislators attended the roundtable luncheon on long-term care. Based on a scale of 1 (*not useful at all*) to 5 (*very useful*), legislators rated the roundtable luncheon at 4.7 (response rate = 70%). The organizers also arrange a separate 90-minute meeting of the speakers with state agency staff. For example, a recent discussion on prescription drugs was attended by 11 people, including the three highest ranking state officials on this issue—the state secretary of Health and Family Services, the administrator of the Division of Health Care Financing, and the director of the Medicaid and Budget Bureau. This meeting began with pointed questions by the state secretary, who had read the entire briefing report. Each participant rated the discussion session a perfect 5 (response rate = 50%).

Following one seminar, 13 personal appointments for speakers were arranged with state policymakers, including the governor; the state secretary of Health and Family Services; the cochair of Joint Finance, Wisconsin's powerful taxing and spending committee; and the senate president. As a result of one appointment with a state legislator, a seminar speaker presented a follow-up meeting for local welfare officials in Milwaukee on employment strategies for unsteady workers and the hard to employ. Seminars are now held only on days the legislature is not in session, so that legislators can participate in discussions or schedule appointments with speakers.

Provide a Neutral Nonpolitical Forum for Fostering Dialogue Among Researchers, Policymakers, Agency Staffers, and Others in the Policy Community

The most frequently cited constraint of linking research and policymaking—mentioned by more than 80% of decision makers, researchers, and committee members who review research proposals—is the lack of direct communication between researchers and policymakers (Weiss & Bucuvalas, 1980). The seminars provide a formal venue that fosters direct communication often extending beyond the event itself. Based on telephone interviews 2 months following the juvenile crime seminar (response rate = 35%), more than one fourth of participants (28%) had contacted a speaker. These linkages are facilitated because contact information is printed in the briefing report.

The communication has been two-way, with researchers presenting their findings to policymakers and policymakers reciprocally influencing the research agenda of the university. Following one seminar, a state legislator requested an evaluation of the effectiveness of a community-based pregnancy prevention program, which a faculty member subsequently conducted. This communication appears to dispel common stereotypes held by both policymakers and researchers. Policymakers are surprised at researchers' practical and down-to-earth manner, and researchers are impressed by policymakers' informed and perceptive questions.

Seminar participants frequently comment on the value of bringing together not only legislators and researchers, but also state agency staffers and other actors in the policy community. For example, following the long-term care seminar, a legislative aide commented that the seminar provided her with an opportunity to meet people at the capitol whom she did not realize were interested in this issue. High-ranking state agency staff report that even if they are familiar with the research presented at the seminar, they welcome having legislators hear the information from an impartial third party, often from out of state. They also welcome the opportunity to interact with representatives of other state agencies, who are too often viewed as competitors for scarce state funds rather than as collaborators for reaching shared goals. One section chief in a state agency wrote,

> The Family Impact Seminars are something we make time for. Many people from around the department, including division administrators, attend regularly. Most important, this is the only time such a broad group gets together to really discuss family-related issues in an atmosphere that encourages good public policymaking over politics.

Perhaps the most surprising finding is reports from state legislators that they have few opportunities to become acquainted with each other, particularly their colleagues on the other side of the aisle. The seminars provide a unique opportunity for some of the state's most liberal and conservative legislators, who often oppose each other on issues, to sit down and discuss policy alternatives. One state legislator wrote that, "The information and the ability for follow-up discussion at the round table portion of the seminar is not available to my knowledge in any other setting." Legislators report that this informal interaction has become even more valuable with the advent of tougher ethics laws. Previously, special interest groups would sponsor receptions, picnics, and other informal gatherings that provided opportunities to socialize with members of the opposition party, but these opportunities have declined precipitously as ethical restrictions have tightened.

By operating outside the political pressures of policymakers' usual environment, the seminars appear to have provided a neutral forum, which may be more conducive to seeking common ground and reaching compromise. One Democratic legislator commented that seminar information was particularly useful for partnering with Republican colleagues because it does not carry "partisan baggage." Smith (1991) contended the most valuable service professionals could provide for policymakers may not be generating novel policy ideas, but rather providing a neutral space for dialogue outside the contentious, interest-group-dominated environment in which policymaking typically takes place. According to one member of Congress, not only the setting but the research itself may defuse divisiveness because "rhetoric flows far more freely in the absence of factual information" (Miller, 1996, p. 339).

Finally, advocates and the media are not invited to the seminars to help foster consensus building and avoid the polarization, posturing, and contentiousness their presence often engenders. Legislators' questions are typically frank and constructive because the absence of the media reduces the grandstanding of headline seekers and allays concerns of genuine information seekers about how the press may misconstrue their questions.

Link up With Academic, Agency, and Legislative Leaders to Legitimize Efforts

One element of the success of FIS is careful attention to legitimization, which began even before launching the Wisconsin seminars. Initially, the organizers interviewed a wide range of potential participants, such as division heads in two state agencies, local policymakers, and state legislators including the majority leader of the senate, the chair of the Assembly Committee on Children and Human Services, the chair of the Standing Committee on College and Universities, and the chair of the Governor's Commission on Families and Children. The organizers decided beforehand to proceed with the seminars only with the enthusiastic support and commitment of these key players.

These interviews initiated a 6-month process of developing the infrastructure for the seminars, which included the formation of a broad-based advisory committee. This committee includes several state legislators and representatives from four state campuses as well as from the following organizations: the Cooperative Extension Service; the Institute for Research on Poverty; the La Follette Institute; the University of Wisconsin–Madison Law School; several university departments, including Human Development and Family Studies; select executive agencies; local units of government; and statewide organizations serving families, including the Wisconsin Association for Marriage and Family Therapy and the Wisconsin Council on Family Relations. The advisory committee provides input into the direction and funding of the seminars and lends credibility to the seminars with committee members' colleagues. For example, to legitimize the seminars with state legislators, invitations are accompanied by a letter from Republican and Democratic legislators in the assembly and the senate encouraging legislative attendance.

Take Advantage of Timing by Responding to Recognized Problems With Politically Viable Solutions

The seminars have illustrated that careful attention to timing is fundamental to the success of policy dissemination efforts. Just as parent educators recognize the existence of sensitive periods for introducing parenting information, policy educators recognize that providing information that is sensitive to political timing is more apt to attract the attention of busy policymakers (Barrows, 1994; Kaufman, 1993; Kingdon, 1995; Weiss, 1986). For example, the welfare reform seminar, held the day before the vote on Wisconsin's welfare legislation, attracted 28 state legislators. One legislator remarked that the seminar helped him decide how to vote and that he was able to use information from the seminar in an assembly floor debate the next day.

One of the most challenging aspects of organizing seminars is that of developing a process for identifying timely seminar topics. In Wisconsin, the process is based on the theoretical notions of Kingdon (1995), which he aptly coined *policy windows*. When policy windows are open, the conditions are right for social change on an issue, and policymakers are willing to invest their time, energy, and political capital because their efforts may pay off. Policy windows may open because of a change in administration or control of the governor's office or legislature, a major crisis or disaster, or shifting public sentiment. The opening of a policy window usually occurs with the convergence of three separate streams: problems, policies, and politics. Specifically, issues rise on the decision-making agenda with the recognition of a problem, the availability of policy solutions, and a political climate supportive of change. No single stream, according to Kingdon, can place an item on the decision agenda. For example, a problem without solutions, solutions without a compelling problem, and problems or solutions that are politically unacceptable quickly result in the closing of a policy window. Typically, more visible policy participants, such as the governor or legislators, influence the legislative agenda, whereas hidden participants, such as academics, legislative aides, and agency staffers, identify policy alternatives.

In Wisconsin, funding has not been tied to the topic of a particular seminar, which has allowed the organizers to develop a three-step planning process based on Kingdon's (1995) framework for linking problems with policies and politics (see Fig. 14.4). First, all seminar participants are asked to identify future seminar topics and to select, from a list of about a dozen problems, those that are or should be highest on Wisconsin's legislative agenda. Seminar organizers prepare brief written descriptions of these top five or six choices and personally interview three to five Democratic legislators, three to five Republican legislators, and the gubernatorial representative on the advisory committee to narrow the list to the single most compelling problem with bipartisan support.

Second, a seminar planning committee comprised of academics, state agency staffers, and legislative service agency personnel with expertise on the problem identifies about five or six themes that could be covered at a seminar on this topic. Typically, experts from across the country are also contacted by phone for their advice on seminar themes such as frameworks for conceptualizing the problem, an overview of the problem, specific program or policy alternatives, and the experiences of other states. Third, seminar organizers assess which themes are on the legislative agenda, their bipartisan appeal, and their political viability by again interviewing legislative and gubernatorial advisors, whose ranking determines the three themes that will be featured at the seminar. The crux of the planning process is that seminars, which entail considerable planning, cannot

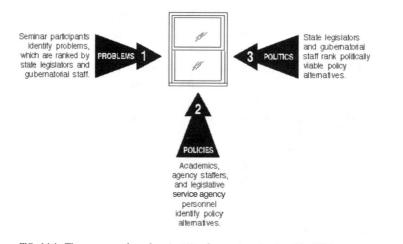

FIG. 14.4. The process for planning timely seminar topics: identifying open policy windows when problems, policies, and politics converge.

be planned too far in advance because policy windows can slam shut with little warning, and the opportune time for an idea may pass before the seminar materializes.

Select Engaging Speakers Who Can Provide Objective, High-Quality Research and Implications for Policy

According to a psychologist who was elected to Congress, what legislators need is not more information, but more objective and valid information (Strickland, 1996). The research that comes to the attention of policymakers may not be the most current or methodologically sound because "no quality control mechanism screens the good and relevant from the partial and the sensational" (Weiss, 1986, p. 219). Decision makers report that two criteria most important to them in evaluating the usefulness of research are objectivity and lack of bias (Weiss, 1986).

Objective, high-quality research is a hallmark of the seminars (see also Wilcox, Weisz, & Miller, 2005). On a scale of 1 (*not objective*) to 5 (*very objective*), each of the last 22 seminars was rated above 4 on objectivity, with an average rating of 4.3 (see Fig. 14.3). When asked what they like best about the seminars, participants frequently comment on the quality of the speakers; one state legislator wrote that the "ability to prepare and present unbiased research based on objective analysis and without political taint is truly refreshing." Compelling evidence of the quality of the research comes from legislators' reports that the information changes their presumptions and helps them form opinions on pending votes. According to Bimber (1996), such legitimacy stems from standards of proof that are based, not on persuasive rhetoric or personal experience, but on the dispassionate methods of science including predetermined probability levels, appropriate research designs, and publication in peer-reviewed journals.

Attaining and maintaining this standard of quality and objectivity depends on adherence to several criteria that seminar organizers developed for selecting speakers: (a) scholarly or practice-based reputation, as evidenced by presentations at professional meetings, awards for research or programs, or recommendations from researchers and practitioners familiar with the field; (b) a record of high-quality research, as indicated by publication in prestigious peer-reviewed journals and review of these publications by members of the planning committee; (c) a reputation of nonpartisanship, with no open affiliations with a particular ideology, political party, or activist organization; (d) prior experience presenting research to policymakers or the ability to draw pragmatic policy implications for lay audiences; and (e) the communication skills to present research in an engaging and understandable style, which are surmised by scouting for appropriate speakers at professional meetings and seeking recommendations from other professionals. Even those speakers who meet these criteria may have limited experience presenting to policymakers. In such cases, seminar organizers brief speakers on what aspects of their research will be most useful to policymakers and what style of presentation is most well received. Adherence to these criteria is time consuming, but is essential to maintaining the seminars' reputation as being above politics and partisanship.

Identifying speakers has proved more difficult than encouraging their participation in the seminars. No honorariums are paid for in-state speakers because benefits may accrue to them or their institution as a result of addressing the legislature. Honorariums to out-of-state speakers are $500 to $1,500 plus expenses, yet leading scholars and policy analysts from across the country seldom refuse an invitation to participate. Smith (1991) surmised that experts' interest in policy may stem from the intrigue of seeing their research and ideas acted on.

Draw Policy Implications That Span the Political Spectrum

A common misperception of academics in working with policymakers is assuming that legislators themselves develop the ideas for new policies. According to interviews conducted by FIS organizers, legislators view themselves not as originators of new ideas, but primarily as conduits for other people's ideas. That is, legislators are requesting assistance in translating research into specific recommendations or policies. To differentiate the seminars from the lobbyists and special interest groups that regularly bombard legislators with specific legislative agendas, the organizers deliberately avoid promoting a specific policy option. Instead, the seminars have maintained a reputation of objectivity and nonpartisanship by presenting several policy alternatives, ranging from liberal to conservative (Barrows, 1984, 1994; Rule, 1978). For example, the briefing report on promoting competent parenting reviewed family support programs in five states as well as 25 policy proposals from agencies, commissions, and organizations that were notably diverse in their political orientation. The seminars offer policymakers a variety of options to study, contemplate, and act on, which we hope helps legislators overcome perceptions that child and family advocates are liberal and Democratic (State Legislative Leaders' Foundation, 1995).

Although advocacy fills an important role in the political process, we argue that the objective, nonpartisan educational approach is preferable for efforts such as the seminars that aim to (a) build bridges across a diverse spectrum of viewpoints, (b) work with policymakers from a range of values and political perspectives, and (c) maintain effectiveness over time regardless of which party is in control (Barrows, 1994; Bimber, 1996; see also chap. 13). In Wisconsin, since we started the seminars, the governorship has changed parties, and the majority has shifted from one party to the other in the assembly and the senate.

Target the Information Needs, Work Culture, and Writing Preferences of Policymakers

A major stumbling block for researchers who work with policymakers is a lack of understanding of the differences between the academic community and that of the policymaker—differences that became increasingly apparent in our work on the seminars. Moreover, the information needs of policymakers in the legislature, governor's office, and leadership of state agencies appear to diverge from the information needs of state agency personnel who administer policies and programs and from front-line staff who deliver programs. A blatant example emerged from the seminar on preventing teenage pregnancy. Because the seminar featured two well-evaluated adolescent pregnancy prevention programs, the seminar organizers expanded their invitation list to include a range of staff involved in program delivery. The difficulty of trying to inform policymakers, state agency personnel, and program staff in the same forum was apparent in the evaluations. Policymakers offered words of praise such as, "Your format was excellent, I have very little free time to attend briefings but can always work around an hour and a half briefing scheduled in advance." In stark contrast, program staff criticized the short length of the seminar, suggesting instead conferences up to 2 days in length, and complained about the presence of policymakers: "Don't invite politicians and people who deal with the real world to the same seminar; they [politicians] deal more with unreal issues and are not reality based."

In retrospect, it appears that, instead of the two communities of researchers and policymakers proposed by Caplan (1979), there are actually three distinct communities routinely involved in the seminars: researchers and two types of policymakers referred to here as *policymakers* and *policy administrators*. For purposes of discussion, we define *policymakers* in the traditional sense of the word as the governor, appointed secretaries of state agencies, and state legislators who actually enact policies. We define *policy administrators* as state agency personnel and directors of nonprofit organizations who develop the practices and procedures that underlie policy implementation. In so doing, they actually determine whether the intent of the policy is carried out. We define *service providers* as front-line workers who actually deliver services. In Shonkoff's (2000) ground-breaking work, he used the term *service providers* more generically to encompass our definitions of both policy administrators, who are a target audience for the seminars, and service providers, who are not.

Extrapolating from our experience and that of Shonkoff (2000) and others, we have identified several differences in the information needs, work culture, and writing preferences of the three primary audiences of the seminars—researchers, policymakers, and policy administrators. We believe that the seminars' success hinges on acknowledging and taking into account these differences. Busy professionals may find it appealing to invite policymakers to their professional conferences or forward to policymakers reprints of journal articles, yet these actions are less likely to be effective than providing information tailored to their preferences. Both Table 14.1 and the following text address the information needs of these three different audiences in more detail.

Information Needs. Academics often focus on the unknown to guide future research and theory development, whereas policymakers prefer focusing on the known to guide policy development. According to Shonkoff (2000), policy administrators focus on what they need to know for successful implementation. Put simply, researchers like questions more than answers, policymakers like answers more than questions, and policy administrators formulate practical questions for which they want concrete answers (Shonkoff, 2000).

The level of detail needed in each community also varies. Researchers value detail on narrow topics in an attempt to move the field forward in small incremental steps. In contrast, policymakers prefer comprehensive overviews that emphasize well-replicated findings with special attention to malleable factors likely to be influenced by policy (Weiss & Weiss, 1996). Policy administrators like some detail, but specifically on pragmatic procedures and best practices for operationalizing policies and programs (Shonkoff, 2000; Unrau, 1993).

For their source of data (Riley, 1997), academics prefer representative samples that produce generalizable data. For policymakers, the preferred focus is a comparison of how their constituency stacks up to a similar city, county, state, region, or nation (Kaufman, 1993). Because policy administrators often believe each community or service area is unique, their focus is local, with emphasis on how program models and best practices can be adapted to different circumstances or to a specific individual who may differ from the norm.

Work Culture. Because they have the luxury of not having to act on information, researchers are trained to advance the knowledge base and contemplate the great truths of the world by being cautious, skeptical, tentative, and reflective (Shonkoff, 2000). Progress in social science research can take years to achieve (Gallagher, 1990). In contrast, progress in policy development can occur within weeks. The policymaker operates in a fast-paced, fluid environment and is rewarded for being reactive and responding quickly to emerging issues. The surest way a policymaker can jeopardize reelection is failing to act; even a misguided response can be remedied

TABLE 14.1

Differences in the Information Needs, Work Culture, and Writing Preferences Among the Three Communities of Researchers, Policymakers, and Policy Administrators

Characteristics	Researchers	Policymakers	Policy Administrators
Information Needs			
Kind of information	Focus on what we do not know; prefer questions	Focus on what we do know; prefer answers	Focus on what we need to know to implement policies; prefer asking questions to get answers
Level of detail	More detail on narrow topics	Comprehensive overviews that emphasize malleable factors policy can influence	Like some detail, but on pragmatic procedures and best practices for operationalizing policies and programs
Source of data	Focus is representative samples that produce knowledge that can be generalized	Focus is often comparison of how a policymaker's constituency stacks up to a similar city, county, state, or region	Focus is local and how program models and best practices can be adapted to different circumstances
Work Culture			
Approach and Timing	Cautious; skeptical; tentative; reflective; progress in research can take years to achieve	Reactive; to enhance reelection chances, must respond quickly in a fast-paced, fluid environment; progress can occur within weeks	Action oriented and pragmatic; often required to respond despite incomplete information and insufficient resources

(Continued)

265

TABLE 14.1
(Continued)

Characteristics	Researchers	Policymakers	Policy Administrators
Criteria for decision making	Statistical probability; sound research methods and designs; publication in peer-reviewed journals	What is possible through negotiation and compromise; persuasive rhetoric and the single anecdote can be powerful	Combination of a decent knowledge base with clinical judgment, observation, and the experience of reputable sources
Views of ambiguity and complexity	Excited by ambiguity and complexity	Counterproductive to embrace complexity because of the need to take firm positions on issues	Energized by complexity, but still have to simplify enough to make decisions
Writing Preferences			
Emphasis	An emphasis on sample, methods, and analysis to improve the quality of future research	Little attention to sample, methods, and analysis because scholars can be trusted to review only high-quality studies	An emphasis on sample to assess similarity to the local context and on methods to allow for replication and adaptation
Organization	Building in a logical progression to the conclusions at the end	Placing the most important conclusions for policy at the beginning	Placing the most important conclusions for practice at the beginning
Writing	In-depth discussions with discipline-specific terminology and technical graphs and illustrations	Concise, easy-to-read reports with accessible language, active voice, short sentences, frequent paragraphing, and simple graphs and illustrations	Reports of moderate length with some technical language and illustrations to allow communicating with researchers and demonstrating accountability to policymakers

in the next legislative session if the policymaker is returned to office (Kaufman, 1993). The policy administrator is action oriented and pragmatic, and is often required to respond even when knowledge is incomplete or resources are insufficient (Shonkoff, 2000).

The criteria for decision making differ in each community (Shonkoff, 2000). Researchers make decisions based on predetermined probability levels, sound research methods and designs, and publication in peer-reviewed journals. Yet research is only one consideration in policymaking, where decisions are often based on what can be achieved through negotiation and compromise. Persuasive rhetoric, common sense, or the single anecdote can sometimes be more powerful than the best scientific evidence. Decisions made by policy administrators are often based on a combination of a decent knowledge base and good clinical judgment, observation, and the experience of reputable sources.

The three communities have distinct attitudes about how to deal with the problem of ambiguity and complexity. Researchers are excited by it, but policymakers shun it because it interferes with taking firm positions on issues (Shonkoff, 2000). Moreover, for policymakers, inconsistencies in one's positions or voting record can be a liability when running for reelection (Weiss, 1989). Policy administrators are somewhat energized by an ambiguous, complex problem because it keeps their jobs interesting, but they must simplify it enough so decisions can be made.

Writing Preferences. The importance of how materials are written was verified in a study in which decision makers rated 29 criteria for using a research study (Weiss & Bucuvalas, 1980). Decision makers reported "understandably written" as one of the two most essential criteria for using a research study; they rated this characteristic even more important than such characteristics as technical quality, direct implications for action, and generalizability. Academic writing often emphasizes methodology and statistical analyses, which allow researchers to assess the rigor of the study and improve the quality of future research. Conversely, writing for policymakers requires little emphasis on methodological issues and statistical techniques, and more attention to preparing brief summaries in understandable language. Policy administrators prefer written materials that have an emphasis on sample, to assess similarity to their target population, and on methods, to allow for replication and adaptation to the local context.

In organizing their written materials, academics typically build their argument systematically in a logical progression, ending with the most important conclusions. In contrast, busy policymakers prefer that the most important conclusions for policy be placed at the beginning of reports. Policy administrators also prefer that reports begin with the most important conclusions, but they prefer conclusions relevant to practice.

Finally, in regard to style, researchers read longer, more in-depth reports with precise, discipline-specific terminology and technical graphs and illustrations. Policymakers request concise, easy-to-read reports that use accessible language, active voice, short sentences, frequent paragraphing, and simple graphs and illustrations (Grob, 1992; Huston, 1994; Newman & Vincent, 1996). The best style for policy administrators is reports of moderate length with some technical language, graphs, and illustrations to allow both communicating with researchers and demonstrating accountability to policymakers.

Applying These Differences to Improve Research Dissemination. Based on these stark differences across several domains, the most effective approach in research dissemination efforts may be to deliberately and strategically target either the policymaker or policy administrator. For the seminars, we clearly target policymakers in the seminars, briefing reports, and some of the discussion sessions. For example, in the seminars and written materials, we provide comprehensive overviews that summarize existing research on an issue, with an emphasis, when possible, on the experiences of other states. We strive to respond to issues on a timely basis by featuring respected researchers—preferably those who can provide rich descriptions, vignettes, or direct quotations from the families they study.

Written materials emphasize the complexity of issues without dwelling on methodology or statistical analysis or without being overly technical in wording and illustrations. Reports begin with the conclusions and implications for policy, and a complete table of contents is provided so readers can easily find the information they need. Policy administrators are also encouraged to attend the seminar; specific discussion sessions and some sections of the briefing report are targeted to their information preferences.

Provide a Broad Interdisciplinary Perspective on Complex Social Problems to Counteract the Specialization and Compartmentalization of Policy Expertise

To the cynic, it appears that society has problems, universities have disciplines, and legislatures have committees (Kellogg Commission, 1999). Legislative policy expertise varies according to legislators' interests and is divided by the narrow jurisdictions of the state legislature's committee structure. Similarly, executive departmental staff often establish expertise in specialized areas (Simmons, 1996).

Yet most social problems are not so easily divided and compartmentalized. The seminars offer a uniquely broad interdisciplinary perspective that, due to the segmentation of expertise, is needed in policy debate

(DeLeon et al., 1996; Weiss & Bucuvalas, 1980). To design comprehensive seminars, organizers attempt to cross disciplinary boundaries by including in the planning faculty who are familiar with scholarship in such diverse fields as economics, education, health, human development and family studies, law, psychology, political science, social work, and sociology. Often seminar panelists are unaware of the research of colleagues studying the same topic in different disciplines. This fact serves as a poignant example that as scholarship becomes more specialized, synthesis and integration become increasingly critical to break through what social critics have called the iron curtain of specialization (Bellah et al., 1985/1996, p. 301).

This comprehensive focus entails balancing two paradoxical tensions. On the one hand, the seminars strive to portray the complexity of problems to avoid any temptation to legislate simple, "magic bullet" solutions. On the other hand, to avoid miring policymakers in complexity, the seminars identify malleable factors and workable solutions that demystify social problems, thereby overcoming the sense of hopelessness that can pervade problems and choke off meaningful response. As evidence of the value of this approach, one participant wrote that the best part of one seminar was "breaking down a very large, diverse problem into manageable pieces"; another wrote, "There's hope."

Another method used by seminar organizers to demystify complex social problems is to provide new frameworks for conceptualizing problems, which can alter the terms of the policy debate. For example, the conceptual framework most frequently requested by seminar participants is Patterson's "vile weed" (Patterson, Reid, & Dishion, 1992; see Fig. 14.5). This illustration visually depicts the research on how violent juvenile crime is rooted in harsh, inconsistent parenting during early childhood and later branches out to rejection by peers, poor school performance, involvement in a deviant peer group, substance use, and early arrest. One state legislator used this analogy, which illustrates the importance of early family intervention, in a debate on the floor of the senate.

Establish and Support Legislative Liaisons Who Assume Leadership for Sustaining Ongoing Linkages Among Researchers, Policymakers, and Policy Administrators

Academics misunderstand policymaking if they think of it as a discrete event in which a particular policy is debated and either passed or defeated. Instead, policymaking is better conceptualized as a process in which policymakers need ongoing access to updated information as issues reemerge because of timing, resources, and shifting priorities (Rist, 1994). Transferring information to policymakers occurs best in the context of relationships built over time and based on familiarity and trust (Bimber, 1996; Caplan,

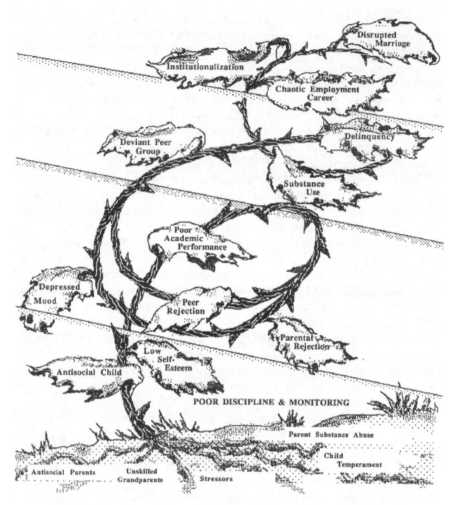

FIG. 14.5. The vile weed: How violent behavior is rooted in early childhood.
Note. From *A Social Learning Approach: Vol. 4. Antisocial boys*, by G. R. Patterson,
J. B. Reid, & T. J. Dishion, 1992, Eugene, OR: Castalia. Adapted with permission.

1979; Simmons, 1996). One important outcome of the seminars is that they
have legitimized the presenters and organizers as credible sources of information and have facilitated ongoing linkages between the legislature and
university. For example, as a direct outcome of the seminars, the organizers
have responded to requests for further information on issues such as day
care, family leave, no-fault divorce, and outcome-based education. Following the initial seminar, the first author was appointed to the Governor's
Commission on Families and Children—an appointment she had sought un-
successfully for several months prior to the seminar.

Establishing a legislative liaison as a point of contact in a university college or department (Kellogg Commission, 1999) may be an important first step for professionals interested in extending research to policymakers. If this work is a responsibility of everyone, it may, by default, be a priority of no one. A critical policy role that every academic can play is to support status and rewards in the university for professionals involved in this time-consuming and often undervalued work (Kellogg Commission, 1999). The tenure and merit systems of universities need to take into account the scarcity of outlets for publishing work geared toward policymakers' unique information needs. Further, university reward structures need to acknowledge the time and expertise it takes to write for policymakers and to implement policy dissemination efforts.

Be Creative in Seeking Time and Funding for Policy Efforts by Tapping Into Universities' and Philanthropists' Interest in Policymakers

Because policymakers are a high-profile audience, public and private funders are often interested in reaching them, particularly with efforts that are not advocacy oriented. Wisconsin secured its initial funding from two Milwaukee foundations—one liberal and the other conservative. University administrators may also be willing to provide seed money, as occurred in Wisconsin, or to provide course releases for policy-related activities, such as conducting seminars or serving as a legislative liaison. Cooperative Extension Service administrators may be particularly interested because the seminars are consistent with their philosophy of policy education, their location in land-grant universities across the country, and their mission of extending research beyond the boundaries of the university.

CONCLUSIONS REGARDING RESEARCH UTILIZATION BY POLICYMAKERS

This experience conducting seminars in Wisconsin over the last 13 years suggests that research produces policy-relevant ideas and that seminars represent one technology for promoting the use of research by policymakers as a guide to social action. This conclusion is strengthened by similar results in other sites that have held or are currently holding seminars—Alabama, Arizona, California, the District of Columbia, Georgia, Illinois, Indiana, Kentucky, Maryland, Michigan, Mississippi, Nebraska, New Hampshire, New Mexico, North Carolina, Ohio, Oklahoma, Oregon, Pennsylvania, Wisconsin, and Wyoming. Wisconsin differs from these other sites in the following respects: (a) leadership is provided in Wisconsin by a university, in California by the research arm of the state library system, and in Indiana by representatives of eight family-serving organizations and three universities; (b) a state-centric system of government in Wisconsin versus one or more large regional city governments in California; and (c) more stability in the legislature in Wisconsin versus legislative term limits in California.

The experience of the seminars lends support to the two-communities theory. This theory posits that the nebulous nexus between research and policymaking can be demystified by careful attention to pragmatic practices and procedures that can enhance the effectiveness of policy dissemination efforts. Similarly, an empirical study concluded that the two-communities theory explained significantly more variance in research utilization than did theories based on policymaking constraints or limitations of social science knowledge (Caplan, Morrison, & Stambaugh, 1975). Yet the experience of the seminars also suggests that extending the two-communities theory into a three-communities theory may more accurately reflect the intricacies of the research–policy nexus by differentiating the information needs, work culture, and writing preferences of researchers, policymakers, and policy administrators. Building on the work of Hayes (1982) and Shonkoff (2000), we propose that efforts to disseminate research may be more effective if strategically targeted either to the unique needs of policymakers, who enact policies, or policy administrators, who develop the procedures and practices that determine whether the intent of the policy is carried out.

Moreover, we argue that the utility of the three-communities theory depends on how it is operationalized. In accord with Grisso and Steinberg (2005), we warn against advocacy approaches that promote a specific policy or ideology and caution researchers about becoming advocates because of apprehensions that "all research begins to looks like advocacy" and "all experts begin to look like hired guns" (Smith, 1991, p. 321). Instead, we recommend an alternatives education approach that presents a range of policy options. As discussed in chapter 13, this educational approach strives for objectivity while fully recognizing that aseptic objectivity is never possible. Nevertheless, we do not reject the ideal of objectivity, just as we would not reject the ideal of love just because it cannot be perfectly expressed or experienced in family relationships.

Based on the tenets of the three-communities framework, research has the potential to inform policymaking in many ways, seven of which have been illustrated by the seminars, briefing reports, and follow-up activities.

1. The seminars portray research as practical and relevant to policymakers and depict researchers not as ivory-tower number crunchers, but as public servants interested in helping decision makers develop sound, effec-

tive policies (Weiss & Bucuvalas, 1980). The most frequent comments on the seminar evaluations refer to the high quality of the speakers and the objective, practical nature of the presentations.

2. The seminars have demonstrated that sound research can rise above politics and partisanship by relying on the dispassionate scientific method. In particular, favorable comments have been received regarding researchers who present results that they acknowledge have contradicted their own hypotheses. Such researchers convincingly model the value of scientific standards of proof, which seminar participants characterize as a refreshing lack of political taint.

3. Research has provided policymakers with conceptual frameworks that have helped reframe the terms of the policy debate. For example, the seminars have raised awareness of the individualistic perspective that has pervaded current policies and programs, and the potential benefit to policymaking if the role of families is taken into account. One Department of Administration official wrote, "It is good to have more of a family focus and address issues from this perspective." Following a parenting seminar, one legislator wrote, "I wasn't sure that the government had a role in parenting, but now I am sure we can no longer stick our head in the sand."

4. Research has helped differentiate fact from myth, an important distinction in decision-making environments in which myth often is treated as fact (Flinchbaugh, 1988; Shonkoff, 2000). For example, one legislator wrote that the seminars "put many of our presumptions in a new light." By offering new facts and frames of reference, research can "counteract the taken-for-granted assumptions, the musty sameness, of existing policy" (Weiss, 1990, p. 107).

5. Research can provide guidance for policy solutions by identifying programs and policies that work, as well as those that have no evidence of effectiveness. This solution-oriented research is most often requested by policymakers and most often praised when it is well presented.

6. Research is often used to support or challenge initiatives that are already underway because high-quality evidence lends credibility to an argument. We do not view this action as using research for political purposes, as academics sometimes do (Bimber, 1996). Instead, we view policymaking as a political process and legitimizing political arguments as an appropriate function of research as long as the researcher does not assume the role of advocate and the results are disseminated widely rather than to select interest groups.

7. The message of hope springs from studies of children and families who succeed against the odds (Werner, 1992) and from evaluations of programs able to ameliorate even complex, seemingly intractable problems. For example, one participant wrote that the research presented at a seminar provides

hope, in keeping with scholars who view one function of universities as once again shaping "a politics of rational hope" (Bevan, 1982, p. 1310).

We do not believe that all attempts to connect research and policymaking will achieve these successes, but rather that success depends on theory-driven planning, strategic legitimization, and precise execution. In an attempt to put some flesh on the bones of the three-communities theory, this chapter identifies 10 pragmatic dissemination practices and procedures that can be summarized into three categories. The first two lessons require a commitment from professionals to research dissemination. Specifically, professionals can develop varied delivery mechanisms geared to the diverse learning styles of policymakers and can provide a neutral, nonpolitical forum for fostering dialogue among researchers, policymakers, agency staffers, and others in the policy community.

Lessons 3 through 8 require a commitment to excellence in tailoring this information to policymakers and the political environment: linking up with academic, agency, and legislative leaders to legitimize efforts; taking advantage of timing by responding to recognized problems with politically viable solutions; selecting engaging speakers who can provide objective, high-quality research and implications for policy; drawing policy implications that span the political spectrum; targeting the information needs, work culture, and writing preferences of policymakers; and providing a broad, interdisciplinary perspective on complex social problems to counteract the specialization and compartmentalization of policy expertise.

Lessons 9 and 10 require changes in the academy. First, legislative liaisons who assume leadership for sustaining ongoing linkages to researchers, policymakers, and policy administrators must be established and supported as a legitimate function of academia no different than serving as a liaison to professional associations and public or private organizations. Two major obstacles in policy work—time and money constraints—may be creatively addressed by tapping into the interest that university administrators and philanthropists have in high-profile audiences like policymakers. The biggest expense in conducting seminars, a one-quarter to one-half time director, may be the easiest for universities to underwrite, because administrators often have the prerogative to reassign time or grant course releases.

LIMITATIONS OF RESEARCH UTILIZATION BY POLICYMAKERS

Despite our enthusiasm, we recognize the danger of overselling the value of research or overpromising the results of even flagship programs and policies (Shonkoff, 2000; St. Pierre, 1985; Wilensky, 1997). Our cautions parallel the three theories that posit structural constraints on research utilization. First, in accord with the theory identifying institutional constraints, researchers must acknowledge the limitations of a democratic system, which inherently resists political decisions by technocrats, strong-arm politicians, or well-funded advocates (Rossi & Wright, 1985). Also, in a free-market system, questions often arise about whether policy alternatives are cost-effective; such analyses are valued by policymakers, but can be difficult to conduct for family policies because of the difficulty of assigning economic values to social outcomes.

Second, in concurrence with the theory positing the limitations of social science knowledge, research is seldom comprehensive and definitive enough to serve as the sole determinant of a policy decision (Weiss & Bucuvalas, 1980). Also, social problems are transformed into public issues when an individual or a group detects a discrepancy between what they perceive as an ideal state of affairs and the actual situation. "While science may contribute significantly to the perception of reality, it contributes little (if at all) to a sense of what is ideal" (Ross & Staines, 1972, p. 20).

Third, echoing reservations about the political nature of the policymaking process, Weiss (1986) warned that only the naive would expect research to have blockbuster effects. Instead, she proposed an enlightenment model, whereby research slowly and continuously seeps into policymaking in obscure ways that are difficult to trace. Support for this enlightenment perspective emerges from Bimber's (1996) account of the rise and the fall of the Office of Technology Assessment (OTA), formed in 1972 to conduct objective in-depth studies of policy problems for congressional committees. In 1995, when the agency was asked to justify its existence, no mention of the OTA could be found in the official Congressional Record, and no single bill or vote could be attributed to the OTA.

In a careful analysis, Bimber (1996) argued that assessing the value of the agency on these criteria, which are the same ones often suggested for evaluating the seminars, is naive for four reasons. First, assessing voting records fails to recognize that voting decisions are complex and multidimensional with no single factor prevailing over all others. Second, the OTA was successful in influencing many bills (e.g., the Brady Bill) by working earlier in the policymaking process to shape the policy agenda. Evidence was provided on effective policy alternatives when bills were being crafted, not when they were being debated or voted on. Third, OTA staff did not always communicate directly with elected officials, but provided information indirectly through their staff, which would not be reflected in voting records, bill sponsorship, or the Congressional Record. Finally, policymakers justify their positions with information from various sources. Over time, this knowledge is incorporated into policymakers' common knowledge, making it difficult to decipher whether and what elements originated from research.

REMAINING CHALLENGES

Embedded in these constraints are several remaining challenges. This chapter is a humble attempt at disentangling the effectiveness of one technology for disseminating research to policymakers, which we hope spawns systematic evaluations of other efforts in the future. These evaluations are important not only because they can enhance the capacity to connect research and policymaking, but also because they can counter a growing cynicism among Americans that politics is more fragmented and less intelligent than it should be (Smith, 1991). Overall, the seminars have taught us the hard lessons of being modest in expectations, cautious in identifying impact indicators, patient in expecting tangible outcomes, and creative in developing methods of evaluating efforts not expected to have large, singular effects. This chapter encourages researchers to be more policy-sensitive in an attempt to entice policymakers to be more research-sensitive. It does not examine how research could be made more relevant, reliable, or generalizable (Mark & Shotland, 1985; Sechrest, 1985), although this is a critical need. Without research of this nature, little is worth applying (Wittrock, 1993).

Finally, scholars and universities need to be willing to make a commitment to strengthening connections between research and policymaking. The return on investment for such a commitment may depend on acknowledging and acting on the lessons learned from conducting Family Impact Seminars in Wisconsin and 20 other sites (see also Wilcox et al., 2005). The goal of more effective policies that strengthen and support families makes these lessons well worth recording, learning, and applying.

15

How Can Professionals Team up With Communities to Influence Local Policymaking? Guidelines From Wisconsin Youth Futures

Never doubt that a small group of thoughtful committed citizens can change the world: indeed, it's the only thing that has.

—Margaret Mead

Of all the policy efforts that I have worked on, the one that resulted in the most policy changes was a community coalition-building initiative known as Wisconsin Youth Futures. Beginning in the fall of 1990, my colleagues and I worked with county Cooperative Extension Service faculty and staff to form coalitions of parents, educators, community leaders, and youth in 22 Wisconsin communities interested in building more supportive environments for youth. In the 7 years that I directed this project, these community coalitions changed more than 30 local policies, including tightening the penalties for selling alcohol to minors, removing alcohol sales from Little League games, delivering parent education programs, developing parent networks, and establishing a parent–school association.

Given the success of Youth Futures in developing new policies and programs, it may seem surprising that my county extension colleagues and I worked with these coalitions as educators, not advocates. As university extension educators, our role was to provide expertise on adolescent development, the latest research on risk and protective processes, and evidence on policies and programs that work and those that do not. Community citizens selected which risky youth behavior to focus on, what programs and policies are needed, and how best to put them in place. The University of Wisconsin–Extension brought to the table the technical know-how to conduct local research and a track record in using research to solve problems.

277

Local citizens brought an intimate knowledge of their community that out-siders seldom have, and the energy and commitment it takes to bring about change.

In this chapter, I briefly describe Youth Futures, its theoretical roots, and its success in enacting local policies and programs to support youth and their families. Then based on my experience across the 22 communities, I extract several principles that undergird the success of these coalitions in influencing local policymaking. These principles can serve as guidelines for professionals interested in working on policy at the grassroots level (see also Bogenschneider, Small, & Riley, 1990). I illustrate these principles with real-life examples from the communities involved in Wisconsin Youth Fu-tures. I must add this caveat to the reader: These coalitions focused on building more supportive environments for an individual member of the family—youth—although many of the efforts were aimed at youth's primary socializing agent—their families. The lessons learned from these 7 years of experience, however, have implications for community efforts that focus on either individuals or families.

HOW WISCONSIN YOUTH FUTURES WORKED

During the 1990s, Youth Futures built 22 coalitions in Wisconsin neighbor-hoods and communities, ranging from a small agricultural community of less than 700 people to a 12-block inner-city neighborhood in Milwaukee. In partnership with county extension faculty who specialize in family living, youth development, agriculture, and community development, Youth Fu-tures formed coalitions of 30 to 35 citizens including judges; school superin-tendents, principals, and teachers; law enforcement officials; presidents of parent–teacher associations; clergy; business leaders; local government of-ficials; representatives of community service clubs; parents; and young peo-ple. The purpose of these coalitions was to build community support for youth by developing comprehensive action plans to promote positive youth development and to prevent specific risky behaviors such as alcohol consumption, depression, prejudice, tobacco use, and youth violence.

These successful community efforts are built on the premises of commu-nity theory—that community citizens may be best positioned to influence lo-cal policymaking because of their intimate knowledge of the community, a vested interest in supporting local youth and families, and a commitment to ensuring that policies are implemented and sustained. Youth Futures was grounded in the tenets of ecological risk-protective theory, which builds on both ecological theory and developmental contextualism (see Bogen-schneider, 1996, for a full review). Ecological theory posits that prevention efforts are most successful if they simultaneously work to address both risk and protective processes, and developmental contextualism posits that prevention programs should be tailored to the unique needs of the neighborhood or community.

Although initially developed and discussed in the context of youth development, the concepts seem readily transferable to family development with only minor modifications in the definitions. When viewed from a family perspective, risk processes are hazards that increase families' vulnerability to future negative outcomes, and protective processes are safeguards that help families resist stressful life events, and promote adaptation and competence. Successful policies and programs should target both risk and protective processes at multiple levels of the human ecology to create a comprehensive, multifaceted effort. For example, building protective processes that help families resist life stresses and promote competent functioning, although important in their own right, seem incomplete without concurrent attempts to make the environment less hazardous for families to negotiate. Similarly, reducing risks in the environment without strengthening a family's ability to resist hazards seems incomplete.

This theoretical framework guided the development, implementation, and evaluation of the Youth Futures process. Initially, extension specialists and county faculty helped communities conduct surveys of local teens to identify the risks and opportunities that confront local youth. Then during five or six meetings, coalition members identified the most critical local youth issues and learned about the latest research on adolescent development, risk and protective processes, effective prevention programs, and community success stories. Next, the coalition assessed what youth resources and supports were available in the community so that they could target their planning to gaps that existed locally. Members developed a comprehensive, multidimensional action plan, and county extension faculty and staff worked with local volunteers to implement the plan. Evaluating the community's efforts involved monitoring risk and protective processes in the short run and tracking changes in youth behavior in the long run.

THE TRACK RECORD OF WISCONSIN YOUTH FUTURES IN CHANGING LOCAL POLICIES

To date, 17 of 22 sites have focused on preventing adolescent alcohol and other substance use. This section reviews some of their preliminary success in reducing documented risks and bolstering proven protective processes associated with adolescent alcohol use. Not only are these processes empirically related to teen alcohol use, their commonsense appeal (i.e., face validity) makes them useful and persuasive with funders, administrators, and community stakeholders. In the interests of brevity, I have included only selected examples of the preliminary effectiveness of our first 15 Youth Futures sites in addressing, first, three risk processes and, then, one protective process that are empirically related to teen alcohol use. I also review other evidence that Youth Futures became a valued entity in the community.

Reducing Documented Risk Processes

Availability of Alcohol. Because underage drinking is related to easy access to alcohol (Hawkins, 1989), Youth Futures volunteers in two communities decreased the availability of alcohol by persuading city officials to deny liquor licenses to convenience stores. In one community, anyone who sells alcohol to a minor is now required to appear in court, so that judges can detect repeat offenders and enforce penalties more uniformly than could arresting officers. In yet another community, the annual family picnic of a major industry was held alcohol free for the first time.

Unclear Family Rules, Expectations, and Rewards. Because youth problems are less likely when parents communicate clear positions and establish consequences if rules are broken (Hawkins, 1989), one community held a parent education program geared to preventing teen drinking; every parent in attendance reported establishing a clear position on teen alcohol use. In another community, half of the parents of high school students joined a parent network and pledged that parties in their homes would be chaperoned and alcohol free; they also promised to support agreed-on curfews and to take steps to ensure that youth activities held outside homes were alcohol free. Another community surveyed all parents of 7th to 12th graders on their worries, parenting practices, and family rules regarding curfews, dating, and drinking. Fact sheets summarizing the findings were mailed to all parents of junior high students.

Complacent or Permissive Community Laws and Norms. Because youth are more apt to engage in risky behaviors when policies are unwritten, unclear, or unenforced (Higgins, 1988), one Youth Futures community located at the hub of five counties took action when they learned that students organized beer parties in the part of the city with the most lenient penalties. The Youth Futures coalition organized a local underage drinking conference with funding from the Wisconsin Department of Transportation. More than 70 participants, representing law enforcement, social services, schools, and prevention organizations, developed specific county plans to create more consistent consequences for underage drinking, with follow-up scheduled. In another site, judges now suspend driver's licenses for under-age drinking, but they reduce the penalties if parents become involved in treatment.

Bolstering Proven Protective Processes

Bonding to Family, School, and Other Social Institutions. Research suggests that when youth successfully participate in meaningful roles, they bond to the community. This bond, in turn, promotes the personal motivation to adhere to family rules, school policies, and community norms (Hawkins, Catalano, Barnard, et al., 1992). In a survey of 15 youth from five sites, teens rated the increase in meaningful roles for youth as one of two top benefits of Youth Futures from a list of 14 possibilities. As examples, older teens in five sites now serve as mentors for elementary students. Two sites have revitalized the high school student council, and 12 students in the National Honor Society in another site operate a homework hotline. As an alternative to jail, one site provides community service and life skills training for first-time youth offenders; of nine referrals, only one has returned to jail.

Becoming a Valued Part of the Community

Other ways to evaluate the effectiveness of Youth Futures are (a) institutionalization of the program in Wisconsin communities, (b) contributions of time and money, and (c) perceptions of local stakeholders. Eight of the first 15 sites incorporated, which indicates those communities were willing to institutionalize Youth Futures as a legitimate local entity. Between 1990 and 1996, volunteers in the first 20 sites donated over 77,000 hours of time, or approximately 9,625 8-hour work days. These efforts were matched by almost 75,000 hours, or about 9,375 8-hour work days, of redirected time from county and state extension faculty (excluding staff hired solely to work on Youth Futures). These community programs generated over $1 million of cash or in-kind services to benefit youth and families at the local level (excluding federal grants to the state).

Views of stakeholders were gathered through interviews. In a survey of 17 adult volunteers (81% response rate) and 15 youth volunteers from five sites, 94% of the adults and 100% of the teens had recommended Youth Futures to another adult or teen in the community. This enthusiasm for citizen coalitions as a mechanism for changing local policy is articulated by a circuit court judge: "I would highly recommend that individuals in their communities get involved in Youth Futures type organizations. I am not saying that it is going to result in any miracles, but when people band together over such issues as underage drinking, abuse of drugs . . . and truancy, that they can make a difference."

PRINCIPLES TO GUIDE COALITIONS IN INFLUENCING LOCAL POLICYMAKING

Given the changes that these coalitions were able to make in a number of diverse communities, my extension colleagues and I extracted several principles and procedures that contributed to this success in influencing local policymaking. The principles are illustrated with the experiences of several Youth Futures communities in preventing adolescent alcohol use, but clearly have implications beyond this issue for other community efforts as well.

Identify the Real Issues or Problems Facing Local Families

Ecological theory suggests that, just as the natural ecology varies from one community to another, the social ecology may vary as well. The problems families face, the etiology of these problems, and the most appropriate responses may differ from one community or neighborhood to the next. Thus, policy efforts may be more successful if coalitions take time to identify those problems that local citizens feel that families in their community or neighborhood face.

One of the first steps in our work with a Youth Futures community was to help them secure data or conduct their own research with local youth and sometimes with local parents. They collected data on local worries and concerns, perceptions of the community, and youth involvement in positive and problematic behaviors through methods such as the Teen Assessment Project (TAP) and the Tapping into Parenting (TIP) Survey (see Small & Bogenschneider, 1998).

Because people are more apt to believe research conducted in their hometown (Riley, 1991), local data can be a powerful way to convince parents and other community members of the relevance of local efforts and to motivate them to action (Baumgartel, 1969). Prior to surveys in their communities, many Wisconsin parents believed that teen use of illicit drugs such as cocaine or crack was the major drug problem. Small's TAP surveys have consistently shown that the major drug problem is alcohol use. Prior to the TIP survey, many parents denied that the problems portrayed in the national media affect their own children. For example, one TIP survey collected matched data from 666 mother–teen pairs and 510 father–teen pairs in one Wisconsin county (60% response rate for parents and 88% response rate for students). Of those teens who reported regular alcohol use, less than one third of their parents were aware of their adolescents' drinking (Bogenschneider, Wu, Raffaelli, & Tsay, 1998).

Mobilizing communities around youth and family issues is difficult, if not impossible, if parents are unaware that their children's development is being compromised by their involvement in potentially risky behaviors. Policymakers are unlikely to enact policies to address problems that they do not know exist, but they often respond when constituents bring issues to their attention. For example, in one Youth Futures community, the Students Against Driving Drunk (SADD) chapter determined through telephone interviews that parents thought the community was issuing too many liquor licenses. This finding was responsible, in part, for the passage of a new city ordinance limiting the number of liquor licenses. In another community, the Youth Futures coalition asked the local park commission to ban alcohol sales at Little League games. When the park commission refused, the Youth Futures committee surveyed all other communities in the county. Faced with data that this was the only community in the county that sold alcohol at Little League games, the park commission recommended, and the village board passed, a permanent ban on alcohol sales at youth events.

Local surveys also provide feedback on what policies and programs are most consistent with the values and beliefs of local youth and parents. For example, in a survey of parents of teens in one Wisconsin community (66% response rate), 93% of parents agreed or strongly agreed that the penalties for selling alcohol to minors should be more strictly enforced, 86% that birth control should be taught in the school, and 83% that the penalties for underage drinking should be more strictly enforced (Bogenschneider, Wu, Thomas, & Wu, 1996). Results like these extend the democratic process by developing policies and programs that reflect the community's collective priorities, not the priorities of a vocal minority.

Establish Well-Defined Goals That Address Proven Risk and Protective Processes

One of the most important steps in planning a successful prevention program is selecting and defining the issue or problem. Without clear goals and outcomes, programs are less apt to succeed for several reasons. First, financial and human resources are often limited, and programs that try to prevent everything may be spread so thin that they end up preventing nothing. Second, success is difficult to assess without well-defined goals that can more easily be translated into measurable outcomes. For example, goals of preventing risky youth behaviors or promoting more positive environments for youth and families are too vague. Communities were encouraged to begin by focusing on one specific goal (e.g., preventing adolescent alcohol use) and three or more proven strategies for reaching this goal (e.g., developing alternative activities for youth at times when alcohol consumption occurs, providing parent education, tightening enforcement of existing laws on underage drinking, or increasing opportunities for youth involvement in the school and community).

By reviewing which policies and programs work and which do not, communities are more apt to invest in programs with evidence of effectiveness and to avoid the latest trendy approaches. "Selling self-esteem to children has become big business" (Dryfoos, 1991, p. 633), despite little evidence that improving self-esteem reduces risky behaviors. Only good programs and policies that target proven risk and protective processes produce good results (Zigler & Styfco, 1993).

Be Comprehensive in Addressing Both Risk and Protective Processes in Several Levels of the Human Ecology

All too often, policymakers look for magic bullets—quick solutions to complex problems that result in piecemeal, Band-Aid approaches. Yet as ecological theory predicts and as a growing body of research supports, most youth and family problems have not a single cause, but many, and have no simple approach for addressing complex problems. Furthermore, the best approach may depend on the teen's personality, age, developmental stage, or context. For example, in a disadvantaged inner-city neighborhood, the best approach may be to focus on protective factors to instill a sense of hope into a seemingly desperate situation. In a rural community or middle-class suburb, the best approach may be one that jars complacency and overcomes denial by emphasizing the risks that even families living behind white picket fences may face.

Moreover, risk and protective processes are not confined to any one part of the human ecology. Programs and policies are more apt to be successful if they are ecological, and thus deal with the child as part of the family and the family as part of the school and community (Lerner, 1995; Schorr, 1991). For example, one of the best predictors of child abuse is not a particular personality trait of the mother, but rather social isolation. Providing mothers with social support resulted in 46% fewer verified cases of child abuse (Olds, 1997). Similarly, school-based substance abuse programs typically have a poor record in reducing student drug use (Bangert-Drowns, 1988). Even when school programs change behavior, this success is short-lived in the absence of family and community norms that support the program goals (Tobler, 1992).

To be successful, programs should address both risk and protective processes at several levels of the human ecology to create a comprehensive, multifaceted effort. For example, in one Wisconsin community working to prevent teen drinking, initial efforts focused on reducing risks—specifically, on strengthening those laws and practices that made it clear their hometown would not tolerate underage drinking. Yet with prompting from the town's young people, the community also began to assess which safeguards existed, what opportunities were available for young people to actively contribute to the community, and whether rewarding alternatives to teen drinking were readily available. After an exploratory survey of local teens and follow-up discussions, the community decided to remodel a building for a teen center. Young people were given opportunities to be involved in meaningful ways: visiting successful teen centers around the state, developing the rules of conduct for the center, interviewing candidates for the center director, and developing the center bookkeeping system.

Another community is focusing on the prevention of chewing tobacco use. Because peer pressure is one of the strongest predictors of chewing tobacco use (Murray, Davis-Hearn, Goldman, Pirie, & Luepker, 1988; Newcomb & Bentler, 1989), several high school students taught all sixth graders in the school a chewing tobacco prevention curriculum that included peer refusal skills. This coalition recognized that building strengths in young people (i.e., bolstering protective factors) is an important strategy.

Yet they simultaneously took steps to reduce the amount of peer pressure that youth must resist and to minimize other risks by establishing clear no-use norms in the community. For example, a parent–teacher network was formed to increase the consistency of messages young people receive from the school and the family. The community opened the school gym for midnight basketball to provide a healthy alternative to chewing tobacco use. The coalition also asked the village board to strictly enforce state laws regarding underage tobacco use. When these initial attempts failed, the coalition, in collaboration with Cooperative Extension, surveyed all parents of 7th to 12th graders to gather their views on this issue and other parenting concerns. With over half of parents responding, 95% agreed or strongly agreed that penalties for selling tobacco to minors should be more strictly enforced. These data were used with the new village board after local elections. Few would argue that stiffening the penalties for chewing tobacco use will work alone, yet it remains an important component of a comprehensive strategy that addresses both risk and protective processes.

Collaborate With Stakeholders in the Community or Neighborhood

Family problems, like youth problems, are much too complex and the solutions much too comprehensive for any one agency or organization to address alone (Albee, 1983). Consistent with the notion that development occurs in context, consensus seems to be emerging that the most appropriate place for solving problems is where they occur—in communities. Local residents are their own best resources for bringing about change in areas important to them (Bellah et al., 1985/1996; Gardner, 1989; Lofquist, 1983; McKnight & Kretzmann, 1992). Involving local citizens in planning helps ensure that prevention programs fit the community and helps generate local ownership and commitment to seeing that the program is implemented and maintained.

Sadly, studies document programs that were extremely effective in statistical terms and human outcomes, yet failed to gain acceptance in the community. Swift and Healey (1986) developed a program that increased stimulation of high-risk infants. However, even as the researchers were packing up their program manuals, the nurses, administrators, and parents were returning to their prior mode of operation. By failing to involve the community in design and implementation, the program failed to generate local acceptance and commitment, thereby limiting the likelihood that this highly successful program would continue.

Thus, even targeting critical needs with proven programs is no guarantee of long-term success. Local citizens need to be involved in program selection, design, and implementation if the program has any hope of becoming institutionalized in the community and generating long-term change (Edelman, 1987; Jenkins, 1989). Sustaining a program may depend less on methodology or staff qualifications than on an understanding of the dynamics of the system in which the program operates (Swift & Healey, 1986) and on steps taken to increase the capacity of community members to continue the program (Lerner, 1995).

According to interviews of 17 Youth Futures coalition members at five sites (81% response rate), the two most important determinants of the success of coalitions are: (a) the composition of the local coalition—specifically, its representativeness and collective power to access resources and influence policy and program development; and (b) the coalition's support from stakeholders in the community, including civic leaders, youth, parents, business groups, and churches or places of worship. In Wisconsin, the list of collaborators is extensive. For example, local program assistants have been supported with financial resources from federal grants, county governments, alcohol and drug abuse funds, city youth and family commissions, school districts, city recreation departments, and private donors.

Educate Coalition Members on Current Theory and Research on Family Development, Prevention Policies and Programs, and Community Process

To encourage comprehensive action plans, coalition members are trained in ecological risk-protective theory, and they use local data to apply these risk and protective processes to the community. This risk and protective approach serves to break complex, seemingly overwhelming problems into manageable pieces, thereby overcoming the sense of hopelessness that often pervades youth issues and chokes off meaningful response. Furthermore, learning which programs and policies have evidence of effectiveness helps coalitions work strategically by focusing their efforts on activities with the greatest potential payoff. Extension specialists in community development have also put together guidelines for selecting a community, recruiting coalition members, prioritizing youth issues, generating prevention strategies, developing action plans, and dealing with pessimistic members who try to discourage progress.

Tailor the Plan to the Community, Reducing Risks That Exist Locally and Building Protective Processes That Do Not Exist

Many effective prevention programs exist, yet developmental contextualism suggests that one standard program cannot be expected to work in all communities. To help communities tailor programs to the local situation (McKnight & Kretzmann, 1992), my colleagues and I wrote several literature reviews on risk and protective processes for specific youth problems and translated them into checklists of community resources and supports needed to prevent risky behaviors and foster positive youth development (see these checklists at http://www.familyimpactseminars.org/cats.htm). Some needs assessments quantify deficiencies and problems (McKnight & Kretzmann, 1992), but in Youth Futures local citizens self-assess their community's needs, but also their community's assets and capacities. In so doing, coalitions identify resources and supports that are already in place and those that are missing. In Milwaukee, for example, at least 35 organizations deliver parent education; another parent education program would be foolish, wasting limited resources and creating competition rather than collaboration (Bogenschneider et al., 1990).

Jessica Mills and I recently tested the validity of one of these checklists, the Youth Support Inventory for Adolescent Alcohol and Other Drug Use, which was used by 17 communities to self-assess the local risk for adolescent substance use: As predicted, communities with higher scores on the checklist (i.e., more community support for youth) had adolescents who reported lower rates of beer and wine use, lower rates of hard liquor consumption, and fewer instances of binge drinking in the past month. Moreover, the checklist guided coalitions to be more strategic in developing programs and policies that filled gaps in community resources and supports. Of the 63 prevention strategies identified by the coalitions, 94% addressed resources that the local self-assessment indicated were not extensively available in the community (see Mills & Bogenschneider, 2001).

To my knowledge, only one checklist is available for local citizens to assess how responsive their community is to family well-being (see http://www.familyimpactseminars.org/ffccheck.pdf). This self-assessment tool, developed by the Premier's Council in Support of Alberta Families, appears to assess many important dimensions of a community's support for families, although its reliability and validity have not yet been empirically verified.

Be Sensitive to Cultural, Ethnic, and Other Forms of Diversity in the Neighborhood or Community

To be consistent with the tenets of developmental contextualism, professionals must be sensitive to differences in assumptions, values, and expectations that are likely to occur across communities. Because social science research is overwhelmingly based on White, middle-class samples (Lerner, 1995), a careful examination of the research on risk and protective processes is essential to determine whether it is valid in different ethnic contexts.

Youth Futures also considers diversity within communities. For example, coalition members represent the racial, ethnic, social class, age, and gender diversity of the community. The coalitions invite representatives of all political persuasions in the community, including those who may oppose community solutions to youth problems such as teaching sex education in school. In one community, the organizers overlooked a less visible aspect of diversity—the length of residence in the community. The coalition was inadvertently comprised of primarily newcomers and included few longtime residents. Including all perspectives allows coalition members the opportunity to learn about different values and beliefs (Camino, 1995) and wins the support and commitment of a cross-section of the community, as evidenced by this comment from one school official: "So they're [coalition members] working really effectively together, and it's really a plus. It's really unusual for a community as diverse as ours and it's a great opportunity for people to become one community when we're thinking of our students and our future."

Proceed When Public Interest Is High

Many communities attribute their success to timing, timing, and timing. Some sites have capitalized on a local event that has mobilized interest on an issue, such as a tragic teen death, a highly publicized sting operation, or a well-attended beer party that police busted. Other sites have created events by releasing survey data, scheduling a news conference, or sponsoring a Youth Futures week with proclamations by the mayor and other dignitaries.

Anticipate How Changes in One Part of the System May Affect Changes in the System or Other Settings

In any ecological system, changing one part of the system usually affects the system or other settings (Segal, 1983). Professionals can use this characteristic of systems to their advantage. The likelihood of extinguishing one behavior is enhanced if alternative behaviors are available. For example, just as people trying to quit smoking often chew gum, teens are less likely to use alcohol if alternatives are available at times when drinking is likely to occur. One young person organized a midnight basketball league as an alternative to weekend drinking; as a result, one teen participant stated, "I'd be out drinking if I wasn't here." Another community planned a dance for youth to coincide with the annual firefighters' celebration; for the first time in 20 years, the police chief reported that no underage drinking took place at this event.

No matter how well intentioned, any prevention program that is powerful enough to change behavior for the better could also have unintended and usually unanticipated adverse side effects (Shaffer, Philips, Garland, & Bacon, 1989). For example, one of the communities planned an after-school event for middle school students that resulted in more students loitering downtown.

Policies need to take steps to foster, not replace or weaken, naturally occurring sources of support for parents in the extended family, neighborhood, and community. Policies can create formal structures to encourage people to develop and rely on their own sources of social support, which in the future will render the formal policies obsolete (Bronfenbrenner & Weiss, 1983).

Evaluate Effectiveness by Monitoring Changes in Risk and Protective Processes

Policy evaluation is often synonymous with program evaluation because programs are often the means through which policies are operationalized. Because many family outcomes are long term in nature and become apparent only after several years of program operation, professionals also need to strengthen their capacity to identify interim indicators of successful programs. In Youth Futures, the short-term evaluations involved monitoring the community's progress in reducing known risk processes and bolstering proven protective processes. These preliminary indicators of effectiveness can be useful to policymakers, because they are more in keeping with brief budgeting cycles and election demands for immediate tangible results.

SUMMARY

The experience of these 22 coalitions in Wisconsin neighborhoods and communities support the premises of community empowerment theory—that the momentum for creating environments to support youth and families stems not only from top-down state or federal policies, but also from grassroots coalitions that engage citizens in public problem solving around common concerns. My colleagues and I observed firsthand how local coalitions developed policies and programs to support local youth and families and, in so doing, created more caring communities. Few professional efforts are more satisfying than helping energetic, enthusiastic citizens make concrete changes they deem important in their communities. What greater reward can there be than seeing a diverse group of people come together to grapple with a common concern, and leave with more tolerance of different views and greater trust that fellow citizens will act in the public good?

I witnessed the utility of ecological risk-protective theory in guiding coalitions to comprehensively assess the local situation and to strategically steer their efforts toward strategies that research suggests may have the highest payoff. I observed the value of developmental contextualism in prompting us to expect many commonalities and idiosyncrasies across communities. Every community had within its midst active, concerned citizens who were willing to work together to create changes of lasting civic value. Yet community concerns also varied, and there were no standard boilerplate policies and programs that fit every community. Despite many similarities, 40% of the prevention strategies developed by the communities were unique to a specific site (see Mills & Bogenschneider, 2001).

From Youth Futures comes the optimism that communities have the capacity to change local policies in ways that support youth and families, but also the realism that changes do not happen overnight. In one community, it took 2 years to get law enforcement officials from seven jurisdictions to sit down around the table. Perhaps the most valuable Youth Futures lesson is this: Thoughtful, committed citizens can change the world, but it takes patience, persistence, sweat, and the confidence it can be done.

Chapter 15 is adapted from Bogenschneider, K. (1996). An ecological risk/protective theory for building prevention programs, policies, and community capacity to support youth. *Family Relations, 45,* 127–138. Copyright 1996 by the National Council on Family Relations, 3989 Central Ave. NE, Suite 550, Minneapolis, MN 55421. Adapted by permission.

CHAPTER

16

Is It Time to Take Family
Policy Seriously?

At present, families are everyone's concern, but nobody's responsibility.
—Ooms (1990, p. 77)

In the preface, I compared family policymaking to Barth's floating opera (Barth, 1967/1983). Family policymaking is like the opera that is being acted out on the deck of a showboat that is floating up and down the river in view of the audience seated along both shores. Those of us in the audience catch part of the plot as the showboat floats by, but we never get the whole story. We sometimes catch sight of family issues, but they drop out of view before we have the time or knowledge to act. The goal of this book is to provide an overview of the whole floating opera—the rationale for and substance of family policy—so that you can better see how the work you already do contributes to family policymaking and what additional expertise you have waiting in the wings that could be brought to center stage.

I contend that the main character in policymaking in this country is individualism and that familism is assigned bit parts and sometimes excluded altogether. If familism was cast in a leading role, policymaking would benefit because families provide a unique quality that no other character, no other interest group, and no other institution provides as well—commitment to others.

Family policy first opened in the 1970s; despite some initial shaky reviews, it has gained renown in policy circles because of a number of philanthropic commitments, federal and state laws, and endorsements by the American people. Family policy has the potential to become a long-running opera that stays on the marquee for quite some time, but its success depends on how much of a following it generates from its devotees.

In its short history, interest in family policy has ebbed and flowed, but now may be at its highest peak in 20 years among the public, policymakers, and professionals alike (Hutchins, 1998; Ooms, 1995; Whitehead, 1992). For example, in recent public opinion polls (Bennett, Petts, & Blumenthal, 1999), a resounding 99% of Americans say that loving family relationships are extremely (91%) or somewhat (9%) important to them—beliefs that appear identical among African Americans and Whites (Wilson, 1999). The leaders of state legislatures across the country—whether Democrat or Republican, liberal or conservative—agree that a vote for child and family issues is a surefire winner (State Legislative Leaders Foundation, 1995). Researchers familiar with hundreds of studies and practitioners who teach or serve scores of families have called for family-focused policymaking in a number of reports issued by federal and state agencies, national commissions, nonprofit organizations, and professional associations (see Fig. 1.1).

Despite the unprecedented popularity that families currently command as a theme in policymaking, *family policy* is still not a term widely used by policymakers, journalists, or the public. Curiously, Americans rate their families as twice as important as their job and one third more important than their financial security (Bennett, Petts, & Blumenthal, 1999), yet examples abound of how family policy takes a back seat compared with economic or environmental policy. It has become standard procedure for policymakers to consider the economic or environmental impact of legislation before they cast their vote, but family considerations are seldom taken into account in policy decisions. Economists cannot predict with a reliable degree of scientific certainty when an economic downturn will occur, yet the government regularly takes actions and enacts policies that are thought to avoid an economic slowdown; for family policies, when the effectiveness of a policy is uncertain, the typical response is this: if it is not proven to work, do not fund it (Zuckerman, 2000).

Economic policy is held in such high regard by policymakers that several formal bodies, including the Council of Economic Advisers and the Joint Economic Committee, were established as long ago as 1945 to help the nation set and reach its economic goals. No such entities exist for families despite specific proposals for their creation advanced to presidential candidates and public officials in the 1988 elections. Economic policies can generate deep-seated passion and controversy, but mechanisms exist (e.g., government shutdowns and interest rate adjustments) to move economic issues forward; mechanisms for overcoming the controversy surrounding family policies are not widely discussed or generally agreed on. The media regularly reports on the country's economic well-being through publicly recognized indicators such as the gross national product, the consumer price index, and the monthly inflation rate, yet barometers of family well-being are fewer in number and attract far less press coverage. In a 13-month analysis of news stories in five major newspapers, 6,700 articles appeared on the stock market, compared to 494 articles on child and family issues such as welfare reform, single-parent families, and teen mothers (Crittenden, 2001).

This conundrum—a politically popular issue with no secure place on the policymaking agenda—deserves the attention of professionals who support families and work on their behalf. In political settings, where timing means everything, clearly the time for action is right. It is time for professionals to take family policy seriously. We have a mandate to proceed, but whether we capitalize on the current enthusiasm for families and family-focused policies depends on our (a) ability to articulate how policymakers can act on their interest in families, (b) our willingness to apply the growing body of knowledge of how policymaking affects families and how professionals can affect policymaking, and (c) our persistence and persuasiveness in making families more than a political icon. A consideration of each of these issues follows.

HOW POLICYMAKERS CAN ACT ON THEIR INTEREST IN FAMILIES

Based on recent polls, policymakers' interest in families is high. Our job as professionals is not to convince policymakers of the power of families in the lives of Americans or the political appeal of family issues in the voting booth. No sales job is required. Instead, we need to clearly communicate to policymakers how they can transform their interest in families into policies and programs that support the important work that families do for their members and for the nation.

Granted, there are many ways that policymakers can exert their influence on behalf of families—in their campaign speeches, press conferences, and communications with constituents. In the interests of brevity, I focus on only two specific actions that we can encourage policymakers to take, actions that parallel the distinction proposed earlier in the definitions of *family policy* and *a family perspective in policymaking*. First, we can encourage policymakers to enact broad-based family policies that would support families in fulfilling their functions. Second, we can encourage policymakers to promote a family perspective in policymaking by assessing the consequences of any given legislation regardless of whether it is explicitly aimed at family functions for its impact on family well-being.

Encouraging Policymakers to Build Family Policy

Of the many functions that families perform, policymaking tends to focus on four: family creation, economic support, childrearing, and caregiving. Professionals can encourage policymakers to routinely ask what policies or programs might be needed to support families in performing these four important functions. For illustrative purposes, I raise four questions, one relating to each of these family functions based on the discussion in chapter 8.

- Because children do well economically, socially, and psychologically if their biological parents have a strong conflict-free marriage, does government have a role in promoting and strengthening marriage?
- Given the growing income disparity between the rich and poor, what policies can encourage parents' economic self-sufficiency without jeopardizing the well-being of children?
- Because family and work conflict is the concern most often voiced by parents, what policies are needed to help parents balance their responsibilities in the workforce with their commitments to their families?
- How much of a role should government play in helping families care for the disabled and frail elderly who experience ongoing difficulties in functioning?

To help policymakers identify which family issues are the most pressing and what policy responses are the most promising, professionals can monitor family trends, gather evidence on the effectiveness of policies and programs, and assess whether policies would be more effective if approached from a family perspective. Professionals need to develop innovative means of providing this information to policymakers in ways that are consistent with their information needs, work culture, and writing preferences (see chap. 14 for a full discussion).

Encouraging Policymakers to Promote a Family Perspective in Policymaking

Many of the issues that land on policymakers' desks are not family policies—they do not deal directly with family creation, economic support, childrearing, or caregiving—yet many would benefit from a family perspective. Zoning laws are not family policies per se because their scope is much larger than families, yet they might benefit from taking families into account. Zoning regulations may determine whether a child-care center can be located next to a senior housing facility (as is required in some European countries). Similarly, development covenants in retirement communities can ban children, which may prohibit grandparents from raising their grandchildren. Health care policies are not typically considered family policies because they are not aimed specifically at families. Yet because of the crucial role that families play in health and illness, policies might be more effective if they took families into account. Moreover, there is reason to believe that a family approach to health care may be more cost-effective than the present approach (see chap. 7 for a full discussion).

For policies that fall outside the family domain, professionals can encourage policymakers to routinely ask the following questions to assess how policies and programs might benefit from a family perspective. These questions sound deceptively simple, yet they can be powerful in developing sound, cost-effective policies.

- Are families part of the policy issue?
- How are families affected by the issue?
- Do families need to be involved in the policy response?
- How could or should families be taken into account in this policy or program?

Appendix A includes a complete list of 34 family impact questions that policymakers can use to develop legislation, to raise questions at hearings, or to evaluate the effectiveness of existing policies and programs. Professionals can help policymakers find the answers to these questions, sometimes with a formal study, but more likely with a paper-and-pencil assessment based on the best research- and practice-based knowledge available. Again, we need to develop lines of communication and working relationships with policymakers so that we can provide timely family information to them and so that they turn to us when family policy questions arise.

Thus, these two approaches are a humble attempt to begin articulating how policymakers can translate their interest in families into concrete policy initiatives. This leads to the obvious question of whether professionals know enough about families and about policymaking to get involved in helping policymakers (a) bring research to bear on policy decisions, and (b) act on their stated interest in families to promote a family perspective in policymaking.

DO PROFESSIONALS HAVE ENOUGH KNOWLEDGE TO MOVE FAMILY POLICY FORWARD?

We know how to build family policy. We possess the knowledge about how families contribute to social problems and in what ways they can be part of solutions. We have access to the latest research regarding which policies and programs work and which do not. We have expertise in what roles professionals can play, how to approach these roles, and which strategies work best. We have tools such as family impact analyses that can assess potential effects on family life, and technologies such as the Family Impact

Seminars and Youth Futures that can transfer this knowledge and information to policymakers.

Perhaps most important, because knowledge is often power in policy decisions, professionals have the potential to wield a unique kind of influence among policymakers and the public. We have the skills to discover new ideas, communicate them clearly, disseminate them broadly, and defend them using not rhetoric or personal anecdotes, but scientific standards of proof. We have the capacity to use this knowledge and expertise to engage our colleagues in family policy efforts; to motivate citizens to support the importance of family policy; to empower families to band together to respond to the challenges they face; to inform policymakers that family problems are often not just individual concerns, but societal responsibilities; and to help policymakers turn good research and good ideas into policy.

This information about ways of connecting knowledge and power is always valuable, but particularly now when experts, leaders, and citizens believe that American politics is less intelligent than it should be (Smith, 1991). If we professionals apply our knowledge, skills, and expertise in the policy arena, we can make inroads on restoring the dignity and legitimacy of American politics. Overcoming public cynicism, powerlessness, and distrust of the policymaking process is particularly important in a representative democracy, which depends on an informed, involved citizenry to make it work (Boyte, 1993a; Tocqueville, 1945). Moreover, by restoring public trust in policymaking, we can once again "shape a politics of rational hope" (Bevan, 1982, p. 1310), the hope that families can succeed against the odds and that policy can play a role in ameliorating the complex, seemingly intractable problems that families and society face.

DO PROFESSIONALS HAVE THE WILL TO TAKE FAMILY POLICY SERIOUSLY?

According to Newt Gingrich (1999), the former speaker of the U.S. House of Representatives, "The fate of our country may well depend upon whether or not scientists recognize that they have real responsibilities as citizens." This mandate extends to all professionals. Family policy is an idea whose time has come. Family policy matters. To date, no group consistently represents family interests, advances family research, or has assumed the leadership needed to shift the discourse from appreciating families to prioritizing them as worthy of study and political action. It is time for family professionals to get serious about our responsibilities to our profession, to families, to the nation. In the now-familiar words of Rabbi Hillel, "If not you, who? If not now, when?" (cited in Turnbull & Turnbull, 2000, p. 231).

The future of family policy appears grim if we dwell on the magnitude of the task, the profound meaning of the mission, and the inadequacies of the bearers of the family banner—how underfinanced, poorly staffed, loosely organized, and overcommitted we are. Yet the future appears bright if we focus on our patient, dedicated progress in moving the field forward—not in giant steps, but slowly and persistently. Those of us who work for families can be heartened to stay the course in the new millennium based on the advice of an anonymous state legislator (State Legislative Leaders Foundation, 1995): "Persist with well-researched and accredited information and keep at it. Politics belongs to the persistent" (p. 29).

In the words of T. S. Eliot (1943):

> What we call the beginning is often the end,
> And to make an end is to make a beginning.
> The end is where we start from.

A

A Checklist for Assessing the Impact of Policies on Families

The first step in developing family-friendly policies is to ask the right questions:

- What can government and community institutions do to enhance the family's capacity to help itself and others?
- What effect does (or will) this policy (or proposed program) have for families? Will it help or hurt, strengthen or weaken family life?

These questions sound simple, but they can be difficult to answer.

The Family Criteria (Ad Hoc) Task Force of the Consortium of Family Organizations (COFO) developed a checklist to assess the intended and unintended consequences of policies and programs on family stability, family relationships, and family responsibilities. The checklist includes six basic principles that serve as the criteria of how sensitive to and supportive of families policies and programs are. Each principle is accompanied by a series of family impact questions.

The principles are not rank ordered and sometimes they conflict with each other, requiring trade-offs. Cost effectiveness also must be considered. Some questions are value-neutral and others incorporate specific values. People may not always agree on these values, so sometimes the questions will require rephrasing. This tool, however, reflects a broad nonpartisan consensus, and it can be useful to people across the political spectrum.

This checklist can be used to conduct a family impact analysis of policies and programs.

For the questions that apply to your policy or program, record the impact on family well-being.

❶
Principle 1. Family support and responsibilities.

Policies and programs should aim to support and supplement family functioning and provide substitute services only as a last resort.
Does the proposal or program:

- ○ Support and supplement parents' and other family members' ability to carry out their responsibilities?
- ○ Provide incentives for other persons to take over family functioning when doing so may not be necessary?
- ○ Set unrealistic expectations for families to assume financial and caregiving responsibilities for dependent, seriously ill, or disabled family members?
- ○ Enforce absent parents' obligations to provide financial support for their children?

❷
Principle 2. Family membership and stability.

Whenever possible, policies and programs should encourage and reinforce marital, parental, and family commitment and stability, especially when children are involved. Intervention in family membership and living arrangements is usually justified only to protect family members from serious harm or at the request of the family itself.
Does the policy or program:

- ○ Provide incentives or disincentives to marry, separate, or divorce?
- ○ Provide incentives or disincentives to give birth to, foster, or adopt children?
- ○ Strengthen marital commitment or parental obligations?
- ○ Use appropriate criteria to justify removal of a child or adult from the family?
- ○ Allocate resources to help keep the marriage or family together when this is the appropriate goal?
- ○ Recognize that major changes in family relationships such as divorce or adoption are processes that extend over time and require continuing support and attention?

❸
Principle 3. Family involvement and interdependence.

Policies and programs must recognize the interdependence of family relationships, the strength and persistence of family ties and obligations, and the wealth of resources that families can mobilize to help their members.
  To what extent does the policy or program:

○ Recognize the reciprocal influence of family needs on individual needs, and the influence of individual needs on family needs?

○ Recognize the complexity and responsibilities involved in caring for family members with special needs (e.g., physically or mentally disabled, or chronically ill)?

○ Involve immediate and extended family members in working toward a solution?

○ Acknowledge the power and persistence of family ties, even when they are problematic or destructive?

○ Build on informal social support networks (e.g., community and neighborhood organizations, religious communities) that are essential to families' lives?

○ Respect family decisions about the division of labor?

○ Address issues of power inequity in families?

○ Ensure perspectives of all family members are represented?

○ Assess and balance the competing needs, rights, and interests of various family members?

○ Protect the rights and safety of individuals in the family while respecting parents' rights and family integrity?

❹
Principle 4. Family partnership and empowerment.

Policies and programs must encourage individuals and their close family members to collaborate as partners with program professionals in delivery of services to an individual. In addition, parent and family representatives are an essential resource in policy development, program planning, and evaluation.
  In what specific ways does the policy or program:

○ Provide full information and a range of choices to families?

○ Respect family autonomy and allow families to make their own decisions? On what principles are family autonomy breached and program staff allowed to intervene and make decisions?

○ Encourage professionals to work in collaboration with the families of their clients, patients, or students?

○ Take into account the family's need to coordinate the multiple services required? Does it integrate well with other programs and services that the families use?

○ Make services easily accessible to families in terms of location, operating hours, and easy-to-use application and intake forms?

○ Prevent participating families from being devalued, stigmatized, or subjected to humiliating circumstances?

○ Involve parents and family representatives in policy and program development, implementation, and evaluation?

❺

Principle 5. Family diversity.

Families come in many forms and configurations, and policies and programs must take into account their varying effects on different types of families. Policies and programs must acknowledge and value the diversity of family life and not discriminate against or penalize families solely for reasons of structure, roles, cultural values, or life stage.

How does the policy or program:

○ Affect various types of families?

○ Acknowledge intergenerational relationships and responsibilities among family members?

○ Justify targeting only certain family types, for example, only employed parents or single parents? Does it discriminate against or penalize other types of families for insufficient reason?

○ Identify and respect the different values, attitudes, and behaviors of families from various racial, ethnic, religious, cultural, and geographic backgrounds that are relevant to program effectiveness?

❻

Principle 6. Support of vulnerable families.

Families in greatest economic and social need, as well as those determined to be most vulnerable to breakdown, should be included in government policies and programs.

Does the policy or program:

○ Identify and publicly support services for families in the most extreme economic or social need?

○ Give support to families who are most vulnerable to breakdown and have the fewest resources?

○ Target efforts and resources toward preventing family problems before they become serious crises or chronic situations?

The Policy Institute for Family Impact Seminars aims to connect research and policymaking and to promote a family perspective in research, policy, and practice. The Institute has resources for researchers, policymakers, and practitioners working to connect research and policymaking.

- To assist researchers and policy scholars, the Institute is building a network to facilitate cross-state dialogue and resource exchange on strategies for bringing research to bear on policymaking.

- To assist policymakers, the Institute disseminates research and policy reports that provide a family impact perspective on a wide variety of topics.

- To assist those who implement policies and programs, the Institute has available a number of family impact assessment tools for examining how responsive policies, programs, and institutions are to family well-being.

- To assist states who wish to create better dialogue between researchers and policymakers, the Institute provides technical assistance on how to establish your own state's Family Impact Seminars.

This checklist was adapted by the Policy Institute for Family Impact Seminars with permission from Ooms, T. (1995). *Taking families seriously as an essential policy tool.* Paper prepared for an expert meeting on Family Impact in Leuven, Belgium. The first version of this checklist was published by Ooms, T., & Preister, S. (Eds.). (1988). *A strategy for strengthening families: Using family criteria in policymaking and program evaluation.* Washington, DC: Family Impact Seminar.

The checklist and the papers are available from Director Karen Bogenschneider or Coordinator Heidi Normandin of the Policy Institute for Family Impact Seminars at the University of Wisconsin–Madison/Extension, 130 Human Ecology, 1300 Linden Drive, Madison, WI, 53706; phone (608) 262-4070; FAX (608) 262-5335; http://www.family impactseminars.org.

B

How to Conduct a Family Impact Analysis

Elizabeth Gross
Karen Bogenschneider
Carol Johnson
Policy Institute for Family Impact Seminars

Policies, programs, and organizations that involve families can have both intended and unintended consequences for the strength and stability of family life. Conducting a family impact analysis provides the opportunity to examine in-depth how sensitive to and supportive of families policies and programs are. A family impact analysis critically examines the past, present, or probable future effects of a policy, program, or service on family well-being. Unlike evaluation research, which assesses whether or not a program carries out its stated goals, family impact analysis examines whether these goals could result in positive or negative outcomes—whether intended or not—for families.

The first step in developing family-friendly policies and programs is to ask three important questions:

1. What can government or communities do to enhance families' capacity to help themselves and others?
2. What effect does (or will) this policy or program have for families?
3. Will this policy or program strengthen or weaken family life and responsibility?

What Tools Are Available to Conduct a Family Impact Analysis?

Family impact analysis checklists are available to examine the family impact of policies, programs, and services. These checklists provide specific criteria that can help in assessing how policies, programs, and organizations can better promote families' stability and commitment. Not all questions on these checklists will be relevant for all topics; the task for those interested in assessing family impact is to evaluate which questions and principles are most applicable to the issue at hand. The checklists were designed to delve both broadly and deeply into the ways in which families contribute to problems, how they are affected by problems, and whether or not families can be involved in solutions.

How Can Family Impact Analysis Be Used?

Family impact questions have proven useful across political party lines for several purposes, including:

1. Reviewing rules, legislation, and laws to point out how legislation does or does not address families' needs.
2. Helping prepare questions or testimony for hearings, board meetings, or public forums.
3. Evaluating programs and operating procedures of agencies or organizations to identify ways in which they are strong in their support of families, and what gaps exist in the services they provide.

Whereas family impact analysis can be used for any of the three purposes, the procedures for conducting these assessments vary according to their intended audience and format. Below we explain the steps involved in using family impact checklists to assess the family-friendliness of policies, programs, or organizations and to help prepare for hearings or testimonies.

I. How to Conduct Family Impact Analysis of a Policy

Policymakers routinely review the economic or environmental impact of a bill, yet far less often are they asked to consider how a bill affects families. Family impact analysis of legislation, laws, and rules can illuminate the ways that legislation is or is not supportive of family strength, functioning, and stability.

To analyze legislation for its family-friendliness, we use the Checklist for Assessing the Impact of Policies on Families originally developed by the Family Criteria (Ad Hoc) Task Force of the Consortium of Family Organizations, and recently revised by the Policy Institute for Family Impact Seminars (see Appendix A). The checklist includes six basic principles of family supportiveness, and reflects a broad nonpartisan consensus so that it can be useful across the political spectrum. For example, a family impact analysis of the Family and Medical Leave Act shows that because the law offers only unpaid leave for parents, spouses, and children to care for one another, it supports families' commitment to caregiving, but limits this commitment to a specific family structure. This could be very problematic if relatives eligible for family leave are unwilling or unable to take unpaid time away from work, or if the family member needing support is a sibling, grandparent, or unmarried partner.

To conduct a family impact analysis involves eight steps, which are detailed below. This procedure is adapted from the writing of Ooms & Preister (1988).

(1) Select a Policy or Program—Selecting a policy or program derived from one's personal interest and expertise, but may also depend upon timing, specifically the likelihood that the analysis will be used by policymakers and practitioners to develop more family-centered policy and practice. Assessing political and organizational readiness often entails consulting with policymakers, advocates, organizational staff, or those who track family policy.

(2) Determine Which Family Types Might be Affected—Policies or programs may have different effects on diverse family types. In the analysis, consider various aspects of diversity such as family structure (e.g., birth family, adoptive family, family of origin, extended family), family life stage (e.g., families with children or elderly dependents, aging families), socioeconomic diversity (e.g., income, education, number of wage earners), heritage (e.g., specific ethnic, racial, or religious affiliations), and community context (e.g., rural, suburban, and urban).

(3) Identify Relevant Family Functions—To assess how a policy or program affects specific aspects of family life, identify the family functions that may be directly or indirectly affected. The four main family functions are (a) family creation (e.g., to marry or divorce, to bear or adopt children, to provide foster care); (b) economic support (e.g., to provide for members' basic needs); (c) childrearing (e.g., to socialize the next generation), and (d) family caregiving (e.g., to provide assistance for the disabled, ill, frail, and elderly). Families also provide members with love and transmit cultural and religious values, but these intimate functions matter to social policy only when they interfere with the four main family functions (Ooms, 1990).

(4) Examine Implementation of the Policy or Program—Because the intent of a policy or program can be affected by implementation, examine how the policy or program has been operationalized. This often entails a broad consideration of relevant laws or court decisions, regulations, appropriations, administrative practices, related programs or policies, and implementation characteristics (e.g., staffing, accessibility, coordination with other programs, family-centered practices).

(5) Select Family Impact Questions—Select the principles and questions that are most appropriate for the issue at hand. Not all principles and questions will be relevant for all topics.

(6) **Gather and Review the Data**—Family impact analysis can entail an in-depth empirical analysis or even a computer simulation. Typically, it is a more informal process of estimating the likely consequences of a particular policy or program. Conducting the analysis may involve such tasks as collecting new data, interviewing informants, or reviewing relevant research.

(7) **Develop Policy Implications**—A family impact analysis may, but often does not, result in overwhelming support or opposition to a program or policy. Typically, the analysis identifies several ways in which a policy or program supports families and others ways it does not. After completing the analysis, policy implications can be drawn regarding the likely effects of the policy or program and its implementation on specific types of families and certain family functions. These implications often raise issues that policymakers and practitioners may wish to take into account in their decision making.

(8) **Apply of the Results**—After the analysis is done, a plan should be made for disseminating the results to those policymakers or practitioners who are in a position to apply the results to policies and programs. Providing the results to the public and to advocacy groups may generate interest and political pressure for family-friendly policies, programs, and implementation practices.

For examples of how family impact analysis can identify specific ways in which policies advantage or disadvantage families, see the Institute Web site at www.familyimpactseminars.org/impact.htm. Family impact analyses are available on the following topics:

- The Mental Health Parity Act.
- The Family and Medical Leave Act.
- The Individuals with Disabilities Education Act.
- Transracial Adoption and the Adoption and Safe Families Act.
- Temperament-Based Parenting Program.
- Home Visiting Programs.
- Program for Bone Marrow Transplantation of Adults.

2. How to Use Family Impact Analysis for Developing Testimony and Preparing Questions for Hearings

Family impact analysis can also be useful in preparing questions or testimony for hearings, board meetings, or public forums. Asking about family impact when policies are being developed, implemented, or evaluated can bring a unique perspective to policy debates or program goals by underscoring the importance of families as institutions that foster commitment to others.

For example, in a hearing on the issue of foster care policy, family impact analysis would suggest the importance of raising questions about whether or not the policy offers incentives—either explicit or implicit—for others to take over family functioning when doing so may not be necessary. Additionally, the family impact checklist would prompt questions about how to involve informal social support networks, such as community, neighborhood, or faith-based organizations in families' lives. Reviewing the family impact questions can help family professionals uncover how policy goals work with or against family well-being and identify questions that may be germane to encouraging a family impact perspective on the issue.

3. How to Conduct Family Impact Analysis of an Organization or Program

The purpose of family impact analysis for organizations or programs is to identify ways in which the services and operating procedures of agencies or organizations are and are not supportive of families. If you are interested in assessing the family-friendliness of your agency or organization, you can use the general checklist or one of the specific checklists.

Family impact analysis of a program or organization is most successful when it is conducted by those involved. These stakeholders not only have a vested interest in seeing the program maximize its potential, but they can also possess intimate knowledge of the program that outside evaluators may not have access to. Of course, you can conduct an analysis with a few strategically selected stakeholders or you can deliberately select a broad group of stakeholders that represent the diversity of the organization. For example, when we conduct a family impact analysis of a middle school using the Family/School Partnership Checklist, we have 25 to 30 individuals from the school complete the instrument. Stakeholders in a school include the following people:

- Parents or caretakers.
- Teachers.
- Administrative staff.
- Principals.
- Students.
- PTA/PTO members.
- Coaches or extracurricular leaders.
- School board members.
- Guidance counselors.

- Library staff.
- School volunteers.
- Community leaders.
- Custodial and maintenance staff.
- Liaisons to strategic planning committees, site councils, or school improvement planning groups.

To obtain a thorough and comprehensive assessment, the team of stakeholders should represent the diversity of the organization or program. The credibility of the family impact analysis will be enhanced if you make a conscientious effort to include representation from all segments of the organization. In the middle school example, we try to give attention to selecting and recruiting stakeholders who:

- Reflect the economic, educational, racial, and cultural diversity of the school community.
- Represent the different viewpoints that may exist in the school community.
- Represent each of the feeder elementary schools.
- Represent newcomers to the community as well as the "old guard"—those who have lived in the community for years.
- Include good representation of men and women.

Stakeholder Meetings. Stakeholders should complete the assessment before the group meets to conduct the organization's family impact analysis. During the stakeholders' meeting, it is helpful to break the 25 to 30 people down into four or five subgroups. These subgroups are assigned different sections of the family impact assessment tool, and should consist of people with knowledge of the particular section. It is important to carefully select the subgroups to make sure that people with the necessary information to complete the questions are in the subgroup. For example, in a school, the group completing the portion of the assessment dealing with communication could consist of a principal, administrative office staff, parents, teachers, school counselors, students, coaches, and extracurricular leaders.

The goal of the small group session is for each group to come to an agreement on each of the items assigned to them. This process involves discussion, and sharing of each individual's experiences and perspectives.

Reporting Findings. After all of the subgroups reach consensus, the entire group reconvenes as a large group to discuss each item of the assessment tool together. Each subgroup selects a leader to record and report the group's responses. As each subgroup reports, stakeholders should pay attention to see if they disagree on any items. At this point, the large group can discuss any changes that should be made to the subgroup's ratings. This provides everyone with an opportunity to give input on every item. After the meeting is complete, preparing a summary of how the organization or agency supports families and what the gaps might be can offer stakeholders a unified and concise look at what the program is doing well, and areas in need of improvement.

Next, stakeholders break into three groups of equal size and brainstorm strategies to address the shortcomings so that the organization can better support and strengthen families. Specifically, stakeholders identify strategies for making the organization more family friendly. Once each group is finished brainstorming strategies, the members should vote silently on their top three choices if less than 25 ideas or top five choices if more than 25 ideas.

The small groups then report their top three strategies to the large group. Members of the large group then vote confidentially on their top three choices. The top three to five vote getters become the priorities for action that will make the agency or organization more family friendly.

Developing a Plan. Finally, stakeholders develop concrete action plans to implement the strategies they have selected to make their organization more family friendly. It is important that the action plans have clear goals, are comprehensive, are informative, address potential pitfalls of implementation, and plan to evaluate and monitor the implementation progress. The purpose of the family impact analysis is not to plan for the sake of planning, but rather to plan for the sake of acting.

Summary

In conclusion, too often families are everyone's concern, but nobody's responsibility. Family professionals, policymakers, and researchers alike can use family impact analysis to move beyond our own families to create the conditions for all families to do their best in what families do best—instilling the responsibility and commitment to others on which the future depends.

References

A conversation with Richard Sennett. (1981, April 27). "You cannot ever make people enjoy being ruled." *U.S. News & World Report*, 79.

Aaron, H. J. (1978). *Politics and the professors: The great society in perspective.* Washington, DC: Brookings Institute.

Aaron, H. J. (2000). Presidential address: Seeing through the fog: Policymaking with uncertain forecasts. *Journal of Policy Analysis and Management, 19,* 193–206.

Abbott, G. (1931). Speech accepting an award from the National Institute of Social Sciences, U.S. Children's Bureau Records, RG 102, National Archives, College Park, Maryland.

Acs, G., & Maag, E. (2005). Irreconcilable differences? The conflict between marriage promotion initiatives for cohabiting couples with children and marriage penalties in tax and transfer programs. *New Federalism* (Series B, No. B-66). Washington, DC: Urban Institute.

Adams, B. (1995, Fall). Building a new political environment. *The Kettering Review*, 16–21.

Albee, G. W. (1983). Advocates and adversaries of prevention. In N. Garmezy & M. Rutter (Eds.), *Stress, coping, and development in children* (pp. 309–332). New York: McGraw-Hill.

Aldous, J., & Dumon, W. (1990). Family policy in the 1980s: Controversy and consensus. *Journal of Marriage and the Family, 52,* 1136–1151.

Aldous, J., Dumon, W., & Johnson, K. (1980). *The politics and programs of family policy: United States and European perspectives.* Notre Dame, IN: University of Notre Dame Press/Leuven University Press.

Amato, P. R. (2000). The consequences of divorce for adults and children. *Journal of Marriage and the Family, 62,* 1269–1287.

Amato, P. R. (2005). The impact of family formation change on the cognitive, social, and emotional well-being of the next generation. *The Future of Children, 15,* 75–96.

Amato, P. R., & Keith, B. (1991). Parental divorce and the well-being of children: A meta-analysis. *Psychological Bulletin, 110,* 26–46.

Anderson, E. (1995). Family policy. In D. Levinson (Ed.), *The encyclopedia of marriage and the family* (pp. 269–275). New York: Macmillan.

Anderson, E. A., & Koblinsky, S. A. (1995). Homeless policy: The need to speak to families. *Family Relations, 44,* 13–18.

Anderson, E. A., & Skinner, D. A. (1995). The components of family policy education. *Journal of Family and Economic Issues, 16,* 65–76.

Anderson, E., Skinner, D. A., & Letiecq, B. L. (2004). *Teaching family policy: A handbook of course syllabi, teaching strategies and resources* (2nd ed.). Minneapolis, MN: National Council on Family Relations.

Andrews, D. (1998, January). *Preventing delinquency through effective parent training and support.* Invited address at the 10th Wisconsin Family Impact Seminar, Building Resiliency and Reducing Risk: What Youth Need From Families and Communities to Succeed, Madison, WI.

Annie E. Casey Foundation. (2003). *Kids count data book 2003.* Washington, DC: Author.

Aos, S. (2003). Using taxpayer dollars wisely: The costs and benefits of incarceration and other crime control policies. In E. Gross, B. Friese, & K. Bogenschneider (Eds.), *Corrections policy: Can states cut costs and still curb crime?* (Wisconsin Family Impact Seminar Briefing Rep. No. 19, pp. 19–30). Madison: University of Wisconsin Center for Excellence in Family Studies.

Aos, S., Phipps, P., Barnoski, R., & Lieb, R. (1999). *The comparative costs and benefits of programs to reduce crime: A review of national research findings with implications for Washington state* (Document No. 99-05-1202). Olympia: Washington State Institute for Public Policy.

Arbuthnot, J., Kramer, K. M., & Gordon, D. A. (1997). Patterns of re-litigation following divorce education. *Family and Conciliation Courts Review, 35,* 269–279.

Arnold, A. D. (1990). *The logic of congressional action.* New Haven, CT: Yale University Press.

Asseo, L. (2001, February 22). Court deals blow to fed disabilities law in 5-4 ruling. *Wisconsin State Journal,* p. A3.

Baker, D. P., & Stevenson, D. L. (1986). Mothers' strategies for children's school achievement: Managing the transition to high school. *Sociology of Education, 59,* 155–166.

Bangert-Drowns, R. L. (1988). The effects of school-based substance abuse education: A meta analysis. *Journal of Drug Education, 18,* 243–264.

Barbarin, O. A., & Chesler, M. A. (1984). Relationships with the medical staff and aspects of satisfaction with care expressed by parents of children with cancer. *Journal of Community Health, 9,* 302–312.

Barratt, M. S. (1993). Early childrearing in Japan: Cross-cultural and intracultural perspectives. *Early Development and Parenting, 2,* 3–6.

Barrows, R. (1984, April). Taking a stand: Extension and public policy issues. *Journal of Extension, 22,* 6–12.

Barrows, R. (1994). *Public policy education.* Madison, WI: North Central Regional Publication, Cooperative Extension Service.

Bartels, P., & Boroniec, P. (1998). Badger Care: A case study of the elusive new federalism. *Health Affairs, 17,* 165–169.

Barth, J. (1983). *The floating opera* (rev. ed.). Toronto: Bantam Books. (Original work published 1967)

Bauder, D. (2004, June 28). Family friendly television group growing at its fifth anniversary. Retrieved on April 5, 2006 from http://www.womenssportsnet.com/EditModule.aspx?tabid=94&mid=703&def=News%20Article%20View&ItemId=3464

Baum, C. G., & Forehand, R. (1981). Long term follow-up assessment of parent training by use of multiple outcome measures. *Behavior Therapy, 12,* 643–652.

Baumgartel, H. (1969). Using employee questionnaire results for improving organizations. In W. B. Eddy, W. W. Burke, V. Dupre, & O. South (Eds.), *Behavioral science and the manager's role* (pp. 300–307). Washington, DC: NTL Institute for Applied Behavioral Science.

Baydar, N., & Brooks-Gunn, J. (1991). Effects of maternal employment and childcare arrangements on preschooler's cognitive and behavioral outcomes: Evidence from the Children of the National Longitudinal Survey of Youth. *Developmental Psychology, 27,* 932–945.

Bayme, S. (1991). A new synthesis on family policy? *Family Affairs, 4*(1–2), 14.

Beaulieu, L. J., Mullis, A. K., & Mullis, R. L. (1998). Building university system collaboration: The Florida Inter-University Center for Child, Family and Community Studies. In R. M. Lerner &

L. K. Simon (Eds.), *University–community collaborations for the twenty-first century: Outreach scholarship for youth and families* (pp. 139–156). New York: Garland.

Becker, P. E., & Moen, P. (1999). Scaling back: Dual-earner couples' work–family strategies. *Journal of Marriage and the Family, 61,* 995–1007.

Belkin, L. (2000, July 23). The backlash against children. *New York Times Magazine,* pp. 30–35, 42, 56, 60–62.

Bellah, R. N. (1990). The invasion of the money world. In D. Blankenhorn, S. Bayme, & J. B. Elshtain (Eds.), *Rebuilding the nest: A new commitment to the American family* (pp. 227–236). Milwaukee, WI: Family Service America.

Bellah, R. N., Madsen, R., Sullivan, W. M., Swidler, A., & Tipton, S. M. (1996). *Habits of the heart: Individualism and commitment in American life.* Berkeley: University of California Press. (Original work published 1985)

Belluck, P. (2005, September 15). Massachusetts rejects bill to eliminate gay marriage. *The New York Times,* p. A14.

Belluck, P., & Zezima, K. (2006, March 31). Massachusetts Court Limits Gay Unions. *The New York Times.* Retrieved March 31, 2006, from the New York Times Web site: http://www.nytimes.com/2006/03/31/us/31gay.html?r+1&th_r=1&th=&oref=slogin&emc=th&pagewanted

Belsky, J., & Eggebeen, D. (1991). Early and extensive maternal employment and young children's socioeconomic development: Children of the National Longitudinal Survey of Youth. *Journal of Marriage and the Family, 53,* 1083–1110.

Bengston, V. L. (2001). Beyond the nuclear family: The increasing importance of multigenerational bonds (The Burgess Award Lecture). *Journal of Marriage and Family, 63,* 1–16.

Bennett, Petts, & Blumenthal. (1999, April). *Adult attitudes towards sexual problems: National survey of American adults aged 25 and older.* Survey conducted for the conference on Gender and Human Sexuality: A Continuing Medical Education Conference, Washington, DC.

Bernard, S. N., & Knitzer, J. (1999). *Map and track: State initiatives to encourage responsible fatherhood, 1999 edition.* New York: Columbia University School of Public Health, National Center for Children in Poverty.

Bevan, W. (1982). A sermon of sorts in three plus parts. *American Psychologist, 37,* 1303–1322.

Bimber, B. (1996). *The politics of expertise in Congress: The rise and fall of the Office of Technology Assessment.* Albany: State University of New York Press.

Blankenhorn, D. (1988a). Cosby for president? *Family Affairs, 1*(1), 1–6.

Blankenhorn, D. (1988b). What are "family values" anyway? *Family Affairs, 1*(2), 6.

Blankenhorn, D. (1990). American family dilemmas. In D. Blankenhorn, S. Bayme, & J. Elshtain (Eds.), *Rebuilding the nest: A new commitment to the American family* (pp. 3–25). Milwaukee, WI: Family Service America.

Blum, R. (1992). Preface. In S. Smith, S. Blank, & R. Collins (Eds.), *Pathways to self-sufficiency for two generations: Designing welfare-to-work programs that benefit children and strengthen families* (pp. 1–2). New York: Foundation for Child Development.

Blum, R. (1993). Critical issues for the family research agenda and their use in policy formulation. In G. E. Hendershot & F. B. LeClere (Eds.), *Family health: From data to policy* (pp. 110–112). Minneapolis, MN: National Council on Family Relations.

Bobbitt, N., & Nelson, M. (2004). *The front line: Building programs that recognize families' role in reentry.* New York: Vera Institute of Justice.

Bogenschneider, K. (1995). Roles for professionals in building family policy: A case study of state family impact seminars. *Family Relations, 44,* 5–12.

Bogenschneider, K. (1996). An ecological risk/protective theory for building prevention programs, policies, and community capacity to support youth. *Family Relations, 45,* 127–138.

Bogenschneider, K. (1997). Parental involvement in adolescent schooling: A proximal process with transcontextual validity. *Journal of Marriage and the Family, 59,* 718–733.

Bogenschneider, K. (1999). Foreword. In R. M. Lerner, E. E. Sparks, & L. D. McCubbin (Eds.), *Family diversity and family policy: Strengthening families for America's children* (pp. vii–xi). Norwell, MA: Kluwer.

Bogenschneider, K. (2000). Has family policy come of age? A decade review of the state of U.S. family policy in the 1990s. *Journal of Marriage and the Family, 62,* 1136–1159.

Bogenschneider, K. (2002). *Family policy matters: How policymaking affects families and what professionals can do.* Mahwah, NJ: Lawrence Erlbaum Associates, Inc.

Bogenschneider, K. (2006). Teaching family policy in undergraduate and graduate classrooms: Why it's important and how to do it better. *Family Relations, 55*(1), 16–28.

Bogenschneider, K., & Corbett T. (2004). Building enduring policies in the 21st century: The past as prologue. In M. Coleman & L. H. Ganong (Eds), *Handbook of family diversity: Considering the past, contemplating the future* (pp. 451–468). Thousand Oaks, CA: Sage Publications.

Bogenschneider, K., & Gross, E. (2004). From ivory tower to state house: How youth theory can inform youth policy making. *Family Relations, 53,* 21–26.

Bogenschneider, K., & Normandin, H. (2005, April). Improving health care quality and cost efficiency. *Family Matters: A Family Impact Seminar Newsletter for Wisconsin Policymakers, 5*(3).

Bogenschneider, K., Olson, J. R., Linney, K. D., & Mills, J. (2000). Connecting research and policymaking: Implications for theory and practice from the Family Impact Seminars. *Family Relations, 49,* 327–339.

Bogenschneider, K., Small, S., & Riley, D. (1990). *An ecological risk-focused approach for addressing youth-at-risk issues* (Wisconsin Youth Futures Tech. Rep. No.1). Madison: University of Wisconsin–Madison/Extension.

Bogenschneider, K., & Steinberg, L. (1994). Maternal employment and adolescents' academic achievement: A developmental analysis. *Sociology of Education, 67,* 60–77.

Bogenschneider, K., & Stone, M. (1997). Delivering parent education to low and high risk parents of adolescents via age-paced newsletters. *Family Relations, 46,* 123–134.

Bogenschneider, K., Wu, C.-R., Thomas, P., & Wu, M.-Y. (1996). *Sun Prairie parents speak out: A report of the findings from the Sun Prairie Tapping Into Parenting (TIP) survey.* Madison: University of Wisconsin–Madison/Extension.

Bogenschneider, K., Wu, M.-Y., Raffaelli, M., & Tsay, J. (1998). Parent influences on adolescent peer orientation and substance use: The interface of parenting practices and values. *Child Development, 69,* 1672–1688.

Bogenschneider, K., Wu, M.-Y, Raffaelli, M. R., & Tsay, J. (1998). Other teens drink, but not my kid: Does parental awareness of adolescent alcohol use protect adolescents from risky consequences? *Journal of Marriage and the Family, 60*(2), 356–373.

Bogenschneider, K., Young, R., Melli, M., & Fleming, M. (1993). *Building policies that put families first: A Wisconsin perspective.* Madison: University of Wisconsin–Madison, Center for Excellence in Family Studies.

Bomar, P. J. (2004). *Promoting health in families: Applying family research and theory in nursing practice* (3rd ed.). Philadelphia: Saunders.

Bonnen, J. T. (1998). The land-grant idea and the evolving outreach university. In R. M. Lerner & L. K. Simon (Eds.), *University–community collaborations for the twenty-first century: Outreach scholarship for youth and families* (pp. 25–70). New York: Garland.

Booth, T. (1988). *Developing policy research.* Brookfield, VT: Gower.

Borman, G. D., Overman, L. T., Fairchild, R., Boulay, M., & Kaplan, J. (2004). Can a multiyear summer program prevent the accumulation of summer learning losses? In G. D. Borman & M. Boulay (Eds.), *Summer learning: Research, policies, and programs* (pp. 231–253). Mahwah, NJ: Lawrence Erlbaum Associates, Inc.

Bowlby, J. (1951). *Maternal care and mental health* (World Health Organization Monograph Serial No. 2). Geneva, Switzerland: World Health Organization.

Boyer, E. L. (1990). *Scholarship reconsidered: Priorities of the professional.* Princeton, NJ: Carnegie Foundation for the Advancement of Teaching.

Boyte, H. (1993a). Practical politics. In B. R. Barber & R. M. Battistoni (Eds.), *Education for democracy* (pp. 172–178). Dubuque, IA: Kendall-Hunt.

Boyte, H. (1993b). Redefining politics, part II. *The Responsive Community: Rights and Responsibilities, 3,* 83–87.

Boyte, H. (2000). *Public engagement in a civic mission: A case study.* Washington, DC: Council on Public Policy Education.

Boyte, H. C., & Etzioni, A. (1993). Redefining politics, part II. *The Responsive Community: Rights and Responsibilities, 3,* 83–88.

Boyte, H. C., & Kari, N. N. (1996). *Building America: The democratic promise of public work.* Philadelphia: Temple University Press.

Brabeck, M., Cawthorne, J., Cochran-Smith, M., Gaspard, N., Green, C. H., Kenny, M., et al. (1998). Changing the culture of the university to engage in outreach scholarship. In R. M. Lerner & L. A. Simon (Eds.), *Creating the new outreach university for America's youth and families: Building university–community collaborations for the twenty first century* (pp. 335–364). New York: Garland.

Braiker, B. (2003, May 23). Q & A: His brother's keeper. *Newsweek* (Web exclusive, Article ID: 052303_braiker_etzioniQA).

Braun, B., & Williams, S. E. (2004). Democratic engagement: A call to family professionals. In C. Anderson (Ed.), *Family and community policy: Strategies for civic engagement* (pp. 1–18). Alexandria, VA: American Association of Family and Consumer Sciences.

Bronfenbrenner, U. (1986, May). *A generation in jeopardy: America's hidden family policy.* Testimony presented at a hearing of the Senate Committee on Rules and Administration on a resolution to establish a Select Committee on Families, Youth and Children, Washington, DC.

Bronfenbrenner, U., & Weiss, H. B. (1983). Beyond policies without people: An ecological perspective on child and family policy. In E. F. Zigler, S. L. Kagan, & E. Klugman (Eds.), *Children, families, and government: Perspectives on American social policy* (pp. 393–414). Cambridge, UK: Cambridge University Press.

Brooks-Gunn, J. (1995, Spring). Research briefs to inform policy. *SRA Newsletter,* p. 1.

Brorsson, A., & Rastam, L. (1993). The patient's family history: A key to the physician's understanding of patients' fears. *Family Practice, 10,* 197–200.

Brotherson, S. E., & Duncan, W. C. (2004). Rebinding the ties that bind: Government efforts to preserve and promote marriage. *Family Relations, 53,* 459–468.

Browning, D. S. (1996). Biology, ethics, and narrative in Christian family theory. In D. Popenoe, J. B. Elshtain, & D. Blankenhorn (Eds.), *Promises to keep: Decline and renewal of marriage in America* (pp. 119–156). Lanham, MD: Rowman & Littlefield.

Browning, D. S., & Rodriguez, G. G. (2002). *Reweaving the social tapestry: Toward a public philosophy and policy for families.* New York: Norton.

Bruner, C. (2004). Rethinking the evaluation of family strengthening strategies: Beyond traditional program evaluation models. *The Evaluation Exchange, 10*(2), 24–25, 27.

Bulmer, M. (1987). *Social science research and government: Comparative essays on Britain and the United States.* New York: Cambridge University Press.

Bumpass, L. L. (1990). What's happening to the family? Interactions between demographic and institutional change. *Demography, 27,* 483–498.

Cairns, R. B. (1983). The emergence of developmental psychology. In P. H. Mussen (Ed.), *Handbook of child psychology* (Vol 1, 4th ed., pp. 41–102). New York: Wiley.

Calabrese, J. R., Kling, M. A., & Gold, P. W. (1987). Alterations in immunocompetence during stress, bereavement and depression: Focus on neuroendocrine regulation. *American Journal of Psychiatry, 144,* 1123–1134.

Califano, J. A. J. (1979). *Healthy people: The Surgeon General's report on health promotion and disease prevention* (DHEW [PHS] Publication No. 79-55071). Washington, DC: U.S. Government Printing Office.

Camino, L. A. (1995). Understanding intolerance and multiculturalism: A challenge for practitioners, but also for researchers. *Journal of Adolescent Research, 10,* 155–172.

Campbell, S. M., & Roland, M. O. (1996). Why do people consult the doctor? *Family Practice, 13,* 75–83.

Campbell, T. L. (1986). Family's impact on health: A critical review and annotated bibliography. *Family Systems Medicine, 4,* 135–328.

Campbell, T. L., & Patterson, J. M. (1995). The effectiveness of family interventions in the treatment of physical illness. *Journal of Marital and Family Therapy, 21,* 545–583.

Caplan, N. (1979). The two-communities theory and knowledge utilization. *American Behavioral Scientist, 22,* 459–470.

Caplan, N., Morrison, A., & Stambaugh, R. J. (1975). *The use of social science knowledge in policy decisions at the national level: A report to respondents.* Ann Arbor: University of Michigan, Institute for Social Research.

Carasso, A., & Steuerle, C. E. (2005). The hefty penalty on marriage facing many households with children. *Future of Children, 15,* 157–171.

Carlson, A. (2001). Theodore Roosevelt's new politics of the American family. *Family in America, 15*(10), 1–8.

Carlson, A. (2002a). Hyphenates, hausfraus, and baby-saving: The peculiar legacy of German-America. *Family in America, 16*(1–2), 1–20.

Carlson, A. (2002b). "Sanctif[ying] the traditional family": The New Deal and national solidarity. *Family in America, 16*(5), 1–12.

Carlson, A. (2005). *Fractured generations: Crafting a family policy for twenty-first-century America.* New Brunswick, NJ: Transaction.

Carter, J. L. (1994). Funding family support programs. In S. L. Kagan & B. Weissbourd (Eds.), *Putting families first: America's family support movement and the challenge of change.* San Francisco: Jossey-Bass.

Carter, N. (1995). *See how we grow: A report on the status of parenting education in the U.S.* Retrieved August 23, 1999 from http://pewtrusts.com/pubs/misc/grow/grow0003.cfm

Caspi, A., Elder, G. H., & Bern, D. J. (1987). Moving against the world: Life-course patterns of explosive children. *Developmental Psychology, 23,* 308–313.

Cassidy, J., & Shaver, P. R. (1999). *Handbook of attachment: Theory, research, and clinical applications.* New York: Guilford.

Cauthen, N. K., Knitzer, J., & Ripple, C. H. (2000). *Map and track: State initiatives to encourage responsible fatherhood, 2000 edition.* New York: Columbia University School of Public Health, National Center for Children in Poverty.

Center on Budget and Policy Priorities. (1998). *Poverty rates fall, but remain high for a period with such low unemployment.* Retrieved December 26, 1998, from http://cpbb.org/9-24-98pov.htm

Chamberlain, P. (1999). Community alternatives for chronic juvenile offenders and emotionally disturbed youngsters: Implications for the foster care system. In K. Bogenschneider & J. Mills (Eds.), *Raising the next generation: Public and private parenting initiatives* (Wisconsin Family Impact Seminar Briefing Rep. No. 13, pp. 18–26). Madison: University of Wisconsin Center for Excellence in Family Studies.

Chamberlain, P., Moreland, S., & Reid, K. (1992). Enhanced services and stipends for foster parents: Effects on retention rates and outcomes for children. *Child Welfare, 71,* 387–401.

Chamberlain, P., & Reid, J. B. (1991). Using a specialized foster care community treatment model for children and adolescents leaving the state mental hospital. *Journal of Community Psychology, 19,* 266–276.

Chamberlain, P., & Reid, J. B. (1998). Comparison of two community alternatives to incarceration for chronic juvenile offenders. *Journal of Consulting and Clinical Psychology, 66,* 624–633.

Chase-Lansdale, P. L., Moffitt, R. A., Lohman, B. J., Cherlin, A. J., Coley, R. L., Pittman, L. D., et al. (2003). Mothers' transitions from welfare to work and the well-being of preschoolers and adolescents. *Science, 299,* 1548–1552.

Cheal, D. (1991). *Family and the state of theory.* Toronto: University of Toronto Press.

Cherlin, A. J. (1997). What's most important in a family textbook? *Family Relations, 46,* 209–211.

Cherlin, A. J., & Krishnamurthy, P. (2004, May 9). What works for mom [Op-Chart]. *The New York Times,* Sec. 4, p. 13.

Children's Defense Fund. (1990). *An advocate's guide to the media.* Washington, DC: Author.

Clark, R. L., King, R. B., Spiro, C., & Steuerle, C. (2001). *Federal expenditures on children: 1960–1997* (Occasional Paper No. 45). Washington, DC: Urban Institute.

Clarkberg, M., & Moen, P. (1999, January). *The time-squeeze: The mismatch between work-hours patterns and preferences* (BLCC Working Paper No. 99-04). Ithaca, NY: Cornell University, Bronfenbrenner Life Course Center.

Cochran, M., & Niego, S. (1995). Parenting and social networks. In M. Bornstein (Ed.), *Handbook of parenting: Vol. 3. Status and social conditions of parenting* (pp. 393–418). Mahwah, NJ: Lawrence Erlbaum Associates, Inc.

Cochran, M., & Walker, S. (In press). Parenting and personal social networks. In L. Okagaki & T. Luster (Eds.), *Parenting: An Ecological Perspective* (2nd ed.). Hillsdale, NJ: Lawrence Erlbaum.

Cohen, E., & Ooms, T. (1993). *Data integration and evaluation: Essential components of family centered systems reform.* Washington, DC: The Family Impact Seminar.

Cohen, S., Frank, E., Doyle, W. J., Skoner, D. P., Rabin, B. S., & Gwaltney, J. M. (1998). Types of stressors that increase susceptibility to the common cold in healthy adults. *Health Psychology, 17,* 214–223.

Cohn, D. (2001, August 22). Count of gay couples up 300%: 2000 census ranks D.C., Arlington, Alexandria among top locales. *Washington Post,* p. A03.

Coleman, M. (1993). Family research: A basis for survey design. In G. E. Hendershot & F. B. LeClere (Eds.), *Family health: From data to policy* (pp. 107–109). Minneapolis, MN: National Council on Family Relations.

Conduct Problems Prevention Research Group. (1999). Initial impact of the Fast Track prevention trial for conduct problems: I. The high-risk sample. *Journal of Consulting and Clinical Psychology, 67,* 631–647.

Conduct Problems Prevention Research Group. (2002a). Evaluation of the first 3 years of the Fast Track prevention trial with children at high risk for adolescent conduct problems. *Journal of Abnormal Child Psychology, 30,* 19–35.

Conduct Problems Prevention Research Group. (2002b). Using the Fast Track randomized prevention trial to test the early-starter model of the development of serious conduct problems. *Development and Psychopathology, 14,* 925–943.

Consortium of Family Organizations. (1988). *A strategy for strengthening families: Using family criteria in policymaking and program evaluation.* Washington, DC: Author.

Consortium of Family Organizations. (1990a). *Family Policy Report, 1*(1).

Consortium of Family Organizations. (1990b). Families and long term care: An issue for the 1990s. *Family Policy Report, 1*(2).

Consortium of Family Organizations. (1992, Winter). Principles of family-centered health care: A health care reform white paper. *The COFO Family Policy Report, 2*(2).

Cook, W. L. (1994). A structural equation model of dyadic relationships within the family. *Journal of Consulting and Clinical Psychology, 62,* 500–510.

Coontz, S. (1997). *What we really miss about the 1950s. The way we really are: Coming to terms with America's changing families* (pp. 33–50). New York: Basic Books.

Coontz, S. (2000, November). *Time after time: Recurring family myths, changing family realities.* Paper presented at the annual conference of the National Council on Family Relations, Minneapolis, MN.

Cooper, C. L. (Ed.). (2005). *Handbook of stress medicine and health* (2nd ed.). Boca Raton, FL: CRC.

Corbett, T. (1993). Child poverty and welfare reform: Progress or paralysis? *Focus, 15*(1), 1–46.

Corbett, T. (2000). From income support to child & family support: Some rather surprising consequences of national welfare reform. In K. Bogenschneider & J. Mills (Eds.), *Helping poor kids succeed: Welfare, tax, and early intervention policies* (Wisconsin Family Impact Seminar Briefing Rep. No. 14, pp. 1–12). Madison: University of Wisconsin Center for Excellence in Family Studies.

Corbett, T., Burkett-Simms, C., Crandall, L., Howard, D., Le, N., Powers, P., et al. (1998). *The Midwest Welfare Peer Assistance Network: Leading the nation beyond welfare reform* (rev. ed.). Madison: University of Wisconsin Institute for Research on Poverty.

Council of Chief State School Officers. (1989). *Family support education, and involvement.* Washington, DC: Author.

Council of Economic Advisers. (1999, May). *Families and the labor market, 1969–1999: Analyzing the "time crunch."* Washington, DC: Author.

Courtney, M. E., Dworsky, A., Piliavin, I., & Zinn, A. (2005). Involvement of TANF applicant families with child welfare services. *Social Service Review, 79,* 119–157.

Covinsky, K. E., Goldman, L., Cook, F., Oye, R., Desbiens, N., Reding, D., et al. (1994). The impact of serious illness on patients' families. *Journal of the American Medical Association, 272,* 1839–1844.

Cowan, P. A. (1993). The sky is falling, but Popenoe's analysis won't help us do anything about it. *Journal of Marriage and the Family, 55,* 548–553.

Cowan, P. A., Field, D., Hansen, D. A., Skolnick, A., & Swanson, G. E. (Eds.). (1992). *Family, self, and society: Toward a new agenda for family research.* Hillsdale, NJ: Lawrence Erlbaum Associates, Inc.

Coyne, J. C., Rohrbaugh, M. J., Shoham, V., Sonnega, J. S., Nicklas, J. M., & Cranford, J. A. (2001). Prognostic importance of marital quality for survival of congestive heart failure. *American Journal of Cardiology, 88,* 526–529.

Crittenden, A. (2001). *The price of motherhood: Why the most important job in the world is still the least valued.* New York: Henry Holt.

Cudaback, D. J., Darden, C., Nelson, P., O'Brien, S., Pinsky, D., & Wiggens, E. (1985). Becoming successful parents: Can age-paced newsletters help? *Family Relations, 34,* 271–275.

Dahl, M. (2005, April 20). *Changes in participation in means-tested programs* (Economic and Budget Issue Brief). Washington, DC: Congressional Budget Office.

Daly, K. J. (2001). Deconstructing family time: From ideology to lived experience. *Journal of Marriage and Family, 63,* 283–294.

Danielson, C. B., Hamel-Bissell, B., & Winstead-Fry, P. (1993). *Families, health, and illness: Perspectives on coping and intervention.* St. Louis, MO: Mosby.

DeLeon, P. H. (1996). Public policy and public service: Our professional duty. In R. P. Lorion, I. Iscoe, P. H. DeLeon, & G. R. VandenBos (Eds.), *Psychology and public policy: Balancing public service and professional need* (pp. 41–55). Washington, DC: American Psychological Association.

DeLeon, P. H., O'Keefe, A. M., VandenBos, G. R, & Kraut, A. G. (1996). How to influence public policy: A blueprint for activism. In R. P. Lorion, I. Iscoe, P. H. DeLeon, & G. R VandenBos (Eds.), *Psychology and public policy: Balancing public service and professional need* (pp. 263–280). Washington, DC: American Psychological Association.

DeSmet, L. (1995, October). *The Bond.* Invited address at the annual Expert Meeting on Family Impact, University of Leuven, Leuven, Belgium.

Dishion, T. J., Andrews, D. W., Kavanagh, K., & Soberman, L. H. (1996). Preventive interventions for high-risk youth: The adolescent transitions program. In R. D. Peters & R. J. McMahon (Eds.), *Preventing childhood disorders, substance abuse, and delinquency* (pp. 184–214). Thousand Oaks, CA: Sage.

Dishion, T. J., French, D. C., & Patterson, G. R. (1995). The development and ecology of antisocial behavior. In D. Cicchetti & D. Cohen (Eds.), *Manual of developmental psychopathology* (pp. 421–471). New York: Wiley.

Dishion, T., Kavanagh, K., Schneiger, A., Nelson, S., & Kaufman, N. K. (2002). Preventing early adolescent substance use: A family-centered strategy for the public middle school. *Prevention Science, 3,* 191–201.

Dishion, T. J., McCord, J., & Poulin, F. (1999). When interventions harm: Peer groups and problem behavior. *American Pscyhologist, 54,* 755–764.

Dishion, T. J., Patterson, G. R., & Griesler, P. C. (1994). Peer adaptation in the development of antisocial behavior: A confluence model. In L. R. Huesmann (Ed.), *Aggressive behavior: Current perspectives* (pp. 61–95). New York: Plenum.

Doherty, W. J. (1992, November). *Family focus on health policy.* Paper presented at the annual meeting of the National Council on Family Relations, Orlando, FL.

Doherty, W. J. (1993). Health and family interaction: What we know. In G. E. Hendershot & F. B. LeClere (Eds.), *Family health: From data to policy* (pp. 98–101). Minneapolis, MN: National Council on Family Relations.

Doherty, W. J. (1994). I'm O.K., you're O.K., but what about the kids? *The Family Therapy Networker, 17,* 46–53.

Doherty, W. J. (1995). *Soul searching: Why psychotherapy must promote moral responsibility.* New York: Basic Books.

Doherty. W. J. (1999). Postmodernism and family theory. In M. B. Sussman & S. K. Steinmetz (Eds.), *Handbook of marriage and the family* (pp. 205–217). New York: Plenum.

Doherty, W. J. (2000). Family science and family citizenship: Towards a model of community partnership with families. *Family Relations, 49,* 319–325.

Doherty, W. J. (2004). *Overscheduled kids, underconnected families: The research evidence.* Retrieved September 1, 2005, from the Putting Families First Web site, http://www.putting familyfirst.org/research.shtml

Doherty, W. J., & Allen, W. (1994). Family functioning and parental smoking as predictors of adolescent cigarette use: A six-year prospective study. *Journal of Family Psychology, 8,* 347–353.

Doherty, W. J., & Anderson, J. R. (2004). Community marriage initiatives. *Family Relations, 53,* 425–432.

Doherty, W. J., & Baird, M. A. (1983). *Family therapy and family medicine: Toward the primary care of families.* New York: Guilford.

Doherty, W. J., & Beaton, J. M. (2000). Family therapists, community, and civic renewal. *Family Process, 39,* 149–161.

Doherty, W. J., Boss, P. G., LaRossa, R., Schumm, W. R., & Steinmetz, S. K. (1993). Family theories and methods: A contextual approach. In P. G. Boss, W. J. Doherty, R. LaRossa, W. R. Schrumm, & S. K. Steinmetz (Eds.), *Sourcebook of family theories and methods: A contextual approach* (pp. 3–30). New York: Plenum.

Doherty, W. J., & Boyte, H. (1999). Family Life 1st: Activating a grass-roots parents' movement. In K. Bogenschneider & J. Mills (Eds.), *Raising the next generation: Public and private parenting initiatives* (Wisconsin Family Impact Seminar Briefing Rep. No. 13, pp. 27–30). Madison: University of Wisconsin Center for Excellence in Family Studies.

Doherty, W. J., & Campbell, T. L. (1988). *Families and health.* Newbury Park, CA: Sage.

Doherty, W. J., & Carroll, J. S. (2002). The families and democracy project. *Family Process, 41,* 579–590.

Doherty, W. J., Kouneski, E. F., & Erickson, M. F. (1998). Responsible father: An overview and conceptual framework. *Journal of Marriage and the Family, 60,* 277–292.

Dowds, B. N., & Bibace, R. (1996). Entry into the health care system: The family's decision-making process. *Family Medicine, 28,* 114–118.

Dryfoos, J. G. (1990, Summer). Community schools: New institutional arrangements for preventing high-risk behavior. *Family Life Educator, 8*(4), 4–9.

Dryfoos, J. G. (1991). Adolescents at work: A summation of work in the field: Programs and policies. *Journal of Adolescent Health, 12*(8), 630–637.

Duncan, G. J., & Magnuson, K. A. (2002). Economics and parenting. *Parenting: Science and Practice, 2,* 437–450.

Dunn, W. N. (1994). *Public policy analysis: An introduction* (2nd ed.). Englewood Cliffs, NJ: Prentice Hall.

DYG, Inc., Civitas, Zero to Three, & Brio. (2000). *What grown-ups understand about child development: A national benchmark survey.* Washington, DC: Author.

Dyk, P. H. (1995, November). *Grassroots-driven family policy.* Paper presented at the annual meeting of the National Council on Family Relations, Portland, OR.

Early, B. P., & Hawkins, M. J. (1994). Opportunity and risks in emerging family policy: An analysis of family preservation legislation. *Children and Youth Services Review, 16,* 309–318.

Eastman, M. (1996). Myths of marriage and the family. In D. Popenoe, J. B. Elshtain, & D. Blankenhorn (Eds.), *Promises to keep: Decline and renewal of marriage in America* (pp. 35–68). Lanham, MD: Rowman & Littlefield.

Edelman, M. W. (1987). *Families in peril: An agenda for social change.* Cambridge, MA: Harvard University Press.

Education Commission of the States. (1996). *Parent involvement in education* (ESC State Notes: Parent/Family). Denver, CO: Author.

Education Commission of the States. (2002). *No state left behind: The challenges and opportunities of ESEA 2001* (ESC Special Rep. GP-02-01). Denver, CO: Author.

Eliot, T. S. (1943). *Little gidding.* London: Faber & Faber.

Elliott, T. R., & Rivera, P. (2003). The experience of families and their carers in health care. In S. Llewelyn & P. Kennedy (Eds.), *Handbook of clinical health psychology* (pp. 61–77). West Sussex, UK: Wiley.

Elrod, L. D. (1995). A review of the year in family law. *Family Law Quarterly, 28,* 541–571.

Elrod, L. D. (1999). Epilogue: Of families, federalism, and a quest for policy. *Family Law Quarterly, 33,* 843–863.

Elrod, L. D., & Spector, R. G. (1997). A review of the year in family law: Of welfare reform, child support, and relocation. *Family Law Quarterly, 30,* 765–809.

Elrod, L. D., & Spector, R. G. (1998). A review of the year in family law: A search for definitions and policy. *Family Law Quarterly, 31,* 613–665.

Elrod, L. D., & Spector, R. G. (2000). A review of the year in family law: Century ends with unresolved issues. *Family Law Quarterly, 33,* 865–907.

Elrod, L. D., & Spector, R. G. (2001). A review of the year in family law: Redefining families, reforming custody jurisdiction, and refining support issues. *Family Law Quarterly, 34,* 607–652.

Elrod, L. D., & Spector, R. G. (2002). A review of the year in family law: State courts react to Troxel. *Family Law Quarterly, 35,* 577–615.

Elrod, L. D., & Spector, R. G. (2003). A review of the year in family law: Increased mobility creates conflicts. *Family Law Quarterly, 36,* 515–558.

Elrod, L. D., & Spector, R. G. (2004). A review of the year in family law: Children's issues remain the focus. *Family Law Quarterly, 37,* 527–575.

Elrod, L. D., & Spector, R. G. (2005). A review of the year in family law: "Same-sex" marriage issue dominates headlines. *Family Law Quarterly, 38,* 777–818.

Elrod, L. D., Spector, R. G., & Atkinson, J. (1999). A review of the year in family law: Children's issues dominate. *Family Law Quarterly, 32,* 661–717.

Elshtain, J. B. (1995). *Democracy on trial.* New York: Basic Books.

Elshtain, J. B., Aird, E., Etzioni, A., Galston, W., Glendon, M. A, Minow, M., et al. (1993). *A communitarian position paper on the family.* Washington, DC: The Communitarian Network.

Epstein, J. L. (1982). *Student reactions to teachers' practices of parent involvement.* Paper presented at the annual meeting of the American Educational Research Association, New York.

Epstein, J. L. (1985). Home and school connections in schools of the future: Implications of research on parent involvement. *Peabody Journal of Education, 62,* 18–41.

Epstein, J. L. (2001). *School and family partnerships: Preparing educators and improving schools.* Boulder, CO: Westview.

Epstein, J. L., Sanders, M. G., Simon, B. S., Salinas, K. C., Jansorn, N. R., & Van Voorhis, F. L. (2002). *School, family, and community partnerships: Your handbook for action* (2nd ed.). Thousand Oaks, CA: Corwin.

Eshleman, R. (1991). *The family: An introduction.* Boston: Allyn & Bacon.

Families and Work Institute. (1995, May). *Women: The new providers. Whirlpool Foundation Study, Part One.* New York: Author.

Family Support America. (2000). *From many voices: Consensus: What America needs for strong families and communities.* Chicago: Author.

Farley, F. (1996). From the heart. *American Psychologist, 51,* 772–776.

Featherstone, J. (1979). Family matters. *Harvard Educational Review, 49,* 20–52.

Finance Project. (1996, December). *Building strong communities: Crafting a legislative foundation.* Washington, DC: Author.

Flinchbaugh, B. (1988). *Two worms: The importance of facts, myth, and values in public policy. Education for public decisions* (Working with our publics: Module 6). Raleigh: North Carolina Agriculture Extension Service and the Department of Adult and Community College Education.

Forehand, R. L., & McMahon, R. J. (1981). *Helping the noncompliant child: A clinicians guide to parent training.* New York: Guilford Press.

Forness, S. R. (2003). Barriers to evidence-based treatment: Developmental psychopathology and the interdisciplinary disconnect in school mental health practice. *Journal of School Psychology, 41,* 61–67.

Forthofer, M. S., Markman, H. J., Cox, M., Stanley, S., & Kessler, R. C. (1996). Associations between marital distress and work loss in a national sample. *Journal of Marriage and the Family, 58,* 597–605.

Fournier, R. (2001, August 4). Bush vows to focus on the family. *Wisconsin State Journal,* p. A1.

Fronstin, P. (2005). The potential impact from consumer health savings accounts as a market-based approach for improving quality and reducing costs. In K. Bogenschneider & H. Normandin (Eds.), *Improving health care quality while curbing costs: How effective are consumer health savings accounts and pay for performance?* (Wisconsin Family Impact Seminar Briefing Rep. No. 21, pp. 13–22). Madison: University of Wisconsin Center for Excellence in Family Studies.

Fuligni, A. J., Tseng, V., & Lam, M. (1999). Attitudes toward family obligations among American adolescents with Asian, Latin American, and European backgrounds. *Child Development, 70,* 1030–1044.

Furstenberg, F. F., Brooks-Gunn, J., & Chase-Lansdale, L. (1989). Teenaged pregnancy and childbearing. *American Psychologist, 44,* 313–320.

Furstenberg, F. F., Jr., & Condran, G. A. (1988). Family change and adolescent well-being: A reexamination of U.S. trends. In A. J. Cherlin (Ed.), *The changing American family and public policy* (pp. 117–155). Washington, DC: Urban Institute Press.

Gagnon, A. G. (1990). The influence of social scientists on public policy. In S. Brooks & A. G. Gagnon (Eds.), *Social scientists, policy, and the state* (pp. 1–18). New York: Praeger.

Gallagher, J. J. (1990). Emergence of policy studies and policy institutes. *American Psychologist, 45,* 1316–1318.

Gallup Organization. (2004, September 13–15). *The Gallup poll: Government.* Princeton, NJ: Author.

Gallup Organization. (2005, August 22–25). *The Gallup poll: Homosexual relations.* Princeton, NJ: Author.

Galston, W. A. (1996). The reinstitutionalization of marriage: Political theory and public policy. In D. Popenoe, J. B. Elshtain, & D. Blankenhorn (Eds.), *Promises to keep: Decline and renewal of marriage in America* (pp. 271–290). Lanham, MD: Rowman & Littlefield.

Galston, W. A. (1997). A progressive family policy for the twenty-first century. In W. Marshall (Ed.), *Building the bridge: 10 big ideas to transform America* (pp. 149–162). Lanham, MD: Rowman & Littlefield.

Ganzglass, E., & Stebbins, H. (2001, April). *Turning good ideas into good policy: Lessons from the National Governors Association in creating comprehensive childhood policy.* Paper presented at the annual meeting of the Society for Research on Child Development, Minneapolis, MN.

Garbarino, J., & Kostelny, K. (1994). Family support and community development. In S. Kagan & B. Weissbourd (Eds.), *Putting families first: America's family support movement and the challenge of change* (pp. 297–320). San Francisco: Jossey-Bass.

Garbarino, J., & Kostelny, K. (1995). Parenting and public policy. In M. H. Bornstein (Ed.), *Handbook of parenting* (pp. 419–436). Mahwah, NJ: Lawrence Erlbaum Associates, Inc.

Gardner, J. W. (1989, Fall). Building community. *The Kettering Review,* pp. 73–81.

Garfinkel, I. (2004). Policy and the family. In D. P. Moynihan, T. M. Smeeding, & L. Rainwater (Eds.), *The future of the family* (pp. 276–282). New York: Russell Sage Foundation.

Gates, G. (2005, November). *Same-sex couples in the United States.* Paper presented at the annual meeting of the National Council on Family Relations, Phoenix, VA.

Gates, H. L., Jr. (2004, August 1). Breaking the silence [Op-ed]. *The New York Times,* Sec. 4, p. 11.

Gergen, K. J. (2001). Psychological science in a postmodern context. *American Psychologist, 56,* 803–813.

Giele, J. Z. (1996). Decline of the family: Conservative, liberal, and feminist views. In D. Popenoe, J. B. Elshtain, & D. Blankenhorn (Eds.), *Promises to keep: Decline and renewal of marriage in America* (pp. 271–290). Lanham, MD: Rowman & Littlefield.

Gingrich, N. (1999, December 28). Scientists must speak out: We depend on it [Op-ed]. *Boston Globe,* p. A19.

Glendon, M. A. (1992). The second national communitarian teach-in. *The Responsive Community, 2*(3), 54–58.

Glenn, N. D. (1993). A plea for objective assessment of the notion of family decline. *Journal of Marriage and the Family, 55,* 542–544.

Glenn, N. D. (1996). Values, attitudes, and the state of American marriage. In D. Popenoe, J. B. Elshtain, & D. Blankenhorn (Eds.), *Promises to keep: Decline and renewal of marriage in America* (pp. 15–33). Lanham, MD: Rowman & Littlefield.

Glenn, N. D. (1997). A critique of twenty family and marriage and the family textbooks. *Family Relations, 46,* 197–208.

Global Strategies Group, Inc. (2000, May 2). *Talking with teens: The YMCA parent and teen survey final report* [Press release]. Retrieved August 24, 2005, from http://www.ymca.net/presrm/research/teensurvey.htm

Goggins, B. K. (1997). Shared responsibility for managing work and family relationships: A community perspective. In S. J. Parasuraman & J. H. Greenhaus (Eds.), *Integrating work and family: Challenges and choices for a changing world* (pp. 220–231). Westport, CT: Quorum.

Gomby, D. S., Culross, C. L., & Behrman, R. E. (1999, Spring–Summer). Home visiting: Recent program evaluations. Analysis and recommendations. *The Future of Children Report, 9*(1), 4–26.

Gordon, L. (1992). Social insurance and public assistance: The influence of gender in welfare thought in the United States, 1890–1935. *American Historical Review, 97,* 19–54.

Gordon, L. (1994). *Pitied but not entitled.* New York: Free Press.

Gordon, R. (1987). An operational classification of disease prevention. In J. A. Steinberg & M. M. Silverman (Eds.), *Preventing mental disorders* (pp. 20–26). Rockville, MD: Department of Health and Human Services.

Gordon, R. A., & Heinrich, C. J. (2005). *Taking a couples rather than an individual approach to employment assistance* (Discussion Paper No. 1294-05). Madison: University of Wisconsin–Madison Institute for Research on Poverty.

Gormley, W. T., Jr., & Phillips, D. (2005). The effects of universal pre-K in Oklahoma: Research highlights and policy implications. *Policy Studies Journal, 33,* 65–82.

Gottlieb, B. H. (1976). Lay influences on the utilization and provision of health services: A review. *Canadian Psychological Review, 17,* 126–136.

Gottman, J. M., & Katz, L. F. (1989). Effects of marital discord on young children's peer interaction and health. *Developmental Psychology, 25,* 373–381.

Governor's Task Force on Family and Children's Issues. (1990). *Report to the governor.* Madison, WI: Author.

Greenstein, R. (2005). *The Earned Income Tax Credit: Boosting employment, aiding the working poor.* Washington, DC: Center on Budget and Policy Priorities.

Grisso, T., & Steinberg, L. (2005). Between a rock and a soft place: Developmental research and the child advocacy program. *Journal of Clinical Child and Adolescent Psychology, 34,* 619–627.

Grob, G. (1992). How policy is made and how evaluators can affect it. *Evaluation Practice, 13,* 175–183.

Gross, E. (2003). *A family impact analysis of the Individuals with Disabilities Act, Part C: Infants and Toddlers with Disabilities* (Family Impact Analysis Series). Madison, WI: Policy Institute for Family Impact Seminars.

Grunfeld, E., Coyle, D., Whelan, T., Clinch, J., Reyno, L., Earle, C. C., et al. (2004). Family caregiver burden: Results of a longitudinal study of breast cancer patients and their principal caregivers. *Canadian Medical Association Journal, 170,* 1795–1801.

Guttmacher Institute. (2004). *U.S. teen pregnancy statistics: Overall trends, trends by race and ethnicity and state-by-state information.* New York: Author.

Hahn, A. J. (1987). Educating citizens and policy makers about public issues. *Human Ecology Forum, 16*(3), 11–14.

Hahn, A. J. (1994). Innovations in public policy. In S. A. Halbrook & T. E. Grace (Eds.), *Increasing understanding of public problems and policies* (pp. 85–92). Chicago: The Farm Foundation.

Harrison, A. O., Wilson, M. N., Pine, C. J., Chan, S. Q., & Buriel, R. (1990). Family ecologies of ethnic minority children. *Child Development, 61,* 347–362.

Hartman, H. (1981). The family as a locus of gender, class, and political struggle: The example of housework. *Signs: Journal of Women in Culture and Society, 6,* 366–394.

Harvard Family Research Project. (1990). *Innovative models to guide family support and education policy in the 1990s: An analysis of four pioneering state programs (Connecticut, Maryland, Missouri, and Minnesota).* Cambridge, MA: Author.

Harvard Family Research Project. (1992a). *Building partnerships: Models of family support and education programs (North Dakota, Iowa, Florida, Vermont, and Massachusetts).* Cambridge, MA: Author.

Harvard Family Research Project. (1992b). *Innovative states: Emerging family support and educational programs (Arkansas, Iowa, Oregon, Vermont, and Washington)* (2nd ed.). Cambridge, MA: Author.

Harvard Family Research Project. (1992c). *Pioneering states: Innovative family support and education programs (Arkansas, Iowa, Oregon, Vermont, and Washington)* (2nd ed.). Cambridge, MA: Author.

Harvard Family Research Project. (1994). *Reinventing systems: Collaborations to support families (California, Colorado, New Mexico, and West Virginia).* Cambridge, MA: Author.

Harvard Family Research Project. (2003). A review of out-of-school time program quasi-experimental and experimental evaluation results. *Out-of-School Time Evaluation Snapshot, 1,* 1–12.

Harvey, E. (1999). Short-term and long-term effects of early parental employment on children of the National Longitudinal Survey of Youth. *Developmental Psychology, 35,* 445–459.

Haskins, R. (1991). Congress writes a law: Research and welfare reform. *Journal of Policy Analysis and Management, 10,* 616–632.

Haskins, R. (1993). Research and the political process. In G. E. Hendershot & F. B. LeClere (Eds.), *Family health: From data to policy* (pp. 61–63). Minneapolis, MN: National Council on Family Relations.

Haskins, R., McLanahan, S., & Donahue, E. (2005, Fall). *The decline in marriage: What to do* (The Future of Children Policy Brief, Fall). Washington, DC: The Future of Children.

Hauser, R. M., Brown, B. V., & Prosser, W. R. (1997). *Indicators of children's well-being.* New York: Russell Sage.

Havas, E. (1995). The family as ideology. *Social Policy & Administration, 29*(1), 1–9.

Hawkins, D. (1989, June). *Risk-focused prevention: Prospects and strategies.* Invited lecture at the Coordinating Council on Juvenile Justice and Delinquency Prevention, Washington, DC.

Hawkins, J. D., Catalano, R. F., Barnard, K. E., Gottfredson, G. D., Holmes, A. B., IV, Miller, J. Y., et al. (1992). *Communities that care: Action for drug abuse prevention.* San Francisco: Jossey-Bass.

Hawkins, J. D., Catalano, R. F., & Miller, J. Y. (1992). Risk and protective factors for alcohol and other drug problems in adolescence and early adulthood: Implications for substance abuse prevention. *Psychological Bulletin, 112,* 64–105.

Hayes, C. D. (1982). *Making policies for children: A study of the federal process.* Washington, DC: National Academy Press.

Health textbooks in Texas to change wording about marriage. (2004). *The New York Times,* p. A20.

Heckman, J. J., & Wax, A. L. (2004, January 23). Home alone. *The New York Times,* p. A14.

Hendershot, G. E., & LeClere, F. B. (1993). *Family health: From data to policy.* Minneapolis, MN: National Council on Family Relations.

Henderson, A. T., & Mapp, K. L. (2002). *A new wave of evidence: The impact of school, family, and community connections on student achievement.* Austin, TX: National Center for Family & Community Connections With Schools.

Henderson, A. T., Marburger, C. L., & Ooms, T. (1986). *Beyond the bake sale: An educator's guide to working with parents.* Washington, DC: National Committee for Citizens in Education.

Henderson, T. L. (2004). Grandparent visitation rights: Successful acquisition of court-ordered visitation. *Journal of Family Issues, 20*(3), 1–31.

Hernandez, D. J. (1994). Children's changing access to resources: A historical perspective. *Social Policy Report, 8*(1), 1–23.

Hernandez, D. J. (2005). Changes in the demographics of families over the course of American history. In J. Heymann & C. Beem (Eds.), *Unfinished work: Building equality and democracy in an era of working families* (pp. 13–35). New York: The New Press.

Hetherington, E. M. (1993). An overview of the Virginia longitudinal study of divorce and remarriage with a focus on early adolescence. *Journal of Family Psychology, 7,* 39–56.

Hewlett, S. A., & West, C. (1998). *The war against parents: What we can do for America's beleaguered moms and dads.* New York: Houghton-Mifflin.

Higgins, P. S. (1988). *The prevention of drug abuse among teenagers: A literature review.* St. Paul, MN: Amherst H. Wilder Foundation.

Hochschild, A. R. (1992, November). *Beyond the second shift: Denying needs at home or contesting rules at work?* Paper presented at the annual meeting of the National Council on Family Relations, Orlando, FL.

Hochschild, A. R. (1997). *The time bind: When work becomes home and home becomes work.* New York: Metropolitan Books.

Hofferth, S. L., & Sandberg, J. F. (2001). How American children spend their time. *Journal of Marriage and Family, 63,* 295–308.

Holmes, T. H., & Rahe, R. H. (1967). The social readjustment scale. *Journal of Psychosomatic Research, 39,* 413–431.

Horn, W. (2004). Marriage, family, and the welfare of children: A call for action. In D. P. Moynihan, T. M. Smeeding, & L. Rainwater (Eds.), *The future of family* (pp. 181–197). New York: Russell Sage Foundation.

Hotz, V. J., & Scholz, J. K. (2000). Not perfect, but still pretty good: The EITC and other policies to support the U.S. low-wage labor market. *OECD Economic Studies, 2000*(31), 26–42.

House, J. S., Landis, K. R., & Umberson, D. (1988). Social relationships and health. *Science, 241,* 540–545.

Howard, G. S. (1985). The role of values in the science of psychology. *American Psychologist, 40,* 255–265.

Huemmert, S. (1995, October). *Implementation of family policy impact assessment in Alberta.* Paper presented at the Expert Meeting on Family Impact, University of Leuven, Leuven, Belgium.

Huston, A. C. (1994, Summer). Children in poverty: Designing research to affect policy. *Social Policy Report: Society for Research in Child Development, 8*(2), 1–12.

Hutchins, J. (1998). *Coming together for children and families: How cabinet-level collaboration is changing state policymaking.* Washington, DC: Family Impact Seminar.

Hyde, J. S., Essex, M. J., Clark, R., Klein, M. H., & Byrd, J. E. (1996). Parental leave: Policy and research. *Journal of Social Issues, 52*(3), 91–109.

Institute for Research on Poverty. (1992). Evaluating comprehensive family service programs: Conference overview. *Focus, 14*(1), 10–13.

Institute of Medicine. (1994). *Reducing risks for mental disorders: Frontiers for preventive intervention research.* Washington, DC: National Academy of Sciences.

International Labour Organization. (1998, February 16). *More than 120 nations provide paid maternity leave: Gap in employment treatment for men and women still exists* [Press release ILO/98/7]. Geneva, Switzerland: Author.

Interview with Gary Becker. (2002, June). *The Region.* Retrieved July 10, 2002, from http://minneapolisfed.org/pubs/region/02-06/becker.cfm

Ittig, M. (2004, April 21). *The power in the process: An examination of the U.S. intercountry adoption policy process in a globalized world.* Unpublished master's thesis, University of Wisconsin–Madison, Madison, WI.

Jacobs, F. H. (1994). Child and family policy: Framing the issues. In F. H. Jacobs & M. W. Davies (Eds.), *More than kissing babies? Current child and family policy in the United States* (pp. 9–36). Westport, CT: Auburn House.

Jacobs, F. H., & Davies, M. W. (1991). Rhetoric or reality: Child and family policy in the United States. *Social Policy Report, 5*(4), 1–25.

Jacobs, F. H., & Davies, M. W. (1994). On the eve of a new millennium. In F. H. Jacobs & M. W. Davies (Eds.), *More than kissing babies? Current child and family policy in the United States* (pp. 277–298). Westport, CT: Auburn House.

Jacobs, F. H., Little, P., & Almeida, C. (1993). Supporting family life: A survey of homeless shelters. *Journal of Social Distress and the Homeless, 2,* 269–288.

James, P. D. (1992). *The children of men.* New York: Warner Vision.

Jenkins, R. (1989). *Youth at risk.* Washington, DC: Youth Policy Institute.

Kagan, S. L., Powell, D. R., Weissbourd, B., & Zigler, E. F. (Eds.). (1987). *America's family support programs: Perspectives and prospects.* New Haven, CT: Yale University Press.

Kaiser Family Foundation. (2005, September 14). *Survey finds steady decline in businesses offering health benefits to workers since 2000* [Press release]. Retrieved September 19, 2005, from http://www.kff.org/insurance/chcm091405nr.cfm

Kamerman, S. B. (1977). Public policy and the family: A new strategy for women as wives and mothers. In J. R. Chapman & M. Gates (Eds.), *Women into wives: The legal and economic impact of marriage* (pp. 195–214). Thousand Oaks, CA: Sage.

Kamerman, S. B., & Kahn, A. J. (1978). Families and the idea of family policy. In S. B. Kamerman & A. J. Kahn (Eds.), *Family policy: Government and families in fourteen countries* (pp. 1–16). New York: Columbia University Press.

Kamerman, S. B., & Kahn, A. J. (1991). Trends, issues, and possible lessons. In S. B. Kamerman & A. J. Kahn (Eds.), *Childcare, parental leave, and the under 3s: Policy innovation in Europe* (pp. 216–224). New York: Auburn House.

Kamerman, S. B., & Kahn, A. J. (2001). Child and family policies in an era of retrenchment. In T. Smeeding & K. Vlemincks (Eds.), *Child well-being and poverty: Policy in modern nations* (pp. 501–525). Bristol, UK: Policy Press.

Kane, R. A., Kane, R. L., & Ladd, R. C. (1998). *The heart of long-term care.* New York: Oxford University Press.

Kane, R. A., & Penrod, J. D. (1995). In search of family caregiving policy: General considerations. In R. A. Kane & J. D. Penrod (Eds.), *Family caregiver applications series: Vol. 5. Family caregiving in an aging society: Policy perspectives* (pp. 1–14). Thousand Oaks, CA: Sage.

Kaufman, I. (1993). Family research in state and local policy making. In G. E. Hendershot & F. B. LeClere (Eds.), *Family health: From data to policy* (pp. 113–115). Minneapolis, MN: National Council on Family Relations.

Kazdin, A. E. (1987). Treatment of antisocial behavior in children: Current status and future directions. *Psychological Bulletin, 102,* 187–203.

Kellogg Commission. (1999). *Returning to our roots: The engaged institution.* Washington, DC: National Association of State Universities and Land-Grant Colleges.

Keyser, J. (2001). County policy that says "yes" to mental health. *Consortium Connections, 10*(2), 7, 9.

Kiecolt-Glaser, J. K., Fisher, L. D., Ogrock, P., Stout, J. C., Speicher, C. E., & Glaser, R. C. (1987). Marital quality, marital disruption, and immune function. *Psychosomatic Medicine, 49,* 13–34.

Kiecolt-Glaser, J. K., Glaser, R., Cacioppo, J. T., MacCallum, R. C., Snydersmith, M., Cheongtag, K., et al. (1997). Marital conflict in older adults: Endocrinological and immunological correlates. *Psychosomatic Medicine, 59,* 339–349.

Kiecolt-Glaser, J. K., Malarkey, W. B., Chee, M., Newton, T., Cacioppo, J. T., Mao, H., et al. (1993). Negative behavior during marital conflict is associated with immunological down-regulation. *Psychosomatic Medicine, 55,* 395–409.

Kiecolt-Glaser, J. K., & Newton, T. (2001). Marriage and health: His and hers. *Psychological Bulletin, 127,* 472–503.

Kiecolt-Glaser, J. K., Newton, T., Cacioppo, J. T., MacCallum, R. C., Glaser, R., & Malarkey, W. B. (1996). Marital conflict and endocrine function: Are men really more physiologically affected than women? *Journal of Consulting and Clinical Psychology, 64,* 324–332.

King, M. (2005, October). Medicaid in a nutshell. In H. Normandin & K. Bogenschneider (Eds.), *Medicaid: Who benefits, how expensive is it, and what are states doing to control costs?* (Wisconsin Family Impact Seminar Briefing Rep. No. 22, pp. 1–12). Madison: University of Wisconsin Center for Excellence in Family Studies.

King v. King, 929 S. W. 2d 630 (Ky, 1992).

Kingdon, J. W. (1995). *Agendas, alternatives, and public policies.* New York: HarperCollins.

Kingston, R. J., & Levine, P. (2004). What is "public" about what academics do: An exchange. In Kettering Foundation (Ed.), *Higher education exchange* (pp. 17–29). Dayton, OH: Kettering Foundation.

Kirby, D. (1997, March). *No easy answers: Research findings on programs to reduce teen pregnancy* [Summary]. Washington, DC: The National Campaign to Prevent Teen Pregnancy.

Klein, L. G. (2004). A conversation with Art Rolnick. *The Evaluation Exchange, 10*(2), 16–17.

Knight, D. K., & Simpson, D. D. (1996). Influences of family and friends on client progress during drug abuse treatment. *Journal of Substance Abuse, 8,* 417–429.

Knitzer, J. (1976). Child advocacy: A perspective. *American Journal of Orthopsychiatry, 46,* 200–216.

Knitzer, J., Bernard, S., Brenner, E., & Gadsden, V. (1997). *Map and track: State initiatives to encourage responsible fatherhood.* New York: Columbia University School of Public Health, National Center for Children in Poverty.

Knitzer, J., & Page, S. (1996). *Map and track: State initiatives for young children and families.* New York: Columbia University School of Public Health, National Center for Children in Poverty.

Knitzer, J., & Page, S. (1998). *Map and track: State initiatives for young children and families, 1998 edition.* New York: Columbia University School of Public Health, National Center for Children in Poverty.

Kochan, T. A. (2004). *Regaining control of our destiny: A working families' agenda for America.* Cambridge, MA: Massachusetts Institute of Technology, MIT Workplace Center.

Koven, S., & Michel, S. (1993). *Mothers of a new world.* New York: Routledge.

Kreider, H. (2004, Winter). A conversation with Jeanne Brooks-Gunn. *The Evaluation Exchange, 10*(4), 12–13.

Kumpfer, K. L. (1993, September). *Strengthening America's families: Promising parenting strategies for delinquency prevention. User's guide* (U.S. Department of Justice Publication No. NCJ140781). Washington, DC: Office of Juvenile Justice and Delinquency Prevention.

Kumpfer, K. L., & Alvarado, R. (2003). Family-strengthening approaches for the prevention of youth problem behaviors. *American Psychologist, 58,* 457–465.

La. Rev. Stat. Ann. § 49:972 (2003).

Ladd-Taylor, M. (1993). "My work came out of agony and grief": Mothers and the making of the Sheppard-Towner Act. In S. Koven & S. Michel (Eds.), *Mothers of a new world* (pp. 321–342). New York: Routledge.

Larin, K. (1998, November). *Income inequities among families in the U.S. and internationally: Problems and policies.* Paper presented at the annual meeting of the National Council on Family Relations, Milwaukee, WI.

Lasch, C. (1977). *Haven in a heartless world: The family besieged.* New York: Norton.

Laue, J. H., & Cormick, G. (1978). The ethics of intervention in community disputes. In G. Bermant, H. C. Kelman, & D. P. Warwick (Eds.), *The ethics of social intervention* (pp. 205–232). New York: Hemisphere.

Leonhardt, D. (2005, August 31). U.S. poverty rate was up last year. *The New York Times,* p. A9.

Lerner, R. M. (1995). *America's youth in crisis: Challenges and choices for programs and policies.* Thousand Oaks, CA: Sage.

Lerner, R. M., & Simon, L. K. (1998a). The new American outreach university. In R. M. Lerner & L. K. Simon (Eds.), *University–community collaborations for the twenty-first century: Outreach scholarship for youth and families* (pp. 3–23). New York: Garland.

Lerner, R. M., & Simon, L. K. (Eds.). (1998b). *University–community collaborations for the twenty-first century: Outreach scholarship for youth and families.* New York: Garland.

Lerner, R. M., Sparks, E. E., & McCubbin, L. D. (1999). *Family diversity and family policy: Strengthening families for America's children.* Norwell, MA: Kluwer.

Lesthaeghe, R. (1995). The second demographic transition in Western countries: An interpretation. In K. O. Mason & A. M. Jensen (Eds.), *Gender and family change in industrialized countries* (pp. 17–82). Oxford, UK: Clarendon.

Lewis, A. C., & Henderson, A. T. (1997). *Urgent message: Families crucial to school reform.* Washington, DC: Center for Law and Education.

Lewis, C. S. (1996). *Mere Christianity.* New York: Touchstone Books.

Lillard, L. A., & Waite, L. J. (1995). 'Til death do us part: Marital disruption and mortality. *American Journal of Sociology, 100,* 1131–1156.

Lindblom, C. E. (1980). *The policy-making process.* Englewood Cliffs, NJ: Prentice-Hall.

Lindenmeyer, K. (1997). *A right to childhood.* Urbana: University of Illinois Press.

Linquist, E. A. (1990). The third community, policy inquiry, and social scientists. In S. Brooks & A. G. Gagnon (Eds.), *Social scientists, policy, and the state* (pp. 21–51). New York: Praeger.

Lipset, S. M., & Pool, A. B. (1996). Balancing the individual and the community: Canada versus the United States. *The Responsive Community, 6*(3), 36–46.

Liptak, A. (2005, April 23). California ruling expands same-sex parental rights. *The New York Times,* p. A10.

Litman, T. L. (1974). The family as a basic unit in health and medical care: A social-behavioral overview. *Social Science and Medicine, 8,* 495–519.

Lofquist, W. A. (1983). *Discovering the meaning of prevention: A practical approach to positive change.* Tucson, AZ: Associates for Youth Development.

Lynton, E. A., & Elman, S. E. (1987). *New priorities for the university.* San Francisco: Jossey-Bass.

Maccoby, E. E., & Martin, J. A. (1983). Socialization in the context of family: Parent–child interaction. In P. H. Mussen (Series Ed.) & E. M. Hetherington (Vol. Ed.), *Handbook of child psychology: Vol. 4. Socialization, personality, and social development* (4th ed., pp. 1–101). New York: Wiley.

Madden, J., Levenstein, P., & Levenstein, S. (1976). Longitudinal IQ outcomes of the mother child home program. *Child Development, 47,* 1015–1025.

Magrath, C. P. (1998). Foreword: Creating the new outreach university. In R. M. Lerner & L. K. Simon (Eds.), *University–community collaborations for the twenty-first century: Outreach scholarship for youth and families* (pp. xiii–xix). New York: Garland.

Maguire, M. C. (1999). Treating the dyad as the unit of analysis: A primer on three analytic approaches. *Journal of Marriage and the Family, 61,* 213–223.

Marcenes, W., & Sheiham, A. (1996). The relationship between marital quality and oral health status. *Psychology and Health, 11,* 357–369.

Mark, M. M., & Shotland, R. L. (1985). Toward more useful social science. In R. L. Shotland & M. M. Mark (Eds.), *Social science and social policy* (pp. 335–370). Beverly Hills, CA: Sage.

Marsh, J. (2004). Reflections of a former editor. *The Responsive Community, 14*(2–3), 18–19.

Marshall, W., & Sawhill, I. V. (2004). Progressive family policy in the twenty-first century. In D. P. Moynihan, T. M. Smeeding, & L. Rainwater (Eds.), *The future of the family* (pp. 198–230). New York: Russell Sage Foundation.

Masnick, G., & Bane, M. J. (1980). *The nation's families: 1960–1990.* Cambridge, MA: Joint Center for Urban Studies of MIT and Harvard University.

Mason, M. A., Carnochan, S., & Fine, M. A. (2004). Family law for changing families in the new millennium. In M. Coleman & L. H. Ganong (Eds.), *Handbook of contemporary families: Considering the past, contemplating the future* (pp. 432–450). Thousand Oaks, CA: Sage.

Mason, M. A., Fine, M. A., & Carnochan, S. (2001). Family law in the new millennium: For whose families? *Journal of Family Issues, 22,* 859–881.

Massad, P. M., Sales, B. D., & Acosta, E. (1983). Utilizing social science information in the policy process: Can psychologists help? In R. F. Kidd & M. J. Sakes (Eds.), *Advances in applied social psychology* (Vol. 2, pp. 213–229). Hillsdale, NJ: Lawrence Erlbaum Associates, Inc.

Matthews, D. (2004). Changing communities through public engagement. In C. Anderson (Ed.), *Family and community policy: Strategies for civic engagement* (pp. 19–29). Alexandria, VA: American Association of Family and Consumer Sciences.

Mayer, R., & Hutchins, V. L. (1998). District of Columbia family policy seminar: A tool for devolution. *Maternal and Child Health Journal, 2,* 59–62.

Mayhew, D. R. (1974). *Congress: The electoral connection.* New Haven, CT: Yale University Press.

Mayne, T. J., O'Leary, A., McCrady, B., Contrada, R., & Labouvie, E. (1997). The differential effects of acute marital distress on emotional, physiological and immune functions in maritally distressed men and women. *Psychology and Health, 12,* 277–288.

McCall, R. B. (1983). Family services and mass media. *Family Relations, 32,* 315–322.

McCall, R. B. (1988). Science and the press: Like oil and water. *American Psychologist, 43,* 87–94.

McCall, R. B. (1993). A guide to communicating through the media. In K. McCartney & D. Phillips (Eds.), *An insider's guide to providing expert testimony before Congress* (pp. 16–22). Chicago: Society for Research in Child Development.

McCall, R. B. (1996). The concept and practice of education, research, and public service in university psychology departments. *American Psychologist, 51,* 379–388.

McCall, R. B., Groark, C. J., Strauss, M. S., & Johnson, C. N. (1998). Challenges of university–community outreach to traditional research universities: The University of Pittsburgh Office of Child Development experience. In R. M. Lerner & L. K. Simon (Eds.), *University–community collaborations for the twenty-first century: Outreach scholarship for youth and families* (pp. 203–230). New York: Garland.

McCartney, K., & Rosenthal, R. (2000). Effect size, practical importance, and social policy for children. *Child Development, 71,* 173–180.

McDaniel, S. H., Campbell, T. L., Hepworth, J., & Lorenz, A. (2005). *Family-oriented primary care* (2nd ed). New York: Springer.

McDaniel, S. H., Hepworth, J. H., & Doherty, W. J. (1992). *Medical family therapy: A biopsychosocial approach for families with health problems.* New York: Basic Books.

McEwen, B. S. (1998). Protective and damaging effects of stress mediators. *The New England Journal of Medicine, 338,* 171–179.

McGurk, H. (1995, October). *Family impact in Australia.* Paper presented at the Expert Meeting on Family Impact, University of Leuven, Leuven, Belgium.

McKnight, J. C. (1996). *The careless society: Community and its counterfeits.* New York: Basic Books.

McKnight, J. L., & Kretzmann, J. (1992). Mapping community capacity. *New Designs for Youth Development, 10*(1), 9–15.

McLanahan, S., & Booth, K. (1989). Mother-only families: Problems, prospects, and policies. *Journal of Marriage and the Family, 51,* 557–580.

McLanahan, S., Donahue, E., & Haskins, R. (2005). Introducing the issue. *The Future of Children, 15*(2), 3–12.

McLanahan, S., Garfinkel, I., & Mincy, R. B. (2001, December). *Fragile families, welfare reform, and marriage* (WR&B Brief No. 10). Washington, DC: The Brookings Institution.

McLanahan, S., & Sandefur, G. (1994). *Why we care about single parenthood: Growing up with a single parent. What hurts, what helps.* Cambridge, MA: Harvard University Press.

McMurrer, D. P., & Sawhill, I. V. (1998). *Getting ahead: Economic and social mobility in America.* Washington, DC: Urban Institute Press.

Meezan, W., & Rauch, J. (2005). Gay marriage, same-sex parenting, and America's children. *The Future of Children, 15*(2), 97–110.

Mellman, M., Lazarus, E., & Rivlin, A. (1990). Family time, family values. In D. Blankenhorn, S. Bayme, & J. B. Elshtain (Eds.), *Rebuilding the nest: A new commitment to the American family* (pp. 73–92). Milwaukee, WI: Family Service America.

Melnick, R. S. (2005, April). *Welfare policies and the strategy of rights.* Paper presented at the conference on Making the Politics of Poverty and Inequality: How Public Priorities Are Reshaping American Democracy, Institute for Research on Poverty, Madison, WI.

Melton, G. B. (1995). Bringing psychology to Capitol Hill: Briefings on child and family policy. *American Psychologist, 50,* 766–770.

Mendel, D. (2001, December–January). Combating delinquency: No place like home. *Youth Today,* p. 59.

Mendenhall, T. J., & Doherty, W. J. (2003). Partners in diabetes: A collaborative, democratic initiative in primary care. *Families, Systems & Health, 21,* 329–335.

Meyer, R. J., & Haggerty, J. (1962). Streptococcal infections in families: Factors altering individual susceptibility. *Pediatrics, 29,* 539–549.

Midwest Welfare Peer Assistance Network. (2002a, January). *Eliminating the silos: Or, it's not just welfare anymore.* Retrieved August 24, 2005, from the Institute for Research on Poverty Web site http://www.irp.wisc.edu/initiatives/outreach/welpan.htm

Midwest Welfare Peer Assistance Network. (2002b, May). *Recreating social assistance: Or, how to use waiver authority to eliminate program silos.* Retrieved August 24, 2005, from the Institute for Research on Poverty Web site http://www.irp.wisc.edu/initiatives/outreach/welpan.htm

Midwest Welfare Peer Assistance Network. (2002c). Welfare then, welfare now: Expenditures in some midwestern states. *Focus 22*(1), 11–14.

Miller, G. (1996). Children and the congress: A time to speak out. In R. P. Lorion, I. Iscoe, P. H. DeLeon, & G. R. VandenBos (Eds.), *Psychology and public policy: Balancing public service and professional need* (pp. 331–342). Washington, DC: American Psychological Association.

Mills, J., & Bogenschneider, K. (2001). Can communities assess support for preventing adolescent alcohol and other drug use? Reliability and validity of a community assessment inventory. *Family Relations, 50,* 355–375.

Mincy, R., Garfinkel, I., & Nepomnyaschy, L. (2005). In-hospital paternity establishment and father involvement in fragile families. *Journal of Marriage and Family, 67,* 611–626.

Moen, P. (1996). Change age trends: The pyramid upside down? In U. Bronfenbrenner, P. McClelland, E. Wethington, P. Moen, & S. J. Ceci (Eds.), *The state of Americans: This generation and the next* (pp. 208–258). New York: Free Press.

Moen, P., & Jull, P. M. M. (1995). Informing family policies: The uses of social research. *Journal of Family and Economic Issues, 16,* 79–107.

Moen, P., & Schorr, A. L. (1987). Families and social policy. In M. B. Sussman & S. K. Steinmetz (Eds.), *Handbook of marriage and the family* (pp. 795–813). New York: Plenum.

Moen, P., & Yu, Y. (1999, January). *Effective work/life strategies: Working couples, gender and life quality* (BLCC Working Paper No. 99-06). Ithaca, NY: Cornell University, Bronfenbrenner Life Course Center.

Monroe, P. A. (1995). Family policy: Introduction to the special collection. *Family Relations, 44,* 3–4.

Moore, K. (1993). Family strengths and youth behavior problems: Analyses of three national survey databases. In G. E. Hendershot & F. B. LeClere (Eds.), *Family health: From data to policy* (pp. 98–101). Minneapolis, MN: National Council on Family Relations.

Moore, K. A. (1999). *Tracking progress in children's well-being.* Retrieved August 27, 2005, from http://www.childtrends.org/ar-tracking.cfm

Moore, K. A., & Brown, B. V., with Scarupa, H. J. (2003, February). *The uses (and misuses) of social indicators: Implications for public policy* (Child Trends Research Brief Publication No. 20003-01). Washington, DC: Child Trends.

Moynihan, D. P. (1941). Foreword to the paperback edition. In *Nation and family: The Swedish experiment in democratic family and population policy* (pp. vi–vii). New York: Harper.

Moynihan, D. P. (1986). *Family and nation: The Swedish experiment in democratic family and population policy.* New York: Harcourt Brace Jovanovich.

Moynihan, D. P. (1996). Congress builds a coffin. *New York Review of Books, 43,* 33–36.

Murray, D. M., Davis-Hearn, M., Goldman, A. I., Pirie, P., & Luepker, R. V. (1988). Four- and five year follow-up results from four seventh-grade smoking prevention strategies. *Journal of Behavioral Medicine, 11,* 395–405.

Myrdal, A. (1941). *Nation and family: The Swedish experiment in democratic family and population policy.* Cambridge, MA: MIT Press. (Original work published in 1941)

National Commission on America's Urban Families. (1993). *Families first.* Washington, DC: Author.

National Commission on Child Welfare and Family Preservation. (1990). *A commitment to change.* Washington, DC: American Public Welfare Association.

National Commission on Children. (1991a). *Beyond rhetoric: A new American agenda for children and families.* Washington, DC: Author.

National Commission on Children. (1991b). *Speaking of kids: A national survey of children and parents.* Washington, DC: Author.

National Council on Family Relations. (2000). *Public policy through a family lens: Sustaining families in the 21st century.* Minneapolis, MN. Author.

National Issues Forum Institute. (1996). *The troubled American family: Which way out of the storm?* Washington, DC: Author.

Neb. Rev. Stat. Ann. § 43-532 (2005).

Neb. Rev. Stat. Ann. § 43-533 (2005).

Neb. Rev. Stat. Ann. § 43-534 (2005).

Nelson, C. E., Roberts, J., Maederer, C. M., Wertheimer, B., & Johnson, B. (1987). The utilization of social science information by policymakers. *American Behavioral Scientist, 30,* 569–577.

Newcomb, M. D., & Bentler, P. M. (1989). Substance use and abuse among children and teenagers. *American Psychologist, 44,* 242–248.

Newman, R., & Vincent, T. (1996). Introduction: Balancing expertise with practical realities. In R. P. Lorion, I. Iscoe, P. H. DeLeon, & G. R. VandenBos (Eds.), *Psychology and public policy: Balancing public service and professional need* (pp. 203–206). Washington, DC: American Psychological Association.

Nock, S. L. (2005). Marriage as a public issue. *The Future of Children, 15*(2), 13–32.

Normandin, H., & Bogenschneider, K. (Eds.). (2005). *Medicaid: Who benefits, how expensive is it, and what are states doing to control costs?* (Wisconsin Family Impact Seminar Briefing Rep. No. 22). Madison: University of Wisconsin Center for Excellence in Family Studies.

Nye, F. I., & McDonald, G. W. (1979). Family policy research: Emergent models and some theoretical issues. *Journal of Marriage and the Family, 41,* 473–485.

Oberst, M. T., & James, R. H. (1985, April). Going home: Patient and spouse adjustment following cancer surgery. *Topics in Clinical Nursing, 7,* 46–57.

Olds, D. (1997). Improving the economic and social well-being of families with home visitation early in the life cycle. In K. Bogenschneider, T. Corbett, M. E. Bell, & K. D. Linney (Eds.), *Moving families out of poverty: Employment, tax, and investment strategies* (Wisconsin Family Impact Seminar Briefing Rep. No. 9, pp. 32–39). Madison: University of Wisconsin Center for Excellence in Family Studies.

Olds, D., Eckenrode, J., Henderson, C. R., Jr., Kitzman, H., Powers, J., Cole, R., et al. (1997). Long-term effects of home visitation on maternal life course and child abuse and neglect: 15-year follow-up of a randomized trial. *Journal of the American Medical Association, 278,* 637–643.

Olds, D., Henderson, C. R., Jr., Cole, R., Eckenrode, J., Kitzman, H., Luckey, D., et al. (1998). Long-term effects of nurse home visitation on children's criminal and antisocial behavior: 15-year follow-up of a randomized controlled trial. *Journal of the American Medical Association, 280,* 1238–1244.

Olds, D., Henderson, C. R., Jr., Kitzman, H. J., Eckenrode, J., Cole, R. E., & Tatelbaum, R. C. (1999). Prenatal and infancy home visitation by nurses: Recent findings. *The Future of Children, 9*(1), 44–65.

Oliver, M. L., & Shapiro, T. M. (1997). *Black wealth/white wealth: A new perspective on racial inequality.* New York: Routledge.

Olson, D. H., & Tiesel, J. W. (1993). Assessment of family functioning. In G. E. Hendershot & F. B. LeClere (Eds.), *Family health from data to policy* (pp. 76–97). Minneapolis, MN: National Council on Family Relations.

Ooms, T. (1984). The necessity of a family perspective. *Journal of Family Issues, 5,* 160–181.

Ooms, T. (1990). Families and government: Implementing a family perspective in public policy. *Social Thought, 16,* 61–78.

Ooms, T. (1995, October). *Taking families seriously: Family impact analysis as an essential policy tool.* Paper presented at the Expert Meeting on Family Impact, University of Leuven, Leuven, Belgium.

Ooms, T. (1998). *Towards more perfect unions: Putting marriage on the public agenda.* Washington, DC: Family Impact Seminar.

Ooms, T. (2002, August). *Marriage and government: Strange bedfellows?* (Couples and Marriage Policy Brief No. 1). Washington, DC: Center for Law and Social Policy.

Ooms, T. (2004, May 5). *The benefits of a healthy marriage.* Testimony presented at a hearing of the Senate Committee on Finance, Subcommittee on Social Security and Family Policy.

Ooms, T. (2005, July). *The new kid on the block: What is marriage education and does it work?* (Couples and Marriage Policy Brief No. 7). Washington, DC: Center for Law and Social Policy.

Ooms, T., Bouchet, S., & Parke, M. (2004). *Beyond marriage licenses: Efforts to strengthen marriage and two-parent families. A state-by-state snapshot.* Washington, DC: Center for Law and Social Policy.

Ooms, T., & Preister, S. (1988). *A strategy for strengthening families: Using family criteria in policy making and program evaluation.* Washington, DC: The Family Impact Seminar.

Ooms, T., & Wilson, P. (2004). The challenges of offering relationship and marriage education to low-income populations. *Family Relations, 53,* 440–447.

Orthner, D. K. (1990). The family in transition. In D. Blankenhorn, S. Bayme, & J. B. Elshtain (Eds.), *Rebuilding the nest: A new commitment to the American family* (pp. 93–118). Milwaukee, WI: Family Services America.

Parasuraman, S., & Greenhaus, J. H. (1997). *Integrating work and family: Challenges and choices for a changing world.* Westport, CT: Quorum.

Parcel, T. L., & Menaghan, E. G. (1994). *Parents' jobs and children's lives.* New York: Aldine de Gruyter.

Partial-Birth Abortion Ban Act, 18 S.S.C. §1531 (2003).

Patterson, C. J. (2000). Family relationships of lesbian and gay men. *Journal of Marriage and the Family, 62,* 1052–1069.

Patterson, G. R. (1986). Performance models for antisocial boys. *American Psychologist, 41,* 432–444.

Patterson, G. R., DeBaryshe, B. D., & Ramsey, E. (1989). A developmental perspective on antisocial behavior. *American Psychologist, 44,* 329–335.

Patterson, G. R., Dishion, T. J., & Chamberlain, P. (1993). Outcomes and methodological issues relating to treatment of antisocial children. In T. R. Giles (Ed.), *Handbook of effective psychotherapy* (pp. 43–88). New York: Plenum.

Patterson, G. R., & Narrett, C. M. (1990). The development of a reliable and valid treatment program for aggressive young children. *International Journal of Mental Health, 19,* 19–26.

Patterson, G. R., Reid, J. B., & Dishion, T. J. (1992). *A social interactional approach: Vol. 4. Antisocial boys.* Eugene, OR: Castalia.

Patterson, G. R., & Yoerger, K. (1993, November). *Differentiating outcomes and histories for early and late onset arrests.* Paper presented at the American Society of Criminology, Phoenix, AZ.

Patterson, K. (2005, March). Australia: Building a virtuous circle. *OECD Observer, 248.* Retrieved April 6, 2005, from http://www.oecdobserver.org/news/printpage.php/aid/1550/Australia.html

Patton, M. (1997). *Utilization-focused evaluation* (3rd ed.). Thousand Oaks, CA: Sage.

Perry-Jenkins, M., Repetti, R. L., & Crouter, A. C. (2000). Work and family in the 1990s. *Journal of Marriage and the Family, 62,* 981–998.

Peterson, E. H. (1985). *Where your treasure is: Psalms that summon you from self to community.* Grand Rapids: William B. Eerdmans Publishing Company.

Pettigrew, T. F. (1985). Can social scientists be effective actors in the policy arena? In R. L. Shotland & M. M. Mark (Eds.), *Social science and social policy* (pp. 121–134). Beverly Hills, CA: Sage.

Pianta, R. (2004, Summer). Transitioning to school: Policy, practice, and reality. *The Evaluation Exchange, 10*(2), 5–6.

Pilling, S., Bebbington, P., Kuipers, E., Garety, P., Geddes, J., Orbach, G., et al. (2002). Psychological treatments in schizophrenia: I. Meta-analysis of family intervention and cognitive behaviour therapy. *Psychological Medicine, 32,* 763–782.

Pittman, K., Irby, M., & Ferber, T. (2000). *Youth policy in the US: Some observations and options.* Takoma Park, MD: The Forum for Youth Investment.

Popenoe, D. (1990). Family decline in America. In D. Blankenhorn, S. Bayme, & J. B. Elshtain (Eds.), *Rebuilding the nest: A new commitment to the American family* (pp. 39–51). Milwaukee, WI: Family Service America.

Popenoe, D. (1993). The national family wars. *Journal of Marriage and the Family, 55,* 553–555.

Pratt, C. C. (1998, September). *Family policy in an era of devolution.* Paper presented at the 1998 National Public Policy Education Conference, Portland, OR.

Pratt, C. C. (2000). Social indicators and social programs: Researcher forges new links in Oregon. *The Child Indicator, 2*(1), 2, 5.

Pratt, C. C., & Katzev, A. (1997). Building results: From wellness goals to positive outcomes for Oregon's children, youth, and families. In K. Bogenschneider, M. E. Bell, & K. D. Linney (Eds.), *Programs and policies to prevent youth crime, smoking, and substance use: What works?* (Wisconsin Family Impact Seminar Briefing Rep. No. 8, pp. 20–28). Madison: University of Wisconsin Center for Excellence in Family Studies.

Preston, S. H. (2004). The value of children. In D. P. Moynihan, T. M. Smeeding, & L. Rainwater (Eds.), *The future of the family* (pp. 263–266). New York: Russell Sage Foundation.

Price, R. H. (1989). Bearing witness. *American Journal of Community Psychology, 17,* 151–165.

Priestley, H. (1980, March). *The skeptical physicist.* Lecture at the Knox College Mortar Board's Last Lecture Series, Galesburg, IL.

Prus, R. (1992). Producing social science: Knowledge as a social problem in academia. In G. Miller & J. A. Holstein (Eds.), *Perspectives on social problems* (Vol. 3, pp. 57–78). Greenwich, CT: JAI.

Ptacek, J. T., Pierce, G. R., Dodge, K. L., & Ptacek, J. J. (1997). Social support in spouses of cancer patients: What do they get and to what end? *Personal Relationships, 4,* 431–449.

Putnam, R. D. (1995). Bowling alone: America's declining social capital. *Journal of Democracy, 6*(1), 65–78.

Putnam, R. D. (2000a). *Bowling alone: The collapse and revival of American community.* New York: Simon & Schuster.

Putnam, R. D. (2000b, September 18). *Bowling alone: The collapse and revival of American community.* University of Wisconsin Hilldale Lectures, Madison, WI.

Putnam, R. (2002). Bowling together: The United State of America. *The American Prospect, 13*(3), 20–22.

Quinn, J. (2001, July–August). The problem with magical thinking. *Youth Today, 10*(7), 54.

Quoss, B. (1992). Teaching family policy through advocacy and empowerment. *Family Relations, 41*(1), 39–43.

Rafael, T., & Pion-Berlin, L. (1999, April). Parents anonymous: Strengthening families. *Juvenile Justice Bulletin,* 1–11.

Ramey, C. T., Campbell, F. A., Burchinal, M., Skinner, M. L., Gardner, D. M., & Ramey, S. L. (1999). Persistent effects of early intervention on high-risk children and their mothers. *Applied Developmental Science, 4,* 2–14.

Ramey, S. L., & Ramey, C. T. (1999). Early experience and early intervention for children at risk for developmental delay and mental retardation. In S. L. Ramey, C. T. Ramey, & M. J. Friedlander (Eds.), *Mental retardation and developmental disabilities research reviews* (pp. 1–10). New York: Wiley.

Rankin-Esquer, L. A., Deeter, A., & Taylor, C. B. (2000). Coronary heart disease and couples. In K. B. Schmaling & T. G. Sher (Eds.), *The psychology of couples and illness: Theory, research, and practice* (pp. 43–70). Washington, DC: American Psychological Association.

Rapp, R. (1978). Family and class in contemporary America: Notes toward an understanding of ideology. *Science and Society, 42,* 278–300.

Rappaport, J. (1981). In praise of paradox: A social policy of empowerment over prevention. *American Journal of Community Psychology, 9*(6), 1–25.

Raver, C. C. (2003). Does work pay psychologically as well as economically? The role of employment in predicting depressive symptoms and parenting among low-income families. *Child Development, 74,* 1720–1736.

Regan, M. C., Jr. (1996). Postmodern family law: Toward a new model of status. In D. Popenoe, J. B. Elshtain, & D. Blankenhorn (Eds.), *Promises to keep: Decline and renewal of marriage in America* (pp. 157–185). Lanham, MD: Rowman & Littlefield.

Reiss, D. (1981). *The family's construction of reality.* Cambridge, MA: Harvard University Press.

Renick, M. J., Blumberg, S. L., & Markman, H. J. (1992). The prevention and relationship enhancement program (PREP): An empirically based prevention intervention program for couples. *Family Relations, 41,* 141–147.

Reno, V. P., Graetz, M. J., Apfel, K. S., Lavery, J., & Hill, C. (Eds.). (2005). *Uncharted waters: Paying benefits from individual accounts in federal retirement policy* (Study Panel Final Report). Washington, DC: National Academy of Social Insurance.

Resnick, D. M., Bearman, P. S., Blum, R. W., Bauman, K. E., Harris, K. M., Jones, J., et al. (1997). Protecting adolescents from harm: Findings from the National Longitudinal Study on Adolescent Health. *Journal of the American Medical Association, 278,* 823–832.

Responsive Communitarian Platform. (1992). *The Responsive Community: Rights and Responsibilities, 2*(2), 4–20.

Reust, C. E., & Mattingly, S. (1996). Family involvement in medical decision making. *Family Medicine, 28,* 39–45.

Reynolds, A. J., & Temple, J. A. (2005). Priorities for a new century of early childhood programs. *Infants and Young Children, 18,* 104–118.

Reynolds, A. J., Temple, J. A., Robertson, D. L., & Mann, E. A. (2001). Long-term effects of an early childhood intervention on educational achievement and juvenile arrest: A 15-year follow-up of low-income children in public schools. *Journal of the American Medical Association, 285,* 2339–2346.

RIA. (2005). *Organization of RIA's complete analysis of the Jobs and Growth Tax Relief Reconciliation Act of 2003.* Stamford, CT: Author.

Rice, R. M. (1977). *American family policy: Content and context.* Milwaukee, WI: Family Service America.

Riley, D. (1991). Creating a local response to children's needs: An empowering approach. *Networking Bulletin: Empowerment and Family Support, 2*(1), 22–24.

Riley, D. (1994). Some principles for designing effective parenting education/support programs. In K. Bogenschneider, D. Riley, K. Morgan, & S. Lundeen (Eds.), *Can government promote competent parenting?* (Wisconsin Family Impact Seminars Briefing Rep. No. 3, pp. 7–14). Madison: University of Wisconsin–Madison Center for Excellence in Family Studies.

Riley, D. (1997). Using local research to change 100 communities for children and families. *American Psychologist, 52,* 424–433.

Riley, D., Meinhardt, G., Nelson, C., Salisbury, M. J., & Winnett, T. (1991). How effective are age paced newsletters for new parents? A replication and extension of earlier studies. *Family Relations, 40,* 247–253.

Rist, R. C. (1994). Influencing the policy process with qualitative research. In N. Denzin & Y. Lincoln (Eds.), *Handbook of qualitative research* (pp. 545–558). Thousand Oaks, CA: Sage.

Rockefeller, J. D., IV. (1998, October 2). *Measuring our success at the turn of the century: A report card on kids and family issues.* Invited address presented to the Georgetown Public Policy Institute, Georgetown University, Washington, DC.

Rolland, J. S. (1994). *Families, illness, and disability.* New York: Basic.

Rosenberg, A. A., & Limber, S. P. (1996). The contributions of social science to family policy. *Journal of Social Issues, 52*(3), 1–9.

Ross, R., & Staines, G. L. (1972). The politics of analyzing social problems. *Social Problems, 20,* 18–40.

Rossi, P. H., & Wright, J. D. (1985). Social science research and the politics of gun control. In R. L. Shotland & M. M. Mark (Eds.), *Social science and social policy* (pp. 311–334). Beverly Hills, CA: Sage.

Rule, J. B. (1978). *Insight and social betterment: A preface to applied social science.* New York: Oxford University Press.

Rumberger, R. W., Ghatak, R., Poulos, G., Ritter, P. L., & Dornbusch, S. M. (1990). Family influences on dropout behavior in one California high school. *Sociology of Education, 63,* 283–299.

Rutter, M. (1995). Maternal deprivation. In M. H. Bornstein (Ed.), *Handbook of parenting: Vol. 4. Applied and practical parenting* (pp. 3–31). Mahwah, NJ: Lawrence Erlbaum Associates, Inc.

Rutter, M., and the English & Romanian Adoptees Study Team. (1998). Developmental catch-up, and deficit, following adoption after severe global early privation. *Journal of Child Psychology and Psychiatry, 39,* 465–476.

Salzinger, S., Kaplan, S., & Artemyeff, C. (1983). Mothers' personal social networks and child maltreatment. *Journal of Abnormal Psychology, 92,* 68–76.

Sarason, S. B. (1978, April). The nature of problem solving in social action. *American Psychologist, 33,* 370–380.

Sawhill, I. V. (1992). Young children and families. In H. J. Aaron & C. L. Schultze (Eds.), *Setting domestic policy: What can government do?* (pp. 147–184). Washington, DC: Brookings Institute.

Scanzoni, J. (1997). A reply to Glenn: Fashioning families and policies for the future—not the past. *Family Relations, 46,* 213–217.

Schattschneider, E. E. (1960). *The semisovereign people: A realist's view of democracy in America.* New York: Holt, Rinehart & Winston.

Schilder, D., Brady, A., & Horsch, K. (1997). *Resource guide of results-based accountability efforts: Profiles of selected states.* Retrieved November 9, 1998, from http://gseweb.harvard.edu/~hfrp/index.html

Schmaling, K. B., & Sher, T. G. (Eds.). (2000). *The psychology of couples and illness: Theory, research, and practice.* Washington, DC: American Psychological Association.

Schor, J. B. (1991). *The overworked American: The unexpected decline of leisure.* New York: Basic Books.

Schorr, L. B. (1991, January). *Successful programs and the bureaucratic dilemma: Current deliberations.* Speech presented at the National Center for Children in Poverty, Columbia University School of Public Health, New York.

Schroeder, P. (1989). *Champion of the great American family.* New York: Random House.

Schweinhart, L. J. (2003, April). *Benefits, costs, and explanation of the High/Scope Perry Preschool Program.* Paper presented at the annual meeting of the Society for Research in Child Development, Tampa, FL.

Scott, K. G., Mason, C. A., & Chapman, D. A. (1999). The use of epidemiological methodology as a means of influencing public policy. *Child Development, 70,* 1263–1272.

Seaberg, J. R. (1990). Family policy revisited: Are we there yet? *Social Work, 35,* 548–554.

Sechrest, L. (1985). Social science and social policy: Will our numbers ever be good enough? In R. L. Shotland & M. M. Mark (Eds.), *Social science and social policy* (pp. 63–95). Beverly Hills, CA: Sage.

Seeley, D. (1985). *Education through partnership.* Washington, DC: American Enterprise Institute.

Segal, J. (1983). Utilization of stress and coping research: Issues of public education and public policy. In N. Garmezy & M. Rutter (Eds.), *Stress, coping, and development in children* (pp. 239–252). New York: McGraw-Hill.

Segerstrom, S. C., & Miller, G. E. (2004). Psychological stress and the human immune system: A meta-analytic study of 30 years of inquiry. *Psychological Bulletin, 130,* 601–630.

Seltzer, J. A. (2000). Families formed outside of marriage. *Journal of Marriage and the Family, 62,* 1247–1268.

Shaffer, D., Philips, I., Garland, A., & Bacon, K. (1989). Prevention issues in youth suicide. In D. Shaffer, I. Philips, N. B. Enzer, & M. M. Silverman (Eds.), *Prevention of mental disorders, alcohol and other drug use in children and adolescents* (OSAP Prevention Monograph No. 2, pp. 443–456). Rockville, MD: Office for Substance Abuse Prevention.

Sherrod, L. R. (1998). The common pursuits of modern philanthropy and the proposed outreach university. In R. M. Lerner & L. K. Simon (Eds.), *University–community collaborations for the twenty-first century: Outreach scholarship for youth and families* (pp. 397–418). New York: Garland.

Shonkoff, J. P. (2000). Science, policy, and practice: Three cultures in search of a shared mission. *Child Development, 71,* 181–187.

Shonkoff, J. P. (2004). Evaluating early childhood services: What's really behind the curtain. *The Evaluation Exchange, 10*(2).

Simich-Dudgeon, C. (1993). Increasing student achievement through teacher knowledge about parent involvement. In N. F. Chavkin (Ed.), *Families and schools in a pluralistic society* (pp. 189–203). New York: State University of New York Press.

Simmons, C. W. (1996, October). *State and local information needs: The California family impact seminar model.* Paper presented at the annual meeting of the Association for Public Policy Analysis and Management Research Conference, Washington, DC.

Skinner, D. A., & Anderson, E. (1993). *Teaching family policy: A handbook of course syllabi, teaching strategies and resources.* Minneapolis, MN: National Council on Family Relations.

Sklar, K. K. (1993). The historical foundations of women's power in the creation of the American welfare state, 1840–1930. In S. Koven & S. Michel (Eds.), *Mothers of a new world* (pp. 321–342). New York: Routledge.

Skocpol, T. (1995). *Social policy in the United States: Future possibilities in historical perspective.* Princeton, NJ: Princeton University Press.

Skocpol, T. (1996, November). *The missing middle: Working parents in U.S. democracy and social policy.* Paper presented at the annual meeting of the National Council on Family Relations, Kansas City, MO.

Skocpol, T. (1997). A partnership with American families. In S. B. Greenberg & T. Skocpol (Eds.), *The new majority: Toward a popular progressive politics* (pp. 104–129). New Haven, CT: Yale University Press.

Skocpol, T., & Dickert, J. (2001). Speaking for families and children in a changing civic America. In C. J. De Vita & R. Mosher-Williams (Eds.), *Who speaks for America's children* (pp. 137–164). Washington, DC: Urban Institute Press.

Skocpol, T., & Greenberg, S. B. (1997). A politics for our times. In S. B. Greenberg & T. Skocpol (Eds.), *The new majority: Toward a popular progressive politics* (pp. 104–129). New Haven, CT: Yale University Press.

Skolnick, A. (1997). A reply to Glenn: The battle of the textbooks: Bringing in the culture war. *Family Relations, 46,* 219–222.

Slack, K. S., Holl, J. L., Lee, B. J., McDaniel, M., Altenbernd, L., & Stevens, A. B. (2003). Child protective intervention in the context of welfare reform: The effects of work and welfare on maltreatment reports. *Journal of Policy Analysis and Management, 22,* 517–536.

Small, S., & Bogenschneider, K. (1998). Toward a scholarship of relevance: Lessons from a land grant university. In R. M. Lerner & L. A. Simon (Eds.), *University–community collaborations for the twenty-first century: Outreach scholarship for youth and families* (pp. 255–274). New York: Garland.

Smeeding, T. M., Moynihan, D. P., & Rainwater, L. (2004). The challenge of family system changes for research and policy. In D. P. Moynihan, T. M. Smeeding, & L. Rainwater (Eds.), *The future of the family* (pp. 1–22). New York: Russell Sage Foundation.

Smith, D. E. (1993). The standard North American family: SNAF as an ideological code. *Journal of Family Issues, 14,* 50–65.

Smith, J. A. (1991). *The idea brokers: Think tanks and the rise of the new policy elite.* New York: Free Press.

Smith, L. (1954). *The journey.* Cleveland, OH: World Publishing.

Smith, M. B. (1968). School and home: Focus on achievement. In A. H. Passow (Ed.), *Developing programs for the educationally disadvantaged* (pp. 87–107). New York: Teachers College Press.

Smith, S., Blank, S., & Collins, R. (1992). *Pathways to self-sufficiency for two generations: Designing welfare-to-work programs that benefit children and strengthen families.* New York: Foundation for Child Development.

Smith, V. (2005, October). What are states doing to control Medicaid costs and why is it so hard? In H. Normandin & K. Bogenschneider (Eds.), *Medicaid: Who benefits, how expensive is it, and what are states doing to control costs?* (Wisconsin Family Impact Seminar Briefing Rep. No. 22, pp. 23–34). Madison: University of Wisconsin Center for Excellence in Family Studies.

Snyder, W., & Ooms, T. (Eds.). (1999). *Empowering families, helping adolescents: Family-centered treatment of adolescents with alcohol, drug abuse, and mental health problems* (Technical Assistance Publication Series, No. 6, DHHS Publication No. SMA-00-3362). Washington, DC: U.S. Government Printing Office.

Society for Human Resource Management (2003, June 22). Rising health care costs force employers to cut some non-essential benefits. Alexandria, VA: Author.

Sokalski, H. J. (1993). The International Year of the Family: The world's support for the smallest democracy. In K. Altergott (Ed.), *One world, many families* (pp. 3–7). Minneapolis, National Council on Family Relations.

Spenner, K. I. (1988). Occupations, work settings and the course of adult development: Tracing the implications of select historical changes. In P. Baltes, D. Featherman, & R. Lerner (Eds.), *Life-span development and behavior* (Vol. 9, pp. 243–285). Hillsdale, NJ: Lawrence Erlbaum Associates, Inc.

Spoth, R. L., Kavanagh, K. A., & Dishion, T. (2002). Family-centered preventive intervention science: Toward benefits to larger populations of children, youth, and families. *Prevention Science, 3,* 145–152.

Stacey, J. (1993). Good riddance to "the family": A response to David Popenoe. *Journal of Marriage and the Family, 55,* 545–547.

Stacey, J. (1996). *In the name of the family: Rethinking family values in the postmodern age.* Boston: Beacon.

Stack, C. B. (1974). *All our kin: Strategies for survival in a Black community.* New York: Harper & Row.

Stack, S., & Eshleman, J. R. (1998). Marital status and happiness: A 17-nation study. *Journal of Marriage and the Family, 60,* 527–536.

Stage, S. (1997). Ellen Richards and the social significance of the home economics movement. In S. Stage & V. B. Vincenti (Eds.), *Rethinking home economics* (pp. 17–33). Ithaca, NY: Cornell University Press.

Stanley v. Illinois, 405 U.S. 645; 92 S. Ct. 1208; U.S. LEXIS 70; 31 L. Ed. 2d 551 (1972).

State Legislative Leaders Foundation. (1995). *State legislative leaders: Keys to effective legislation for children and families.* Centerville, MA: Author.

Staton, J., Ooms, T., & Owen, T. (1991). *Family resource, support, and parent education programs: The power of a preventive approach.* Washington, DC: The Family Impact Seminar.

Steinberg, L. (1996). *Beyond the classroom: Why school reform has failed and what parents need to do.* New York: Simon & Schuster.

Steinberg, L., & Brown, B. B. (1989, March). *Beyond the classroom: Parental and peer influences on high school achievement.* Paper presented at the annual meeting of the American Educational Research Association, San Francisco.

Steinberg, L., Lamborn, S. D., Dornbusch, S. M., & Darling, N. (1992). Impact of parenting practices on adolescent achievement: Authoritative parenting, school involvement, and encouragement to succeed. *Child Development, 63,* 1266–1281.

Steiner, G. (1980, Fall). The family as a public issue: Many causes with many votaries. *Carnegie Quarterly, 28*(4), 1–5.

Steiner, G. Y. (1981). *The futility of family policy.* Washington, DC: Brookings Institute.

Stevenson, D. L., & Baker, D. P. (1987). The family–school relation and the child's school performance. *Child Development, 58,* 1348–1357.

Stone, R. I. (1999). Long term care: Coming of age in the 21st century. In R. Butler, L. Grossman, & M. Oberlink (Eds.), *Life in an older America* (pp. 49–73). New York: Twentieth Century Fund.

Stormshak, E. A., Dishion, T. J., Light, J., & Yasui, M. (2005). Implementing family-centered interventions within the public middle school: Linking service delivery to change in student problem behavior. *Journal of Abnormal Child Psychology, 33*(6), 723–733.

Stormshak, E. A., Kaminski, R. A., & Goodman, M. R. (2002). Enhancing the parenting skills of Head Start families during the transition to kindergarten. *Prevention Science, 3,* 223–234.

St. Pierre, R. G. (1985). Are the social sciences able to answer questions about compensatory education programs? In R. L. Shotland & M. M. Mark (Eds.), *Social science and social policy* (pp. 195–218). Beverly Hills, CA: Sage.

St. Pierre, R. G., Layzer, J. I., & Barnes, H. B. (1996). *Regenerating two-generation programs.* Cambridge, MA: Abt Associates.

Strach, P. (2006). The politics of family. *Polity, 38*(2), 151–173.

Strein, W., Hoagwood, K., & Cohn, A. (2003). School psychology: A public health perspective: I. Prevention, populations, and systems change. *Journal of School Psychology, 41,* 23–38.

Strickland, T. (1996). Moving psychology toward (self) recognition as a public resource: The views of a congressman psychologist. In R. P. Lorion, I. Iscoe, P. H. DeLeon, & G. R. VandenBos (Eds.), *Psychology and public policy: Balancing public service and professional need* (pp. 369–389). Washington, DC: American Psychological Association.

Swift, M. S., & Healey, K. N. (1986). Translating research into practice. In M. Kessler & S. E. Goldston (Eds.), *A decade of progress in primary prevention* (pp. 205–234). Hanover, MA: University Press of New England.

Szapocznik, J., Rio, A., Murray, E., Cohen, R., Scopetta, M. A., Rivas-Vasquez, A., et al. (1989). Structural family versus psychodynamic child therapy for problematic Hispanic boys. *Journal of Consulting and Clinical Psychology, 57,* 571–578.

Thomas, A., & Sawhill, I. (2005). For love and money? The impact of family structure on family income. *The Future of Children, 15,* 57–74.

Tittle, C. R. (1985). Can social science answer questions about deterrence for policy use? In R. L. Shotland & M. M. Mark (Eds.), *Social science and social policy* (pp. 265–294). Beverly Hills, CA: Sage.

Tobler, N. S. (1992). Drug prevention programs can work: Research findings. *Journal of Addictive Diseases, 11*(3), 1–28.

Tobler, N. S., & Stratton, H. H. (1997). Effectiveness of school-based prevention programs: A meta-analysis of the research. *Journal of Primary Prevention, 18,* 71–128.

Tocqueville, A. (1945). *Democracy in America* (Vol. 2). New York: Vintage Books.

Todd, C. M., Ebata, A. T., & Hughes, R., Jr. (1998). Making university and community collaborations work. In R. M. Lerner & L. K. Simon (Eds.), *University–community collaborations for the twenty-first century: Outreach scholarship for youth and families* (pp. 231–254). New York: Garland.

Tough, A. (1971). *The adult's learning projects* (Research in Education Series No. 1). Toronto: Ontario Institute for Studies in Education.

Trattner, W. I. (1999). *Poor law to welfare state.* New York: Free Press.

Triandis, H. C. (1994). Theoretical and methodological approaches to the study of collectivism and individualism. In U. Kim, H. C. Triandis, C. Kagitcibasi, S.-C. Choi, & G. Yoon (Eds.), *Individualism and collectivism: Theory method, and applications* (pp. 41–51). Thousand Oaks, CA: Sage.

Triandis, H. C. (2001). Individualism and collectivism: Past, present, and future. In D. Matsumoto (Ed.), *The handbook of culture and psychology* (pp. 35–50). New York: Oxford University Press.

Triandis, H. C., Bontempo, R., Villareal, M. J., Asai, M., & Lucca, N. (1988). Individualism and collectivism: Cross-cultural perspectives on self-ingroup relationships. *Journal of Personality and Social Psychology, 54,* 323–338.

Triandis, H. C., McCusker, C., Betancourt, H., Iwao, S., Leung, K., Salazar, J. M., et al. (1993). An etic–emic analysis of individualism and collectivism. *Journal of Cross-Cultural Psychology, 24,* 366–383.

Trzcinski, E. (1995a). An ecological perspective on family policy: A conceptual and philosophical framework. *Journal of Family and Economic Issues, 16,* 7–33.

Trzcinski, E. (1995b). The use and abuse of neoclassical theory in the political arena: The example of family and medical leave in the United States. In E. Kuiper & J. Sap (Eds.), *Out of the margin: Feminist perspectives on economics* (pp. 231–248). London: Routledge.

Tubbesing, C. (1998). The dual personality of federalism. *State Legislatures, 24*(4), 14–19.

Turnbull, J. R., & Turnbull, A. P. (2000). Accountability: Whose job is it, anyway? *Journal of Early Intervention, 23,* 231–234.

Turner, H., Nye, C., & Schwartz, J. (2004–2005, Winter). Assessing the effects of parent involvement interventions on elementary school student achievement. *The Evaluation Exchange, 10*(4), 4.

Tweedie, J. (1999). Eight questions to ask about welfare reforms. *State Legislatures, 25,* 32–35.

Uchino, B. N. (2004). *Social support and physical health: Understanding the health consequences of relationships.* New Haven, CT: Yale University Press.

Uchino, B. N., Cacioppo, J. T., & Kiecolt-Glaser, J. K. (1996). The relationship between social support and physiological processes: A review with emphasis on underlying mechanisms and implications for health. *Psychological Bulletin, 119,* 488–531.

Uhlenberg, P., & Eggebeen, D. (1986). The declining well-being of American adolescents. *The Public Interest, 82,* 25–38.

Unrau, Y. A. (1993). Expanding the role of program evaluation in social welfare policy analysis. *Evaluation Review, 17,* 653–662.

U.S. Department of Education. (2002, January). *Executive summary: No Child Left Behind Act.* Retrieved September 11, 2005, from http://www.ed.gov/nclb/overview/intro/execsumm.pdf

U.S. Department of Education, Office of Educational Research and Improvement. (1991). *Policy perspectives: Parental involvement in education* (Publication No. PIP 91-983). Washington, DC: U.S. Government Printing Office.

U.S. Department of Health and Human Services. (2000). *Healthy people 2010: Understanding and improving health* (2nd ed.). Washington, DC: U.S. Government Printing Office.

Utah Code Ann. § 62A-4a-119 (2006).

Vandivere, S., Gallagher, M., & Moore, K. A. (2004). Changes in children's well-being and family environments. *Snapshots of America's Families* (Vol. 3, No. 18). Washington, DC: The Urban Institute.

Vitaliano, P. P., Zhang, J., & Scanlan, J. M. (2003). Is caregiving hazardous to one's physical health? A meta-analysis. *Psychological Bulletin, 129,* 946–972.

Waite, L. (1995). Does marriage matter? *Demography, 32,* 483–507.

Walker, T. B., & Elrod, L. D. (1993). Family law in the fifty states: An overview. *Family Law Quarterly, 16,* 319–421.

Walsh, F. (1995). From family damage to family challenge. In R. H. Miskell, S. H. Lusterman, & S. H. McDaniel (Eds.), *Integrating family therapy: Handbook of family psychology and system theory* (pp. 587–606). Washington, DC: American Psychological Association.

Webster-Stratton, C. (1982). Long-term effects of a videotape modeling parent education program: Comparison of immediate and 1-year-follow-up results. *Behavior Therapy, 13,* 702–714.

Webster-Stratton, C. (1990). Long-term follow-up of families with young conduct-problem children: From preschool to grade school. *Journal of Clinical Child Psychology, 19,* 114–149.

Weiss, C. H. (1986). Research and policy making: A limited partnership. In F. Heller (Ed.), *The use and abuse of social science* (pp. 214–235). Newbury Park, CA: Sage.

Weiss, C. H. (1989). Congressional committees as users of analysis. *Journal of Policy Analysis and Management, 8,* 411–431.

Weiss, C. H. (1990). The uneasy partnership endures: Social science and government. In S. Brooks & A. G. Gagnon (Eds.), *Social scientists, policy, and the state* (pp. 97–112). New York: Praeger.

Weiss, C. H., & Bucuvalas, M. J. (1980). *Social science research and decision making.* New York: Columbia University Press.

Weiss, H. B. (1993). Home visiting. *The Future of Children, 3,* 113–128.

Weiss, H. B., & Halpern, R. (1989, April). *The challenges of evaluating state family support and education initiatives: An evaluation framework.* Presentation for the Public Policy and Family Support and Education Colloquium, Cambridge, MA.

Weiss, J. A., & Weiss, C. H. (1996). Social scientists and decision makers look at the usefulness of mental health research. In R. P. Lorion, I. Iscoe, P. H. DeLeon, & G. R. VandenBos (Eds.), *Psychology and public policy: Balancing public service and professional need* (pp. 165–182). Washington, DC: American Psychological Association.

Weissbourd, B. (1987). A brief history of family support programs. In S. L. Kagan, D. R. Powell, B. Weissbourd, & E. F. Zigler (Eds.), *America's family support programs: Perspectives and prospects* (pp. 207–227). New Haven, CT: Yale University Press.

WELPAN (2002a). Developing a workable cross systems waiver authority: Perspectives of the WELPAN network. Madison, WI: Institute for Research on Poverty.

WELPAN (2002b). Eliminating the silos: Or, it's not just welfare anymore. Madison, WI: Institute for Research on Poverty.

WELPAN (2002c). Recreating social assistance: Or, how to use waiver authority to eliminate program silos. Madison, WI: Institute for Research on Poverty.

Werner, E. E. (1992). The children of Kauai: Resiliency and recovery in adolescence and adulthood. *Journal of Adolescent Health, 13,* 262–268.

Wertheimer, R. (2003). *Poor families in 2001: Parents working less and children continue to lag behind* (Child Trends Research Brief No. 2003-10). Washington, DC: Child Trends.

Westat. (2000). *Trends in the well-being of America's children and youth.* Retrieved April 6, 2003, from the U.S. Department of Health and Human Services Web site, http://aspe.hhs.gov/hsp/00trends.

Westat & Policy Study Associates. (2001). *The longitudinal evaluation of school change and performance in Title 1 schools: Vol. 1. Executive summary.* Washington, DC: U.S. Department of Education, Office of the Deputy Secretary, Planning and Evaluation Service.

Westman, J. (2003, December 13). Families are missing link in economic development. *Wisconsin State Journal,* p. A8.

What's the problem? (1999, August 1). *New York Times,* p. 4.

White, L., & Rogers, J. (2000). Economic circumstances and family outcomes: A review of the 1990s. *Journal of Marriage and the Family, 62,* 1035–1051.

Whitehead, B. D. (1992). A new familism? *Family Affairs, 5*(1–2), 1–5.

Wickrama, K. A. S., Lorenz, F. O., Wallace, L. E., Peiris, L., Conger, R. D., & Elder, G. H. (2001). Family influence on physical health during the middle years: The case of onset of hypertension. *Journal of Marriage and Family, 63,* 527–539.

Wiener, J. M., & Sullivan, C. M. (1995). Long-term care for the younger population: A policy synthesis. In J. M. Weiner, S. B. Clauser, & D. L. Kennell (Eds.), *Persons with disabilities: Issues in health care financing and service delivery* (pp. 291–324). Washington, DC: Brookings Institute.

Wilcox, B. L., & Kunkel, D. (1996). Taking television seriously: Children and television policy. In E. Zigler & N. W. Hall (Eds.), *Children, families and government: Preparing for the 21st century* (pp. 333–352). New York: Cambridge University Press.

Wilcox, B. L., & O'Keefe, J. E. (1991). Families, policy, and family support policies. In D. G. Unger & D. R. Powell (Eds.), *Families as nurturing systems: Support across the life span* (pp. 109–126). New York: Haworth.

Wilcox, B. L., Weisz, V. P., & Miller, M. K. (2005). Practical guidelines for education policymakers: The Family Impact Seminar as an approach to advancing the interests of children and families in the policy arena. *Journal of Clinical Child and Adolescent Psychology, 34,* 638–645.

Wilensky, H. L. (1997). Social science and the public agenda: Reflections on the relation of knowledge to policy in the United States and abroad. *Journal of Health Politics, 22,* 1241–1265.

Williams, N., Himmel, K. F., Sjoberg, A. F., & Torrez, D. J. (1995). The assimilation model, family life, and race and ethnicity in the United States: The case of minority welfare mothers. *Journal of Family Issues, 16,* 380–405.

Wilson, W. J. (1987). *The truly disadvantaged: The inner city, the underclass, and public policy.* Chicago: The University of Chicago Press.

Wilson, W. J. (1991, November). *Urban poverty, joblessness, and social isolation: Challenges to the inner-city ghetto family?* Paper presented at the annual meeting of the National Council on Family Relations, Denver, CO.

Wilson, W. J. (1997). The new social inequity and affirmative opportunity. In S. B. Greenberg & T. Skocpol (Eds.), *The new majority: Toward a popular progressive politics* (pp. 57–77). New Haven, CT: Yale University Press.

Wilson, W. J. (1999). *The bridge over the racial divide: Rising inequality and coalition politics.* Berkeley: University of California Press.

Winkler, A. (1994, November–December). Communitarianism. *Utne Reader, 66,* 105–108.

Winton, P. J. (2000, Summer). Early childhood intervention personnel preparation: Backward mapping for future planning. *Topics in Early Childhood Special Education, 20,* 87–94.

Winton, P. J., & Crais, E. R. (1996). Moving towards a family-centered approach. In P. J. McWilliams, P. Winton, & E. Crais (Eds.), *Practical strategies for family-centered interventions* (pp. 155–193). San Diego, CA: Singular.

Wisensale, S. K. (1997). The White House and Congress on child care and family leave policy: From Carter to Clinton. *Policy Studies Journal, 25,* 75–86.

Wisensale, S. K. (2001a). *Family leave policy: The political economy of work and family in America.* Armonk, NY: Sharpe.

Wisensale, S. K. (2001b). Twenty years of family policy: From Carter to Clinton. In S. Garasky & J. Mercier (Eds.), *Redefining family policy implications for the 21st century* (pp. 3–20). Ames: Iowa State University Press.

Wisensale, S. K. (2005a, July 18). Force corporations to focus on the family. *Baltimore Sun,* p. 9A.

Wisensale, S. K. (2005b, Spring). Think tanks and family values. *Dissent.* Retrieved July 29, 2005, from http://www.dissentmagazine.org/article/?article=257

Wittrock, B. (1993). Social knowledge and public policy: Eight models of interaction. In P. Wagner, C. H. Weiss, B. Wittrock, & H. Wollman (Eds.), *Social sciences and modern states: National experiences and theoretical crossroads* (pp. 333–353). New York: Cambridge University Press.

Wolfe, A. (1989). *Whose keeper? Social sciences and moral obligation.* Berkeley: California Press.

Wolfe, A. (1998). Developing civil society: Can the workplace replace bowling? *The Responsive Community: Rights and Responsibilities, 8*(2), 41–47.

Wollman, N., Yoder, B. L., Brumbaugh-Smith, J. P., & Gross, H. (2005, September 3). *Despite rise in overall poverty in 2004, gaps between races, age groups, and gender continue to drop: Widening income gap also examined* [Press release]. North Manchester, IN: Manchester College Peace Studies Institute.

Wright, L. M., Watson, W. L., & Bell, J. M. (1996). *Beliefs: The heart of healing in families and illness.* New York: Basic Books.

Yankelovich, D., interviewed by R. C. Nelson. (1989). America's values are changing. In D. L. Bender & B. Leone (Eds.), *American values: Opposing viewpoints* (pp. 110–118). San Diego, CA: Greenhaven.

Yankelovich, D. (1995, Fall). Three destructive trends. *The Kettering Review,* pp. 6–15.

Yoshikawa, H. (1994). Prevention as cumulative protection: Effects of early family support and education on chronic delinquency and its risks. *Psychological Bulletin, 115,* 28–54.

Zaslow, M., Tout, K., Smith, S., & Moore, K. (1998). Implications of the 1996 welfare legislation for children: A research perspective. *Social Policy Report, 12*(3), 1–35.

Zautra, A. J., Hoffman, J. M., Matt, K. S., Yocum, D., Potter, P. T. Castro, W. L., et al. (1998). An examination of individual differences in the relationship between interpersonal stress and disease activity among women with rheumatoid arthritis. *Arthritis Care and Research, 11,* 271–279.

Zigler, E. (1993). Communicating effectively before members of Congress. In K. McCartney & D. Phillips (Eds.), *An insider's guide to providing expert testimony before Congress* (pp. 11–15). Chicago: Society for Research in Child Development.

Zigler, E. (1998). A place of value for applied and policy studies. *Child Development, 69,* 532–542.

Zigler, E. F., & Gilman, E. P. (1990). An agenda for the 1990s: Supporting families. In D. Blankenhorn, S. Bayme, & J. B. Elshtain (Eds.), *Rebuilding the nest: A new commitment to the American family* (pp. 237–250). Milwaukee, WI: Family Service America.

Zigler, E., & Styfco, S. J. (1993). *Using research and theory to justify and inform Head Start expansion.* Ann Arbor, MI: Society for Research on Child Development.

Zigler, E., Taussig, C., & Black, K. (1992). Early childhood intervention: A promising preventative for juvenile delinquency. *American Psychologist, 47,* 997–1006.

Zill, N. (1993). A family-based approach to analyzing social problems. In G. E. Hendershot & F. B. LeClere (Eds.), *Family health: From data to policy* (pp. 32–42). Minneapolis, MN: National Council on Family Relations.

Zill, N., & Daly, M. (1993). *Researching the family: A guide to survey and statistical data on U.S. families.* Washington, DC: U.S. Department of Health and Human Services.

Zimmerman, S. L. (1995). *Understanding family policy: Theoretical approaches.* Newbury Park, CA: Sage. (Original work published 1988)

Zimmerman, S. L. (1998). Educational policy and the role of advocacy. In M. L. Fuller & G. Olson (Eds.), *Home–school relations: Working successfully with parents and families* (pp. 332–352). Needham, MA: Allyn & Bacon.

Zuckerman, A. (2000, July–August). Youth employment programs do work. *Youth Today, 9*(2), 52.

Zuckerman, D. (1999). Research watch. *Youth Today, 8*(8), 16–17.

Author Index

M

Maag, E., 18, 313
MacCallum, R. C., 88, 328
Maccoby, E. E., 69, 70, 330
Madden, J., 68, 330
Madsen, R., 13, 315
Maederer, C. M., 247, 249, 332
Magnuson, K. A., 46, 322
Magrath, C. P., 218, 330
Maguire, M. C., 27, 330
Malarkey, W. B., 88, 328
Mann, E. A., 50, 336
Mao, H., 88, 328
Mapp, K. L., 47, 204, 326
Marburger, C. L., 20, 326
Marcenes, W., 88, 330
Mark, M. M., 249, 276, 330
Markman, H. J., 82, 105, 323, 336
Marsh, J., 138, 330
Marshall, W., 18, 20, 51, 58, 61, 62, 123,
    135, 330
Martin, J. A., 69, 70, 330
Masnick, G., 11, 330
Mason, C. A., 152, 337
Mason, M. A., 8, 19, 27, 40, 60, 106,
    180, 330
Massad, P. M., 256, 330
Matt, K. S., 88, 343
Matthews, D., 215, 330
Mattingly, S., 89, 336
Mayer, R., 223, 330
Mayhew, D. R., 247, 330
Mayne, T. J., 88, 330
McCall, R. B., 196, 197, 220, 249, 330
McCartney, K., 181, 331
McCord, J., 6, 321
McCrady, B., 88, 330
McCubbin, L. D., 111, 329
McCusker, C., 16, 132, 340
McDaniel, M., 102, 338
McDaniel, S. H., 86, 90, 331
McDonald, G. W., 170, 177, 178, 187, 201, 226,
    228, 241, 333
McEwen, B. S., 88, 331
McGurk, H., 202, 331
McKnight, J. C., 92, 331
McKnight, J. L., 285, 287, 331
McLanahan, S., 10, 33, 102, 105, 106, 120, 129,
    180, 326, 331

McMurrer, D. P., 56, 101, 103, 104, 110, 111,
    139, 331
Meezan, W., 10, 26, 104, 107, 108, 109, 331
Meinhardt, G., 74, 336
Melli, M., xxviii, 19, 60, 316
Mellman, M., 40, 45, 331
Melnick, R. S., 19, 331
Melton, G. B., 245, 331
Menaghan, E. G., 99, 334
Mendel, D., 49, 331
Mendenhall, T. J., 93, 94, 331
Meyer, R. J., 88, 331
Midwest Welfare Peer Assistance Network,
    186, 331
Miller, G., 245, 249, 258, 331
Miller, G. E., 88, 337
Miller, J. Y., 52, 281, 326
Miller, M. K., 261, 342
Mills, J., xxviii, 12, 245, 276, 287, 290,
    316, 332
Mincy, R., 102, 332
Mincy, R. B., 33, 331
Minow, M., 43, 322
Moen, P., 11, 16, 26, 27, 29, 30, 35, 36, 45,
    98, 99, 164, 315, 319, 332
Moffitt, R. A., 102, 318
Monroe, P. A., 27, 29, 117, 332
Moore, K., 25, 57, 332, 343
Moore, K. A., 120, 178, 179, 188, 189,
    332, 341
Moreland, S., 82, 318
Morrison, A., 272, 318
Moynihan, D. P., x, 10, 79, 80, 104, 153, 157,
    332, 338
Mullis, A. K., 221, 314
Mullis, R. L., 221, 314
Murray, D. M., 285, 332
Murray, E., 78, 340
Myrdal, A., x, 332

N

Narrett, C. M., 78, 79, 334
National Commission on America's Urban
    Families, 7, 82, 83, 332
National Commission on Child Welfare and
    Family Preservation, 7, 82, 83, 332
National Council on Family Relations, 7, 59,
    64, 81, 95, 169, 200, 209, 210, 276,
    290, 332

Subject Index